M000218362

Bhagavad Gītā

Home Study Course

(Text in Sanskrit with transliteration, word-to-word and verse meaning, along with an elaborate commentary in English based on Śaṅkara-bhāṣyam)

Volume 2

Chapter 2

Swami Dayananda Saraswati
Arsha Vidya

Arsha Vidya
Research and Publication Trust
Chennai

Published by :
Arsha Vidya Research and Publication Trust
4 'Srinidhi' Apts 3rd Floor
Sir Desika Road Mylapore
Chennai 600 004 INDIA
Tel : 044 2499 7023
Telefax : 2499 7131
Email : avrandpt@gmail.com
Website: www.avrpt.com

ISBN : 978-93-80049-31-1
ISBN : 978-93-80049-39-7 (Set of 9 Volumes)

New Edition & Format :	July	2011	Copies : 1200
1st Reprint :	July	2012	Copies : 1000

Design & Layout :
Graaphic Design

Printed at :
Sudarsan Graphics
27, Neelakanta Mehta Street
T. Nagar, Chennai 600 017
Email : info@sudarsan.com

Preface

I am very happy that the 'Bhagavad Gītā Home Study Course' will now be available in nine compact volumes so that one can carry a given volume while travelling. As I said in my foreword for the last edition, I want the readers to be aware that these books do not constitute another set of books on the *Bhagavadgītā*. They are different in that they are edited transcript-pages of classroom discussions; they are presented to the reader as a program for self-study. If this is borne in mind, while reading, one can enjoy the same attitude of a student in the classroom, making oneself available to the whole process of unfoldment of the content of the words of Bhagavān. The study will then prove to be as rewarding as directly listening to the teacher. This attitude would prove to be *ātma-kṛpā*. Once this *kṛpā* is there, the other two, *śāstra-kṛpā* and *īśvara-kṛpā* would follow.

The enormous job of patient editing of the pages, thousands of them, and presenting them, retaining the original words and content without any compromise, was done by Dr. Martha Doherty. These books have created a number of committed students of the *Bhagavadgītā*, thanks to Martha's invaluable contribution to the teaching tradition of Vedanta. I also congratulate the staff of our Publication division ably led by Ms. K. Chandra, a dedicated student of Vedanta.

Swami Dayananda Saraswati
Arsha Vidya
June 19 2011

KEY TO TRANSLITERATION AND PRONUNCIATION OF SANSKRIT LETTERS

Sanskrit is a highly phonetic language and hence accuracy in articulation of the letters is important. For those unfamiliar with the *Devanägari* script, the international transliteration is a guide to the proper pronunciation of Sanskrit letters.

अ	*a*	*(but)*
आ	*ā*	*(father)*
इ	*i*	*(it)*
ई	*ī*	*(beat)*
उ	*u*	*(full)*
ऊ	*ū*	*(pool)*
ऋ	*ṛ*	*(rhythm)*
ॠ	*ṝ*	*(marine)*
लृ	*ḷ*	*(revelry)*
ए	*e*	*(play)*
ऐ	*ai*	*(aisle)*
ओ	*o*	*(go)*
औ	*au*	*(loud)*
क	*ka*	*(seek)* 1
ख	*kha*	*(blockhead)**1
ग	*ga*	*(get)* 1
घ	*gha*	*(log hut)**1
ङ	*ṅa*	*(sing)* 1
च	*ca*	*(chunk)* 2
छ	*cha*	*(catch him)**2
ज	*ja*	*(jump)* 2
झ	*jha*	*(hedgehog)**2
ञ	*ña*	*(bunch)* 2
ट	*ṭa*	*(true)**3
ठ	*ṭha*	*(anthill)**3
ड	*ḍa*	*(drum)**3
ढ	*ḍha*	*(godhead)**3
ण	*ṇa*	*(under)**3
त	*ta*	*(path)**4
थ	*tha*	*(thunder)**4
द	*da*	*(that)**4
ध	*dha*	*(breathe)**4
न	*na*	*(nut)**4
प	*pa*	*(put)* 5
फ	*pha*	*(loophole)**5
ब	*ba*	*(bin)* 5
भ	*bha*	*(abhor)**5
म	*ma*	*(much)* 5
य	*ya*	*(loyal)*
र	*ra*	*(red)*
ल	*la*	*(luck)*
व	*va*	*(vase)*
श	*śa*	*(sure)*
ष	*ṣa*	*(shun)*
स	*sa*	*(so)*
ह	*ha*	*(hum)*

ं	*ṁ*	*anusvāra*	(nasalisation of preceding vowel)
ः	*ḥ*	*visarga*	(aspiration of preceding vowel)
*			No exact English equivalents for these letters

1.	Guttural	–	Pronounced from throat
2.	Palatal	–	Pronounced from palate
3.	Lingual	–	Pronounced from cerebrum
4.	Dental	–	Pronounced from teeth
5.	Labial	–	Pronounced from lips

The 5th letter of each of the above class – called nasals – are also pronounced nasally.

Contents

Chapter 2

साङ्ख्ययोगः

Sāṅkhya–yogaḥ
Topic of knowledge

Verse 1

Sañjaya speaks

सञ्जय उवाच ।
तं तथा कृपयाविष्टमश्रुपूर्णाकुलेक्षणम् ।
विषीदन्तमिदं वाक्यमुवाच मधुसूदनः ॥ १ ॥

sañjaya uvāca
taṁ tathā kṛpayāviṣṭam aśrupūrṇākulekṣaṇam
viṣīdantam idaṁ vākyam uvāca madhusūdanaḥ (1)

sañjayaḥ – Sañjaya; *uvāca* – said;
madhusūdanaḥ – Madhusūdana (Kṛṣṇa); *tathā* – thus; *kṛpayā āviṣṭam* – overwhelmed by compassion; *aśru-pūrṇa-ākula-īkṣaṇam* – whose eyes were filled with tears and showed distress; *viṣīdantam* – one who was sad; *tam* – to him; *idam* – this; *vākyam* – sentence; *uvāca* – spoke

Sañjaya said:

To him – who was thus sad and overwhelmed by compassion, whose eyes were filled with tears and showed distress – Madhusūdana (Kṛṣṇa) spoke these words.

The use of the third person in this verse reminds us that Sañjaya, the narrator of the *Gītā*, was continuing his report to Dhṛtarāṣṭra. The dialogue between Arjuna and Kṛṣṇa, on the other hand, is always in the first person and second person. As the second chapter begins, Kṛṣṇa, referred to as Madhusūdana, had been patiently listening to Arjuna. Because he knew the importance of listening, he let Arjuna talk.

A therapist also listens a lot and nods his or her head at the appropriate time, speaking only enough to keep the person talking. People do not generally listen in this way. They begin advising right away and do not know how to listen. Kṛṣṇa was a good listener. He had already listened to one complete chapter! Only when Arjuna laid down his bow, arrows, and sat back in the chariot, did Kṛṣṇa think it was time for him to respond.

The word '*madhu*' in the name Madhusūdana refers to the ego. It means honey, something that is very dear, very sweet to us. The *ahaṅkāra*, ego, is very dear to us. Everyone wants to boost the *ahaṅkāra*. No one wants to give it up. We have already seen that Madhusūdana refers to Kṛṣṇa as the destroyer of demons. The ego here can be seen as a demon. Therefore, the one whose grace destroys *ahaṅkāra*, the one knowing whom the *ahaṅkāra* is destroyed, is called Madhusūdana.

Arjuna was described as being overwhelmed, overpowered by sympathy, compassion and affection. His eyes were filled with tears because he had placed himself in such a situation. There was more here than mere compassion; there was conflict too, because of his sense of duty. Arjuna was confused about having to destroy people who were his *guru*s and relatives.

Because he was a man of discipline, Arjuna did not allow the tears to flow. There are three reasons why the eyes can be filled with tears. Pepper can certainly do it. When you are ecstatic also, you may shed tears. When you are sad, the tears can well up. Any disease causing tears is usually due to an irritation and is therefore covered under the first of these three. Thus, the tear glands are stimulated by these kinds of situations. We know that Arjuna's tears were not due to ecstasy because he was described here as one who was sad.

Arjuna who was sad, whose eyes were glistening with tears, and whose heart was overwhelmed by compassion, was being addressed by Śrī Bhagavān. The word '*vākya*' usually means a sentence, a group of words. Here, it refers to the whole subject matter of this particular section.

Verses 2&3

Lord Kṛṣṇa speaks to Arjuna

श्रीभगवानुवाच ।
कुतस्त्वा कश्मलमिदं विषमे समुपस्थितम् ।
अनार्यजुष्टमस्वर्ग्यमकीर्तिकरमर्जुन ॥ २ ॥

śrībhagavān uvāca
kutastvā kaśmalam idaṁ viṣame samupasthitam
anāryajuṣṭam asvargyam akīrtikaram arjuna (2)

śrībhagavān – Śrī Bhagavān (The Lord); *uvāca* – said; *arjuna* – O Arjuna!; *viṣame* – in this crisis; *idam* – this; *anārya-juṣṭam* – that which is not becoming of an upright man; *asvargyam* – that which does not lead to heaven; *akīrti-karam* –

that which does not add to your fame; *kaśmalam* – despair; *tvā* – upon you; *kutaḥ* – from where; *samupasthitam* – has come

> Śrī Bhagavān said:
>
> Arjuna! In such crisis from where has this despair come upon you? It is unbecoming of an upright man and does not add to (your) fame. Nor does it lead you to heaven.

'Hey, Arjuna, where did you pick up this despair, this sorrow?' asked Kṛṣṇa. Arjuna had been talking in a way that did not sound like him at all. Because it was totally unexpected, Kṛṣṇa's response did not take the form of helpful advice. He did not let Arjuna know that he understood his position and the difficulties he was facing. Instead, he whipped him with his tongue saying, 'Where did this despair come from, Arjuna? It does not befit you at all!'

To expand Kṛṣṇa's words, 'You have missed your calling, Arjuna. You should have been a great actor. How could you have hidden this from me all these years? I never expected that you could get into this kind of a state. We all knew you to be the bravest, the most courageous, and now I hear your talk that betrays only sorrow, sorrow at the thought of the imminent destruction that this war will bring. It may have been all right if you had mentioned all this before we came to the battlefield. We could have sat down and discussed it, but we cannot do that here. It is both the wrong time and the wrong place.' Thus, Kṛṣṇa admonished Arjuna.

This was when Arjuna should have been spending his time on the strategies of the war such as deciding with whom he should fight and how to proceed, etc. He was in the battlefield, standing in the midst of the two armies, having requested Kṛṣṇa to be his driver. Kṛṣṇa had fulfilled his end of the bargain, but now it looked as though he had backed a horse that would not even start! 'Not only are you sick, Arjuna,' Kṛṣṇa went on, 'but you have made me also sick. This is a time for brave deeds, not for this kind of lamenting. It is neither the time nor the place for such talk.' Kṛṣṇa, therefore, demanded to know where all these had come from.

The verse contains three adjectives describing Arjuna's despair, *anārya-juṣṭa, asvargya* and *akīrti-kara. Anārya-juṣṭa* derives its meaning from *ārya,* meaning an upright man, one who does the right thing at the appropriate time. Arjuna was reminded by Kṛṣṇa that he had always been an *ārya,* a man who did what was to be done. From such a man, despair is not expected. Therefore, this behaviour is *anārya-juṣṭa,* not befitting or becoming an *ārya.* It is not that an *ārya* does not cry. He will cry when the occasion warrants it, but not in the battlefield where he has to act. Thus, Kṛṣṇa told Arjuna that his despair, his wailing and lamentations, here in the battlefield, were totally inappropriate, *anārya-juṣṭa,* not becoming at all.

Kṛṣṇa also told him that what he was contemplating was *asvargya,* not the way to heaven. Arjuna said that he had heard of people who destroyed the family, and thereby the *dharma,* would live in hell, *naraka,* an abode of pain, for a length of time. He thought that by doing his duty, of fighting this war, he would go to *naraka* and by not doing it, by retreating, he would go to heaven, *svarga.* He was therefore prepared to sacrifice everything and go to *svarga.* Kṛṣṇa was now telling him that, if this were to be his thinking, it would not work. Not fighting would amount to a dereliction of duty because he was supposed to protect the law and order of the kingdom. Therefore, when he talked like this, it was *asvargya*. Kṛṣṇa also told him in a later verse that, in addition to living with sorrow and privations due to not having a kingdom, this dereliction of duty would gnaw at his heart. Furthermore, when he died, he would go only to *naraka* and not to *svarga*.

To this, Arjuna might have said that he did not care about going to heaven. He did not even know if there was a heaven or a hell. Being cornered, he might have said, all that he cared about was the here and now. If this were Arjuna's thinking, Kṛṣṇa tells him that it would prove to be *akīrti-kara*, a disgrace even in this life. He says, "This sorrow, leading to your running away from the battlefield, is not going to redound to your credit in the society. People are going to look at you and say, 'That is Arjuna, the one who ran away from the battlefield.' If you go to Rishikesh and sit under a tree, pilgrims will come to see you before going to the Ganges, saying, 'I want to see Arjuna, the one who ran away from the battlefield.' Everyone will talk lightly of you."

Kṛṣṇa might have said further, "They will say, 'How great was Arjuna! How courageous he was! He was the master archer, until the battle began!' Nobody is going to give you any credit for such an action, Arjuna." Kṛṣṇa may then have said, "Not only will they talk lightly of you, they will criticise and belittle all your powers and prowess. Even ordinary people will talk ill of you. If you run away from the battlefield,

Dharmaputra, your older brother, crestfallen, will follow you. Bhīma, of course, will be angry, but being helpless, he too will go away. The whole army will fizzle out; everyone will leave and some may even heave a sigh of relief that they have escaped."

Everyone in Arjuna's rank was afraid of Bhīṣma and Droṇa, and those in the opposite camp were afraid of Arjuna and Bhīma. They would all be greatly relieved. The Pāṇḍavas, along with their entire army, would be gone and Duryodhana would be handed the victory on a platter. He would be able to say, 'Hands down, without a shot, I won.'

Kṛṣṇa would therefore have admonished Arjuna even further, "After you have gone to the forest, what will Duryodhana do? There will be parties everywhere. Duryodhana will let the entire army drink as much as it wants. Much more than a happy hour, it will be a happy day. Because the media is with him, Duryodhana will see to it that people think you are a coward. He will say that Arjuna asked Kṛṣṇa to station his chariot in such a way that he could see Duryodhana's army, and seeing it he ran away in fear. The headlines will read, 'Arjuna saw, shivered, and ran.' There will even be photographs of you running away." "Of course," Kṛṣṇa may have continued, "Duryodhana will present it in the worst possible light because Duryodhana cannot afford to have citizens looking upto Arjuna as a man of sacrifice. He will belittle you, Arjuna, even though he knows in his heart that your sacrifice was due only to compassion for the people, to save their families and so on, he will not allow anyone to know that. He will cover it all up, saying that you ran away out of sheer fear for your precious life. Duryodhana will not be the only one to present it this way. Arjuna, even the ordinary soldiers who normally had nightmares about you, those who had been so afraid of you, those who were recruited only a few days ago will also talk like this. Over drinks, one will boast to others that 'Kṛṣṇa stopped Arjuna's chariot right in front of me. And when Arjuna's eyes fell upon me, all I did was twist my moustache, give him that special look, and Arjuna ran away in terror.' Who will not tell such stories? Not only the great warriors, but also yesterday's recruits, will talk like this. People will talk so ill of you, Arjuna, that it will be impossible for you to be happy in this world." This, then, was what Kṛṣṇa meant by *akīrti-kara*.

Kṛṣṇa would have also reminded Arjuna of the many wonderful titles that had been lavished upon him over the years. He was a role model for every soldier and now he was thinking of running away! It would be something like a Nobel laureate who, having been honoured for the great work he had done for the downtrodden, the poor and the ill of the society, is found to have committed a multiple murder for the sake of money. This news, of course, would blare out from the headlines of all the newspapers. The Nobel laureates of the world will then immediately surrender their scrolls because the Nobel Prize will no longer have any meaning. This was exactly what happened when a group of rock singers was knighted. One of the old knights surrendered his knighthood because he did not want to be in the same ranks as these young singers.

'Therefore, Arjuna, your name, fame, credibility, and everything will be destroyed,' Kṛṣṇa tells Arjuna. *Kīrti-kara* means that which adds to one's name. *Akīrti-kara* is that which does not add to one's credit at all. 'Your sorrow, Arjuna, is *akīrti-kara*. I see in it the seed for all further reactions,' says Kṛṣṇa. Arjuna had already dropped his bow and arrows and sat down. Kṛṣṇa, therefore, had to tell Arjuna that his thinking was confused and that he should get up and do what had to be done.

क्लैब्यं मा स्म गमः पार्थ नैतत्त्वय्युपपद्यते ।
क्षुद्रं हृदयदौर्बल्यं त्यक्त्वोत्तिष्ठ परन्तप ॥ ३ ॥

klaibyaṁ mā sma gamaḥ pārtha naitattvayyupapadyate
kṣudraṁ hṛdayadaurbalyaṁ tyaktvottiṣṭha parantapa (3)

parantapa – O scorcher of enemies!; *pārtha* – Arjuna; *klaibyam* – unmanliness; *mā sma gamaḥ* – do not yield to; *etat* – this; *na tvayi upapadyate* – does not befit you; *kṣudram* – lowly; *hṛdaya-daurbalyam* – weakness of heart; *tyaktvā* – giving up; *uttiṣṭha* – please get up

Pārtha (Arjuna)! Do not yield to unmanliness. This does not befit you. The scorcher of enemies! Give up this lowly weakness of heart and get up.

By calling Arjuna as *pārtha*, the son of Pṛthā, Kṛṣṇa was saying, 'This is definitely not the time for behaving like a child, a mama's boy. Kṛṣṇa also used the word *klaibya*, meaning one who is neither male nor female. In other words, the mental state of a eunuch. Men fight in a certain way, and when women have to fight, they too fight in a way that is peculiar to them.

Eunuchs, on the other hand, are a problem in any society because they are in between, neither man nor woman. Kṛṣṇa advised Arjuna against that state. 'Do not proceed in this way. Do not let this emotion take you over, *klaibyaṁ mā sma gamaḥ*.'

Arjuna was known to be a man of great discipline, perseverance, dexterity and skill. Therefore this thinking like a *klība* did not fit him at all. He was a soldier and, as Kṛṣṇa said, it was his duty not to talk in this way. More than a soldier, he was a *kṣatriya* who was supposed to protect *dharma*. By birth, this duty was enjoined upon him. In addition, because he was a prince, he had to set an example. Nor was he an ordinary prince; he was the most exalted among princes. There was no one like him in this kingdom or elsewhere. He was the role model. Whatever he did, others would follow.

Kṛṣṇa says, 'Arjuna, you are a role model, a leader. You are not a *sādhu*. Nor you are a dropout, a hobo, who can do as he likes. You are a responsible person and what is more, a leader. You are one of the five crowned princes and your older brother is supposed to rule. You are committed to doing what is to be done and there is no escape. To run away is not fitting for any soldier and for you, Arjuna, it is definitely not fitting.'

Kṛṣṇa continued, 'Giving up, being overcome by emotional weakness at this time, Arjuna, is base and lowly. Please get up.' Although he addressed him politely, Kṛṣṇa ordered Arjuna up, in fact. In the first line of this verse he called him Pārtha and then, to remind him who he was, he called him Parantapa, the one who destroys the enemy. 'Do not run away,' he said. 'Get up and face the battle.'

Kṛṣṇa told Arjuna to do what had to be done. For Arjuna, it happened to be a battle. The whole *Gītā* is going to point out that what is to be done must be done, unless one is a *sannyāsī*. Doing what is to be done can be *yoga*, requiring only a change of attitude on your part. So, this part of the *Gītā* is a set-up for the whole *dharma* that is to be unfolded, the seed for what is to come later in terms of *karma-yoga*.

Being ordered to get up in this way, Arjuna felt that he was not understood, much less was his sympathy understood. He then began again to explain himself. So much respect did he have for Kṛṣṇa!

Kṛṣṇa's admonitions were not meant as criticisms, but were only to show Arjuna that a particular type of thinking led to his sorrow and that now he should change his thinking. Sympathy for others is a virtue, but what is to be done has to be done. The whole teaching is about another type of thinking and Arjuna's thinking process was triggered off by Kṛṣṇa's whipping words, as evidenced by his reply.

Verses 4-8

Arjuna's response

अर्जुन उवाच ।
कथं भीष्ममहं सङ्ख्ये द्रोणं च मधुसूदन ।
इषुभिः प्रतियोत्स्यामि पूजार्हावरिसूदन ॥ ४ ॥

arjuna uvāca
kathaṁ bhīṣmamahaṁ saṅkhye droṇaṁ ca madhusūdana
iṣubhiḥ pratiyotsyāmi pūjārhāvarisūdana (4)

arjunaḥ – Arjuna; *uvāca* – said;
arisūdana – O destroyer of foes (Kṛṣṇa)!; *madhusūdana* – O destroyer of the demon, Madhu!; *aham* – I; *saṅkhye* – in this battle; *pūjā–arhau* – who are worthy of worship; *bhīṣmam* – Bhīṣma; *droṇam* – Droṇa; *iṣubhiḥ* – with arrows; *katham* – how; *pratiyotsyāmi* – fight against

Arjuna said:

Madhusūdana (Kṛṣṇa)! The destroyer of foes! How will I, in this battle, fight with arrows against Bhīṣma and Droṇa, who are worthy of my worship?

In this verse, Arjuna said what amounted to, 'You cannot understand what I am saying. You cannot appreciate where I am coming from. I have been placed in a very unenviable situation. I have to fight and I am quite accustomed to that. That I have to fight against people known to me is also not the real problem. I probably could manage to fight against my own people. But how can I fight against these two stalwarts, Bhīṣma and Droṇa, for whom I have such great reverence, to whom I owe everything?'

By addressing Kṛṣṇa as Madhusūdana and Arisūdana, Arjuna was reminding Kṛṣṇa that he had destroyed only demons and enemies, not his teachers and family. But those whom Arjuna was now supposed to destroy were his *gurus*, who deserved only worship from him. Instead of weapons, he should have brought flowers and been making garlands to offer them. Droṇa was the one from whom he had learned the art of archery. He had grown up on Bhīṣma's lap and learned everything he knew from him. Bhīṣma was Arjuna's role model, his inspiration, idol, and hero. 'How can I use my arrows against these two men?' he asked.

Arjuna could also talk the way Kṛṣṇa was talking. He too could deliver a pep talk and tell others that they should behave like men and do what had to be done. But Bhīṣma and Droṇa were two people for whom he had the greatest respect, which they deserved, and Arjuna did not think he could destroy them. This thinking was what led him to ask Kṛṣṇa to teach him what was right.

The process of Arjuna's thinking is revealed in these verses very beautifully. The *Gītā* still has not begun. Kṛṣṇa's advice to get up was that of a friend. What Arjuna intended to do was not going to take him to heaven, muchless add to his credit and Kṛṣṇa told him so. Everything else Kṛṣṇa said was just to boost Arjuna's morale. Naturally, Arjuna was surprised that Kṛṣṇa was saying things like, 'Do not get into this eunuch-like state,' and so on, since he was not accustomed to be spoken to as a weakling.

Given the words he used, Kṛṣṇa seemed to be thinking of Arjuna as a coward, someone who had to be told to get up and do what had to be done. Arjuna had never heard such words in his lifetime and had certainly never expected to hear them from Kṛṣṇa, of all people. So, he wanted to counter all of Bhagavān's statements. Therefore, he said, 'It is easy for you to tell me not to have this weakness. However, the problem here for me is not fear. That is not why I want to leave the battlefield. I want to leave because of compassion and my concept of *dharma*, which holds that *dharma* can be protected only by protecting the *dharmīs*. The only way I can win this war is by destroying all the *dharmīs*. Therefore, none of this makes any sense.'

Arjuna's problem was something like that of a student who wanted to protect his *guru* from a fly that was bothering him while he slept. He took a big stone and killed the fly, also killing his *guru* in the process. Here too, in the name of protecting *dharma*, the very people who were supposed to live *dharma* and hand it over to the next generation, were all going to be destroyed. Arjuna was anguished and amazed that all the Pāṇḍavas could have armed themselves to fight such a war. Thus, he asked, 'How could we have decided to do anything so insensible?'

In Arjuna's perception, this war would not protect *dharma*. It was also very clear to him that the result of this battle would definitely not give him any happiness in this lifetime. Nor did he see any kind of heaven for himself after death, because, to destroy the entire *kula-dharma* was an act of sin. More than that, for the rest of his life, he would have to live with the thought that he had destroyed all these people. Therefore, there would be neither *dṛṣṭa-phala* nor *adṛṣṭa-phala* in such an action.

Since this was Arjuna's view, he did not understand how Kṛṣṇa could say that he was frightened. He went on to explain that the people standing there were not unknown to him. They were his own people, people for whom he had the greatest respect and reverence. Unless he killed people like Bhīṣma and Droṇa, there would be no question of his gaining victory. In addition, if they were destroyed, assuming that Arjuna was going to destroy them, what kind of happiness would he possibly have? He had to live with the thought that he had destroyed those he revered the most, those from whom he had learned all that he knew! 'How can I send arrow for arrow against them,' he asked Kṛṣṇa.

Even if Kṛṣṇa had argued that Bhīṣma and Droṇa did not seem to have the same concern for him, Arjuna did not feel that he was in a position to make any such judgement. Their choosing to fight against him may have been wrong but at the same time, they no doubt had their own logic for doing so. Because of his respect and reverence for these two stalwarts, Arjuna did not feel that he had the right to say anything about their decision to support Duryodhana. The point he was making to Kṛṣṇa was that he himself could not sin by exchanging arrows with them. He would rather die than draw the arrow that would destroy Droṇa and Bhīṣma, his teachers.

Arjuna therefore told Kṛṣṇa that he did not know the meaning of fear, as was very well known to Kṛṣṇa. A brave man can be sympathetic, but a coward who is sympathetic has a problem because the sympathy ends in distress. This kind of sympathy is of no use, whereas, when a resourceful, courageous, skilful person is sympathetic, the sympathy can be useful to the other person. A brave man should be sympathetic. So too, a rich man should be magnanimous and a knowledgeable man humble. Knowledge and humility, money and magnanimity, power and justice, strength and gentleness, these go together. A person having only one of these two attributes, such as power or strength, without justice or gentleness that goes with it, is capable of destroying others.

Arjuna was brave, courageous, and a mature person. A mature person can be sympathetic. However, a problem arises when there is confusion. Arjuna's confusion was that of a mature person. Vedanta cannot be taught to an immature person. Instead, he or she can be taught something else, something that will resolve a particular problem. A mature person can be taught Vedanta, thereby solving the problem more fundamentally. This is where the *Gītā* comes in, as we will see.

Arjuna presented his case very well. Kṛṣṇa destroyed demons and enemies, but here, those who were to be destroyed were Arjuna's teachers and relatives. Droṇa was a teacher who was not against Arjuna in any way. The only problem was that he was obliged to Duryodhana because of all the help he had received from him. Bhīṣma was also obliged for the same reason. However, it did not mean that they were against Arjuna. Perceiving this particular situation properly, Arjuna told Kṛṣṇa, 'Destroying demons and enemies, as you have done, is right, but destroying one's teachers is not right.' It was fine that Kṛṣṇa was known as a destroyer of demons, Madhusūdana. However, Arjuna definitely did not want to be known as a destroyer of teachers, *gurusūdana*.

It would be better to live on alms than to kill my *guru*s.

गुरूनहत्वा हि महानुभावान् श्रेयो भोक्तुं भैक्ष्यमपीह लोके ।
हत्वार्थकामांस्तु गुरूनिहैव भुञ्जीय भोगान् रुधिरप्रदिग्धान् ॥ ५ ॥

gurūnahatvā hi mahānubhāvān
śreyo bhoktuṁ bhaikṣyam apīha loke
hatvārthakāmāṁstu gurūn ihaiva
bhuñjīya bhogān rudhirapradigdhān (5)

mahānubhāvān – most revered; *gurūn* – teachers; *ahatvā* – not killing; *iha* – here; *loke* – in this world; *bhaikṣyam* – food collected from others by begging; *api* – even; *bhoktum* – to eat; *śreyaḥ* – better; *hi* – indeed; *tu* – whereas; *gurūn* – teachers; *hatvā* – killing; *iha eva* – here itself; *rudhirapradigdhān* – stained with blood; *artha-kāmān* – security and pleasure; *bhogān* – enjoyments; *bhuñjīya* – I would experience

> It would be better indeed to eat food collected from others here in this world than to kill these most revered teachers. If I kill them, the pleasures I would experience in this world will be stained with (their) blood.

Arjuna also looked upon his grandfather, Bhīṣma, as a *guru* because he had been taught by him as he grew up. Bhīṣma and Droṇa were not ordinary *guru*s of the world. They deserved the status of highly exalted people. In this verse, Arjuna told Kṛṣṇa that it would be preferable to live on alms than to kill his own people.

Bhaikṣya means collecting food from others, something that only *sādhu*s are entitled to do. They take only a little from each person so as not to be a liability on anyone. The whole process of Arjuna's thinking was changing. In fact, his mind had already gone to this way of life, rather than to fighting the war.

Arjuna knew that if he left the battlefield, he would have to go to the forest. Previously, he had counted on this day to retrieve the kingdom and he had been looking forward to it for a long time. He had gathered all the weapons he needed, but when the day came, he decided not to fight. What else was left for him to do but go to the forest and live a life of alms? He could not remain in the kingdom. Only from the distant mountain people could he hope to collect a little food on which to live. This was all that was open to him and he was ready for it. He wanted it, in fact.

Only two types of people can take *bhikṣā*, students, *brahmacārī*s, and renunciates, *sādhus*. *Brahmacārī*s can take *bhikṣā* because they are not earning members in the society. They leave home and go to the *gurukula* to live with a teacher. Therefore, they are allowed to go for *bhikṣā*, if they have to. *Sādhus* or Swamis are renunciates and they live on alms. Arjuna's mind had now turned in this direction.

Because he was already a father and grandfather, Arjuna could not become a *brahmacārī*. Therefore, all that was available to him was the life of a *sādhu*. This was what he wanted and it was the basis for the only question he asked again and again in the *Gītā*, 'Which is better of the two, *karma-yoga* or *sannyāsa*? Why do you ask me to do *karma* when there is this other lifestyle?' He asked this question in the third chapter and again in the fifth chapter. Then, perhaps because he was a little shy about asking it again, he asked some other questions in between. And then, slowly, he slipped it in again in the eighteenth chapter in a different form, 'What is the difference between *tyāga* and *sannyāsa*?'

Thus, Arjuna always kept the same thought in his mind. He wanted to be a *sādhu* and all of his arguments were directed to this end. Although Bhīṣma and Droṇa had come to the battlefield, not as teachers but to cast their lot with Duryodhana for the sake of the kingdom, Arjuna's point was that if these people were destroyed, what kind of kingdom would he have? Any enjoyment he would experience would be soaked in blood. The sight of the blood of his teachers would haunt him. Nothing would remove it from his mind, he was sure.

The more one tries to remove a fixation, the more it becomes fixed. There is no way of removing it. If it could be removed, it would not be a fixation. Thus, Arjuna knew that the sight of Bhīṣma and Droṇa bleeding to death would be permanently imprinted in his mind. The impact would be so powerful that it would remain a fixation. Therefore, any pleasant experience he gathered would be sullied by the thought of having killed his own people. Any enjoyment he might have had would always be conditioned by the memory of the cost–the blood of Bhīṣma, Droṇa, and others who were killed in the battle.

Arjuna expresses his confusion:

न चैतद्विद्मः कतरन्नो गरीयो यद्वा जयेम यदि वा नो जयेयुः ।
यानेव हत्वा न जिजीविषामस्तेऽवस्थिताः प्रमुखे धार्तराष्ट्राः ॥ ६ ॥

na caitadvidmaḥ kataranno garīyo
yadvā jayema yadi vā no jayeyuḥ
yāneva hatvā na jijīviṣāmaste'vasthitāḥ
pramukhe dhārtarāṣṭrāḥ (6)

naḥ – for us; *katarat* – which of the two; *garīyaḥ* – better; *etat* – this; *na ca vidmaḥ* – and we do not know; *yad vā* – if; *jayema* – we should conquer them; *yadi* – if; *vā* – or; *naḥ jayeyuḥ* – they should conquer us; *yān eva* – indeed whom; *hatvā* – having slain; *na jijīviṣāma* – we will not like to live; *te* – those; *dhārtarāṣṭrāḥ* – the sons of Dhṛtarāṣṭra; *pramukhe* – in front of (us); *avasthitāḥ* – stand

> And, we do not know which of the two will be better for us–that we should conquer them or that they should conquer us. The sons of Dhṛtarāṣṭra, after slaying whom we will indeed not like to live, stand facing us (to be killed).

In this verse, Arjuna told Kṛṣṇa that he did not know which was better, to win the battle against the enemies, who were his own people, or to be defeated by them. Regardless of who was victorious, the problem would remain. To be victorious, Arjuna had to destroy all these people. He would have the pleasures of a kingdom but would be unable to enjoy them. For Arjuna, then, the choice was meaningless. Because Kṛṣṇa was telling him to get up and fight, he was confused about how the victory could be good for him. If, on the other hand, Duryodhana won, the Pāṇḍavas would have to go to the forest and live a life of *bhikṣu*. Although this lifestyle was arduous and there would be no enjoyments, Arjuna thought that it was definitely the better of the two alternatives.

Arjuna said that the Pāṇḍavas did not want to live by destroying the sons of Dhṛtarāṣṭra and those connected to them,

Bhīṣma, Droṇa, Kṛpa and so on, all of whom were standing in front of him on the battlefield. He called the war a 'no-win' situation. It would be one big loss and he had no interest in it. But Kṛṣṇa had told him that, what he was thinking of doing was wrong. Therefore, Arjuna argued that whether it was wrong or right, the situation was such that he could not see anything good coming to him from fighting.

Then, Arjuna explained himself further:

कार्पण्यदोषोपहतस्वभावः पृच्छामि त्वां धर्मसम्मूढचेताः ।
यच्छ्रेयः स्यान्निश्चितं ब्रूहि तन्मे शिष्यस्तेऽहं शाधि मां त्वां प्रपन्नम् ॥ ७ ॥

kārpaṇyadoṣopahatasvabhāvaḥ
pṛcchāmi tvāṁ dharmasammūḍhacetāḥ
yacchreyaḥ syānniścitaṁ brūhi tanme
śiṣyaste'haṁ śādhi māṁ tvāṁ prapannam (7)

kārpaṇya-doṣa-upahata-svabhāvaḥ – overcome by faint–heartedness; *dharma-sammūḍha-cetāḥ* – confused about (my) duty; *tvām* – you; *pṛcchāmi* – I ask; *me* – for me; *yat* – which; *niścitam śreyaḥ syāt* – is truly better; *tat* – that; *brūhi* – please tell me; *aham* – I am; *te* – your; *śiṣyaḥ* – student; *tvām prapannam* – one who has taken refuge in you; *mām* – me; *śādhi* – please teach

Overcome by faint-heartedness, confused about my duty, I ask you: Please tell me that which is truly better for me. I am your student. Please teach me, who has taken refuge in you.

न हि प्रपश्यामि ममापनुद्याद् यच्छोकमुच्छोषणमिन्द्रियाणाम् ।
अवाप्य भूमावसपत्नमृद्धं राज्यं सुराणामपि चाधिपत्यम् ॥ ८ ॥

na hi prapaśyāmi mamāpanudyād
yacchokamucchoṣaṇam indriyāṇām
avāpya bhūmāvasapatnam ṛddhaṁ
rājyaṁ surāṇām api cādhipatyam (8)

bhūmau – on the earth; *asapatnam* – unrivalled; *ṛddham* – prosperous; *rājyam* – kingdom; *surāṇām* – of the denizens of heaven; *api* – even; *ādhipatyam* – sovereignty; *ca* – and; *avāpya* – obtaining; *mama* – my; *indriyāṇām* – of the senses; *ucchoṣaṇam* – that which dries up; *śokam* – sorrow; *yat apanudyāt* – that which would remove; *na hi prapaśyāmi* – I do not see

> Indeed, I do not see anything that would remove the sorrow that dries up my senses, even if I were to obtain an unrivalled and prosperous kingdom on earth and sovereignty over the denizens of heaven.

We will now look at the second of the two verses. Here, Arjuna described how his sorrow had dried up his sense organs so that they could not function. His arms and legs also seemed to have atrophied. The energy in them had been totally sapped by this incapacitating sorrow. Nor could he see any way of removing it. Even if he found the courage to fight because of his commitment to *dharma* and because Kṛṣṇa asked him to fight, Arjuna did not think his sorrow would ever go away. He saw it as something inside of himself.

A sorrow that cannot be alleviated.

In fact, only the sad become sad. No one suddenly becomes sad. Just as the angry become angry, the sad become sad. If you are already angry inside, all that you require is a reason to become angry. Similarly, the jealous become jealous and the lonely become lonely. These feelings indicate that there is a problem already there underneath.

Arjuna recognised an inner, unwept sadness and felt sad. Sometimes the sadness that is underneath comes out. Otherwise, it always remains hidden. In between the bouts of sadness that come out, there is some laughter, not because of your effort but in spite of it. Sadness seems to be something that is identical with the person. Arjuna concluded that even gaining an unrivalled kingdom on earth would not allay his sorrow.

A kingdom is usually surrounded by enemies, making it a rivalled kingdom, that is, its ruler cannot sleep peacefully. It is like having a nice house, which you cannot enjoy because it is in an inimical neighbourhood. Similarly, in a kingdom that all the rivals want to occupy and go on encroaching upon, one rival nibbles away at the east while another nibbles away at the west. This continual encroachment, nibbling, makes the ruler of the kingdom miserable. Therefore, in order to be happy, a ruler must have a kingdom that is unrivalled.

Even by being the emperor of an empire, this could not be accomplished, Arjuna knew. There can be such severe drought and poverty in an empire that people will begin to eat each other or, at least, will be ready to do so. Arjuna saw his situation in this way. *Dharma* is very difficult to follow when a man is hungry and continues to be hungry. Eventually, he will begin to compromise his *dharma* in order to relieve his hunger. The ruler of a kingdom is no different except that he must become a national beggar. If you are the head of a family, you have to beg for the whole family, not a big problem. However, if you are the ruler of a whole nation and its citizens are hungry, you must go to UNESCO and America to plead for assistance.

A kingdom that is poor, is not a happy kingdom and if it is prosperous, rivals will definitely be there. Having commented on earthly kingdoms, Arjuna then extended his thinking to the kingdom of the gods. 'I do not see that even ruling the kingdom of heaven will enable me to cross this sorrow,' he said.

Arjuna saw his mind as having been destroyed by *kārpaṇya*, miserliness. A person who has no money and does not spend is practical, whereas one who has no money but spends is not. Neither is a miser. A miser is one who has money and will not spend it. He or she is always waiting for retirement, which is not related to a job, but to the time when he can no longer take care of himself. Always worrying about who will take care of him, he keeps his money for later time/days. If he does fall ill, he still hangs on to it out of his concern for a more serious illness later! Then, when he dies, his brother-in-law gets everything! Such a person is a miser. He does not spend on himself or others. He is a very unfortunate person, like a child holding on to all of his toys. He is immature; he does not know himself and dies not knowing.

The *Bṛhadāraṇyakopaniṣad* talks about a *kṛpaṇa*, a miser, from another standpoint. It describes the person as a miser, leaving this world without gaining the knowledge of *ātmā*.

It says:

यो वा एतदक्षरं गार्ग्यविदित्वास्माल्लोकात्प्रैति स कृपणः

yo vā etadakṣaraṁ gārgyaviditvāsmāllokātpraiti sa kṛpaṇaḥ

(Bṛhadāraṇyakopaniṣad 3. 8.10)

O Gārgī! The one who departs from this world without knowing this 'Immutable One' is a *kṛpaṇa*.

The real wealth of a human being is more than external wealth. It is *viveka* knowing what is real and what is unreal, what is right and what is wrong. This wealth distinguishes the human being from all other beings. The one who has this *viveka* is not a *kṛpaṇa*, whereas the one who does not have it naturally holds on to things, which have no real content because his or her value structure is confused. Arjuna is referring to this kind of miserliness, when he says that he has been overcome by *kārpaṇya*.

Arjuna now saw that although he had opportunities to do so, he had not made proper use of his mind. Otherwise, he would not have had this problem and knowing what was right and wrong would have been easy. He knew he could only decide this when he was not caught in the very concept of right and wrong. He had to know a little more than *dharma* and *adharma* in order to decide about right and wrong. When right and wrong itself is an issue, one whose mind is deluded with reference to right and wrong cannot resolve it. Because he knew something more was needed, Arjuna asked Kṛṣṇa to tell him what was best for him. He wanted Kṛṣṇa to teach him that which is more than *dharma* and *adharma*.

Two pursuits are open to a person, *śreyas* and *preyas*. *Śreyas* is something that is good for all, something that is above *dharma* and *adharma*. Whereas *preyas* is the result of *dharma*. Any good action produces a result for you, such as prosperity, pleasure, and so on. *Śreyas* is other than this, more than this; it is *mokṣa*. Arjuna therefore asked, 'Please teach me *śreyas* alone.'

Kṛṣṇa could have said, 'Why should I teach you? I came here to drive your chariot and you are asking me to teach. That was not the original contract. I said I would drive; I told you I would not fight. I did not tell you that I would teach. You wanted me to drive your chariot and I accepted. Now you are asking your driver to teach you!' Kṛṣṇa responded in this way because Arjuna was telling him something that he had never told him before. He was saying, 'I am your student.'

If someone tells you that he or she is your student, *śiṣya*, you have to decide whether the person deserves to be a *śiṣya*. Whether you will be his or her *guru* is something for you to decide. Thus Arjuna left it in Kṛṣṇa's hands. He seems to say, 'The ball is in your court now, Kṛṣṇa. You do whatever you like. I do not care, but I am your *śiṣya*.' Until now, Arjuna had not told Kṛṣṇa that he was his student, which is why Kṛṣṇa had not taught him so far. Only for the asking is the teaching given and Arjuna had never asked for it, although he had asked for a variety of things. He had asked him to come and drive his chariot, which Kṛṣṇa did. But he had never asked him to teach.

What does it mean to be a śiṣya?

The words *śiṣya* and *śreyas* go together. Once you say, 'I am a *śiṣya*,' and you ask for *śreyas*, there is only one meaning for that *śreyas*. Although it can mean anything good, any topical solution to a topical problem, any medicine or treatment, *śreyas* here has an absolute meaning. Because Arjuna says, 'I am your *śiṣya;* please teach me,' the absolute meaning is conveyed.

Śiṣya can also mean many things. There is an archery *śiṣya*, a dance *śiṣya*, both of which apply to Arjuna, as well as many others. In all of them, one factor is missing, the surrender. By asking Kṛṣṇa to teach him, Arjuna became a *śiṣya*, a disciple. As a student, he surrendered himself to Kṛṣṇa.

As we saw earlier, there are three words in Sanskrit for the student, *vidyārthī*, *antevāsī* and *śiṣya*. *Vidyārthī* can be anyone having a desire for knowledge. Everyone wants to know everything, but it does not mean that effort is made to gain knowledge. An *antevāsī* is the one who makes this effort. This type of student goes to a teacher, joins the ranks, joins the courses, and enrolls in the university. It does not mean that he or she understands what is being taught in the class. The student may simply be sitting there, accomplishing nothing.

The third word '*śiṣya*' refers to a student who is qualified to be taught based on his or her capacity to understand. By using the word *śiṣya*, Arjuna was stating that he thought he was prepared to learn what Kṛṣṇa had to teach. His compassion indicated that he was mature, but because of certain lack of understanding, there was confusion with reference to *dharma* and *adharma*. Arjuna wanted to solve this problem much more fundamentally. He could not but think of his sorrow, which is a human problem. He had discerned sorrow in a situation where sorrow was not expected. He could not proceed with the battle because he did not see any favourable outcome, nothing that he could be proud of and thus his mind went elsewhere.

Where does the mind go in such circumstances? It comes back to oneself. This is where culture comes in. Without culture, one becomes a hobo. In Arjuna's case, his culture, maturity, his upbringing, his lifelong commitment to the values of *dharma*, the various privations he underwent for the sake of *dharma*, all of these had paid off in this particular coming back to himself and saying, 'I do not think that even a heavenly kingdom could remove this sorrow that is in me.'

Sorrow was, therefore, the problem and Arjuna had always heard that there was only one way of removing it. He had to become a *śiṣya* and gain *śreyas* or *mokṣa*, liberation. He did both of them. 'To be a *śiṣya*,' he told Kṛṣṇa, 'I have surrendered to you. You are the one who is going to deliver the goods. I am your student.' In this way, Arjuna surrendered so that Lord Kṛṣṇa could do what was to be done.

Verse 9

Sañjaya narrates the events to Dhṛtarāṣṭra

सञ्जय उवाच ।
एवमुक्त्वा हृषीकेशं गुडाकेशः परन्तपः ।
न योत्स्य इति गोविन्दमुक्त्वा तूष्णीं बभूव ह ॥ ९ ॥

sañjaya uvāca
evamuktvā hṛṣīkeśaṁ guḍākeśaḥ parantapaḥ
na yotsya iti govindam uktvā tūṣṇīṁ babhūva ha (9)

sañjayaḥ – Sañjaya; *uvāca* – said;
parantapaḥ – the scorcher of foes; *guḍākeśaḥ* – Arjuna; *hṛṣīkeśam* – to Lord Kṛṣṇa; *evam* – in this manner; *uktvā* – having spoken; *na yotsye* – I shall not fight; *iti* – thus; *govindam* – to Govinda (Lord Kṛṣṇa); *uktvā* – saying; *tūṣṇīm babhūva* – became silent; *ha* – indeed

Sañjaya said:
Having spoken to Hṛṣīkeśa (Lord Kṛṣṇa) in this manner, Guḍākeśa (Arjuna), the scorcher of foes, said, 'I shall not fight'. Speaking thus to Govinda (Lord Kṛṣṇa), he became silent.

With these words Sañjaya informed Dhṛtarāṣṭra of the most recent events on the battlefield, as he had been asked to do.

Wanting Kṛṣṇa to teach him *śreyas*, Arjuna had said, 'I am your *śiṣya*. Please teach me.' Arjuna seemed to know the profundity of the word *śreyas*, a word mentioned often in the *śāstra*.

In the *Kaṭhopaniṣad*, there is a story about a young boy, Naciketas, who went to Yama, the Lord of Death, and received three boons. He encashed the first in favour of his father, who was angry with him. For the second boon, he asked to be taught the ritual for gaining heaven. This boon, too, was for the sake of others. Lord Yama granted Naciketas both of these boons.

Naciketas encashed the third boon for himself. He wanted to know whether there was a self, an *ātmā* other than the body, because some people said there was, and others said there was not. He told Lord Yama that he wanted to be taught about this *ātmā* and that there was no one more qualified to do it than Lord Yama himself. At first Lord Yama discouraged him, but finally he decided to teach Naciketas.

Lord Yama told Naciketas that there were always two things available to a human being, *śreyas* and *preyas*. *Śreyas* is chosen by one who is wise, a *vivekī*. Whereas everyone else generally chooses *preyas* – prosperity and pleasure, *artha* and *kāma*. *Dharma* also comes under *preyas*. *Śreyas*, on the other hand, is *mokṣa*, liberation, the freedom brought about by self-knowledge. Naciketas asked Lord Yama for this *śreyas*. Because *śreyas* can be used in both a relative and an absolute sense, it is important to know what it was that Arjuna was asking for. Whether Arjuna wanted it, Kṛṣṇa understood Arjuna's request only in terms of absolute *śreyas* and not in the ordinary sense. The absolute meaning of *śreyas* is absolute fullness, that which is good for me, good for you, good for everyone, at any time and place. That which was good for Arjuna was equally good for Duryodhana, if only he had ears for it. If Duryodhana had said to Kṛṣṇa, 'I am your *śiṣya,* please teach me,' and if Kṛṣṇa had considered Duryodhana a qualified student, he would have taught him in the same way.

Whenever and to whomever *śreyas* is taught, it is always taught the same way because it is knowledge, *jñāna*. From Kṛṣṇa's point of view, the *śreyas* Arjuna asked for was this knowledge, which is *mokṣa*. In the wake of this knowledge, there is no sorrow. Because this is the teaching of the *Gītā,* from beginning to end, the *Gītā* is *mokṣa-śāstra,* a body of teaching meant to destroy *śoka*, sorrow.

Knowledge is something that cannot be personal. Although it has to be gained by a person, knowledge, any knowledge, is always true to the nature of the object of knowledge. It is not something that is centred on your personal will, but on the object of knowledge. For example, if the object is a flower, it is a flower; there is no choice in knowing it as anything other than a flower. If there is something more to know about the flower, then you can know it such as its botanical name, which includes its family and so on. Whatever more you come to know about the flower is always *jñāna*. Because knowledge is always as true as the object, it is not determined by your will. Therefore, knowledge of a thing is not going to differ from person to person.

Relative śreyas

Usually, what is good for you at a given time may be not good for you at another time. For example, a particular drug may be a cure for your illness, although it is also a poison. So, what is good for you at one time is not good for you at another time. Also, certain medicine may be good for only one problem and not any other. Alternatively, the drug that treats your problem may not be good for someone else with the same problem, because of the other person's allergic reaction to it. This kind of goodness is what is meant by relative goodness, something that is not always applicable in the same way. It keeps on changing.

Something that is good is determined by place, *deśa*; time, *kāla*; and *nimitta*, situation. Even ethics and values, *dharma-śāstra*, which we generally consider as absolute, have to be interpreted from time to time. Because *dharma-śāstra* is to be interpreted, it cannot be considered absolutely good.

Absolute śreyas

If there is something that is absolutely good, it must be something that does not change at any time and is always the same for any person. That is what is meant by *śreyas* here. Arjuna's sorrow led him to ask for this *śreyas* and Kṛṣṇa understood what he wanted as absolute *śreyas*.

Absolute *śreyas*, called *mokṣa*, is the complete acceptance of oneself. Self-acceptance implies a self that is already acceptable. If I am not acceptable to myself, positive thinking cannot give me self-acceptance. The self is unfolded in the *Gītā* as already acceptable, along with how it is acceptable and how it is free from all limitations.

The one who is happy with oneself has nothing more to do. Such a person is one who has checked off all the items to be completed, to be fulfilled that are on the list. He or she is a free person. Throughout the *Gītā* we are told that the self is acceptable and this acceptable self alone is what everyone is seeking in life.

When Duryodhana wanted the kingdom, he wanted only self-acceptance. He wanted to see himself as a person who was acceptable to him. Without a kingdom, he could not see himself in this way. Therefore, he wanted the kingdom. In the process, of course, he had conflicts. He was cavilled at by so many people and he had wronged so many people. How could he be acceptable to himself under such circumstances?

You should be acceptable to yourself without a kingdom, without any addition, without even the physical body and its condition. Only then can you accept yourself. If the body is something based on which you have self-acceptance, you are in trouble because the body will change. It is not going to remain the same. The self might have been acceptable yesterday, but not today, because the body has picked up a problem. The body is time-bound; it is subject to change and it keeps changing. In the morning it is acceptable and in the evening, it is not. We find, then, that if the self depends on any other factor for its acceptability it is not an acceptable self at all. The self by itself, in its own glory, should be acceptable to you, for which it has to be free from any limitation whatsoever.

The self is the whole. In reality, there is nothing other than the self. This vision is unfolded in the *Gītā* in such verses, '*...matsthāni sarvabhūtāni na cā'haṁ teṣvavasthitaḥ,* all beings exist in me and I do not exist in them.' *(Gītā 9.4)* and, '*na ca* *matsthāni bhūtāni...* in me there are no beings...' *(Gītā 9.5)*. It means that while I do not depend on any one of them, they all depend upon me. This is the vision of the whole, unfolded in the *śāstra* as the meaning of the word *śreyas*.

Śreyas is you. Until it is gained, *śreyas* is an end, as it were. Once gained, it is not separate from you. It is you alone. You are *śreyas*. Arjuna asked for it and he got it. If Arjuna had wanted ordinary *śreyas*, he would not have told Kṛṣṇa that he was his *śiṣya*. Nor would he have told him that he was surrendering to him. All this indicated that Arjuna wanted to gain absolute *śreyas* at this particular stage of his life. Having surrendered to Kṛṣṇa, Arjuna left everything to him. Kṛṣṇa then had to decide whether he would teach Arjuna or merely urge him to stop blabbering and fight! Fortunately, Kṛṣṇa taught him. Had he opted not to, we would not have the *Gītā*.

Arjuna's attraction to sannyāsa

In asking that Kṛṣṇa teach him, there was a prayer, a surrender in Arjuna that calmed the storm within him. When there is a doubt or indecision, the mind is restless. When there is a possibility of a solution, or a decision is made, then the mind quietens down. There is definitely restlessness when there is a conflict between *dharma* and *adharma*.

In Arjuna's mind there was a conflict between right and wrong, *dharma* and *adharma*, and there was the emotion of sympathy, leading to his sorrow. Affections being involved, his mind was in an even greater state of confusion than it would have been had he merely been concerned about his duty.

Arjuna's confusion naturally led to certain sadness. Lord Kṛṣṇa was a good listener and perhaps the two verses wherein he tried to whip Arjuna into action also helped to trigger Arjuna's thinking.

While trying to prove to Kṛṣṇa that he was not frightened, Arjuna had to tell him that he could not handle this particular situation. He now saw himself as someone who was not as dispassionate as he was expected to be. Arjuna concluded that he would be better off living a life of alms, a lifestyle mentioned in the *śāstra* for a *sādhu*, a person who gives up the pursuit of all desires.

The life of a *sādhu* is meant purely for the pursuit of knowledge, *jñāna*, and is free from all social, national, religious or familial obligations. As a *sannyāsī* you are a non-competitor in the society. You do not have a job. Nor are you interested in anything in the next life like heaven and so on. Self-knowledge is pursued to the exclusion of everything. A *sannyāsī* is respected by society, and lives on *bhikṣā*, alms. The Vedic society has a value for this lifestyle and it is one of the four stages, *āśrama*s, of a person's life.

Sannyāsa was exactly what Arjuna had in mind. He thought that a life of *bhikṣā* would mean *sannyāsa* and he talked about it constantly. He knew that *sannyāsa* was meant for *jñāna*, *mokṣa*, and that it was not for securities and pleasures, *artha*, *kāma* and *dharma*.

Having lived in the forest, Arjuna had met many great people, *mahātmā*s. What a period it was! Even though some

Duryodhanas were there, it was an excellent era. Certainly, it is a rare privilege to have as one's contemporaries, people like Vyāsa, Śuka, Bhīṣma, Vidura and Balarāma.

Although Arjuna had lived in such times, he had been a prince with his own predominant desires and ambitions. Naturally, he had not been committed to the pursuit of *mokṣa* although he had access to it. He knew all about *śreyas*, but now the time had come for him to pursue it.

When Arjuna had first come to fight, he had no conflict whatsoever. All he wanted to know was with whom he would be fighting. Even when he saw his own people on both sides, his conflict was simple. It was, 'Should I fight? How can I fight my own people?' But then, as he thought about it, he became completely unnerved, believing that he was committing some kind of self-destruction. What had started out as a simple conflict had now gained a different proportion altogether. A simple topical problem had become a fundamental problem.

This can happen to anyone. A time comes when death draws our attention and we ask, 'What is this death?' Perhaps, the Buddha thought he had to be a monk in order to find an answer to such a question. He was a prince and had not seen death or anyone who was crippled. Or, perhaps, since such events had not touched him personally, he had simply not paid any attention to them. Only when he began noticing them, did the big question hit him, 'There is so much sorrow and pain in life. Can there be a solution?' Having asked this question, it is said that he left the palace in search of the answer.

When you go off in search of truth, you do not carry a truckload of belongings with you. Since he was interested only in truth, he just walked out.

Similarly, seeing simple pain, there is an empathy that turns into something else because a question has been triggered. In fact, all problems in life are connected to those that are much more basic, the basic problems being inherent in ordinary small problems.

The small sorrows and pains, which are mental in nature, have their basis in the core personality. One who is angry becomes angry and one who is not angry does not. Similarly, only the sad become sad. In order to determine why you are sad, a psychotherapist may take you into regression, back into a period of time when you picked up various notions about yourself and the world. In this way, your neurosis is accounted for, which is psychology. There is a core personality, which is psychologically traceable by an informed specialist.

Tracking back, however, in itself, is not enough. One more step has to be taken, a step that is psychologically fundamental. No psychologist says that it is improper to think, 'I am a mortal, I am subject to sorrow, that I have to prove myself.' In fact, they all agree that you should get angry if the situation warrants it. 'Cry it out, do not suppress it,' they say. The teaching, however, says we must take one more step because there is a more basic problem that must be addressed. Because 'I am subject to sorrow' is a basic problem, there is something more basic about you, which you had better know. Any small problem can be traced if you ask a few more questions.

Inevitably, you will come to appreciate that there is a basic problem. If you ask the question, 'Am I really sad?' you end up reading the *Gītā* because the *Gītā* is the answer.

The answer is not something you can figure out because if you are sad, you are sad. It is something that needs to be recognised. To ask, 'What is the basis of sadness?' means that it is something to be understood and not a particular condition or experience. The experiences of both happiness and sorrow have always been there, one alternating with the other, now I am sad; now I am happy. It seems, therefore, that happiness is a visitor and sadness is the person.

You need to understand whether the self is subject to sorrow, what sorrow is, and so on. There is a whole gamut of questions involved here. A simple frown by someone can trigger some small pain in you. It can be traced to a fundamental self-ignorance and self-confusion, or at least a self-question, 'Am I seeing myself rightly?'

This kind of questioning is called *ātma-vicāra* and is what happened in Arjuna's mind. Therefore, he told Kṛṣṇa that he was his *śiṣya* and he wanted *śreyas*. 'If you think the battlefield is not a good place for us to be in, then just drive the chariot somewhere else. Do whatever you like. I have handed over the horses and chariot to you. You decide. If you want a quiet place, drive to a quiet place. And if you think you can teach in this din and roar, then I too can listen. I do not mind.' Saying this and leaving everything to Bhagavān, Arjuna became quiet.

Arjuna's surrender

Not only had Arjuna handed over his horses and chariot to Kṛṣṇa, but also his life. Having found the possibility of a solution to his problem in the form of *śreyas* and in the form of Kṛṣṇa's teaching, Arjuna became silent. The storm in his mind had blown over. Although it was not enlightened, his mind was at least silent with some hope. Even though the storm was over, Arjuna was still overcome with an intense inner torpor. Where did it come from? He had been so enthusiastic, armed, and ready to fight. Now, right in the middle of the battlefield, his sorrow was so much that his eyes glistened with tears.

When you are in sorrow, you are present as a whole person. In fact, sorrow cannot come unless you are there as a whole person. Some people have a feeling of deadness due to some emotional problem and, in order to relieve it, to feel alive, they work themselves into sorrow. Only then do they feel that they exist. Only then is there some reality for them. Artists sometimes have this problem. They feel dull and think they should be either ecstatic or in pain. They say that pain produces music or some other art form. However, it is not the pain that does it. It is because the whole person comes out of the pain and then something is produced. The result of such pain then becomes someone else's pain or joy, perhaps, depending on the product!

Similarly, Arjuna became a whole person because a storm had occurred. There was now no chance of sleep or any other expression of torpor, only silence. Having found this possibility of a solution, there was a lull in his mind now that the storm had blown over. What a silence it was!

Verse 10

Sañjaya speaks

तमुवाच हृषीकेशः प्रहसन्निव भारत ।
सेनयोरुभयोर्मध्ये विषीदन्तमिदं वचः ॥ १० ॥

tamuvāca hṛṣīkeśaḥ prahasanniva bhārata
senayorubhayormadhye viṣīdantam idaṁ vacaḥ (10)

bhārata – O Bhārata!; *ubhayoḥ senayoḥ madhye* – in the midst of both armies; *viṣīdantam* – the one who is sad; *tam* – to him; *hṛṣīkeśaḥ* – Kṛṣṇa; *prahasan iva* – as though smiling; *idam* – this; *vacaḥ* – sentence; *uvāca* – said

Bhārata (Dhṛtarāṣṭra)! To him who was sad in the midst of both armies, Hṛṣīkeśa (Kṛṣṇa), as though smiling, said these words.

In this verse, Sañjaya addressed Dhṛtarāṣṭra as Bhārata, a name that applied to all of these people, including Arjuna and his brothers, because they were born in the Bharata family. He told him that Lord Kṛṣṇa, about to respond to Arjuna's silence, was 'as though laughing.' Why did he not simply say Kṛṣṇa was smiling? Being an opportunity for interpretation here, many interpretations have been put forward.

Was Kṛṣṇa smiling because he had been waiting for this day? Previously, Arjuna had used the words, 'my chariot.' Now Arjuna had surrendered, an attitude that Kṛṣṇa would no doubt have found preferable. Kṛṣṇa was quite satisfied with the outcome of Arjuna's outpourings. The discussion had not been just a simple dialogue with a person in despair. Arjuna had asked to be Kṛṣṇa's *śiṣya*. Perhaps Kṛṣṇa was smiling because it was now going to happen.

Whatever the reason, Kṛṣṇa was smiling. The knowledge he was about to teach was not a grim knowledge. He did not have to say, 'Please listen to me. I am a *vedāntī* and this is a very serious matter. You are all bliss, fullness, *ānanda*. Please, therefore, do not take this knowledge lightly,' and so on. The subject matter being what it was, it was a smile, laughter, all the way. We find that Kṛṣṇa always had a good time while teaching Arjuna, whereas Arjuna, of course, did have a hard time now and then. One can find a number of different meanings for this expression, 'as though laughing.'

Kṛṣṇa did not drive the chariot to a quieter place. He kept the chariot where it was, right in the middle of the battlefield. For gaining this knowledge, you do not require a particular time or place. You only require a particular person or persons. There should be someone like Kṛṣṇa who, in the din and roar of the battlefield, had all the composure necessary to talk to Arjuna. Arjuna too had the necessary composure to listen to Kṛṣṇa; the appropriateness of his questions indicates that he listened well. Therefore, who is learning and who is teaching are important, whereas the time and place are not.

Because the words to be spoken by Kṛṣṇa to Arjuna comprise the teaching, the *Gītā* is said to begin with the next verse. Kṛṣṇa began by telling Arjuna that there was no reason for grief, *aśocyān anvaśocaḥ tvam*, and concluded the *Gītā* saying, 'Grieve not, *mā śucaḥ*.' In between there is only removal of grief, to put it more accurately, removal of the reason for grief. The cause of grief, ignorance and error, is removed totally. Therefore, the entire *gītā-śāstra* is a *śāstra* that removes sorrow, *śoka*.

Sorrow refers to any complaint. Any uneasiness about me, centred on the self, is sorrow. Physical pain is not sorrow, but complaining about such pain is sorrow. The problem is in thinking that everyone else is well and I am not. This self-centred sorrow, *śoka*, is purely the brood of ignorance, wrong thinking stemming from wrong notions about oneself and the world. Kṛṣṇa's words, Bhagavān's *Gītā*, addressed this very problem.

Verse 11

The teaching begins

श्रीभगवानुवाच ।
अशोच्यानन्वशोचस्त्वं प्रज्ञावादांश्च भाषसे ।
गतासूनगतासूंश्च नानुशोचन्ति पण्डिताः ॥ ११ ॥

śrībhagavān uvāca
aśocyān anvaśocastvaṁ prajñāvādāṁśca bhāṣase
gatāsūn agatāsūṁśca nānuśocanti paṇḍitāḥ (11)

śrībhagavān – Śrī Bhagavān; *uvāca* – said;
tvam – you; *aśocyān* – those who are not to be grieved for; *anvaśocaḥ* – grieve; *prajñāvādān* – words of wisdom; *bhāṣase* –

you speak; *ca* – and; *paṇḍitāḥ* – the wise; *gatāsūn* – those from whom the breath has left; *agatāsūn* – those from whom the breath has not yet left; *ca* – and; *na anuśocanti* – do not grieve

Śrī Bhagavān said:

You grieve for those who are not be grieved for. Yet you speak words of wisdom. The wise do not grieve for those who are gone and who are not yet gone.

Arjuna, confused about *dharma* and *adharma*, overwhelmed by sorrow, became a *śiṣya* and asked for *śreyas*. Wanting to help Arjuna out of his sorrow for good and knowing that relative *śreyas* was useless here, Kṛṣṇa's teaching was for imparting self-knowledge alone.

The subject matter of the rest of the *Gītā* is self-knowledge, *ātma-jñāna*, the cause for the removal of sorrow. Śaṅkara's commentary starts with this verse since it marks the beginning of the teaching.

While the word '*tvam*, you,' refers to Arjuna, it can also apply to any second person. The word is significant given that the whole *vedānta-śāstra* is nothing but '*tat tvam asi*, that thou art.' The first six chapters of the *Gītā* deal with 'you' alone. What is 'you' in the equation, *tat tvam asi*? You are 'that' means you are equated to 'that.' 'That' has to be presented and the meaning given is the Lord, Īśvara. Therefore, '*tat tvam asi*' means 'you are Īśvara.'

That there is a difference between you and the Lord is obvious. But, because the statement, '*tat tvam asi*' is an equation, it seems as though 'you' are equated to the Lord. The vision of the *śruti* is that you are that Īśvara who is the cause for the entire creation. That Brahman you are. The '*tat tvam asi*' equation is a statement, a *vākya*, of this vision.

There are two elements involved here. One is Īśvara, the Lord, which is the meaning of the word *tat;* and the other is the *jīva*, the individual, which is the meaning of the word *tvam*, you. Unless the meaning of 'you' is properly understood, the equation cannot be understood because there is a contradiction. If the statement, 'You are Brahman' were to be a self-evident fact, there would be no necessity for the teaching at all. Since there is a contradiction between *jīva* and Īśvara, we have to resolve it. Unless there is absence of contradiction, there is no identity. Unless you recognise the real meaning of the word 'you,' which means 'I' there is no way of discovering the identity between you and Īśvara that the '*tat tvam asi*' equation reveals. Therefore, the first six chapters of the *Gītā* emphasise 'you.' The next six chapters deal with 'that' the Lord, and the last six chapters deal with the identity between the two. You will find, as you proceed, that the whole subject matter in the seventh chapter changes and that the last six chapters are significantly different.

Arjuna's sorrow, the subject matter of the first chapter, is the sorrow of any *jīva*, the individual, one who is subject to sorrow. That Arjuna was sad is not unusual. In fact, we are all with Arjuna. His sorrow seems to be very legitimate. If this situation could not cause sorrow, what could? We can well appreciate and sympathise with Arjuna because for much lesser reasons, we find ourselves in even deeper trouble.

This is the condition of the *jīva*. That the *jīva* is desirous of getting rid of sorrow is also obvious.

Generally, people seek relief through escapes. What is significant here is that Arjuna wanted to resolve the sorrow for good, which is the reason we have a *gītā-śāstra*. Arjuna was told straight away by Kṛṣṇa, 'You, Arjuna, grieve unnecessarily.' Over the shoulders of Arjuna, you too are being addressed. You too have entertained sorrow, the state of mind known as *śoka*.

What is deserving of grief?

Śocya is that which deserves grief, that which has legitimate basis for sorrow. In the society, we have universally accepted that certain events are matters for sorrow, while others are not. For example, when someone is about to be married, we do not send condolences. We send congratulations. Marriage is a matter for joy and laughter, not for sorrow. It is the case in any culture. For a death, on the other hand, even when there is relief involved because the person was suffering extreme pain and required constant care, there is a tinge of sadness when someone dies. Therefore, death is synonymous with mourning and can be called *śocya*, universally.

There is also personal *śocya*. You may be sad because of something that has come or gone, whereas another person may not be sad at all. A man may be very happy that his mother has come, whereas his wife is a pack of nerves. For him the event is not *śocya*, but for her it is a great *śocya*. Because this woman has walked into their home, one person becomes a pack of nerves. The other is ecstatic because he can show off his accomplishments to his mother. The event is the same for both of them, but for one person it is *śocya* and for the other it is *aśocya*. Thus, we find that some things are *śocya* universally and others are *śocya* only for an individual.

Culturally, there may also be peculiar situations that are *śocya*s. In some cultures the birth of a girl is *śocya*, whereas in other cultures the birth of a boy may cause sorrow since too many boys are definitely a problem. Thus, an object of sorrow, *śoka* is called *śocya* just as an object of knowledge, *jñāna*, is called *jñeya*. An object of sorrow means a situation that causes sorrow, be it an event or an experience. A situation that does not cause sorrow is called *aśocya*. Here, Kṛṣṇa's contention is that whatever may be the situation, you have no legitimate reason for grief. In the coming verses he will establish that there is no legitimate cause for sorrow both from the relative and the absolute standpoints.

The wise do not grieve

Here, Kṛṣṇa told Arjuna that he had picked up sorrow where it was not warranted at all and that people of knowledge, *paṇḍita*s, do not entertain any grief. *Paṇḍā* means self-knowledge and a *paṇḍita* is one in whom self-knowledge is born.[1] Kṛṣṇa also acknowledged in this verse that, although Arjuna was grieving over that which did not deserve any grief, he had also spoken words of wisdom. Bhagavān remembered all of

---

[1] पण्डा । आत्मविषया बुद्धिः येषां ते पण्डिताः । (शङ्कर भाष्यम्)

paṇḍā, self-knowledge; the one who has this self-knowledge is a *paṇḍita*

Arjuna's words from the first chapter when he spoke so eloquently about who would go to *naraka* and why the *dharma* would be in trouble, etc. While acknowledging the wisdom of Arjuna's words, Kṛṣṇa told him that people of wisdom do not grieve.

Arjuna was not a wise man and that was his whole problem, Kṛṣṇa knew that all he had to do was make Arjuna a *paṇḍita* so that he would not see a problem where there was not one, as he was presently doing. The sorrow itself was unwarranted which was why he was aggrieved.

With reference to what, do the wise not grieve? Lord Yama, death, can interfere at any time. There are many breaths and any one of them could be the last. One breath alone does not last for eighty years. Between every inhalation and every exhalation, there is a gap. Therefore, how do you know which breath will be the last? Only when the next breath comes do we know that the last breath was not the last.

The verse makes a distinction between one who has breathed his or her last and one who has not. Men of wisdom do not entertain any grief either for the dead or for the not yet dead. Why was death referred to here? Because all of Arjuna's arguments revolved only around death. He was always talking about the imminent death of his teachers and members of his family. Destruction was involved because there was a battle ensuing. This was one reason. In addition, death is the only event that uniformly, universally, evokes sorrow. But we would never send condolences to the devotees of a *mahātmā*; we only seek his continued blessings.

To use an analogy for why death was used here, a boxer who wants to become the heavyweight champion of the world has only to fight one person, the present champion and knock him out. Similarly, if death is one event which invariably evokes sorrow in all, with reference to which the wise do not grieve, certainly the loss of hair or the loss of a relationship or marriage will not be the cause for sorrow.

Finally, death is an appropriate event that is used here in order to discuss about sorrow and its removal when what is to be discussed is *ātmā*, which is not subject to death. Kṛṣṇa told Arjuna, that anything he might look upon as a source of sorrow was not. Nor would any wise man look upon anything as a source of sorrow because there is no source of sorrow.

Source of sorrow

What is it that can cause you sorrow? There can be only two sources, yourself, *ātmā* or a source other than yourself, *anātmā*. If *ātmā* is the source of sorrow, then there is no problem. You will always be sad because sadness is your nature, your *svabhāva*. In fact, when you are sad, you will be very happy because to be sad is your nature.

A restless monkey is a healthy, happy monkey because restlessness is its nature. A quiet monkey is a problem and should be cause for concern. If you are taking care of a monkey who suddenly becomes very quiet, do not think he has become a *sādhu* and is meditating. He definitely has a problem and may require attention. Similarly, what is natural to you cannot be a source of sorrow. If sorrow is our own nature, then we have no cause for sorrow at all. We should all be happy being sad. Thus, if *ātmā* is the source of our sorrow, then sadness is not a problem.

Since sadness is the problem, we must analyse whether it is the *ātmā* or the *anātmā* that is the source of your sadness. It means that either the world that you come across is the source of your sorrow or you yourself are its source; in other words, you are a source of sorrow to yourself. To put it more technically, you have to analyse whether *ātmā* is a source of your sorrow or *anātmā* is a source of sorrow. This analysis is the sole subject matter of the *Gītā*.

*Paṇḍita*s are those who know the *ātmā* and *anātmā*. If you know the *ātmā*, then you naturally know the *anātmā* also because what is not *ātmā* can only be *anātmā*. Conversely, if you know what *anātmā* is, you will also know what *ātmā* is. Therefore, knowing one implies knowing the other.

Arjuna's grief was due to not knowing the difference between *ātmā* and *anātmā*. That is, he did not have *ātma-anātma-viveka*. Knowing the difference, *viveka*, resolves the problem. This verse identifies the subject matter of the *Gītā* as *ātma-anātma-viveka* and states the result of such knowledge, knowing themselves the wise do not grieve.

The *gītā-śāstra* is the connection between the subject matter and the result in that it reveals what the *ātmā* is, thereby enabling one to become wise. And who is qualified for this knowledge? A qualified person is one who has a good degree of dispassion, *vairāgya*, with reference to his or her likes and dislikes and who has a desire for liberation, *mumukṣā*. Here, Arjuna is the qualified student and Kṛṣṇa is the teacher.

A pragmatic view of this verse

This verse can be viewed from the standpoint of a pragmatist who has no belief in any scripture or its statements. Or, it can be viewed from the standpoint of a person who has faith, *śraddhā*, in the survival of the soul after death, from the standpoint of a believer, *āstika*, a follower of the Veda. It can also be viewed from the standpoint of the vision of the *Gītā*, the standpoint of *ātmā* itself.

The practical person's standpoint is that any sorrow, if analysed, has no legitimacy. Legitimate sorrow is sorrow that is commonly accepted. The question is, is there a sorrow that can be called legitimate? For a simple, practical person, if sorrow produces a result that you want, then it is legitimate for you. Otherwise, it is not. That we all have sorrow is not in question for the practical person, but the point is that it does not produce any result.

When a person is sad because someone very near and dear has died, what does this sadness produce? Does it alter the fact that one's friend is dead and gone? No. Sadness does not alter any fact. A woman is crying because someone has died. Crying, she gets up and lights the stove. Crying, she boils water and makes coffee. Crying she adds milk and sugar. Crying, she drinks it. Nothing changes. Previously, she drank coffee and now also she is drinking coffee. All that is new is the crying. She is not taking coffee to cry better. No fact is altered.

From a pragmatist's point of view, sorrow is not going to help you and it certainly does not help the dead. If I am dead and gone, I have no problem. Even if I am dying, can I afford to be sad? The heart generally does not give up easily. It keeps trying even when there is pain, even when it misses beats, or even when one artery is gone. It does not give up. However, when you become sad, the heart may think, 'this fellow is sad. Why should I continue to work?' Because you have already decided, it too will give up. The will also seems to have a way of moving the limbs and organs to make them tick. If the will is gone, if you are sad, the fighting system will necessarily give up.

There is a story about three men who, in the doctor's opinion, were dying of terminal diseases. The doctor therefore asked each of them what he wanted. The first man asked for a priest so that he could make his confession and this was arranged. The second man wanted to see his family and the doctor arranged this as well. When the third man was asked what he wanted, he replied, 'I want another doctor!' The third man was practical and wanted to live. He had something about him that perhaps would make the heart try harder. Because he required all the strength he had in order to live, he definitely could not afford to be sad.

We have already seen that sadness with reference to someone who is dead produces no result in that it does not alter the fact. But, should you not be sad if someone is seriously ill? If you cry when you visit such a man, he will think he is going to die, although all the doctors may have been telling him that his condition is not serious and that he should not worry. The doctors may even have some hope; but your crying is going to make him doubt what the doctors have been saying. In other words, he will read his own death in your crying and then give up. Anyone who is ill requires strength and therefore cannot afford to be sad. Instead of crying, you have to boost the person's morale in whatever way you can, which, in turn, can boost his or her strength.

Thus, crying does not alter the fact that the dead have gone and the dying do not require your crying. If you yourself are dying, crying is also useless. Why then this sorrow? Sorrow still takes place. It is born of confusion, *aviveka*. What is subject to change will change. Why then sit and say, 'They are changing. They are changing.' The changing is always changing.

One who dies is one who is subject to death. Therefore, the one who will die, dies, and the one who will not die, does not die. What is not subject to death will always remain and what is subject to death will not. Death may come earlier than expected, but it is always expected, although we do not know which breath will be the last.

Grief, therefore, is never legitimate. From the practical person's standpoint, sorrow is useless and for the one who believes that the *jīva* continues after the death of the body, sorrow is also not a problem because the *jīva* itself does not die.

Two-fold teaching methodology – pravṛtti and nivṛtti

The first portion of the Vedas is in the form of *pravṛtti*, meaning you engage yourself in positive pursuits in order to accomplish certain ends, which you do not have now and want to accomplish. These pursuits may be in the form of progeny, wealth, another world, a better birth, and so on, all of which require appropriate effort to achieve the desired ends. This subject matter of the Vedas in the form of effort-based pursuit in terms of action, *karma*, is called *pravṛtti-ātmaka-śāstra*.

The *karma* enjoined in the first portion of the Vedas is three-fold from the standpoint of the means of doing it – *mānasa*, mental activity; *vācika*, speech; and *kāyika*, physical activity involving the limbs. For example, repeating the Vedas is a prayer employing both mind and speech. Chanting the *Puruṣa-sūkta* is also a prayer in praise of the Lord, the *puruṣa*, who is everything. The *Puruṣa-sūkta* also gives you the knowledge of the Lord. Any *sūkta* is both a prayer and something to be understood.

Chanting is a *karma* which is *vācika*. However, chanting can also be an *aṅga*, a part of a ritual. For instance, a *paṇḍita* may chant the *Puruṣa-sūkta*, line by line, while offering a flower or some other oblation. Thus, the same *mantra*s can be chanted, themselves forming a prayer, or used as part of a ritual. This three-fold *karma* namely *kāyika*, *vācika* and *mānasa*, is the subject matter of the first portion of the Vedas and is what is meant by *pravṛtti*, what you must do to accomplish certain desirable ends.

The last portion of the Vedas, called Vedanta, is *nivṛtti-ātmaka-śāstra*, that is, it is purely in the form of negation. The first quarter of the verse we are presently studying, *aśocyān anvaśocaḥ tvam*, which reveals the entire subject matter of the *Gītā*, is also in the form of negation. In *pravṛtti*, the doer, the *kartā*, is retained. The *kartā* is told to do certain things in order to accomplish certain results. Whereas, in the Vedanta portion, the very notion, 'I am the doer' is questioned and negated. Here also there is something to be accomplished – that which is not already accomplished by you, the *kartā*. The accomplishment is negation of the doership in the wake of the knowledge of the *ātmā*.

This portion of the Veda, which says that you are the reality of everything, that you are the whole, is in the form of negation, *nivṛtti*, in the sense that all the notions that you superimpose upon the self, the *ātmā*, are negated. Therefore, this part of the Veda is in the form of knowledge, *jñāna*, leading to the negation and recognition of what I am not, and an appreciation of what I am.

Sorrow is something that is superimposed upon the *ātmā* due to the non-recognition of the nature, the reality, *svarūpa*, of the *ātmā*. Therefore, any sorrow is really without reason because sorrow itself has its roots only in the non-recognition of the self and confusion. The world, *anātmā*, cannot cause you sorrow, nor can *ātmā* be a source of sorrow. So, this verse starts with the negative particle *nañ*, meaning 'not'– *aśocyān*, which means *na śocyān*.

Generally, a *nañ* would not be the first word of any *śāstra*, negation not being an appropriate beginning. A *śāstra* should begin with something positive. Here, the *śāstra*, being in the form of *nivṛtti*, begins with *nañ* – it begins with the word, *aśocyān*, meaning that nothing is deserving of grief. Because Arjuna was in sorrow, the word *aśocyān* is extremely relevant here.

The Lord is called Hari because he is the one whose grace removes everything. The Lord is a robber, a remover of all your problems, of everything that you do not want. Lord Viṣṇu is called Hari and Lord Śiva is called Hara. Both their names originate from the same root, '*hṛ*'– to rob, to remove.

Arjuna is told, 'You are aggrieved for no reason. You have entertained grief with reference to situations that do not demand any grief on your part. Bhīṣma and Droṇa can take care of themselves. You need not have any grief on their behalf or for any other reason.' If you understand everything from the standpoint of *ātmā* there is no sorrow. From any other standpoint also, sorrow is not reasonable.

It is not that Arjuna was advised to have no sorrow. Such advice would not have been proper. Therefore, we should not say that we should not be sad because the *Gītā* says so. Nor does the *śāstra* say that it is not proper to be sad. It says there is no reason for sadness, meaning that sadness, sorrow is something to be enquired into and understood.

The *Gītā* says that you have entertained grief for which there is no reason because neither *ātmā* nor *anātmā* is the source of sorrow. This statement must then be proved, which the *gītā-śāstra* does by revealing that *ātmā*, whose nature is fullness, *ānanda-svarūpa*, cannot be affected by *anātmā*, *mithyā*, because the very existence of *anātmā* depends on *ātmā*, *satya*, the truth of everything. So *ātmā* is not going to be affected by *mithyā* just as the imaginary snake you see on the rope cannot affect the rope. If the rope is wet, it is wet, but it has not been made so by the sliminess of the snake you see sitting on top of it! So too, *ātmā* is not affected by anything that has been superimposed upon it.

Therefore, the basis, the *adhiṣṭhāna, satya,* is not affected by *mithyā. Mithyā* depends upon *ātmā* for its existence and sustenance, for its fuel, its very fibres of being. The only thing that could affect *ātmā* would be something enjoying the same order of reality. When two entities belonging to the same order of reality, such as the father-in-law and the son-in-law, come together in a relationship, the dependency of one will affect the other. If the son-in-law does not have a job and finds it necessary to move in with his father-in-law, the son-in-law's dependency will definitely affect the father-in-law. This dependence is entirely different and is not what is under discussion here.

What we are discussing is *ātmā* which is *satya* and *anātmā* which is *mithyā*. Just as the *svarūpa* of water is not affected by the wave, the *svarūpa* of *ātmā, sat-cit-ānanda,* is not affected by *anātmā*. This subject matter is discussed throughout the *Gītā* starting with this verse. Although the verse starts with a negative particle, *nañ*, it is not an improper beginning because the whole *Gītā* is *nivṛtti-ātmaka*.

Before beginning the *Mahābhārata*, Vyāsa saluted the Goddess of Knowledge, Sarasvatī, and he started the first chapter of the *Gītā* with the word Dhṛtarāṣṭra, meaning the one who sustains the entire universe. In this way, prayer for an auspicious beginning was well taken care of and nothing more was required. To begin the teaching with the statement,

'There is no room for sorrow,' as he did in this verse, is therefore a very effective beginning, although a negative particle was used.

Verse 12

In the vision of the Gītā there is no birth and death

न त्वेवाहं जातु नासं न त्वं नेमे जनाधिपाः ।
न चैव न भविष्यामः सर्वे वयमतः परम् ॥ १२ ॥

na tvevāhaṁ jātu nāsaṁ na tvaṁ neme janādhipāḥ
na caiva na bhaviṣyāmaḥ sarve vayam ataḥ param (12)

aham – I; *jātu* – ever; *na tu āsam* – did not exist; (*iti*) *na eva* – not indeed; *tvam* – you; (*āsīḥ* – did not exist); (*iti*) *na* – not; *ime* – these; *janādhipāḥ* – kings; (*na āsan* – did not exist); (*iti*) *na* – not; *ataḥ param* – hereafter; *sarve* – all; *vayam* – we; *bhaviṣyāmaḥ* – shall not exist; *ca* – and; (*iti*) *na eva* – not at all

There was never a time I did not exist, neither you nor these kings. Nor will any of us cease to exist in the future.

If all these people are going to die, how can it be said that they do not cause sorrow for the bereaved? Surely, since they are going to die, they must be the cause of sorrow, *śocya*. Even those who are not on the battlefield are *śocya*s because they too are eventually going to die. Addressing this doubt, Kṛṣṇa shifted the discussion to the vision of the *ātmā*. His statements were not meant as an argument to kill but rather, to provide an understanding of *dharma* so that what was to be done could be done. Since Arjuna also wanted absolute *śreyas*, Kṛṣṇa talked about the nature of *ātmā*.

He said 'There is no time that I did not exist. To say that I did not exist at some time is not true. I always existed.' Kṛṣṇa was obviously, therefore, not an ordinary person. He was an *avatāra*. He could say, 'I always existed.' Could the same thing be said of a *jīva* like Arjuna? Kṛṣṇa said, 'That you did not exist before is also not true. You too always existed.'

Being a prince, Arjuna was also not an ordinary person. Kṛṣṇa therefore went on to say that all the stalwarts standing before them on the battlefield, leaders of the people, chieftains, commanders-in-chief, and all the other soldiers had also always existed. What Kṛṣṇa is saying in this verse is that all of us are eternal, 'I was there before and you were there before, as were all these other people.' In his vision, they were all there before.

The next question would be, what about later? I might have existed before, but I might not exist later. Will there be a time in the future when I am not? Kṛṣṇa says, 'No! After the destruction of the body you will continue to exist.'

We have a concept that everyone is born and we have a horoscope to prove it. You know that you were born at a given time and take this to mean that there was a time when you were not. This is a very well-entrenched notion about the 'I'– that I was born, that I am getting old, that I am going to die and so on. If you are born, you will naturally get old. The notion that you are getting old is going to be there as long as you think you are born.

In the vision of the *Gītā* there is no such thing as birth for you. *Ātmā,* 'I' is not born. The notion that you are born is negated here by using double negatives. That you celebrate the birthday of Kṛṣṇa does not confirm the non-existence of Kṛṣṇa before. It only confirms that on this particular day, in this particular name and form, *nāma-rūpa,* Kṛṣṇa was born. To say that he was born in this *nāma-rūpa* is correct and creates no problems. But to say that Kṛṣṇa was not there before, despite what people might think, is not true. Therefore, Kṛṣṇa was not really born. He was 'as though' born.

Kṛṣṇa went on to say that it is also not true to think that you were not there before. There was no time that you were not there. Kṛṣṇa told Arjuna that he too essentially was timeless and that everyone else was as eternal, as existent, as Kṛṣṇa was.

Similarly, you always think that you will not exist later, a conclusion that calls for lamentation. This notion is also not true, Kṛṣṇa said. Whatever form you take yourself to be, you definitely exist. As an individual, *jīva,* you definitely exist. The *jīvatva,* individuality, may not exist later, but as *ātmā* you will always exist. Because the *jīvatva* goes when a person is enlightened, only *ātmā* is meant to be taken here. It is in this sense that Kṛṣṇa said to Arjuna, 'There was never a time when I was not, there was never a time when you were not, nor was there ever a time when all these leaders were not. Similarly, there will never be a time when all of us will not be.'

Does it mean that this feud will continue forever because all these *ātmā*s are going to be eternally there? No, the use of plural here was only with reference to forms, *upādhis*.[2] There was never a time when we were not there. Nor will there ever be a time when we will not be there. We can use pots and pot space as an example–the pots will come and go, but all the pot spaces will always be there because there is only one space. The words used in this verse – I, *aham*, you, *tvam*, we, *vayam*, kings, *janādipāḥ*–are all with reference to the bodies seemingly enclosing one *ātmā*, like many pots enclosing one space.

Ātmās are not many

Śaṅkara makes this important observation here in the last line of his *bhāṣya*, commentary –'*deha-bheda-anuvṛttyā bahuvacanam, na ātma-bheda-abhiprāyeṇa*, the plural has been used here with reference to the various bodies and not with reference to *ātmā*, the self.' The people standing before Kṛṣṇa and Arjuna had different physical bodies. Only from the standpoint of the physical bodies, there is plurality, and not from the standpoint of *ātmā*. There are no differences in *ātmā*. It is not that a Kṛṣṇa-*ātmā* existed, an Arjuna-*ātmā* existed, other *ātmā*s existed, and all of these having existed before will continue to exist forever. It is not the contention here at all.

*Ātmā*s are not many; there is only one *ātmā*. *Ātmā* that is not subject to time, *nitya-ātmā* being without form and attributes, can only be one. *Anitya* is that which is subject

---

[2] उप समीपे स्थित्वा स्वीयं धर्मं रूपम् अन्यत्र आदधाति इति उपाधिः ।

upa samīpe sthitvā svīyaṁ dharmaṁ rūpam anyatra ādadhāti iti upādhiḥ – that which imparts its qualities to another by staying close to it, is called an *upādhi*.

to time; it means anything that has a form with attributes, with an *upādhi* is subject to time. But an *ātmā* that is subject to time is not the *ātmā* we are talking about. *Ātmā* is the very basis, the *adhiṣṭhāna*, of time and therefore is not subject to time. Because it is not subject to time, it is *nitya*.

Because the forms, *upādhi*s, are many, there are many people, whereas *ātmā* is one whole consciousness, *caitanya*, not bound by time. In that consciousness alone is my mind, your mind, and any other mind. These minds differ, as do the bodies. When we count, the bodies are many, but not from the standpoint of consciousness, *cit*. Thus, what is necessary is the negation of a notion. Instead of telling Arjuna that *ātmā* is *nitya*, thereby creating a concept in his mind, Kṛṣṇa removed the notion of his being time-bound. When we are told that *ātmā* is eternal, we think of *ātmā* as having a long, long life. Here, instead, the concept of *ātmā* being time-bound is knocked off; it is negated. There was never a time when I, you, or anyone else was not. Nor will there be a time when we will not be, *ātmā* being timeless. Since we cannot cry for the timeless, *ātmā* is not a cause for sorrow; it is *aśocya*. *Anātmā* alone is subject to change; it is *anitya*. Even if we want to stop this present second, we cannot because it is already gone. Therefore, crying for *anātmā* is foolish. Both *ātmā* and *anātmā*, therefore, are *aśocya*.

Anything time-bound is always time-bound. You cannot expect constancy from something whose nature is change itself. If you are aggrieved or sad because something that changes by nature is non-constant, what you need is proper understanding of the nature of *ātmā* and *anātmā*, neither of which is a matter for sorrow. Either way you take it, this fact remains.

Therefore, the first line of the previous verse becomes increasingly true as our understanding of *ātmā* and *anātmā* increases.

Verses 13-15

Knowing the ātmā the wise do not come to grief

Kṛṣṇa provides an example in the following verse to help Arjuna understand how *ātmā* is always the same and never changes.

देहिनोऽस्मिन्यथा देहे कौमारं यौवनं जरा ।
तथा देहान्तरप्राप्तिर्धीरस्तत्र न मुह्यति ॥ १३ ॥

dehino'smin yathā dehe kaumāraṁ yauvanaṁ jarā
tathā dehāntaraprāptirdhīrastatra na muhyati (13)

yathā – just as; *dehinaḥ* – for the indweller of the body; *asmin dehe* – in this body; *kaumāram* – childhood; *yauvanam* – youth; *jarā* – old age; *tathā* – so also; *deha-antara-prāptiḥ* – the gaining of another body; *tatra* – there (with reference to that); *dhīraḥ* – a wise person; *na muhyati* – does not come to grief

> Just as, for the *jīva*, the indweller of this body, there is childhood, youth and old age, similar is the gaining of another body. With reference to that, a wise person does not come to grief.

Where does the person, the *jīva*, exist? The *jīva*, the one who makes the body conscious, is the indweller of this body. In other words, the *jīva* referred to in this verse as the *dehī*, is nothing but *ātmā* with a body, mind and senses. In this verse,

Kṛṣṇa refers to the three-fold states that the body undergoes, each of which is distinct from the other two. For instance, in boyhood there is no need for shaving, whereas in youth and adulthood, there is. Nor is a person likely to require a cane in either of these two states, unlike in old age.

When childhood passes, does the one dwelling in the body survive or not? If there were no survivor, an old man could not talk about his earlier exploits and accomplishments. His voice is certainly no longer the voice of his boyhood, having become very shaky due to the changes brought about by age, but the 'I' is the same. The 'I' is solid, not shaky. Thus, the one who was in childhood is the one who was in youth and is the one who is now. That 'I' does not change at all.

As each state comes and goes, the 'I' remains the same. Although each state is destroyed, the *ātmā* is never destroyed. The body is said to undergo a metamorphosis every seven years, but the person remains the same. The birth of a later state does not imply a new birth and a new life for the person, the *ātmā*. Nor does death of the previous state spell death for the *ātmā*. These states come and go whereas *ātmā* remains the same in a given body.

The same *ātmā* sees all three states – childhood, adulthood and old age. One need only ask an elderly person what he or she had for lunch! In response to this simple question, an elderly man may start with his first marriage! The *ātmā* is the same through all the experiences of life.

Just as each of these states is taken for the *ātmā*, another body can also be taken for the *ātmā*, even though *ātmā* itself remains the same. Like even a person who does not remember his or her first three years, so too, previous lifetimes in other bodies are also not remembered – which is just as well, since there would only be that many more problems! If we all knew our own and each other's previous births, we would be blaming people from those lifetimes just as we do in this one. There would then be far too many situations and people to blame!

Known or unknown, *ātmā* is the same, be it with reference to the first three years of this birth or to previous births. Thus, from the standpoint of *ātmā*, there is no reason for sorrow born of self-decimation. It is the same even from the standpoint of the simple *jīva*, the one who has a body. Where is the reason, then, for getting into a state of delusion that you will be absent at any time? The *jīva* will continue, with or without a body. Without a body, there is no problem. I am *ātmā* and, therefore, timeless. As a *jīva*, gaining a new body gives you a new and better start. If you did not make proper use of the previous body, now you can make better use of the new one.

Because a wise person has the knowledge of *ātmā* and *anātmā* there is no question of he or she being sorrowful. Such a person knows that, what does not change cannot be changed and what changes cannot be stopped. When the facts are clear, there is no sorrow. The wise person is one who knows what is real, *ātmā* and what is unreal, *anātmā*. Further, Kṛṣṇa said:

मात्रास्पर्शास्तु कौन्तेय शीतोष्णसुखदुःखदाः ।
आगमापायिनोऽनित्यास्तांस्तितिक्षस्व भारत ॥ १४ ॥

mātrāsparśāstu kaunteya śītoṣṇasukhaduḥkhadāḥ
āgamāpāyino'nityāstāṁstitikṣasva bhārata (14)

kaunteya – O son of Kuntī (Arjuna)!; *mātrā-sparśāḥ* – the contacts of the sense organs with the sensory world; *tu* – indeed; *śīta-uṣṇa-sukha-duḥkhadāḥ* – which give rise to cold and heat, pleasure and pain; *āgama-apāyinaḥ* – which have the nature of coming and going; *anityāḥ* – not constant; *bhārata* – O descendant of Bharata (Arjuna)!; *tān* – them; *titikṣasva* – endure

> Kaunteya (Arjuna)! The contacts of the sense organs with the sensory world which give rise to cold and heat, pleasure and pain, which have the nature of coming and going, are not constant. Endure them, Bhārata (Arjuna)!

Given that the *ātmā* never dies, that it always survives, as Kṛṣṇa said, it seems that the sorrow caused by the death of a person is not reasonable and therefore not very legitimate. That there may be no sorrow for the person who knows the *ātmā* to be eternal and the *anātmā* to be non-eternal is also possible. However, in this life, sorrow does occur because of certain changes that take place.

Situations do not go your way all the time. You do not call all the shots. Things keep changing, some of them favourably and many of them not so favourably. Some situations are pleasant, others unpleasant. That which is pleasant does not last, while the unpleasant seems to stick to you most of the time. Therefore, there is both pleasure, *sukha*, and pain, *duḥkha*. The pleasant arrives and must pass away for the unpleasant to come.

For instance, people begin to wail about winter long before it actually comes. As the summer ebbs away, they wail about that too. Even when summer is there, it is going. Thus, when winter is not there, it is coming and when it is there, it seems not to be going at all! Half the summer is gone because of clouds and another part of it is frittered away by rain. When it is hot, it is too hot. Because the seasons keep on changing, we find that *sukha* and *duḥkha* keep on occurring. The pleasant has gone and the unpleasant has come accompanied by sorrow. The sorrow is not due to *ātmā* going and coming, but purely because of the situational contact and so on. So will there not be a legitimate sorrow?

Kṛṣṇa talked here about the nature of the sense organs and the sensory world. The sense organs, *mātrā*s, contact sense objects. And these contacts, *sparśāḥ*, give you the experience of cold, heat, pleasure, pain, etc., *śīta-uṣṇa-sukha-duḥkhadāḥ*. The knowledge that something is cold or hot produces a response–this is pleasant, *sukha*, or this is unpleasant, *duḥkha*. Cold can be either pleasant or unpleasant and so can anything hot. For instance, you do not go to the fireside on a hot day as you would when it is cold. Thus, heat is not always pleasant and cold is not always unpleasant.

We find that there is uniformity in our responses and also, to a certain extent, universality. The world is one of opposites like even heat and cold that give us *sukha* and *duḥkha*, pleasure and pain. Categorically, we may say that certain situations make us happy, like a pleasant, sunny day. At the same time, however, there are people who want rain so much that they are praying for it. Therefore, the rain that you do not want, someone else may be praying for. These, then, are our responses that seem to give rise to *sukha* and *duḥkha,* all due to contact of the sense organs with their objects. One may argue that if contacting heat and cold gives rise to sorrow, perhaps we should avoid contact with sense objects. But how can we?

Kṛṣṇa did not say we have to avoid the contacts. We need only understand them. Most of our problems are like this; they only need to be understood. What is to be understood here is the tendency to come and go is the nature of opposites–heat and cold, pleasant and unpleasant and so on. If you keep on saying it is hot, a time will come when the heat will be gone. It is the same with the cold. Therefore, they are not constant. They do not remain for you to complain about. Even if you want them to stay, they will not. They are always in a flux, constantly changing. And this nature of their being in constant flux does not change.

You cannot totally remove yourself from the opposites or remove them from you. This is not to say that you should not make an attempt to improve a situation. But if things must always be pleasant for you, Lord Kṛṣṇa was making it very clear here that they would not be. Because things are both pleasant and unpleasant, they are not always going to be as you want. Nor are they always going to be unpleasant either.

If death is said to be incapable of causing you sorrow, where does that leave all of the other situations that seem to make you unhappy? The world can cause you some physical pain because the physical body belongs to the physical world. One physical entity can, therefore, hurt another. Arjuna's problem is not physical. It is purely sorrow *śoka,* and *śoka* is a type of thinking. While physical pain is something to be endured and cured, sorrow is something you build on.

Physical pain is not something that is totally avoidable, The body is subject to pain and will be affected by one force or the other such as the sun, rain, winter, and so on. You can protect the body to the extent possible, but because it is *anitya*, constantly changing, it is subject to pain. This is the nature of the body. Sorrow, on the other hand, is something you build on to the pain because of a particular way of thinking. This is exactly where we have to change, cognitively. Therefore, Kṛṣṇa said, 'Take every situation as it comes, Arjuna, cheerfully, in your stride, with a sense of humour.'

Kṛṣṇa later told Arjuna how these opposites cannot really do anything to you because, by nature, they have no independent existence apart from yourself, the *ātmā*. There is some kind of 'lumping' that occurs due to confusion between orders of reality. The mind, senses, and body have similar realities, whereas the *ātmā* is of another order of reality. When you say you are sad, you involve the *ātmā*, I, in the sadness as though the *ātmā* belongs to the same order of reality as the mind, which it does not. In this way, *ātmā* is taken to be *anātmā* and it becomes one among the many. Because *anātmās* in the world are too many and so varied, you cannot cope with them all, even though they are all *anātmā*. Even the small bugs create so many problems, let alone the more powerful forces.

If *ātmā* is really one among the many, nothing can be done. However, the vision is that *ātmā* is unlike any of them. Sorrow is not possible without *ātmā*, 'I.' Every time there is sorrow, it is because *ātmā* is somehow involved. Mere mind with its thought processes cannot create sorrow. Therefore, ignorance is the cause for imputing sorrow to *ātmā*.

The coming and going of the opposites is a fact. Thus, when Kṛṣṇa told Arjuna, 'Endure them, *titikṣasva*,' he was not offering advice; he was being objective. What is the need for this objectivity? There is a need because situations are constantly changing, the pleasant as well as the unpleasant. To think that only the pleasant ones change and not the unpleasant is not correct.

What, then, is there to worry about? For a person who is objective, who has an appreciation for what the world and its situations are all about, there is no reason for sorrow. There are just situations to face and act upon, whether inner or outer. There is nothing to be sad about.

Further, Kṛṣṇa said:

यं हि न व्यथयन्त्येते पुरुषं पुरुषर्षभ ।
समदुःखसुखं धीरं सोऽमृतत्वाय कल्पते ॥ १५ ॥

yaṁ hi na vyathayantyete puruṣaṁ puruṣarṣabha
samaduḥkhasukhaṁ dhīraṁ so'mṛtatvāya kalpate (15)

puruṣa-ṛṣabha – O the prominent among men (Arjuna)!; *ete* – these two (*sukha-duḥkha*); *sama-duḥkha-sukham* – the one who is same in pleasure and pain; *dhīram* – one who is discriminative; *yam puruṣam* – the person whom; *na vyathayanti* – do not affect; *saḥ* – he; *hi* – indeed; *amṛtatvāya* – for gaining liberation (*mokṣa*); *kalpate* – is fit

Arjuna, the prominent among men! The person whom these (*sukha* and *duḥkha*) do not affect, who is the same in pleasure and pain, and who is discriminative, is indeed fit for gaining liberation.

In this verse, Kṛṣṇa addresses Arjuna as a *puruṣa-ṛṣabha* whose literal meaning is a bull, *ṛṣabha*, among men. Among large herds of cattle, the stud bull always stands out because of its size and the big hump on its back. Just as a bull cannot be missed among hundreds of cows, so too, Arjuna stood out as the most exalted of men. Even those who did not know who Arjuna was would have acknowledged him because of his brilliance, *tejas*. He was a man of great accomplishment and a highly recognised person in the society. So he was addressed as *puruṣa-ṛṣabha*, the most prominent among men.

A discriminative person remains the same with reference to the opposites. Pleasant and unpleasant situations do not affect the person. Such a person is aware of their coming and going, of their constantly changing nature. In the *bhāṣya*, Śaṅkara makes it clear that this is not just a matter of practicality. A wise person knows himself as *ātmā*, one who cannot be affected by any situation. Such a person is called *dhīra*, meaning one who is discriminating, one who has knowledge of the *nitya-ātmā*. The word *paṇḍita*, used in an earlier verse, is replaced here by the word *dhīra*, meaning one who is not affected by the opposites and, who therefore gains *mokṣa*, *amṛtatva*. *Mṛtatva* means being subject to mortality, whereas *amṛtatva* is to be free from mortality. Knowing *ātmā* as the one that is *nitya*, the wise gain *mokṣa*.

One who is discriminative, who accepts situations happily, and who does not allow oneself to be swayed by either pleasant or unpleasant situations is one who is fit for self-knowledge or who already has this knowledge. Kṛṣṇa obviously wanted to make this fact clear at the outset.

Verse 16

Analysis of existence and non-existence

नासतो विद्यते भावो नाभावो विद्यते सतः ।
उभयोरपि दृष्टोऽन्तस्त्वनयोस्तत्त्वदर्शिभिः ॥ १६ ॥

nāsato vidyate bhāvo nābhāvo vidyate sataḥ
ubhayorapi dṛṣṭo'ntastvanayostattvadarśibhiḥ (16)

asataḥ – for the unreal (*mithyā*); *bhāvaḥ* – being; *na vidyate* – is not there; *sataḥ* – for the real; *api* – also; *abhāvaḥ* – non-being (absence); *na vidyate* – is not there; *ubhayoḥ anayoḥ* – of these two (the real and the unreal); *antaḥ* – the ultimate truth; *tattva-darśibhiḥ* – by the knowers of the truth; *tu* – indeed; *dṛṣṭaḥ* – is seen

> For the unreal (*mithyā*), there is never any being. For the real, there is never any non-being. The ultimate truth of both (the real and the unreal) is seen by the knowers of the truth.

This is a very important verse even though cryptic. For the *asat*, a word we shall use as it is, there is no *bhāva*, being. In other words, being is not there for *asat*. And for *sat*, there is no non-being. In the second line of the verse, Kṛṣṇa went on to say that this fact is known by those people who know the ultimate truth about *sat* and *asat* The first line is the crux of the verse.

Asat means something that does not exist independently and *sat* is what exists independent of anything else. What is it that exists independently? Cold and heat, for example, do not exist independently because they depend upon a number of factors. There is no absolute cold existing by itself. That something is cold depends upon something else. The temperature cannot reveal itself to you unless you have a perception. Therefore, your perception is essential in order to understand that something is cold and something else is hot.

When you say, 'This is a pot,' does the word 'pot' reveal an object that exists by itself or does the object indicated by the word 'pot' depend for its existence upon something else? If it depends on something else, clay, because of which the pot is there and unto which it will go back, that clay becomes the cause, *kāraṇa*, for the pot. The word 'pot' has no real object outside of the word itself; it has no existence apart from clay. That which has a cause, which depends upon something for its existence, which does not independently exist, is called *asat*.[3]

---

[3] This explanation is from the *Chāndogyopaniṣad* where, in one particular sentence, it is said that before this creation there was only one thing, the *sat-vastu* , which was non-dual, one without a second, undifferentiated. Nothing else was there. From that *sat-vastu*, Brahman, alone everything has come and is non-separate from it. Nothing exists apart from *sat*. This knowledge was revealed in this *Upaniṣad* to Śvetaketu who had been sent by his father to a *gurukula* at the age of twelve. He returned at the age of twenty-four, very proud of his accomplishments, having studied the Vedas for twelve years.

Śaṅkara explains *asat* further. When we try to prove the existence of things that are dependent upon causes for their existence, such as cold and heat or any given object, we find there is no self-existent thing at all among the objects of the world. Why? Because what is there is only a *vikāra*, form, that keeps changing, *vyabhicarati*; it is never the same, nor can it be the same.

Śaṅkara goes on to prove a point here. Suppose there are many pots made of clay. If one knows the truth of one pot, that it is but clay, one knows the truth – all clay pots are but that clay.

Then what is pot? It is purely a name for a form. Other than this, there is no pot that exists separate from clay. Nor is the clay the pot. If it were, you would not need to make the pot again, the clay being there already. Therefore, clay is not pot. If you remove the clay, where is pot? Is it something that you have to search for its location? No. All that is there for the name 'pot' is a form recognised as such.

Anything that is time-bound, like a pot, will change and you cannot stop it because its nature is to keep on changing.

Śvetaketu's father was a great man. He could not stand his son's arrogance. So he asked his son, 'Did you ask your teacher for that knowledge gaining which everything is known?' The boy replied that he did not think his teacher knew this. Later, he asked his father if there was such a knowledge. And he said, 'How can you know one thing and thereby know everything else? If there is such a knowledge, please teach me, O Lord!' The same topic is discussed in the *Muṇḍakopaniṣad*. The only difference being that there the student asked this question to the teacher, whereas in the *Chāndogyopaniṣad*, the father asked Śvetaketu, who said he did not know. Then Śvetaketu asked his father to teach him.

When and how are you going to stop it? Therefore, what are you crying for? What are you sad for? Are you sad for something eternal because it is eternal? No.

Sat is that which never changes; it has no *abhāva*, non-existence, at all. *Sat* is never negated at any time, whereas *asat* never enjoys a being of its own. Therefore, *sat* is all, it cannot create any sorrow for you and *asat* is incapable of doing so because it does not exist in its own right.

How can *asat* create sorrow? In the vision of the Veda, you are *sat* and everything else is *asat*. *Asat* cannot be a source of sorrow to *sat*, and *sat* cannot be a source of sorrow to you because it is you. The whole problem is one of confusion between *sat* and *asat*, between *ātmā* and *anātmā*.

Asat has no being, no *bhāva*. It has no existence. Thus, it cannot be *bhāva*, that which exists in all three periods of time. The word '*bhāva*' comes from the root '*bhū*' used in the sense of 'existence.'

Tuccha is another word for *abhāva* and refers to some combinations that do not exist at all. For example, man's horn, *manuṣya-sṛṅga*, does not exist. Horn exists and man exists. Both are *bhāva*; both exist. For these words, there are objects in the world, which I know exist. But when I combine the two as 'man's horn,' there is no such thing.

Does the word *asat* in the verse mean *tuccha*, non-existent? No. Because it is unnecessary to say that something that is non-existent has no being. In some modern commentaries on the *Gītā*, however, we do find *asat* being translated as and equated to non-existent that is *tuccham*. What purpose is served by this sentence, the non-existent, such as the man's horn, has no existence? No purpose.

That which we refer to as *asat* has an order of reality, which is neither *satya, bhāva,* nor *tuccha*. There is another type of *abhāva* between these two, a non-existence that we call *asat* here. For instance, we cannot dismiss the sense organs and sense objects as totally non-existent, *tuccha*. Are they, then, *sat*? Let us analyse them.

A sense organ cannot be called a sense organ unless it perceives something. Eyes are a sense organ only because they see a form. Ears are a sense organ because they hear a sound and the senses of smell, taste, and touch are all called sense organs because they perceive their sense objects. How can you call eyes a sense organ if they do not see? If ears do not hear, there is no sense organ even though the earlobes may be used for earrings or for catching hold of someone. The earlobes, etc., are just the anatomical aspects of the sense called hearing. It is hearing that makes the ears a sense organ and there is no such thing as sound without the ears. Which establishes what?

To establish the existence of one, we need to establish the existence of the other. Then there must be some other basis for the existence of both. Thus, all of them depend on something that is self-existent called *sat*. Because we cannot dismiss the sense organs and their sense objects as non-existent, we say they are *asat*. They are not totally non-existent, *atyanta-abhāva*. The sense organs and the sense objects do exist.

All the responses of *sukha* and *duḥkha*, pleasure and pain, exist. You cannot dismiss them as non-existent nor can you take them as independently existent.

Therefore, for something that cannot be dismissed as non-existent, *tuccha*, and cannot be taken as independently existent, *sat*, we have to have a word and that word is *asat*. Another word for *asat* is *mithyā*. *Asat* or *mithyā* is that which has no *bhāva*, and which depends upon *sat*. Only when there is *sat*, is *asat* possible. Therefore, *mithyā* or *asat* is something whose existence depends upon another thing and, because it has no independent existence, it is not separate from that upon which it depends.

All objects in the world are time-bound

When a pot is made, before it is baked, there is only clay. Thus, once upon a time, the pot was clay. When it became a pot, it was clay in the form of pot. Even though it has been baked, it is nothing but clay. All that has happened is that the clay now has an added attribute, *guṇa*, the pot-form. This added attribute is what is meant by creation. Creative possibilities are there, but there is no such thing as clay pot without clay.

When we look at anything in this world, we always find that it is a form with a name, depending on some other substantive, *vastu*. A particular *rūpa*, form, is called *asat*. It has the nature of its substantive, but in itself has no *bhāva*. By the time you see an object, it has already changed. It is never the same in the next moment. It is like seeing a film projected on a white screen. It looks as though someone is standing there, but in fact, the frame is continuously changing. Similarly, the frame in one's mind keeps on changing, exactly like the film. It is what makes it possible for us to see motion.

Because what you have seen is already gone and you do not see it again in the same form, an object has no real *bhāva*. In a flowing river, you do not get the same water at the same place. It is over, gone, flowing constantly in the flow of time. Similarly, any perception you have is conditioned by time and therefore has the nature of being merely an appearance. It is 'as though' there and not really there because it is always changing; it is 'as though' all the time.

All objects in the world are time-bound. When you see an object, that object is not seen by you as an independent object. You always see some other thing along with it. When you see a shirt, for example, you also see cloth and when you see the cloth, you see a particular material. So, you find that the shirt has no existence apart from its cause, *kāraṇa*, the cloth. Not only can you not create a shirt without cloth, you cannot imagine one either. Cloth here refers to any material with which the shirt is made. Without cloth, paper, or some other material, it is impossible to make a shirt, even in your imagination. You can imagine an elephant entering your ear by seeing yourself as very big, but you cannot imagine making a shirt without cloth. No object exists by itself, apart from its cause.

An object that does not exist independent of something else cannot have the word *sat* imputed to it. It can only be called *asat* because *sat* will be the one upon which the object depends for its *bhāva*. If you remove the cloth, can you wear the shirt? All you will have is the 'emperor's clothes!'

There is no such thing as shirt without the material with which it is made. For the word 'shirt,' there is no corresponding object at all. *Bhāva* means it must independently exist and, because the cloth is the *bhāva*, the shirt has no independent substantive status.

Nor can you say the cloth with which the shirt is made is *sat* because it too depends upon something else. Then what is the real *sat*? That which exists by its own glory and does not depend on anything else for its existence is called *sat* or *satya*. Just because something is a cause does not mean it is *satya*. Causes themselves depend on their causes and therefore are also *asat*.

If everything that we experience is *asat*, how is it that we see the world as real, as *sat*? We say 'the world is.' We do not look at it as something that is not. It is because in every perception, there are two *buddhi*s. Here *buddhi* means knowledge, cognition. One *buddhi* is with reference to the object and the other is with reference to its *sat vastu*, the self.

The problem is that we take the 'is-not' as 'is' and get confused. This confusion leads to *sukha* and *duḥkha*. When we see a pot, there is a pot-*buddhi*, pot cognition and we say, 'The pot is.' That *buddhi*, cognition whose object is pot, undergoes a change similar to the changing frame in a moving film. This *buddhi* is called *asat-buddhi*. That which does not undergo a change is called *sat-buddhi*. Suppose the pot that is seen is replaced by another object, a tree. The pot is gone and the tree is there in its place. Previously, we said, 'The pot is,' and now we say, 'The tree is.' If we analyse these two cognitions, we can see that the is-*buddhi* never goes. The pot goes because it is *asat* and the *sat* that is always there is now with the tree. When the tree-*buddhi* goes, branch-*buddhi* may be there and when the branch-*buddhi* is gone, leaf-*buddhi* is there. When the leaf-*buddhi* is gone, chlorophyll-*buddhi* is there and when the chlorophyll-*buddhi* is gone, particle-*buddhi* is there. When particle-*buddhi* is gone, whatever *buddhi* that is left will still be there.

What is it that remains? *Sat*, the 'is,' is always there. 'Is' always is. Therefore, it is called *sat*, that which does not change, whereas the object whose *buddhi* changes is called *asat* The object is *asat* because the *buddhi* keeps changing. We recognise it differently each time it changes. So in every perception, there are two *buddhi*s – the object-*buddhi* and the is-*buddhi*.

When we say, 'blue pot, *nīlaḥ ghaṭaḥ*,' both words indicate the same object. The object that is blue is pot and object that is pot is blue. Similarly, when I say, 'Please meet this person, the musician,' both the person and the musician are one and the same object. When we say, '*arjunaḥ, pāṇḍavaḥ*, there is only one person, Arjuna, and he is a Pāṇḍava. In all these situations, there is a substantive-adjective relationship. The word blue is an adjective to pot in the expression, 'blue pot.' However, this is not so when we say, 'the existent pot,' or 'this is a pot.' Here, it seems as though the 'is-ness' is an adjective to pot; it is not correct. The pot is adjective to existence; the 'pot-ness' qualifies 'is-ness.'

Here, there is *sat-buddhi*, meaning that the pot exists, and there is also pot *buddhi*, that is, the object-*buddhi*, which are two different things. To say, 'This is a pot,' definitely implies 'is-ness,' since the word 'is' is used. There are, therefore, always two *buddhis*, *sat-buddhi* and *asat-buddhi*, the object-*buddhi*. Only *asat-buddhi* changes, meaning that the existent *sat-buddhi* is conditioned by an object as its attribute. 'Is' is always there. When the tree is, 'is' is in the form of a tree. Similarly, 'is' can be in the form of a pot, a person, a nose, a body, or anything.

Existence is also in the form of thought. Therefore, if there is no thought, what is there is existence minus thought. Existence minus the body, existence minus the world, is existence. That existence, *sat*, is always there not affected by any addition to or subtraction from it.

The is-buddhi always remains

The way in which the *sat-buddhi* is conditioned is what undergoes change, whereas the *sat-buddhi* itself never changes. Therefore, Śaṅkara says in his *bhāṣya* that the object of the thought, 'This is a pot,' is *asat* because it is always changing. It never remains the same. The *sat-buddhi*, on the other hand, is *satya* because, whatever that *sat* is, does not undergo any change.

A doubt being possible here, Śaṅkara clarifies the point in the *bhāṣya* by raising and answering an objection, *pūrva-pakṣa*. Suppose a pot is gone, destroyed, and the pot *buddhi*, *ghaṭa-buddhi* is gone, you say, 'The pot was and now the pot is no more.' The pot being destroyed, the pot *buddhi* goes and the pot proves to be *asat*. However, along with the destroyed pot, does not the is-*buddhi*, *sat-buddhi* also go? Śaṅkara's response is that the is-*buddhi* never goes; 'is' is always there. We say, 'The pot is destroyed, the destroyed pot is, the pot is no more.' Because something else is, the is-*buddhi* never goes, only the conditioned *sat-buddhi* is gone.

The *sat-buddhi*, the 'exists-*buddhi*,' is conditioned by *nāma-rūpa*, a name and form. And when the pot is destroyed, that *nāma-rūpa* is gone, but the *sat-buddhi* is not gone. It is there to join anything. The is-*buddhi* can join the broken pot; the broken pot 'is' or anything else 'is.' Only *asat* keeps on changing. The varieties of objects seen by you keep on changing, while you remain the same person. That 'is' existence, remains; it never goes away. If this aspect of the teaching is not clear, you could conclude that *ātmā*, the *sat-vastu* is zero!

Ātmā alone is, and everything else is *nāma-rūpa*, only an addition to the *sat-buddhi*, an addition that does not bring about any addition. Just as the pot form does not bring about an addition to the clay, so too, the addition of *nāma-rūpa* to the *sat-buddhi* does not bring about any change to it. This is the vision. The *sat-buddhi* is always qualified by an attribute – 'is' in the form of a tree, 'is' in the form of a pot, 'is' in the form of something, and that form keeps on changing. That which changes is *asat*, *mithyā* whereas *sat* remains ever the same.

What is that *sat*? *Sat-buddhi* is existence-consciousness, *sat-cit*. Existence is consciousness. Consciousness, the *sat-buddhi*, always joins with something in the form of knowledge and reveals. For example, the pot is. When the pot is gone, the tree is. When the tree is gone, something else is. When everything is gone, I am, *aham asmi*.

Consciousness between two thoughts

Between two thoughts, everything is gone except consciousness. Although everything does go between two thoughts, consciousness does not require everything to go in order to be. Consciousness is always there. Whatever comes, consciousness is and if everything goes, consciousness is. There is only one thing that is *sat* and it is consciousness.

It was said that the pot is *mithyā, asat,* because the pot-*buddhi* changes. Then it was said that when the pot is destroyed, the *sat-buddhi,* the pot-is-*buddhi* is also destroyed. Therefore, is not your *sat-buddhi* also *asat*? No, Śaṅkara replies. Even when the pot is gone and the cloth is there, you see the *sat-buddhi* in the cloth. Only the attribute has changed. Previously the *sat-buddhi* was conditioned by the pot, whereas now it is conditioned by the cloth.

Again, an objection is raised. Even though one pot is gone, we may still have pot *buddhi* in some other pot. In this other pot we recognise, 'This is a pot.' Since pot *buddhi* does not change, does it not prove that it is *sat*? To this, Śaṅkara said that, although pot *buddhi* may be seen in another pot, it is not seen in the cloth. Only in another pot can you have pot *buddhi.* In a piece of cloth, the only *buddhi* you have is cloth *buddhi,* not pot *buddhi.* Whereas the *sat-buddhi* is always there, in the pot, in the cloth, in anything you see, and in anything you say is non-existent.

We say the man's horn does not exist. It does not mean there is no *sat-buddhi* here. When we say, 'The horn is' and 'The man is,' it is *sat-buddhi*. To say, 'Man's horn is,' is wrong, whereas to say, 'Man's horn is not,' is right. The latter expression indicates that 'Man's horn is not,' which is *sat-buddhi*. Therefore, *sat-buddhi* does not change in any way.

Sat in the *sat-buddhi*, which is the *sat* of *ātmā*, is always there even in deep sleep. It is obvious in the light of our discussions that the *asat-buddhi* of the pot has no existence independent of the *ātmā*. So this *sat-buddhi* joins the pot. How is this combination possible? Between two equally existent objects there can be a combination, but how can there be a combination between *sat* and *asat*? You may see a reflected face in the mirror, but you cannot feed that person because there are two orders of reality involved. The spoon belongs to one order of reality and the reflection in the mirror to another. That is why the mouth in the reflected face, even though it is open, cannot combine with the spoon. Similarly, then, if the *ātmā* is the object of this *sat-buddhi* how can it go and join anything? To this, Śaṅkara said that there was no problem. *Sat* can join anything.

Mirage water in the desert makes you feel happy. But whether water is there or not, it is only *sat*. Even if there is no water and you only imagine it to be there, you still say, 'The water is.' Here, the *sat-buddhi* joins the mirage water which is *asat*. The is-*buddhi*, the *sat-buddhi*, thus joins anything and everything. There is no rule that prevents *sat-buddhi* and *asat-buddhi* from joining because *sat* is not opposed to anything–everything being a superimposition upon the *sat*. The *sat-buddhi* lends itself to any type of object such as an imagined pot or a real pot, a mistaken snake superimposed on a piece of rope, or a real rope.

Imagination is something different from mistake. If you are aware that you are imagining something, then it is imagination. Either way, an imagined pot is, snake is, even though it is later found to be a rope, a rope is. The *sat-buddhi* joins in any and every situation. The object of the *sat-buddhi, sat-buddhi-viṣaya,* is *ātmā* and is *sat,* which has no non-existence, *abhāva, sataḥ abhāvaḥ na vidyate.*

Anything that depends upon something else is *asat.* If you look at your body, *deha,* on that, it is *asat.* Therefore, there is no cause for sorrow. It is the same with any thought. When we say, 'Thought is,' that 'is-ness' is consciousness, *ātmā.* Consciousness is and the thought is incidental to the consciousness. A thought is *nāma-rūpa.* A thought that has an outside object is called perception. If there is an object perceived outside sense perception, then it is inferential knowledge, imagination, or memory. Whatever it is, the thought 'is' and it is nothing but consciousness conditioned by *nāma-rūpa.* And if there is no *nāma-rūpa,* then what 'is' is still consciousness.

Existence is consciousness

Sat is always only *cit-ātmā* and the word *satya* can only mean *cit.* Self-existent consciousness alone can be *sat.* Either word, *sat* or *cit,* will bring in the other word because what has to be *cit* has to be *sat* and what has to be *sat* has to be *cit.* Thus, *sat* will bring in *cit* and *cit* will bring in *sat.*

Because everything depends upon this *sat-cit, sat-cit* becomes limitless, *ananta, ānanda. Ananta* means limitless, and consciousness is *ananta.* It is also said to be *ānanda;* people are always looking for *ānanda*. If everything depends upon *sat-cit*, is there any limitation for *sat-cit-ātmā*? There is no limit because everything is *sat-cit-ātmā*. Therefore from the standpoint of the *sat-cit-ātmā*, there is no distance between itself and everything else nor is anything separate from it. In any cognition, the subject is *sat-cit-ātmā*, the object is *sat-cit-ātmā*, and the means of knowledge, the thought *vṛtti*, is also *sat-cit-ātmā*. All three are *sat-cit-ātmā* alone. Thus, *sat-cit-ānanda* is the *svarūpa* of *ātmā*. *Sat* is not going to be non-existent at any time, and *asat* cannot be kept as it is because it is constantly changing. *Sat* is the meaning, the content of *sat-buddhi*, and the content of *asat-buddhi* is name and form. When we say, 'The pot is, the chair is, the table is, the man is, the woman is, the tree is,' the 'is' in all of them is *sat-buddhi*. That 'is' is common and is always qualified by the name and form called tree, pot, chair, table, and so on. Why do we say name and form? Because whatever you consider depends on something else, which depends on something else, and so on. Whenever we say, 'Something is,' the 'is' is the basis, the *satya*, and the *nāma-rūpa* is *mithyā*, depending on this *sat*.

Sat-buddhi viṣaya is *satya* Therefore, the 'am-ness' in 'I am, *aham asmi*,' the 'are-ness' in 'you are, *tvam-asi*,' and the 'is-ness' in 'he is, *saḥ asti*,' and 'that is, *tad-asti*,' are all one and the same. The 'is-ness' that each implies is the common basis for all things that exist. Therefore, it is the *kāraṇa*, the cause for everything and is *satya*. The effect, *kārya* is recognised as *asat*, *mithyā*, because it is dependent on the *kāraṇa* for its existence. As mentioned earlier, Vedanta is nothing but a discussion of this cause and effect, *satya* and *mithyā* – *kāraṇa-kārya-vāda*.

A product and its cause

A product, a creation, a *kārya*, a *vikāra*, is entirely dependent upon *satya* that which is self-existent. If *satya* itself depended upon something else, it would not be *satya*. The self-existent *satya* is called *kāraṇa*, cause. Depending on what it is you want to prove, *kāraṇa* can also be said to be *satya* – *yat kāraṇaṁ tat satyam*. That which is *satya* is said to be a cause, like clay with reference to a pot. Because clay is the cause for the pot, it is *satya*, but only for the pot, please understand. Another example is thread as the *satya* for the cloth. Thus from these two examples, we see that *satya* is *kāraṇa* and *kāraṇa* is *satya*.

With reference to a product, a creation, we are going to prove something. In Śaṅkara's *bhāṣya* on this verse, he says that a product is *mithyā* – *yat kāryaṁ tat mithyā*. *Mithyā* means *asat*, the word used in the current verse. Such statements reflect a style that we will be coming across later. A product is *mithyā* because it is dependent upon a cause, as is the case for cloth. Whereas, *sat* is not dependent upon anything else and undergoes no change whatsoever, *sataḥ abhāvaḥ na vidyate*.

Because the object of *sat-buddhi* is *sat* and the object of *asat-buddhi* is *asat*, we have the *sat-buddhi* at all times. The *asat-buddhi* depends upon the *sat-buddhi*. The object of the *asat-buddhi*, the pot, depends upon the object of *sat-buddhi*, clay, which itself depends upon something else. When you say, 'Clay is,' the clay, depends upon another *sat-buddhi*-object, atom. When you say, 'The atom is,' the atom depends upon particles, which depend upon a concept. When you say, 'A concept is,' the concept depends upon the witness of the concept, *sākṣī* which is consciousness. And when you say, 'Consciousness is,' what does it depend upon? It does not depend upon another consciousness because it is *svataḥ-siddha*, self-existent.

Therefore, nothing can be *satya* except that which is self-existent. This is all that is being said here. That which is self-existent is *ātmā* and that alone is *satya*. Everything else, being dependent upon *satya*, is *asat*. For the *satya-ātmā*, there is no non-existence, *abhāva*, whereas for the *asat*, there is no real existence. The experience of seeing objects is there, but these objects are all in the transactional world, *vyavahāra* and, therefore, have only an empirical reality.

About *sat* and *asat*, a final understanding, an ascertained knowledge is arrived at by the seers of the truth of Brahman, *tattvadarśibhiḥ anayoḥ ubhayoḥ api antaḥ tu dṛṣṭaḥ*. The *tattvadarśī* is the one who is capable of seeing the truth, *tattva* of everything. *Tattva* is the abstract form of the pronoun *tat*. The pronoun *tat*, means 'that' and can stand for anything from apple to zebra as indicated by the word in Sanskrit for pronoun, *sarva-nāma*, meaning the name for everything. Therefore, the word *tattva*[4] means, the truth, the intrinsic nature of a thing. Śaṅkara further explains its meaning by saying, 'Because all that is here is only Brahman, the name for that Brahman is *tat*. The abstract noun of *tat*, *tattva*, means the truth, the *svarūpa* of Brahman.[5]

---

[4] तस्य भावः तत्त्वम् । (शङ्कर भाष्यम्) – *tattva* is the nature of a thing.

[5] तत् इति सर्वनाम, सर्वं च ब्रह्म, तस्य नाम तत् इति, तद्भावः तत्त्वं – ब्रह्मणः याथात्म्यम् । (शङ्कर भाष्यम्)
tat is the name for everything, that is, it includes everything. It is because Brahman is everything. And it is called '*tat*' here. The nature of this '*tat*,' that is, Brahman, is called *tattva*, the true nature of Brahman.

Here Śaṅkara uses the etymological meaning of the word *sarva-nāma* to his advantage to define Brahman. Here the word *sarva-nāma* is not a pronoun.

The truth of Brahman

Tattva is often said to mean reality but, in fact, it is the *svarūpa* of Brahman. That Brahman is *satya*, unqualified existence; *jñāna*, knowledge; *ananta*, limitless; *śuddha*, pure; *nitya*, timeless and so on, can be understood through the various implied meanings, *lakṣaṇa*s of each of these words. Brahman is the cause of the world, *jagat-kāraṇa* and at the same time is itself *satya*, *jñāna* and *ananta*. This, then, is the *svarūpa* of Brahman and is called *tattva*. Brahman is not only *satya* but is the *kāraṇa* for everything. Therefore, everything is Brahman. Brahman plus all names and forms is all that is here.

So, the *tattva-darśinaḥ*, who know the truth of Brahman, understand both *sat* and *asat*. Both must be known. *Sat* is *sat* and *asat* is *asat*. *Asat* depends upon *sat*, but *sat* does not depend upon *asat*. Those who know the truth of everything, *tattva-darśinaḥ* are called *paṇḍita*s, the ones who, as we saw earlier, do not come to grief. Why? Because they know the truth.

Now, why are you sad? Is it due to *asat* or *sat*? If you say you are sad because *asat* is going, you must see that going is the nature of *asat* and that it is not real. Therefore, you cannot cry for the *asat*. When your understanding of *satya* is lacking then *mithyā* becomes *satya*, resulting in confusion. Without *satya* there is no *mithyā*. *Mithyā* must be understood as *mithyā* and *satya* as *satya*. Only then does everything fall into its own place. *Satya* does not elicit any sorrow, and *mithyā* does not have the status to cause sorrow. If there is sorrow, it is *mithyā*.

The confusion between satya and mithyā

There is a well-known story that illustrates the confusion between *satya* and *mithyā*. It is as follows.

In the court of a particular king, there were two scholars. One was an *advaitī* who said that Brahman was *satya* and the world, *jagat*, was *mithyā*. He talked about this constantly, Vedanta being nothing but a discussion of *satya* and *mithyā*, cause and effect, *kāraṇa-kārya-vāda*. He told the king that *kāraṇa* was *satya* and *kārya* was *mithyā*. The whole world, including one's body, was *kārya* and therefore *mithyā*. There was nothing away from that Brahman, and that *satya*, Brahman, was independent of everything.

The king did not understand what this scholar was saying, but he liked the idea. There was a fascinating aspect to it because it said that he was wonderful, that he was Brahman, and so on. The king found this pleasant to get up to each morning. It was good for his mental health, at least.

The second scholar was a dualist, *dvaitī*, who kept telling the king that he was not Brahman, the *jagat-kāraṇa*, the cause of the world, and that he was a product, subject to *puṇya* and *pāpa*. If he did the right things, he would gain some time in heaven and if he did not, he would go to more unpleasant places such as *naraka*. This scholar maintained that what he was saying was the truth as stated in the *śāstra*. He even backed up his statements by quoting Vedanta in his daily teaching.

The king listened to both these scholars because he wanted to be impartial, although he generally slept in the second scholar's class! This made the second scholar a little jealous of the other one, who seemed to be getting more attention from the king.

The time came when the king went on a big pilgrimage accompanied by a large retinue, including his two teachers. As they walked through a forest, which was infested with many wild animals, a huge elephant with enormous tusks confronted them. The first scholar spied the elephant first and cried out, 'Elephant, Maharaj, elephant!' He then began to run and, of course, everyone else ran, too.

It should be remembered that these *advaitī*s are all very alert people and, because they understand things as they are, they are absolutely practical, also. Because they are not encumbered by projections, problems, or shadows, they are free to deal with things objectively. So, this scholar was the first to see the elephant and run. The king also ran along with everybody including the *dvaitī.*

After this adventure was over, the king decided to camp and start out again the next day when there had been time to check for safety. While the king was relaxing, the second scholar went to him and said, 'O Lord! Did you see how our *advaita-guru* ran?' The king remarked that he indeed had run very well. In fact, he reached safely before the others.

'That is what I mean,' said the *dvaitī*. He says the world is *mithyā* and yet he ran away from the elephant. If this world is *mithyā*, then the elephant must also be *mithyā*. Why did he run from a *mithyā* elephant? Everything he has been teaching is all verbal nonsense! That is why, Maharaj, I told you that there is no *mithyā*. Everything is *satya*.

The second scholar then pressed his point a little further. 'I do not understand his running, given what he teaches. Perhaps Maharaj understands it better.' The king also found that it did not make sense to him. So he summoned the *advaita-guru* and asked him to explain himself. Out of respect for his teacher, the king gave him an opportunity to explain himself. He asked, 'Sir, you said everything is *mithyā*. Therefore, the elephant is also *mithyā*, is it not?' The scholar agreed that this was correct. 'Then why did you run away from the elephant?' the king asked.

'Maharaj,' the scholar replied, 'the elephant is indeed *mithyā*. But when did I tell you that running was *satya*? Running is also *mithyā*! Do you find any sorrow or fear in me? There is none. I just did what was to be done.'

This is the vision. Vedanta says that everything is *satya* from the standpoint of the *sat-buddhi*, and everything is *mithyā* from the standpoint of the *asat-buddhi*. The vision does not exclude anything. We have to understand everything. Any *karma*, action, is *mithyā*. For example, we talk of 'running' as an action. But if we do some enquiry into this so-called action, we see that we cannot categorically say what is 'running.' Whether lifting the leg is 'running' or placing the foot is 'running,' we cannot say. This is true of any action. Therefore, it is *mithyā*. The person performing the action, the *kartā* is *mithyā*, as is the action, *kriyā*. Therefore, the whole thing is *mithyā*. Only *ātmā* is *satya*.

Once you see both *satya* and *mithyā* very clearly, as the *paṇḍitas* do, there is no reason for sorrow. Lord Kṛṣṇa has shown that what is *sat*, self-existent, does not have *abhāva* at any time, meaning that there is no end, no non-existence for it, *sataḥ abhāvaḥ na vidyate*. And *asat* being only a name and form, depending upon the *sat* has no real *bhāva*, no real being. Therefore, it is *mithyā*.

What is *mithyā* then? It is neither *bhāva* nor *abhāva*. It does not have an existence of its own nor is it totally non-existent. It is something in between, which is what we mean when we say that *mithyā* is inexplicable. There are others who say that reality, the *vastu* or *sat*, is inexplicable. The vision of Vedanta is just the opposite. Only the *vastu* can be unfolded, albeit by implication, and everything else is inexplicable.

Can truth be defined?

It is generally thought that truth cannot be defined, whereas we say that truth alone can be defined. Everything else can be only conditionally defined and so requires further definition. Therefore, any definition of an object, which is *asat*, *mithyā*, is a point of view subject to further definition. Being neither *sat*, existent, nor *tuccha*, totally non-existent, how can *mithyā* be defined? There is no explicability for *mithyā*. That there is no explicability is its explanation. We are not just getting lost in *mithyā* and then saying it is not explainable at all. It is inexplicable in the sense that it cannot categorically be defined as, 'This is *satya*,' because our definition of *satya* is that which is not negated at any time. Because what is never negated at any time is *satya*, we cannot say that an object such as a pot is *satya* because it does not always exist. Furthermore, it may be broken tomorrow. Nor is it always the same pot, since yesterday it was in one form and today it is in another.

The pot is also not *tuccha*, totally non-existent, because if it were non-existent, it would not be perceived or known to hold any water. Therefore, there is such a thing as pot.

Between *sat* and *tuccha*, therefore, there is a reality, which is referred to as *asat*. In fact, the technical word for *asat* is generally *mithyā*. Although the words *asat*, *mithyā* and *māyā*, are used in the *śāstra*, the ontological definition for this order of reality is *mithyā*. What is not subject to negation in all three periods of time, past, present and future, is *satya*. And that which does not exist at all in all three periods of time is *tuccha*. Therefore, what is in between becomes *mithyā* or *asat*.

Verse 17

The indestructibility of the non-dual

Further Kṛṣṇa said:

अविनाशि तु तद्विद्धि येन सर्वमिदं ततम् ।
विनाशमव्ययस्यास्य न कश्चित्कर्तुमर्हति ॥ १७ ॥

avināśi tu tadviddhi yena sarvam idaṁ tatam
vināśam avyayasyāsya na kaścit kartum arhati (17)

idam sarvam – this entire world; *yena* – by which; *tatam* – is pervaded; *tat* – that; *tu* – indeed; *avināśi* – indestructible; *viddhi* – know; *asya avyayasya* – of that which does not change; *vināśam* – destruction; *na kaścit* – no one; *kartum* – to bring about; *arhati* – is able

Know that, by which this entire world is pervaded, to be indeed indestructible. No one can bring about the destruction of that which does not change.

Here, *tat* refers to *sat*, for which there is no *abhāva* and is understood by the *tattva-darśī*, knower of the truth, as stated in the previous verse. *Sat* is not subject to destruction; it is *avināśi*. Moreover, everything that is here, the entire world, is pervaded by this indestructible *sat* – *sat-ātmā*. Being subject to destruction, the world is *asat*, not *sat*.

In this verse, *sat* and *mithyā* are made very clear. *Sat* is other than *asat*, whereas *asat* is not other than *sat*. *Sat-vastu* is called *viṣṇu*, a word that is being quietly introduced here by *bhāṣyakāra*, Śaṅkara. That which pervades everything, meaning the entire world including space is called Viṣṇu. This is *sat*. Since there is no *asat* without *sat*, the *bhāva* of the *asat* is nothing but the *bhāva* of the *sat*. For example, because the existence of clay pot is inherent in the existence of the clay, the *bhāva* belongs to the clay and not to the pot. And when we say, 'The pot is,' that 'is' is *sat*. Therefore, wherever there is *asat*, there is *sat*.

How do we get to the *sat*? We do not have to get rid of the *asat* in order to get to the *sat*. Nor is the *asat* sitting upon *sat*, covering it up, just as the pot does not cover the clay by sitting on it. We need not destroy the pot in order to know the clay. It is just a question of understanding.

Another question then arises. When the entire world is pervaded by *sat-vastu*, is the *sat-vastu* destroyed when the world is destroyed? No. One is *sat* which is not subject to destruction and the other is *asat*. When the *asat* is destroyed, the *sat* is not destroyed. There is both difference and non-difference here, non-difference in the sense that all there is, is *bhāva*, *sat*, and difference in the sense that, while *asat* depends upon *sat*, *sat* does not depend upon *asat*. Therefore, we say that there is both non-difference and difference. Because there is no real difference, there is non-duality. The crux of the matter here is that B is A, whereas A is not B.

Is it possible that *sat*, like time, destroys itself by its own nature, creating itself and then going away? No, because it is *avyaya*, not subject to change. Can anything else, other than itself, destroy *sat*? No. *Sat* pervades everything and there is nothing other than *sat*. Since *sat-vastu* is *ekam advitīyam*, one without the second, there is no second thing that can destroy *sat*. Any 'other' is dependent upon this *sat-vastu* and, therefore, has no independent *bhāva* at all. How is it going to destroy the *sat*? This would be like the pot destroying the clay. The pot cannot say to the clay, 'I am bored with you. You are always hanging around me. You never give me any privacy. Wherever I go, you come too. I am going to get rid of you.' The pot cannot get angry at the clay. It cannot get out of the clay and destroy it. Such a possibility does not exist. Therefore, Kṛṣṇa said here that the *vastu*, *sat-ātmā*, which does not change at any time, cannot be destroyed by anyone or anything. There is no one to effect destruction and no one capable of destroying it, *asya avyayasya vināśaṁ na kaścit kartum arhati*.

Regardless of the number of people or objects, *ātmā* is always non-dual. No number or condition, activity or connection to activity brings about a change in the *ātmā*. In fact, there is no *sambandha*, connection, for *ātmā*, just as there is no connection between clay and pot because all that is there is clay. If there were a pot other than clay, then the clay could establish a relationship with it. But when a pot is clay, there can be no relationship between them. This, therefore, is the nature of *ātmā*.

At the end of his commentary on this verse, Śaṅkara says that no one can destroy this *ātmā*, not even Īśvara, the Lord. But should not God be able to destroy anything? Śaṅkara is not trying to belittle God here. He was merely pointing out that Īśvara cannot destroy *sat-cit-ānanda-ātmā*, not because he is not almighty, but because Īśvara is *ātmā*. *Ātmā* is Brahman and Īśvara is Brahman; therefore, *ātmā* and Īśvara are the same Brahman; the destroyer, Īśvara is *ātmā*. What is to be destroyed is also *ātmā*. How, then, can there be destruction when there is no distinction between the agent and object of destruction?

A *kartṛ-karma-sambandha*, subject-object relationship, is not possible between Īśvara and *ātmā*. But is there not a relationship between the devotee and Īśvara? Yes, if the word 'devotee' means an individual, *ātmā*, identified with a given body-mind-sense complex. Īśvara can destroy or help a devotee, elevate or give punishment, but Īśvara cannot destroy the *sat-ātmā* because both are identical; they have no subject-object relationship.

Perhaps it might be argued that one part of the subject can destroy the other part, just as we can take a knife in our hand and destroy ourselves. If one hand can amputate the other hand, why cannot one part of the subject, *ātmā*, destroy the other part? Cannot *ātmā* also commit suicide in this way? Such destruction could only happen if *ātmā* had parts, which it does not have. It is *avyaya*, indeclinable, indestructible.

Verse 18

The physical body is mithyā

अन्तवन्त इमे देहा नित्यस्योक्ताः शरीरिणः ।
अनाशिनोऽप्रमेयस्य तस्माद्युध्यस्व भारत ॥ १८ ॥

antavanta ime dehā nityasyoktāḥ śarīriṇaḥ
anāśino'prameyasya tasmādyudhyasva bhārata (18)

anāśinaḥ – of the indestructible; *aprameyasya* – of that which is not available as an object of knowledge; *nityasya* – of that which is not subject to change; *śarīriṇaḥ* – of the embodied one (the self); *ime* – these; *dehāḥ* – bodies; *antavantaḥ* – subject to end; *uktāḥ* – are said; *tasmāt* – therefore; *bhārata* – O descendent of Bharata (Arjuna)!; *yudhyasva* – fight

> These bodies of the embodied one (the self), which is not subject to change and destruction, and which is not available as an object of knowledge, are said to be subject to end. Therefore, Bhārata (Arjuna)! (get up and) fight.

Kṛṣṇa unfolded the *sat-vastu*, showing that no one can destroy this *ātmā*, including Īśvara, because it is indestructible and itself sustains everything. Now, what about *asat*? If *sat* is indestructible and pervades everything, and if everything depends upon *sat*, does that which depends upon *sat* not become as true as *sat*? Is it not said that you acquire the same qualities as the company you keep? Is it not also true that if you string roses and then remove them all, the string will continue to smell like roses because of its previous association with them?

Similarly, here, since *asat* is always with *sat*, is there not some kind of attribute-transference because of this association and then, will not *asat* gain the same attribute of being indestructible? No, because there is no association. The string is different from the rose but both enjoy the same empirical reality. What we call string has an empirical reality, as does the rose. Both of them enjoy the same degree of reality and, therefore, one can lend its attributes to the other because association is possible between objects belonging to the same order of reality.

Between *sat* and *asat*, however, such an association is not possible, just as it is not possible between pot and clay. There is only one thing here, clay, which is *sat*. Therefore, *asat* cannot gain indestructibility by association with *sat*.

When you say, 'This is the body,' what is it exactly? Is it the skeletal structure, the skin, the flesh, the marrow, the blood, a given cell, or the DNA? There is no one thing that we call 'body.' All of this put together is the body. You can look at it in many different ways. You can look at it biologically or simply from the standpoint of being nothing but minerals, calcium, phosphorous, and so on. Because each component depends upon so many other things, the physical body is *mithyā*. Or, if you take the body as a whole, it depends upon the five elements, according to the model in Vedanta. However you look at it, the body is *mithyā*.

The physical body is a product created at a given time and is subject to modification. Because it has been created, it has an end, *antavat*. Kṛṣṇa, pointing out all the bodies standing before them, including his own, described them as *antavantaḥ*.

To whom do these bodies belong? The body, *śarīra*, is given existence and consciousness by *ātmā* alone. *Sat-vastu* lends its existence equally to the *sthūla-śarīra*, physical body, and to the *sūkṣma-śarīra*, subtle body. Because the subtle body can reflect consciousness, the body is conscious. Therefore, the *śarīra* belongs to and has its being in *ātmā*, which is the indweller of the body.

Two words were used with reference to the physical body in this verse, *dehāḥ (ime dehāḥ)* which is plural, and *śarīrī (nityasya-śarīriṇaḥ)* which is singular. *Nitya* means eternal, that which is not subject to change, the one who indwells this body as *ātmā*, the meaning of the word 'I.' Because there is only one *ātmā* the singular *śarīrī* is used, whereas with reference to all these bodies that undergo change and come to an end, the plural *dehāḥ* is used.

Who can be destroyed?

In one stroke, three facts have been conveyed here. One is that the bodies are many and *ātmā* is one. Secondly, *ātmā* does not come to an end and is behind every *śarīra*. Thirdly, *ātmā* cannot be destroyed. This being so, whom can you kill? You can only kill something that is subject to destruction. The destructible alone is destroyed. The one that cannot be destroyed is the real person – you, he or she, the 'I' the *ātmā* that is always there.

'Therefore, do what is to be done. Fight, *yudhyasva*!' Kṛṣṇa told Arjuna. What Arjuna had to do at the time was to protect *dharma* by fighting this war. A war was at hand and he had to fight, because this was his *dharma* as a *kṣatriya*.

There are two types of destruction, *nāśa*. One is destruction in a relative sense. 'He is destroyed because she walked out on him.' This is not real destruction. It is figuratively used here. A person who has terminal cancer is destroyed, more or less. Although the final rites may not yet have been done, we say the person is finished; his life is over. Then, when it is literallyover, when the person has died, there is another type of destruction. We have, thus relative destruction and total destruction.

Similarly, there are two types of eternity, relative and absolute. In order to point out that which always is and is never destroyed at all, two words are used in this verse, *nitya* and *anāśī*. Both words mean that which is absolutely free from any form of change or death and, therefore, absolutely free from time, timeless.

There is also another adjective used here, *aprameya*. *Prameya* means that which is to be known, that which can be known. The knower, *pramātā*, gains the knowledge, *pramā*, of an object, *prameya*, through a means of knowledge, *pramāṇa*. *Ātmā* is said here to be *aprameya*, something that is not an object to be known.

Any *prameya* that is seen by you, any object that is available for your *pramāṇa* as an object, *dṛśya*, is non-eternal, *anitya*. Why? Because anything that is seen is within the time-space framework alone and is therefore *anitya*. You cannot say a pot, for example, is *dṛśya* and also *nitya*. To say that something is *dṛśya*, seen, means that it is changing every second. It is never the same because it is within time, and time is an element, which keeps on effecting change. Any object, therefore, is never the same; it is always different. What is available for you to know is therefore always *anitya* and never *nitya*.

Because *ātmā* is not available as an object of knowledge, it is *aprameya*. But if *ātmā* is not an object of knowledge, why are you doing all this study? What is the *gītā-śāstra* for if not for knowing *ātmā*?

The nature of perception

Here, Śaṅkara enters into a short discussion, which he picks up again in more detail elsewhere in the *Gītā*. All these bodies are said to be *anitya*, subject to destruction, whereas *ātmā*, the *śarīrī* who obtains in all bodies, is *nitya*. *Ātmā* is *aprameya*, not available as an object of knowledge.

Anything subject to distinct understanding is called *paricchedya*. There are three words used with reference to our understanding of a distinct object, *paricchedya*, *paricchedaka*, and *pariccheda*. *Paricchedya* means that which is subject to limitation, *pariccheda*. *Paricchedaka* is what brings about this *pariccheda*.

Through the sense organs you perceive objects. The eyes, for example, perceive the form and colour of an object. So the sense organs all become *paricchedaka*s for varieties of *paricchedya*s. Each of the sense objects such as sound, touch, form, taste, and smell, is distinct from one another and, therefore, *paricchediya*. The form that the eyes see is *paricchedya* because it is perceived as distinct from all other things. Therefore, any *pramāṇa* that picks up a distinct piece of knowledge becomes *paricchedaka* and what is picked up is *paricchedya.*

Any object of knowledge that can be known in the form of a cognition such as, this is a pot, this is a cloth, this is a tree, this is a man, this is a woman, is *paricchedya* because an object of knowledge is conditioned or limited in nature and perceived as such through the sense organs. Therefore, the sense organs become *paricchedaka*s and the objects are *paricchedya*s. That which is not known in a determinate form, as an object, by all these *pramāṇa*s, is what is meant here by *aprameya.*

Brahman is not one more object that you see, like the pot or the tree. If Brahman is also *paricchedya,* then it becomes one of the objects in the world and, therefore, becomes *anitya.* However, Brahman cannot be known by *pratyakṣādi-pramāṇa*s, the various means of knowledge that are available to us, such as perception, inference etc. The 'etc., *ādi*' here includes words, *śabda,* meaning that the Veda is also a *pramāṇa.*

When the Veda is a *pramāṇa,* then, *svarga,* heaven, for example, is a *prameya* and therefore a *paricchedya.* Knowledge gained by *śabda-pramāṇa* is again determinate knowledge. Because heaven is not hell, earth, or any other, it is a distinct object. Thus, there is limitation. If heaven is mentioned by the Vedas, then it is something that can be known distinctly.

Similarly, when you say *puṇya,* it is not *pāpa.* It is not produced by wrong *karma.* It is produced by right *karma.* In this way, we understand what *puṇya* is and what it does, purely by *śabda,* the word. Therefore, *śabda* is also a *pramāṇa,* a means of knowledge.

Ātmā is not established by a pramāṇa

If *ātmā* cannot be known even by *śabda*, why, then, do you study the *gītā-śāstra*? If it is not an object of knowledge for the *pratyakṣādi-pramāṇa*s, how can Vedanta be a *pramāṇa* for the *ātmā*? Addressing this question, Śaṅkara first says that *ātmā* is not known by any *pramāṇa*, including the Veda, because it is not an object of knowledge.

Thinking that *ātmā* could be known through this *pramāṇa*, a person goes to a *guru*, does a lot of service, and at the end of it the *guru* says, '*ātmā* is not known even through the Veda.' Since the *guru* teaches only the Veda, what is the use of all this? Naturally, such a person thinks it has all been a waste. He or she also thinks that *ātmā* is understood perhaps through the *pratyakṣādi-pramāṇa*s. Śaṅkara refuted this notion here by saying that *ātmā* is not known by the *pratyakṣādi-pramāṇa*s including the Veda.

Before you listen to the *vedānta-śāstra*, *ātmā* must be there. The existence of *ātmā* is not established by a *pramāṇa* like the Veda, nor can it be established by *pratyakṣa*, perception or *anumāna* inference. If the existence of *ātmā* were to be established by any of the *pramāṇa*s resulting in such knowledge as, here is a pot, here is a table, here is the Swami sitting, etc., then we would be using perception, of course. But we would not be establishing the *ātmā* behind the perception. Only when the knower is already established, can there be an enquiry through a *pramāṇa*.

Vedānta-vicāra, enquiry, can only be done when there is an *ātmā* to enquire. If Vedanta were to establish the *ātmā*, it would mean that until one enquired into Vedanta, *ātmā* did not exist. It means you were not there! Who is it then, that goes to Vedanta, which says that *ātmā* is limitless? Moreover, who listens to this Vedanta? The *ātmā*.

The one who wants to know is the same as the one who can use any of the *pramāṇa*s to enquire into what is to be known. Even before the *pramāṇa*s are pressed into service for gathering such knowledge, there must be a self-evident *ātmā*. Therefore, the Veda does not establish *ātmā*, as it does any other existent thing like heaven, *svarga*, and so on. A *svarga* that is unknown to you is made known to you by the *śāstra*. You come to know of something called *puṇya* that is said to be dormant in a *karma* that can be invoked through the *śāstra* alone. Thus, you find these unknown things discussed in the *śāstra* as potentially existent things.

Similarly, there are many unknown things in the world that you come to know through the various *pramāṇa*s, a new disease, for example. Having come to know about it, you say the disease 'is.' After discovering it, you look for its cause. Then, after finding the cause, you say the cause 'is' and the treatment for the cause 'is.' After treatment, you say the side effects 'are.' Like this, with the help of *pramāṇa*s, you keep on discovering things that exist but which were so far not known.

Although *ātmā* is not available as an object of knowledge, it is not totally unknown. In fact, Śaṅkara says that *ātmā* is not something unknown to anyone. It is always *svataḥ-siddha*, self-evident, self-established. No one's *ātmā* is unknown; everyone's *ātmā* is known. Only then is the operation of the *pramāṇas* possible. The *ātmā* is not established by a *pramāṇa;* it is *svataḥ-siddha.*

Śāstra as a pramāṇa

Then the problem would be, what about the *śāstra*? 'If I already know *ātmā,* how can the *vedānta-śāstra* be a *pramāṇa*?' Here, Śaṅkara says that the *śāstra* is definitely a *pramāṇa*. How? Revealing the existence of *ātmā* is not what establishes the *śāstra* as a *pramāṇa*. But, the *śāstra* has the status of a *pramāṇa* because it removes the wrong notions you have about *ātmā.*

Ātmā by nature is *paraṁ-brahma* and that *paraṁ-brahma* is not known to you. The *pramāṇas* available to you are only good for knowing things other than yourself. *Ātmā* is already *svataḥ-siddha* and it is this *svataḥ-siddha-ātmā* that is mistaken for a *jīva,* a doer, *kartā,* an enjoyer, *bhoktā,* one who is happy one moment and sad the next, *sukhī* and *duḥkhī*. That I am a *jīva,* an individual, means that I am someone who is limited, as good as the body, etc. This is the natural conclusion of every *jīva* because of *avidyā,* ignorance.

The status of being a *jīva, jīvatva* has been superimposed upon the *ātmā*. In other words, the seeking person is born of *avidyā*. It is an error of self-identity, which only the *śāstra* can resolve. One's own *pramāṇas* are of no use here. The *śāstra* does not prove the existence of *ātmā;* it only removes the confusion. For this reason, it has the status of being a *pramāṇa*, that is, it has *pramāṇatva*. It does not bring to your recognition the *ātmā* as an object that is totally unknown, as it does for other unknown things like heaven, for instance.

When the *śāstra* says there is a heaven, heaven as an unknown thing is brought to your understanding. You understand that there is such a thing as heaven. When the *śāstra* says that this particular ritual will produce this particular result, it is definitely bringing an unknown thing to your recognition. That this ritual has this efficacy is not known to you by any other *pramāṇa* Therefore, the *śāstra* has the status of being a *pramāṇa* by bringing to your recognition something that is totally unknown to you, which cannot be known by you through any other *pramāṇa*.

When it comes to *ātmā*, the *śāstra* has *pramāṇatva* only insofar as it removes all superimpositions upon the *ātmā*. Knowledge is nothing but the removal of ignorance. It cannot be a superimposition upon ignorance. If ignorance is not removed, there is no knowledge at all, ignorance being opposed to knowledge. Only the removal of ignorance is necessary. Ignorance of *ātmā* is present and the *śāstra* has the capacity to remove it, meaning that it removes all the confusions centred on *ātmā*. But, *ātmā* is self-evident, which is why there is confusion. *Ātmā* is self-evident but that it is limitless is not known. Hence, all the limitations of the body, mind and so on, are superimposed on it.

Ātmā is already known but not as an object

If *ātmā* were to be totally unknown, like heaven, you would not say that you are a *sukhī* or a *duḥkhī* or a *samsārī*. To say, 'I am finished,' is possible only because you have concluded that you are a *samsārī*. Therefore, the *ātmā*, 'I' is already self-evident. However, it is taken for something other than what it is and the *śāstra* makes the necessary correction, thereby proving itself to be a *pramāṇa*.

Śaṅkara quotes the *śāstra* saying that this *brahma-ātmā* is self-evident, *aparokṣa*. That which is self-evident is *ātmā*, Brahman; everything else becomes evident to the self. In this verse, Kṛṣṇa says that all bodies are subject to destruction, whereas *ātmā*, the indweller of the body, is not subject to destruction because it is the subject, not an object, *aprameya*. This is the point here. Any object is subject to destruction, whereas *ātmā*, not being an object, is *nitya*. Anything *aprameya* is *nitya* and only one thing is *aprameya*, the *svataḥ-siddha-ātmā*. Therefore, *ātmā* is not subject to time and, thus, not subject to destruction.

Kṛṣṇa concluded by saying, '*Tasmāt yudhyasva bhārata*, therefore, fight, Arjuna.' What does it mean? There is nothing for you to be sad about. Things that die and are dying, die. Things that remain permanent remain permanent. If Arjuna wanted to destroy Bhīṣma's *ātmā* he could not. Had he wanted to stop Bhīṣma's body from dying, he could not. Either way, Arjuna could not do anything. Therefore, what is to be done is to be done.

Śaṅkara says here that Kṛṣṇa was not giving Arjuna an order to fight. It is not the point here. The meaning here was, 'Do not entertain the idea of withdrawing from this battlefield.' What is the difference between this statement and an order to fight? Śaṅkara says there is a difference. This was not a command that one should actually fight. If it was not a command, then was it a request? No. Arjuna was already prepared to fight. He had come with his entire armoury; but then found himself obstructed by sorrow and delusion; he was *śoka-moha-pratibaddha*, which is why he became silent. He could not proceed because he was completely paralysed psychologically and emotionally for various reasons. Therefore, he was no longer interested in fighting and turned his attention to something else.

All that Bhagavān was doing here was removing the sorrow and delusion that were the obstructions, *pratibandha*s. Afterwards, if the fighting was to be done, then it was to be done. Therefore, *yudhyasva* was not a command; it was only asking Arjuna to do what was to be done. It was only a restatement of what he was planning to do. Bhagavān does not ask people to fight each other. Śaṅkara states, *gītā-śāstra* is not a *pravṛtti-śāstra* like the *karma-kāṇḍa*, which enjoins people to perform various rituals and other actions. It is a *nivṛtti-śāstra, mokṣa-śāstra*. To have asked Arjuna to fight would have been a *pravṛtti-śāstra* whereas the *nivṛtti* here is the removal of the cause of *saṁsāra*, sorrow and delusion which is ignorance.

Removing the obstacles to knowledge

The *gītā-śāstra* is meant to remove the ignorance, which is the cause for *saṁsāra* consisting of *śoka* and *moha*. This should be understood well. It was sorrow and delusion that clouded Arjuna's mind and for that alone the *gītā-śāstra* was given by the Lord. Therefore, Kṛṣṇa was not asking Arjuna to fight. Arjuna was already fighting. He was simply saying that

Arjuna should do what was to be done. In other words, he was saying, 'Do not give me these kinds of arguments in order not to fight.'

Suppose someone were to say, 'I will not take care of my child because it takes so much time to take care of a child. It consumes too much of my personal life. I want to pursue *ātmā* and to take care of this child will take seventeen years, perhaps longer. I cannot wait for *mokṣa*.' If such a person were to go to Kṛṣṇa and Kṛṣṇa happened to teach the *Gītā*, he or she would be told, 'Take care of your child.' Or, if a man were to tell Kṛṣṇa that he wanted to get rid of his wife so that he could become a *sannyāsī*, or that he wanted to become a *sannyāsī* in order to get rid of her, he would be told not to use *sannyāsa* for this purpose. There are smaller solutions available. And if this man thinks that by getting rid of his wife, he will become a *sannyāsī*, Kṛṣṇa would say, 'I am sorry. Such an idea is quite useless. It will not work. You had better take care of your wife.'

Arjuna had been talking to Kṛṣṇa and they happened to be in the battlefield. Therefore, the expressions like 'Fight!' and 'Get up!' are only contextual. Kṛṣṇa was not interested in a battle as such; he was only interested in *dharma*. He was not interested in engaging anyone in a fight. We should not think, 'The *Gītā* says that I should fight; therefore, I am going to fight it out.' This is not what was said here. That the situation may amount to a fight is one thing. But removing sorrow is the real issue. There are some points in the *Gītā*, like this one, that are important to understand well because they are areas where people often misunderstand the intended meaning.

Verse 19

Ātmā does not kill – nor is it killed

य एनं वेत्ति हन्तारं यश्चैनं मन्यते हतम् ।
उभौ तौ न विजानीतो नायं हन्ति न हन्यते ॥ १९ ॥

Ya enaṁ vetti hantāraṁ yaścainaṁ manyate hatam
ubhau tau na vijānīto nāyaṁ hanti na hanyate (19)

yaḥ – the one who; *enam* – this (the self); *hantāram* – killer; *vetti* – thinks; *ca* – and; *yaḥ* – the one who; *enam* – this (the self); *hatam* – killed; *manyate* – thinks; *ubhau tau* – they both; *na vijānītaḥ* – do not know; *ayam* – this (self); *na hanti* – does not kill; *na hanyate* – is not killed

The one who thinks this (self) to be the killer and the one who thinks of it as the killed, both do not know. This (self) does not kill; nor is it killed.

This verse and the next are quoted from the *Kaṭhopaniṣad*, put a little differently by Lord Kṛṣṇa. He need not have quoted an *Upaniṣad* since he had the authority to propound the vision in his own way, but he respected the *Upaniṣad* because it is a means of knowledge, a *pramāṇa-grantha*. Therefore, whatever he says should have the sanction of the *Upaniṣad*. Kṛṣṇa does point out elsewhere in the *Gītā* that the *Upaniṣad*s were his own creation. He says, 'I am the one to be known through the Vedas. I am the one who initiated these Vedas.'[6] Thus, throughout the *Gītā*, Kṛṣṇa always talks as Īśvara.

---

[6] *Gītā* 15.15

Whether we accept him as Īśvara, Kṛṣṇa talks as Īśvara. The entire dialogue in the *Gītā* was between Īśvara, in the form of Kṛṣṇa, and Arjuna. That is how Vyāsa presented it. As Īśvara, Kṛṣṇa naturally does not need to substantiate his statement. At the same time, however, the *Gītā* has a historicity in that it came from a given mind, Kṛṣṇa's mind, at a given time.

What is heard and received by one generation from another is called *śruti*, whereas what is born of someone's mind is called *smṛti*. What Kṛṣṇa says has the status of *smṛti* and not *śruti*. Any *smṛti* must have the sanction of the *śruti*. And if it is against the *śruti*, the *smṛti* is to be looked at again to see whether it has some other meaning that will conform to the *śruti*. If it does not conform in all areas, from the beginning to the end, then the *smṛti* has to be dismissed.

This being the tradition, Bhagavān, in so many words, confirms the *śruti*. He did not say, this is what the *śruti* says. But he did put the words of the *śruti* in a different form here. There are several instances in the *Gītā* where such verses have been taken from the *Upaniṣad*s, mainly the *Kaṭhopaniṣad*, for the purpose of validating what is being said.

Śaṅkara begins his commentary of this verse by saying that Bhagavān presents the next two verses, taken from the *Kaṭhopaniṣad*, to support what he has been saying, meaning that the *śruti* is a *pramāṇa* that is like a witness. Generally, to validate an event that took place, you have a witness who says, 'Yes, I saw that happen.' Similarly, to validate what he was saying, Bhagavān needed a witness and called upon one. The *śāstra-pramāṇa* has the status of a witness here. The *śruti*, being a *pramāṇa*, is self-valid. It does not require any validation by any other *pramāṇa*. All that is necessary is that it does not contradict any other *pramāṇa*.

If the *śruti* can be contradicted by any other means of knowledge, it ceases to be a *pramāṇa*. In other words, the *śruti* need not be validated by any other *pramāṇa* for it to be established as a *pramāṇa*. That is why reasoning is required, so that you can prove that it is not contradicted in any way. If someone says the *śruti* is contradicted by his or her experience, then reasoning is used to show how the person's conclusion regarding the *śruti* or one's experience is wrong. By reasoning, then, we show that what the *śruti* says is not contradicted by any other means of knowledge and is, therefore, a *pramāṇa*.

The word '*enam*,' in this verse, refers to *ātmā* which is self-evident, which is *sat*, the very basis, the truth of all *asat*, and which is *nitya*, *aprameya*, all of which has been stated previously. *Yaḥ* refers to the one who looks upon this *ātmā* as the agent of the action of killing, *hantā*.

Even though the action of killing, *hanana-kriyā*, does not have the same context in the *Kaṭhopaniṣad* as in the *Gītā* where there was going to be a war, it was nevertheless used in the *Upaniṣad* where there was no war at all. To understand the reason for this, the analogy of a world champion wrestler or boxer is helpful. In order to become the world champion, you need not fight against everyone in your neighbourhood. Nor do you need to fight all of humanity. You need only knock out the current world champion. Nothing more is required. Similarly, of all actions that a human being is capable of doing, the one that is universally considered to be the most unbecoming is killing. This is why this action is cited here.

With reference to killing, *ātmā* is looked upon in two different ways in this verse. One person may consider the *ātmā* to be the killer, *hantā,* the doer of the action of killing, and another person may consider himself or herself to be the object of the killing. One thinks *ātmā* is the *kartā,* the doer, of the *hanana-kriyā,* the act of killing. The other thinks *ātmā* is the *karma,* the object of the *hanana-kriyā,* meaning that he or she is subject to destruction. The one who looks upon *ātmā* as subject to destruction thinks that *ātmā* can be objectified. Kṛṣṇa says here that both of them do not know the *ātmā* – *ubhau tau na vijānītaḥ.*

Ātmā does not perform the act of killing; nor is it destroyed by anyone else. It is neither a killer nor the object of anyone's killing, *na ayaṁ hanti na hanyate.* It means that *ātmā* is neither *kartā* nor *karma.* If *ātmā* can neither kill nor be killed, again the question must be asked, how can one grieve? No one can harm *ātmā* nor can *ātmā* harm itself. It is not a *kartā.* Not even Īśvara can destroy the *ātmā,* as Śaṅkara pointed out.

In the previous verse, we saw that *kartṛ-karma,* the subject-object division, is not possible for *ātmā* and this statement is validated in the present verse, which is a replica of the *śruti.* *Ātmā,* therefore, is neither the subject of an action nor the object of an action. The status of doership, *kartṛtva* is imposed upon the *ātmā* while *ātmā* itself is *akartā.* Some insight can be gained here by looking at the meaning of the word, *sarva-karma-sannyāsa.* In fact, there are two types of *sannyāsa* – *sannyāsa* as a lifestyle and *sarva-karma-sannyāsa.*

Karma-sannyāsa is present in both types of *sannyāsa*. When *sannyāsa* is taken as a lifestyle, all obligatory duties, including religious duties, are given up by performing a ritual. This ritual is the last ritual a *sannyāsī* performs, one that absolves him or her from those rituals and duties that are enjoined by the Vedas. This is *karma-sannyāsa*, the renunciation of all enjoined *karma*s. However, this *karma-sannyāsa* does not remove the doership, the *kartṛtva*, in the person. *Sarva-karma-sannyāsa* is knowing the *ātmā*, the 'I' *aham*, as free from action. The knowledge that 'I perform no action, *aham na kiñcit karomi*, I am not a doer, *aham na kartā*,' frees me from all actions. This freedom is called *sannyāsa* here.

Ātmā does not perform any action

Later, we will see in the *Gītā* that a person who, by knowledge, gives up all *karma*s, knows well that *aham*, the *ātmā*, does not perform any action, *na karma karoti*. The doership that one has can be with reference to either an enlightened doer or an unenlightened doer. An enlightened doer is one who knows, 'I am not the *kartā*,' even though he or she still performs actions.

This is not to say that there is no doer; there is a doer, but its reality with reference to the person is negated. No one can perform an action without a sense of doership. Everyone has to recognise, 'I perform this action.' Even to speak, one has to identify with the body and the organ of speech and, thus, there is a *kartā*. There is a subject and an action done like a talker and the act of talking. Whether it is Kṛṣṇa talking, Vyāsa writing, Śaṅkara commenting, or any enlightened person doing anything, there is definitely a *kartā*. But he or she is an enlightened *kartā*, meaning that the person does not look upon oneself as the *kartā*. The *ātmā* is no longer mistaken to be the *kartā*. So, there is an enlightened *ahaṅkāra* and an unenlightened *ahaṅkāra*.

The *ahaṅkāra* is not something to be afraid of. All that we are aiming at is the removal of the ignorance, which makes the *ātmā* a *kartā*, a doer. *Ātmā* is free from all action and this is not recognised by the one who looks upon *ātmā* as the *kartā*. The one who thinks, 'I subject myself to the influence of the world' or 'The world is too much with me,' does not know the *ātmā*. The world is not too much with you. The world is you and you are free from the world.

That 'I am the basis, the *sat*, of the whole creation and, at the same time, I am free from everything,' is something that I must understand. It is this *jñāna* that is taught in the *Gītā*, the essence of which appears in the next verse.

Verse 20

Ātmā is not born – nor does it die

न जायते म्रियते वा कदाचिन्नायं भूत्वा भविता वा न भूयः ।
अजो नित्यः शाश्वतोऽयं पुराणो न हन्यते हन्यमाने शरीरे ॥२० ॥

na jāyate mriyate vā kadācin-
nāyaṁ bhūtvā bhavitā vā na bhūyaḥ
ajo nityaḥ śāśvato'yaṁ purāṇo
na hanyate hanyamāne śarīre (20)

ayam – this; *kadācit* – ever; *na jāyate* – is not born; *vā-* – or; *na mriyate* – does not die; *vā-* – or; *bhūtvā* – having been; *na abhavitā* – does not cease to be; *bhūyaḥ* – again; *ajaḥ* – unborn; *nityaḥ* – eternal; *śāśvataḥ* – that which undergoes no change whatsoever; *purāṇaḥ* – ever new; *śarīre hanyamāne* – when the body is destroyed; *ayam* – this; *na hanyate* – is not destroyed

> This (self) is never born; nor does it die. It is not that, having been, it ceases to exist again. It is unborn, eternal, undergoes no change whatsoever, and is ever new. When the body is destroyed, the self is not destroyed.

Ātmā does not perform any action nor does it subject itself to any action as an object of action because it is unchanging, *avikriya*. There must be some change on the part of the one who performs the action for an action to occur. Also, to subject oneself to an action is to undergo some change because whatever has been subjected to an action does not remain the same. For example, when water is heated, it is an object of the act of heating and is not the same after subjecting itself to that action. So too, if *ātmā* were subject to change, it would be possible for it to be a subject or an object, a *kartā* or *karma*. It would be able to perform actions and also subject itself to an action. But, since the *ātmā* is not subject to any form of change, it is neither *kartā* nor *karma*. It does not change nor does any other condition bring about a change to it. This verse from the *śruti* was cited here to uphold this particular vision that *ātmā* is *avikriya*, unchanging.

The previous verse, also taken from the *Kaṭhopaniṣad* and put in Kṛṣṇa's own words, was in the *anuṣṭubh* metre, the more common of the two metres found in the *Gītā*, whereas this verse is in the *triṣṭubh* metre. The *Mahābhārata* and the *Rāmāyaṇa* generally follow the *anuṣṭubh* metre, it being a very popular one and easy to chant. Because the verse is in the *triṣṭubh* metre, it cannot be chanted in the same way as the other verses. Each metre demands its own style when chanting or reciting it and the tune has to be discovered.

Kṛṣṇa wanted to make two points here, *ātmā* is not born, *na jāyate;* nor does it die, *na mriyate.* There is no such change as birth or death for *ātmā*. Birth means that certain changes have taken place and such changes are not for *ātmā*. There are many types of births. For instance, previously something was not and then afterwards it came into being, like a pot. Or, previously something was in one form and now it is in another, like a seed, having been in a seed form, is now in a plant form. There has been a sprouting and something new is born, but only the form has changed.

So, for the *ātmā*, there are no such births. There is no birth from *abhāva* to *bhāva*, non-existence to existence. It also does not have a birth from *bhāva* to *bhāva*, existing in one form and then assuming another. *Ātmā* undergoes no change at all, meaning that it neither dies nor is born.

These are two basic types of *vikriyā*s, changes. One is the change of being born and the other is the change that spells death. Neither of these *vikriyā*s are there for *ātmā* at any time, *na jāyate na mriyate vā kadācit*. It means, then, *ātmā* being existent now, does not become extinct later. And it was not non-existent before it came into being. Nor, having existed in another form, does it assume a new form now. The first change implying birth and the last change implying death, both having been negated, all the other changes in between – growth, metamorphosis, and decline–are also dismissed for *ātmā* because there is no *vikriyā* whatsoever.

Kṛṣṇa also said in this verse that *ātmā*, having been before, does not again become non-existent, *ayam-bhūtvā abhavitā vā na bhūyaḥ*. What is the sense of 'again' here? Again, having been, *ātmā* does not become non-existent. Death is 'having been, one is no more.' Such a situation is not there for *ātmā*. *Ātmā* was, is, and will ever be the same. Because *ātmā* is not subject to time, it is *avikriya*, not subject to change. This is one meaning.

A person who was there before and is no more is said to be dead. Such a person is gone and no one can say where he or she went. However, you cannot say the same for the son of a barren woman. He never existed at any time. Therefore you cannot say that having existed he ceases to exist now. A non-existent thing does not die. The barren woman dies, but her son does not. Death only applies when, having been, something goes away. A similar change does not happen to *ātmā*. *Ātmā* is not subject to a futuristic extinction, which means that it is not subject to time in terms of the future in any way. Nor is it subject to time in terms of the past. That something did not exist before and has now come into being is another situation, called birth. Having not been before, it came into existence.

The one who is born is the one who, having not been before, comes into being, *abhūtvā bhavitā*. Previously it was non-existent and later it comes into existence. This also does not apply to *ātmā*. Therefore, the words in the verse can also be put differently, *ātmā* was not non-existent previously and there will be no time when it does not exist. Either way you can take it – *bhūtvā abhavitā na* or *abhūtvā bhavitā na*. Both meanings are given by Śaṅkara here for the same line because both meanings are there in the verse.

Having not been, and then coming into being, which is called birth, is not there for *ātmā, na jāyate*. Having been and disappearing, which is called death, is also not there for *ātmā, na mriyate*. This being so, *ātmā* is unborn, *aja*. Because it is not subject to death, the word also implies that *ātmā* is not bound by time. It is not an object within time. It is something on which time depends for its existence and is, therefore, *aja* and *nitya*. The word '*śāśvata*,' meaning that which is always the same, that never undergoes any change, was also necessary here to eliminate the possibility of *ātmā* being taken for something eternal, *nitya*, but continuously changing, eternally changing.

The changing and the changeless

So, the changes that the physical body is subject to between birth and death, growth, metamorphosis, and decline, are also not there for *ātmā*. Another word describing the *ātmā* in this verse, *purāṇa*, generally means ancient, but here it refers to that which is ever fresh. *Ātmā* was always fresh, is still fresh and will always be fresh. *Ātmā* is timeless and is the very content of the meaning of the word new, *nava*. It was *nava* then and it is *nava* now.[7] Previously it was new and now also it is new. It is always new; it does not grow old. There is no *vṛddhi*, ageing, no *apakṣaya*, decline, for the *ātmā*. In other words, even when the *śarīra*, the body is destroyed, *ātmā* is not destroyed, *hanyamāne śarīre na hanyate*. It is always the same.

We have seen, then, that *ātmā* is neither the subject nor the object of any action, which is why it cannot be affected by *puṇya* and *pāpa* or destroyed by anyone, not even Īśvara. If it were the subject of an action, it would necessarily undergo a change in order to perform the action. A new action cannot emanate in any other way. The subject, the doer of the action has a thought or a desire, *saṅkalpa* and undergoes whatever change is necessary to perform the action. For example, the desire to see something, 'Let me look at the book,' means that the person becomes a *kartā*. There is a *saṅkalpa* and the one with the *saṅkalpa* becomes the subject, the doer, and the doer undergoes a change. The change is in the form of a *saṅkalpa*, anxiety, and so on, on the part of the doer, the subject. That subject performs the action. If *ātmā* is a *kartā*, then *ātmā* itself must undergo this *vikriyā*, change. That this self-evident *ātmā* undergoes no change and is therefore neither *kartā* nor *karma* was made clear in the previous verses. Therefore, only an *ātmā* that undergoeschange, a *vikriyāvān-ātmā*, can be a *kartā*. Similarly, if *ātmā* is the object of any action, it would be affected by any action perpetrated by someone towards it, you, the *ātmā*. A *karma*, action, is that which brings about a change to the object of action. For instance,

---

[7] *purā eva navaḥ purāṇaḥ* – even before it was new.

if we hit an object with a hammer, that object, the recipient of that action, must undergo some kind of change and that change is the result of that particular *karma*, hitting. Similarly, if *ātmā* is the object of any kind of action, it must also undergo a change. Therefore, we would have a *vikriyāvān-ātmā*, an *ātmā* that is subject to change. But *ātmā* is *avikriya*.

The physical body, on the other hand, is subject to change. When the *ahaṅkāra*, ego, identifying with the body, performs an action, it is the physical body that performs the action in keeping with the *ahaṅkāra*'s intention. The legs move, the hands move, the body shrinks or expands, to a certain extent, in that you can stretch it in order to reach something or you can shrink yourself in order to get out of a tight place. Thus, the body undergoes all kinds of contortions. The body is at the disposal of the *kartā* and undergoes a lot of change. It also becomes an object of action when someone else pushes it. The body is, therefore, *vikriyāvān;* not only does it undergo change, but it is meant to do so.

The body is *jāyate*, born; *asti*, it exists; *vardhate*, grows; *vipariṇamate*, undergoes certain modifications; *apakṣīyate*, declines; and *vinaśyati*, dies because it is *vikāravān*, that which is subject to change.

Due to lack of understanding, this physical body and the *ātmā* are taken together. *Ātmā* is taken to have a physical body as an intrinsic attribute. Therefore, I become as good as the physical body. Here, the *viveka*, discrimination, required is that while the *deha* is subject to change, *ātmā* is not. It is neither born nor does it die. The first and last *vikāra*s for the body, birth and death, are negated in *ātmā* by this verse.

Ātmā was not born because there was not a time when it was not in order to be born. It was always there. Nor will it die because, having not come into being, there will never be a time when it will not be there. Thus, it is not subject to birth or death; therefore it is *nitya*. Nor does it undergo the other changes that happen between birth and death; therefore it is *śāsvata*.

The question may then be asked, if *ātmā* does not decline, does it grow? Is it that when you are born, there is a nascent *ātmā*, a baby *ātmā*, which then becomes a child *ātmā*, adult *ātmā*, and so on? No, *Bhāṣyakāra* Śaṅkara said, it does not grow either. Here, he introduced a small definition for growth, *vṛddhi*. Any growth means that something that was not earlier should come into being. For instance, a young man previously did not have a moustache and therefore did not have to shave. Now he has both a beard and a moustache and has to shave every day. This is *vṛddhi*, growth. Something new has happened.

In any growth, there are always new features introduced. Either something is added to what is already there or it expresses itself in some new way. Either way, the arrival of a new feature makes the thing grow. For instance, a small sprout begins to grow. It branches out into leaves and flowers, and becomes a full-grown tree. Therefore, growth always implies new features added to a given stem and the new feature that has been gained means that which grows is no longer the same.

Ātmā was always ever grown, meaning that it never grows. Only that which has a feature, an attribute, can grow and decline, wax and wane, bulge and contract. If it is a colour, for example, it will fade or a new colour may come. Something can happen to it, whereas *ātmā*, having no features whatsoever, no limbs or attributes, is *purāṇa*, ever new. Even when the body is destroyed, *hanyamāne śarīre*, *ātmā* is not destroyed. 'Not destroyed' is to be taken here in the sense of change so as not to confuse its meaning with the use of *hanti* and *hanyate*, to kill and be killed, in the previous verse. All that is being said is that *ātmā* undergoes no change whatsoever.

Śaṅkara concludes his commentary of this verse by saying that, with reference to *ātmā*, Kṛṣṇa negated the six-fold modifications that we see in any given physical body, namely birth, existence, growth, modification, decline and death. The meaning of these two verses taken from the *śruti*, therefore, is that *ātmā* is free from any manner of modification. In no way is it subject to change.

No one can effect a change on *ātmā* because it is not available for objectification and does not have any *avayava*, feature or attribute, to receive such an action. Nor does *ātmā* itself undergo a change to perform any action. Therefore, being both *akartā*, not a doer of the action, and *akarma*, not an object of the action, *ātmā* is *aśocya*, not a source of sorrow.

Where is *śocya*, then? There should be an object available for sorrow, a situation capable of causing sorrow. *Ātmā* cannot cause sorrow because it does not undergo any change, nor does it subject itself to change. How, then, can it be *śocya*? *Ātmā*, whose *svarūpa*, nature, is *ānanda*, fullness, can only be *aśocya*.

Verse 21

Ātmā is neither subject nor object of action

वेदाविनाशिनं नित्यं य एनमजमव्ययम् ।
कथं स पुरुषः पार्थ कं घातयति हन्ति कम् ॥ २१ ॥

vedāvināśinaṁ nityaṁ ya enam ajam avyayam
kathaṁ sa puruṣaḥ pārtha kaṁ ghātayati hanti kam (21)

pārtha – O son of Pṛthā (Arjuna)!; *enam* – this (*ātmā*); *avināśinam* – indestructible; *nityam* – timelss; *ajam* – unborn; *avyayam* – that which does not undergo decline; *yaḥ veda* – the one who knows; *saḥ* – that; *puruṣaḥ* – person; *katham* – how; *kam* – whom; *hanti* – kills; *kam* – whom; *ghātayati* – causes to kill

> Pārtha (Arjuna)! The one who knows this (self) to be indestructible, timeless, unborn, and not subject to decline, how and whom does that person kill? Whom does he cause to kill?

The one who thinks that *ātmā* performs the action of killing, or any action for that matter, does not know *ātmā* and the one who looks upon *ātmā* as an object of the action of killing or any other action also does not know the *ātmā*. This is because, as we saw in an earlier verse, *ātmā* does not kill nor is it killed, *na hanti, na hanyate*. To put it positively, one who takes *ātmā* to be neither the subject nor the object of action, knows the *ātmā*.

What has been pointed out so far was summed up here by Kṛṣṇa. His initial statement was that *ātmā* does not become the *kartā* or *karma* of any *kriyā*, including killing, *hanana-kriyā*.

Having introduced this point, he explained that this is because *ātmā* is not subject to change. Having given the reason, he concluded, stating that one who knows the *ātmā* knows it to be *avināśī*, not subject to death or destruction.

The body's change is called *bhāva-vikāra*, a technical expression to include *jāyate*, is born, *vardhate*, grows, *vipariṇamate*, metamorphoses, *apakṣīyate*, wanes or declines, and *vinaśyati*, dies. Because *ātmā* does not have this last *bhāva-vikāra*, it is referred to here as *avināśī*. The one who knows *ātmā* as one that is not subject to death and therefore timeless, *nitya*, is called an *ātmajña*, the knower of *ātmā*.

Ātmā is also known by the *ātmajña* as *aja*, unborn, and as that which does not undergo any kind of *avyaya*, decline. Unlike *ātmā*, the body is expended as the years go by, which is why it is described as a 'spent force,' the job being done, the game is over! All that is then discussed is in the past tense, 'I was like this, I was like that, and I would have been like that, and so on.' This is *vyaya*, expenditure, whereas *ātmā* is *avyaya*. In Sanskrit grammar also, an indeclinable word is called *avyaya*, that which does not change in any situation, regardless of number, gender or case.

Bringing up one more point in his summary Kṛṣṇa asks, '*Kaṁ hanti*, whom does that person destroy? *Kaṁ ghātayati*, whom does he impel to kill?' There are two types of action reflected here. One is the action that you do and the other is the action that you make others do. In a robbery, for example, there is the accused number one and the accused number two. One may have performed the act of driving the get-away car, while the other performed the act of driving the driver. There is someone who performs the felony and there is someone else behind it. The one behind the felony is the accused and the one who performed it is only an accomplice. The accused is an important person, the kingpin, whereas the other one is only a pin! But both of them perform action.

How can one who knows *ātmā* perform the action of killing and whom does he or she kill? Where is the person being killed? Where is that action? A question is not really being posed here. For instance, we are not trying to find out by what means the killing is done. Nor are we trying to find out why the person does it or whether he or she kills. It is not the intent here. Rather, how can one kill and whom does one kill is being looked into. There should be some *vikriyā* on one's part in order to perform the action and *ātmā* is *avikriyā*.

A doubt may arise here. If there is no *vikriyā* for *ātmā* and the *ātmajña* knows that *ātmā*, the I, is not the performer of any action, how, then, can that person perform any action? What is to be understood here is that *ātmā* does not perform any action. It does not kill nor cause anyone to kill because *ātmā* does not even wish. It is the *svarūpa* of every wish. The wish is a *nāma-rūpa*, a thought, and if you press the thought, it ends up in *ātmā*, wherein there is no thought anywhere. Thus, any given thought or desire is *mithyā* and the doership is also *mithyā*.

If you analyse who the doer is, you find that the doer is nothing but consciousness, *caitanya*. That is, the doer disappears in the *caitanya* and is not there at all. When the doer is there, *caitanya* is there, whereas in the *caitanya* there is no doer.

Therefore, there is only drama. There is no real doer, only an 'as though' doer. It is 'as though' he or she hears, 'as though' listens, 'as though' talks, 'as though' walks, and 'as though' stands.

There is no doership in *ātmā* because *ātmā* is always free. The notion that 'I am the performer of the action,' is the source of action we talk about here. Where is an action without a *kartā*? Without the doership, *kartṛtva,* there is no real action at all. Therefore, the doership is the one that gives the blood, bones, and flesh necessary for the action to be an action and for the *karma-phala* to be the *karma-phala,* the result you enjoy. The whole cycle is based upon the kingpin, the *kartā.*

Without the *kartā,* there is no *karma* or *karma-phala.* The *kartā* is defined as the one who decides and performs action. He or she has *kriyā,* etc. and, therefore, can choose from the hundreds of verbal roots for 'doing' that are available. The doer can choose to kill, to speak, or to do any of the varieties of actions possible, but for the *ātmā,* which is *avikriya,* free from any change, there is no *kartṛtva.* Where, then, is the question of how and whom, with reference to killing, *kathaṁ ghātayati, kathaṁ hanti, kaṁ ghātayati kaṁ hanti*!

A sarva-karma-sannyāsī

The word '*hanti,*' here, is only contextual and has nothing to do with killing as such. Śaṅkara says that the expression is purely with reference to action. What kind of action does the person perform and what kind of action does he or she cause anyone else to perform? A question may then arise here.

If a person is a *sarva-karma-sannyāsī*, and has given up all *karmas*, will he or she not perform any action at all? Does the person not continue to perform actions? Does he or she not teach? Does the person not do anything, not even eat, walk or talk? How can you say that one who still performs these actions is a *sarva-karma-sannyāsī*?

Sarva-karma-sannyāsī is the one who does not have the notion that 'I am the doer,' that is, the one who does not have *kartṛtva-buddhi*. For such a person, there is no doership in the *ātmā*. One is not a *sarva-karma-sannyāsī* by merely not doing *karma*. One may be a *karma-sannyāsī* but not a *sarva-karma-sannyāsī*. Even if one does not do any *karma*, if one has *kartṛtva-buddhi*, one is still a *saṁsārī*. A *sarva-karma-sannyāsī* is a *jñānī*, one who is totally free from all *karmas*. Even if *karmas* are performed, the *jñānī* does not perform any action. In this, one has no doubt whatsoever because, with reference to *ātmā*, the self, the notion of doership is not there. All that takes place for the *jñānī* is that the sense organs, backed by the mind, engage themselves in their own fields of activity. The *jñānī* does not look upon himself or herself as the *kartā*. This is the actual meaning of *sarva-karma-sannyāsī*.

A *sarva-karma-sannyāsī* is called a *vidvān*, one who is wise. All the *karma* that the *vidvān* has done so far, the prayers, *yoga*, and other forms of discipline, and even a life of *sannyāsa*, have found their fulfilment in this *sarva-karma-sannyāsa*. Thereafter, Śaṅkara said, there is no question of such a person doing certain *karmas* in order to create some result. There is nothing more to do. All the prayers have been fulfilled in this particular discovery and it is for this discovery alone that the prayers and other *karma*s were performed. In this way, Śaṅkara connected *vedānta-śāstra* to the *karma-śāstra. Karma-yoga* is meant for this alone. Thus, *sannyāsa* is really *sarva-karma-sannyāsa.*

For the *sarva-karma-sannyāsī* there are no *karma*s to be performed. The point here is that the rituals enjoined by the *śāstra* need not be performed any longer by the *sarva-karma-sannyāsī*. If the person continues to be a house-holder, he or she is purely playing out previous *karma, prārabdha-karma* and whatever one was doing is continued.

King Janaka was a case in point. Although he was considered a wise man, he continued to be the ruler of a kingdom and was not bothered by the role at all. Like Janaka, one can be a wise person and be in the world or be a *sannyāsī* without playing any roles, having given up everything to pursue knowledge. Either way it is possible. Being a *jñānī* has nothing to do with what the *jñānī* seemingly does and does not do. This is what is meant by *sarva-karma-sannyāsa*, as established in the *śāstra* and elaborated upon here by Śaṅkara.

When one says, 'I am affected,' then *ātmā* is looked upon as an object, a *karma*, that has something affecting it. This object can be a person, an event, or even Īśvara. Anyone who looks upon *ātmā* as an object does not know *ātmā*. The *saṁsārī*'s *ajñāna*, ignorance, is such that not only does the person look upon himself or herself as a *karma*, object, but also as a *kartā*, which only heightens the *ajñāna*. One looks upon oneself as a doer; otherwise, one could not be a sinner. Unless a person performs action, there is no way of sinning; nor is there any way of gathering *karmas* and *karma-phalas*.

Some people do not take the body as *ātmā*, but believe that there is a survivor of this body. Most religious people believe this to be so. Even the nihilists, Buddhists, believe that you are born again and again. Therefore, *mokṣa*, for them, is realising that the *ātmā* is a zero, non-existent. They believe in the survival of the *ātmā* until enlightenment, whatever their concept of enlightenment may be.

All religions talk of an *ātmā* other than the physical body, referred to as the soul, that which survives death. Any given soul is the *kartā;* he or she is the sinner, and so on. It is a belief but, at the same time, people do look upon that *ātmā*, the survivor, the soul, as one who is subject to all kinds of *karma*, all kinds of *puṇya*, *pāpa*, imperfections, and so on, and as one who may get some kind of bliss experience later. Kṛṣṇa negated all these beliefs here. *Bhāṣyakāra* mentioned specifically those who consider themselves to be great scholars and yet say there is no way of knowing the *ātmā*. They say that knowledge of the *ātmā* free from *kartṛtva*, doership, is not possible and, therefore, *sarva-karma-sannyāsa* is also not possible.

There is no kartṛtva for ātmā

It was pointed out that *sarva-karma-sannyāsa* is only possible if *ātmā* is not a doer, that is, *akartā*. Only when you understand, '*aham akartā*, I am not the doer,' does the renunciation of all *karmas* take place naturally. If the knowledge that 'I am neither a doer nor an enjoyer' has arisen in someone, then *sarva-karma-*

sannyāsa is accomplished by that person. Only if the knowledge itself cannot take place, is *sarva-karma-sannyāsa* an impossibility. But on what basis can you say this knowledge cannot take place? Are you saying such an *ātmā* is not there and, if so, upon what do you base your statement?

You cannot say that *ātmā* is not there, since the very act of saying so presupposes an *ātmā*. Because you are existent, you are talking. Therefore, no one can say, 'I am not there.' In the existence of *ātmā*, then, there is no doubt whatsoever. If the doubt is not with reference to the existence of the *ātmā*, then it is with reference to the *ātmā* being *akartā*. It is easy to assume that there can be no *akartṛ-ātmā* because *ātmā* is known as *kartā* and not as *akartā*. And if there is an *ātmā* that is *akartā*, there is no way of knowing it. This could be the contention of most people who do not understand that there is no *kartṛtva* for the *ātmā*.

To this, we answer as follows. If *ātmā* is the *kartā* it must always be the *kartā*. If *ātmā* is always the *kartā*, if *kartṛtva* is the very nature of *ātmā* then as a doer it should be doing all the time. But that is not what happens. Sometimes you fall back and do nothing at all; you only enjoy. Then you see only enjoyership, *bhoktṛtva* and no *kartṛtva*. Similarly, if enjoyership were the nature of *ātmā*, then *ātmā* would be a *bhoktā* all the time. *Ātmā* is neither *kartā* nor *bhoktā*.

There are also moments when neither doership nor enjoyership is there, when there is no 'I' sense at all because this 'I' notion, *ahaṅkāra* is absent at times, like between two thoughts. How then are you going to account for this experience?

You cannot. Nor can you say that the *śāstra* says *ātmā* is a *kartā*. Because, it says *ātmā* is *akartā* and we have no data whatsoever to contradict this statement.

You may agree with the *śruti* that *ātmā* is *akartā*, but may say that knowledge of such an *ātmā* is not possible because it is not the object of your mind. But *śāstra* says that such knowledge has got to be gained by the mind alone, for which there is a *pramāṇa*, the *śāstra*. You have a mind that is capable of the knowledge that will destroy the *ajñāna*, the ignorance. This is all that we are talking about and you say it is not possible. Is it that it is not possible for you or is it because it is not possible at all?

Can *ātmā* be known?

How can I gain the knowledge of the *akartṛ-ātmā*? I cannot see the *akartṛ-ātmā*. Here, Śaṅkara says that knowledge of *ātmā* is not similar to the knowledge of an object, but is rather the removal of ignorance about the subject itself. There is a knower who has ignorance about himself or herself and removal of that ignorance is the only knowledge being discussed here. This knowledge, *vṛtti-jñāna*, is '*aham-akartā*, I am not the doer.' This *vṛtti*, thought, is capable of destroying the ignorance about oneself. The fact that I am *ātmā*, the non-doer, is not known, and ignorance of this fact is removed by the *vṛtti* brought about by *upadeśa*, teaching. The *vṛtti*, having done its job, goes along with the ignorance.

Where is the problem here? We have a complete methodology, *prakriyā* for it, how exactly the knowledge takes place, and so on.

If you say, that it does not take place in your *antaḥ-karaṇa*, mind, then we will say that a certain type of *antaḥ-karaṇa* is necessary and that there are ways for you to gain it. This is why the *Gītā* talks so extensively about *yoga* and so on. Because you do not want to accept something, you keep on talking about its impossibility. It is because of your commitment to a belief. You are not committed to truth. First, you commit yourself to a belief, to a faith, and then you explore for confirmation of that belief in the *śāstra*. You should have *śraddhā* in the *śāstra* and explore it to find out what it has to convey.

Two types of negation

If you are honest, committed to truth, all you need to do is look back at what has been said here. You will find nothing that you can disown or disprove. All that has been said is something that you have to see, as it is. We are not proposing anything speculative. We are not making a promise. We say that you are an *akartā*, that you are *avināśī*, indestructible. How can such a person perform any action, there being no action really?

There are two types of negation. One is a physical negation, *niṣedha*, and the other is *bādhā*, negation by knowledge. The *kartṛtva-buddhi* is there and it is negated. You may see the same person performing an action, talking, for example, and at the same time saying that *ātmā* is *akartā* and so on. You could say that Kṛṣṇa was talking and was, therefore, a *kartā*. Arjuna could have said to Kṛṣṇa, 'You are performing the action of talking to me. How, then, can you tell me that *ātmā* is *akartā*?'

To say, the one who knows *ātmā* does not perform any action means that you do not know *ātmā*. Kṛṣṇa was definitely performing actions. For one thing, he was driving Arjuna's chariot. Does this not make him an *ajñānī*? And if he is an *ajñānī*, what does he have to teach? This kind of question arises only because *ātmā* is not understood.

When you see the sun rise, you enjoy it and negate it also, because you know that the sun does not actually rise. There is a conclusion that the sun rises and because you see it rising. You say that the conclusion is true. You perceive it; therefore, the sun rises in the eastern sky. By further knowledge, however, you understand the whole process of why the sun appears as though it is rising. The sun rising becomes only an appearance and therefore is not a real rising in that there is no real action of rising on the part of the sun. Thus, seeing the sunrise, you negate it, knowing that it does not rise at all. This is negation by *bādhā*, knowledge, you see and still you negate.

Similarly, you see a variety of colours in a peacock's feather, but there are no such colours, in fact. The appearance of colour is due to different prism-like structures that reflect light in a particular manner. This is purely *bādhā*, negation by knowledge. It does not mean that you are negating the perception of colour, only that you are negating colour being there.

In fact, all science is purely *bādhā*. It goes on negating. It sees something and then finds that it is not true, and that something else is true instead. When you go after the substance of a given substance, what was previously considered to be the substance is found to have no substance because it has to depend on another substance for its existence. In this way, we find that any substantive loses its substance and still continues to exist. Although you have negated its existence, you may even use it!

Bādhā is a kind of negation that is done by everyone. A physicist will say that gold is nothing but some quanta of energy. Copper is also some quanta of energy. However, this does not mean that he will give his fiancee a copper engagement ring! Buying a gold ring does not, in any way, alter his knowledge that both gold and copper are but energy. This is also *bādhā*, negation. Seeing it, you negate it.

Bādhā, then, is a different type of negation and that is how the *kartṛtva-buddhi* in the *ātmā* is negated. *Bādhā* is not a simple negation. Once *bādhā* is there, regardless of what the *jñānī* does, he or she knows that, 'I perform no action.' This is *jñāna*, knowledge, and there is no way of losing it. This is what we call *sarva-karma-sannyāsa*. It does not mean that a person will not do any action; it means that the *sat-cit-ānanda-ātmā* does not perform any action.

There is nothing more to be done

While performing *karma*, the *sarva-karma-sannyāsī* sees that there is freedom from action. In action, one sees actionlessness. The one who knows this is called *buddhimān;* such a person has the knowledge, *buddhi*, and has done everything that has to be done, *kṛtsna-karmakṛt*, because one knows that *ātmā* is *akartā*, *pūrṇa*, always full.

Śaṅkara spends a lot of time here quoting from later verses because of the importance of these two sentences. He said that it would be shown that the one who has *ātma-jñāna*, self-knowledge, alone is qualified for *sarva-karma-sannyāsa*. Such a person is not bound any more by *karma*. Therefore, whatever a *sarva-karma-sannyāsī* does, he or she does only because it has to be done and not because of any desired result. Because of the person's *prārabdha-karma*, certain actions may be performed. This will be seen repeatedly throughout the *gītā-śāstra*. What is relevant here is the initial conclusion that *ātmā* is not subject to any change or destruction.

Verse 22

The body as a suit of clothes

वासांसि जीर्णानि यथा विहाय नवानि गृह्णाति नरोऽपराणि ।
तथा शरीराणि विहाय जीर्णान्यन्यानि संयाति नवानि देही ॥२२॥

vāsāṁsi jīrṇāni yathā vihāya
navāni gṛhṇāti naro'parāṇi
tathā śarīrāṇi vihāya jīrṇān–
yanyāni saṁyāti navāni dehī (22)

naraḥ – a person; *yathā* – just as; *jīrṇāni* – old; *vāsāṁsi* – clothes; *vihāya* – giving up; *aparāṇi* – others; *navāni* – new; *gṛhṇāti* – takes; *tathā* – so too; *dehī* – the indweller of the body; *jīrṇāni* – old; *śarīrāṇi* – bodies; *vihāya* – giving up; *anyāni* – others; *navāni* – new; *saṁyāti* – takes

Just as a person gives up old clothes and takes up new ones, so does the self, the one who dwells in the body, give up old bodies[8] and takes others, which are new.

Nara means a human being, or etymologically, one who cannot be destroyed, who always survives somehow! If a person is enlightened, he or she survives eternally, as eternal Brahman. If not, the person merely survives. How?

The word '*yathā*,' meaning 'just as' indicates that an illustration is about to be presented. Here, the illustration used is the discarding of old clothes for new or better ones, *vāsāṁsi jīrṇāni vihāya aparāṇi navāni gṛhṇāti*. Similarly, the old body, *śarīra*, is given up and a new one is taken. *Śarīra* means that which is subject to disintegration. Bodies, therefore, become useless in time because of the natural ageing process, disease, or abuse. The abuse may be caused by someone's wrong action, like murder, for instance, or by your own abuse. By slow suicide, like drinking and so on, a person destroys the body and thus it is rendered old and useless, *jīrṇā*.

You are the one wearing the clothes and you keep on wearing them on this *śarīra*. They are with you only, as long as you find them useful and, when they are useless, you throw them away and take on new clothes. This process is repeated again and again. Similarly, there is a wearer of this body who is the indweller of it. The *dehī*, indweller, is the one who has a *deha*, body. Just as the body is within the clothes, so too, within this body, which is itself a costume, is the person, the indweller,

---

[8] This is the general rule *(utsarga)* and every rule has exception *(apavāda)*. One may die young due to many reasons.

Mr., Mrs., or Miss So-and-so, who takes new bodies, *anyāni navāni saṁyāti*. Giving up the old, one takes on the new.

The idea here is that either way *ātmā* is *nitya*; it does not die. It always keeps on going. Even when the *jīvatva* dies, the *jīva* does not die; only the notion dies. Kṛṣṇa wants to point out here that *ātmā* is always *nitya*. Never does the *ātmā* subject itself to disappearance; the *dehī*, the indweller, continues to be.

Here, certain questions can be asked. When a person is really old, the body is no longer useful. A man, for example, may be ninety-eight years old and unable to hear, see, walk, or do anything. He cannot digest his food or even open his mouth and, even if he can, he has no teeth. Such a body is definitely useless, like an old Cadillac. The only difference is that certain parts are salvaged from the Cadillac, whereas the old body has nothing to donate. Everything is so old and worn out that to receive a donation from such a person, one would need to be at least one hundred and fifty years old!

Because this old body is no longer useful, the person gives it up. That he lets it go and takes a new body is understandable, just as giving up of old clothes and taking on to new ones is understandable. However, the example does not seem to hold in all cases, given that we see people dying away in the prime of youth with cancer and so on.

We can understand that accidents are due to someone's mistake, carelessness or whatever. Someone dying because of a homicide is also understandable in that another person abused his or her free will by performing a destructive action against a body, which can be objectified by others. For example, a bullet can destroy the *sthūla-śarīra*, physical body, and once ruptured, the *sūkṣma-śarīra*, subtle body, can no longer live in it. Just as a car needs a few things with which to operate, spark plugs and so on, so too, there is a minimum requirement for the *sūkṣma-śarīra* to be able to operate within the physical body. For instance, there must be a heart and kidney. If these are ruptured, the body is useless, regardless of its age. Just as the new car you bought yesterday can become a wreck today, so too, this body can also be wrecked. And, because the *dehī* can no longer run it, a new body has to be found.

However, when a young person dies of leukemia, or due to some unknown reason, we cannot say that he or she did anything wrong to bring about this disease. The person may have done one or two things wrong, but nothing sufficient to develop cancer. Crib death is but one of the many ways a child may die. People are also struck down in youth and middle age in any number of ways. Energetic, ambitious people with a lot of plans and many irons in the fire, do succumb to heart attacks. Why do people die away like this when the body is not yet worn out? The answer to these questions is as follows.

What is said is that, the death of the physical body depends on the *dehī*. If the *jīva* has taken this body and is a survivor of death, then there must be some cause which has brought this body into being. If you accept that there is a *dehī* other than this body who survives death, then that *dehī* having survived not only this death but also the previous ones, is always a survivor. The *dehī*, then, must have come to this body because of his or her own *karma*, not because of God's will or for any other reason.

A God who willed suffering to people would be some kind of a tyrant, a sadist, and would definitely require psychological treatment. Why else would he put so much sadness into people? One person is born with leprosy, another with syphilis, AIDS, and what not, for no fault of the person. What kind of God would sit there and give people such sadness from the very start? Not only for the growing child, but for everyone around as well, since seeing such suffering is a sickness in itself. Anyone who is responsible for doing such things is a sadist and is the first one who should be brought to justice. We could never sing in praise of such a Lord!

Only a sadistic God could be a tyrant, enjoying the suffering of people for no reason. Some are born with wooden spoons in their mouths, others with silver and golden spoons, and some are born with no mouth at all. What kind of God would do this? Some are born to become orphans. Why then are they even born? 'Do not ask,' we are usually told. This is what is called double justification. God is first justified by what he does and then we are told not to question his actions. Why even talk about such a God then? Let us settle our account with ourselves. We have our own lot. You have a body here, which has its own problems. You do not require God at all for this and, if there is such a tyrant, it is better not to think of him at all.

On the other hand, perhaps, the explanation is that we have asked for our particular lot in life. God is the law. We asked for it and we got it. The Lord says, 'I am the one who made you and, at the same time, I have not made you.'

This is like putting your finger into the fire and then asking the fire,

'Did you burn me?'

'Yes, I burned you,' says the fire.

'Why?'

'I did not burn you at all.'

'You just told me you burned me and then you say you did not. How can you say both? You are blowing hot and cold. I thought you blew only hot and now I find you blow both hot and cold. Why is that?'

'When you stuck your finger into me, I burned. To burn is my nature, my *svabhāva*, and I burned. I cannot say that someone else burned; I burned your finger. But then, I did not go after your finger, did I? I remained in my place. You stuck your finger into me and got burnt. In other words, you asked for it.'

This is the law and is what is meant by the law of *karma*, *prārabdha-karma*. It is the *jīva*'s *karma*, the law of *karma* being there. If you accept a soul that survives the body, then you definitely have to account for the varieties of situations that you face. Thus, *prārabdha-karma* is the reason why a person, a *dehī*, comes with a particular *deha*, which dies when the job is done.

What is it that is new?

With reference to taking on a new body, who is to decide what is new? Car rental people always buy new cars and after one year sell them. For them, a one-year-old car is old, but the one who buys it thinks of it as new. Others may buy a much older car and also think of it as new, whereas the seller thinks of it as old. Of course, there are even others who buy very old cars, fix them up, and are very happy that they have the oldest car available because it is a valuable antique. Who, then, is to decide which of these is new?

Similarly, the king of Tiruvanantapuram, in the south of India, must walk to the temple everyday wearing new clothes. The clothes he wears one day are considered old the next day, and are given away. Of course, the one who receives the clothes thinks of them as new. This person may wear them for a year or two and then also think they are old. There is always someone who will take them. That is why it is said that there is a buyer for everything. You have to decide what is new.

Similarly, here, what is old or new has to be decided by the *dehī* and not by you, the onlooker. For the onlooker, the body may not be ready for death, but for the *dehī* the job is done. Those who are bereaved may look at a particular death as something that is premature, but this is not the case from the standpoint of the *dehī*, unless the death is caused by some wrong action, the abuse of free will on the part of oneself or someone else. Otherwise, it is for the *dehī* to decide when the body's job is done; in other words, when the purpose for which the body was taken has been accomplished.

Even though the *dehī* may like to live on, the job for which this body was taken is done. When it is done the tenure is over. Whatever had to happen here has already happened. Therefore, death takes place. Just as, in the world, a person takes on new clothes and gives up the old ones, so too, the one who indwells in the body, the *jīva*, gives up the old body and takes on the new. What is meant by 'old bodies' is to be understood properly.

Therefore, for the *dehī*, the one who indwells the *deha*, there is no death at all and for the *deha*, there is no survival. The body is bound by time, subject to change, and it keeps changing all the time. There is no time when the body does not change. Because it is always changing, it is called *śarīra* or *deha*. *Deha* means that which is subject to cremation and *śarīra* means that which is subject to disintegration, that which is buried. The choice, then, is only between these two!

The *deha* is always subject to death and is always dying. It is not that suddenly one fine day it dies; rather, it keeps on dying all the time. You cannot stop it, whereas in the case of the *dehī*, you cannot destroy it. Both facts must be seen clearly. This being so, there is no cause for grief, *aśocyān anvaśocaḥ tvam*, a theme that continues and is the conclusion.

That there is no cause for grief is the vision of the *śāstra* and, being so, has a bearing upon the entire dialogue between Kṛṣṇa and Arjuna. As we proceed, we shall see that there are topical connections, sectional connections, and a total connection with this theme throughout the *Gītā*.

Verse 23

Ātmā is indestructible

नैनं छिन्दन्ति शस्त्राणि नैनं दहति पावकः ।
न चैनं क्लेदयन्त्यापो न शोषयति मारुतः ॥ २३ ॥

nainaṁ chindanti śastrāṇi nainaṁ dahati pāvakaḥ
na cainaṁ kledayantyāpo na śoṣayati mārutaḥ (23)

śastrāṇi – weapons; *enam* – this (the self); *na chindanti* – do not slay; *pāvakaḥ* – fire; *enam* – this; *na dahati* – does not burn; *āpaḥ* – waters; *enam* – this; *na kledayanti* – do not wet (or drown); *mārutaḥ ca* – and the wind; *na śoṣayati* – does not dry

Weapons do not slay this (self); nor does fire burn it.
Water does not wet (or drown) nor does wind dry it.

In verse 16, and again in verse 20, Kṛṣṇa said that for the self, which is *sat*, real, there is no absence. It is not subject to negation in any of the three periods of time, *abādhitaṁ satyam*. This statement cannot be shaken because that which is not subject to negation cannot be negated and truth, *satya*, is not subject to negation. You yourself are this truth. If you have any doubt, try to negate yourself. The very person doing the negation is the one you are trying to negate. Therefore, you find that it is impossible to negate yourself.

Anything that is negatable is not *satya*. The one who goes on negating is *satya*, the only one who cannot be negated; everything else is subject to dismissal. That which is not subject to negation can only be *ātmā*, the self. Thus, there is no *abhāva*, absence, for the *ātmā*.

Only that which is subject to time can be *asat*. That which is not subject to time is *sat*. *Sat* cannot be dismissed because dismissal implies prior existence and posterior non-existence, both of which are in terms of time alone, past, present and future. That which is not subject to time and for which time itself is a dismissible object is called *satya, ātmā*. This is Kṛṣṇa's constant refrain.

Just as one gives up old clothes and takes on new ones, the one who dwells in this body, *deha*, gives it up and assumes another body. Neither the *jīva* nor *ātmā* is subject to negation, the *jīva* and *ātmā* being one and the same. What can be negated, however, is the notion that 'I am limited' – the *jīvatva*. The *svarūpa* of the *jīva* cannot be negated, only the notion that 'I am a *jīva*' can be negated.

The same point was also made by Kṛṣṇa in another form when he said that *ātmā* is not an object for any act of destruction, *na ayaṁ hanti na hanyate*.[9] It is neither the performer of an action nor the object of anyone's action. In other words, *ātmā* is not subject to negation because it is not subject to destruction. No action can destroy it.

In the present verse, Kṛṣṇa mentioned a few methods of destruction, none of which affects *ātmā*. At first, he talks of weapons, which cannot destroy *ātmā*. Later he enumerates the elements that can bring about destruction. Generally weapons are of two types. Those weapons that are released from one's

---

[9] *Gītā* 2.19

hand are called *astra*s like a rock, a bullet or an arrow. Those held in the hand are called *śastra*s like a stick, hammer, or sword. Here in the verse, the word *śastra* implies both types of weapons.

With reference to weapons, then, *ātmā* does not subject itself to any type of objectification. It is so because *ātmā* objectifies everything. That which objectifies everything cannot be objectified by anything. *Ātmā*, yourself, objectifies the whole world. The world does not reveal itself to you unless you objectify it. And *ātmā* cannot be objectified by anything.

What is objectified is not going to objectify the objectifier because everything else shines after *ātmā*. There is only one source of consciousness and that is *ātmā*, you. Everything else is an object of consciousness. How, then, is an object of consciousness going to destroy consciousness? Consciousness has no particular form. If it had a heart, it could have an attack, but it does not. If it does, we have had it! *Ātmā* is the one because of which we are aware of the beating of the heart. It is the subject of every object. Because *ātmā* is not subject to objectification, it is not subject to any type of action, including destruction. Thus, weapons do not slay this *ātmā*.

Fire also cannot destroy *ātmā* – *na enaṁ dahati pāvakaḥ*. It can burn the body, but it cannot burn *ātmā*. Fire cannot even destroy *sūkṣma-śarīra*, the subtle body, let alone the *ātmā*. Similarly, water cannot wet the *ātmā*, let alone drown it, *āpaḥ enaṁ na kledayanti*, because it does not become an object that is subject to drowning. Nor can the wind dry it up, *na enaṁ śoṣayati mārutaḥ*, meaning that *ātmā* cannot be dehydrated.

Thus, Kṛṣṇa brings out all the elements. *Pṛthivī*, earth, implied by the weapons and the metals with which they are made, does not destroy the *ātmā*. Nor do fire, water, and air. *Vāyu*, air, does not bring about the death of *ātmā* through dehydration. The word '*māruta*' refers to the hot air of the tropical country, which can cause dehydration.

The five-element model of the world

Throughout the *śāstra* we find a particular model that presents the world as made up of five elements–*ākāśa*, space; *vāyu*, air; *agni*, fire; *āpaḥ*, water; and *pṛthivī*, earth. In their subtle and gross forms, these elements account for everything that is here. The subtle elements account for the mind, senses, and so on, and the gross elements account for the physical body and the physical world.

Your physical body comprises of five gross elements. It occupies *ākāśa*, space. It contains *vāyu*, air, oxygen being present wherever there is blood. The body has *agni*, temperature or heat, and its shape is due to *āpaḥ*, the water, it has as part of its composition. Finally, the body contains the same minerals that are found in *pṛthivī*, the earth, calcium, carbon, magnesium, and so on.

The physical universe can be defined in many ways. This elemental model is simply for understanding. Each of the *bhūta*s, elements, enjoys the same degree of reality because they are all elements. Whatever the nature of reality is, *ākāśa* has a certain degree of that reality. The same degree of reality is also enjoyed by the other four elements, *vāyu*, *agni*, *āpaḥ* and *pṛthivī*.

Only objects belonging to the same degree of reality can affect each other. For example, one physical body can definitely destroy another physical body. Similarly, a body and a weapon, both physical objects, belong to the same degree of reality. Therefore, the weapon can hit the body and injure or destroy it.

Suppose, you want to destroy a tree with the shadow of another tree. It is impossible. Nor can you hit a dog with the shadow of a rock. This is because the object and the shadow belong to two different orders of reality and are, therefore, incapable of destroying each other. If one is to affect the other, both must enjoy the same degree of reality.

The nature of destruction

Objects belonging to the same order of reality need not affect each other. Space, for example, belongs to the same order of reality as the other four elements but is not affected or destroyed by any of them. Air cannot dehydrate space, fire cannot burn it, and water cannot drown it. Nor can you take a sword in hand and destroy space. Space cannot be destroyed by bombing it, much less with a pistol. It cannot even be polluted. There is no such thing as space pollution; only the atmosphere is polluted.

The other four elements cannot destroy space because space has no form. Air, on the other hand, can be destroyed in the sense that one form can be changed into another. Air implies atoms and atoms imply a structure, which can always be changed into a new structure. If hydrogen and oxygen are brought together in a certain way, water is created. Any structure is always available for change. It can become entirely different. One metal can be converted into another metal simply by changing its atomic weight. A base metal can be changed into gold in this way, although it is not economically feasible to do.

The word 'death' applies to a particular structure that no longer exists because it has been changed in some way. Śaṅkara argues that anything that has limbs, attributes or structure can be destroyed. Space, having none of these, cannot be destroyed, even by other elements that share the same order of reality.

Ātmā is also free from limbs, attributes or structure; it is pure consciousness. I am aware of everything, including my thoughts, which objectify this entire world. Therefore, this consciousness, *ātmā*, cannot be destroyed by any weapon or any other instrument of destruction because it is not available for objectification. Nothing can get at this *ātmā*. Furthermore, nothing else belongs to the same order of reality.

Ātmā is *satya*. *Ātmā* alone is self-evident and everything else is evident to it. *Ātmā* is self-shining and everything else shines after *ātmā*. The one that shines of its own accord is *ātmā*. It requires no evidence for its existence. What is self-evident is self-existent, depending on nothing for its existence, whereas what is not self-evident is not self-existent and depends entirely upon that which is self-existent.

In this way, any given object depends upon another object. A clay pot depends upon clay, which is nothing but mud and mud is nothing but atoms. Atoms depend on particles and so on.

Thus, everything depends upon something else and that something else depends upon your concept, which depends upon consciousness. Consciousness, alone, depends on nothing.

Therefore, everything shines after this self-evident, self-existent *ātmā*. Naturally then, the whole creation, the whole world, is equal to *asat* only. When everything is *asat* and *ātmā* alone is *sat*, how can the *sat* be destroyed by *asat*? Air, fire, water and earth exist because of *ātmā*. Because *ātmā* is *sat* and the elements are *asat*, they are incapable of destroying the *ātmā*.

The reflection cannot come out of the mirror to tease and destroy you, anymore than your own shadow can. If your reflection looks ferocious and frowning, that is only because you look so. There is no need to become anxious because your reflection is frowning and looks as though it is going to destroy you. If you run away from it and it comes chasing after you, any chasing that is done is all in your mind! The reflection is not going to affect you because it is *asat* and you are *sat*. Since all of the elements are *asat*, they cannot do anything to *ātmā*, which is *sat*.

However a problem may arise here. Since a non-existent thing also cannot be destroyed by anyone, perhaps this *ātmā* is non-existent, *śūnya*, zero. In the expression, '*vandhyā-putra*,' the son of a woman who cannot give birth to a child, the son cannot be destroyed by anything. We are not talking here of an adopted son or a surrogate son, but of a non-existent son. There is no son to be burnt or drowned. Similarly, perhaps there is no *ātmā*. This doubt could arise but, the next verse, along with Śaṅkara's commentary, puts this doubt to rest.

Verse 24

Ātmā alone is self-evident

अच्छेद्योऽयमदाह्योऽयमक्लेद्योऽशोष्य एव च ।
नित्यः सर्वगतः स्थाणुरचलोऽयं सनातनः ॥ २४ ॥

acchedyo'yam adāhyo'yam akledyo'śoṣya eva ca
nityaḥ sarvagataḥ sthāṇuracalo'yaṁ sanātanaḥ (24)

ayam – this; *acchedyaḥ* – cannot be slain; *ayam* – this; *adāhyaḥ* – cannot be burnt; *akledyaḥ* – cannot be drowned; *aśoṣyaḥ eva ca* – and also cannot be dried; *ayam* – this; *nityaḥ* – changeless; *sarvagataḥ* – all-pervading; *sthāṇuḥ* – stable; *acalaḥ* – immovable; *sanātanaḥ* – eternal

This (self) cannot be slain, burnt, drowned, or dried.
It is changeless, all-pervading, stable, immovable,
and eternal.

Ayam in this verse refers to the self-evident, self-existent *ātmā*, not a non-existent *ātmā, śūnya*. Self-evident means that which does not require any means of knowledge to prove its existence. *Ātmā* alone is self-evident. Everything else becomes evident to the self.

To say, 'I am' does not require perception, inference, presumption, illustration, or the means of knowledge called *anupalabdhi*, that which helps you understand what does not exist. Even to understand what does not exist requires someone who is existent to use the *anupalabdhi-pramāṇa*. For example, in order to know that there is no pot in my hand, there must be perception and a person who wields the perception.

Inference, a means of knowledge based on perception, also presupposes a person who wields the inference. Whatever the means of knowledge, there must be someone to wield it. To say that the object in your hand is a feather and it belongs to a peacock requires a means of knowledge, your own perception and your prior knowledge of a peacock feather. You perceive the object directly and recognise it as a feather. Similarly, to prove the existence of any object, a means of knowledge is necessary.

Even to perceive that your physical body is not the same as it was yesterday requires a means of knowledge. How do you know you have a stomachache, back pain, or that you ache all over? Since you cannot show the ache to anyone, no one can verify it, which is why bodyache and back pain are so useful in applying for leave! Even an orthopaedic specialist cannot say whether there is an ache or not because it is purely your own experience. You alone are the witness. *Sākṣi-pratyakṣa*, witness perception, is another type of perception that does not involve the senses, but still is a perception.

You can only talk about these various conditions of the body if you have a way of knowing them. Similarly, since you talk about your mind, you must have some way of knowing it. There must be some perception by which you know the mind. That you have certain memories is purely because the programming is there, even though it might not always serve your purpose. Even to know that you have forgotten something is a perception.

Everything is evident to me because I have a means of knowing. But by what means do I know that 'I am'? Is it by perception, by a scripture, by the senses, by inference? No. 'I' am there before them all. Because I am, I can infer. I am and, therefore, I can see and hear. That I am is self-evident and, because I am, all knowledge is possible.

One thing, *ātmā* alone, is self-evident, *svataḥ-siddha*. Therefore, *ayam* is a very important word here, referring as it does to that which is not the object of any destruction, *acchedya*. Kṛṣṇa kept repeating it because the *ātmā* is not zero. It is not non-existent like the son of a barren woman. *Ātmā* is all-existent, self-existent, and is not subject to being slain, burnt, drowned, or dehydrated. It is *nitya*, timeless, and thus *sarvagata*, all-pervasive.

Anything that is *anitya*, time-bound, is not *sarvagata*. Even space is not all-pervasive. Space is all-pervasive only with reference to the world, but it does not pervade the *ātmā* because *ātmā* is consciousness and in the consciousness there is no space. But then, when space is there, consciousness is also there. Therefore, space does not pervade *ātmā*, but *ātmā* pervades space; it is *sarvagata*.

Then, again, *ātmā* cannot move, it is *sthāṇu*. How can it move? Where can it move? It can only move to a place where it is not. Since *ātmā* is *sarvagata*, it is *sthāṇu*. It does not move, it is always the same. Here one may think, perhaps the *ātmā* is like a tree, staying in one place, but swaying. No, we are told. Unlike the tree, it does not sway, it is *acala*. Kṛṣṇa also describes *ātmā* as that which remains the same always; it is *sanātana*. It is not brought into being by some force or cause. Because it is not affected in any way by anything, *ātmā* is always the same, always fresh, always new.

Knowing *ātmā* in this way, there is no reason for you to entertain any grief. But you may say, 'I do not cry for *ātmā*, I cry for *anātmā*.' To which, Kṛṣṇa would ask, 'Why would you cry for *anātmā*?' It is always changing, *anitya*. *Anātmā* is always going and you cannot stop it even if you want to, whereas the *ātmā* is *nitya* and there is no way of destroying it. 'For what do you grieve, Arjuna?' Kṛṣṇa asked. 'There is no room for grief at all. There is something to be done, do it!' This constant refrain is again sounded in the next verse.

Verse 25

Ātmā has no attributes

अव्यक्तोऽयमचिन्त्योऽयमविकार्योऽयमुच्यते ।
तस्मादेवं विदित्वैनं नानुशोचितुमर्हसि ॥ २५ ॥

avyakto'yam acintyo'yam avikāryo'yam ucyate
tasmādevaṁ viditvainaṁ nānuśocitum arhasi (25)

ayam – this; *avyaktaḥ* – unmanifest; *ayam* – this; *acintyaḥ* – not an object of thought; *ayam* – this; *avikāryaḥ* – not subject to change; *ucyate* – is said; *tasmāt* – therefore; *evam* – thus; *enam* – this; *viditvā* – knowing; *anuśocitum* – to grieve; *na arhasi* – you ought not

> This (self) is said to be unmanifest, not an object of thought, and not subject to change. Therefore, knowing this, you ought not to grieve.

Vyakta refers to anything that is manifest, that which is an object of perception, an object of the sense organs. And that which is not manifest, not an object of the sense organs, is *avyakta*. Therefore, *ātmā* is referred to here as *avyakta*.

If *ātmā* is not an object of one's perception, is it, perhaps, an object of inference? 'No,' says Lord Kṛṣṇa. *Ātmā* cannot be an object of inference because it is not an object of thought, it is *acintya*. *Ātmā* is self-evident. Thus, the word '*acintya*' does not mean that *ātmā* is not available for understanding. Also, *ātmā* cannot be an object of inference or perception because, without *ātmā*, inference and perception are not possible.

In addition to not being an object of sense perception, *avyakta*, nor an object of any inference, *acintya*, *ātmā* also does not undergo any modification whatsoever; it is *avikriya*. It is not like milk that undergoes a change to become yoghurt. The milk gains a new taste, sourness, and its smell as well as form, undergoes a change. Because milk is subject to change, it is said to be *vikārya*. Previously, it was in one form and now it is in another. The same object that was milk before is yoghurt now.

Unlike milk, *ātmā* undergoes no change. You cannot say that previously *ātmā* was happy and now it is sad because, no change is possible for *ātmā*. Due to *aviveka*, however, you take *ātmā* to be subject to change. But, because it has no *avayava*, attribute, it cannot undergo any change.

One may say that *sat*, *cit*, *ānanda* and are attributes of *ātmā*. Why not *sat* become *asat*, *cit* become *acit*, and *ānanda* become *duḥkha*? This does not happen because *sat*, *cit* and *ānanda* are not attributes as such. They are the *lakṣaṇa*s, words that convey their meaning by implication, for *ātmā*. *Ātmā* is the *lakṣya*, that which is being implied. The implied meaning is the very nature, *svarūpa* of *ātmā*. Attributes are something other than the *svarūpa* of an object. That which is *cit* is *sat* and also *ānanda*.

Ātmā is not a substantive enjoying certain attributes. In fact, it is free from all attributes.

If *sat* were to be an attribute, what would the substantive be? The substantive itself is *sat*, so its *svarūpa* is *sat*. Thus, *sat* is not an attribute of *ātmā*. Similarly, *cit* is also not an attribute. *Sat* is *cit*; *cit* is *sat*. *Cit* stands for consciousness and this is what we call *sat*. Because *ātmā* is limitless, the word *ānanda* also comes in to imply its *svarūpa*.

Ātmā is said to be *avikārya*, not subject to modification at any time, because it does not have attributes to subject itself to change. Another reason that *ātmā* cannot undergo change is because it is not in time. *Ātmā* has always been as it is now.

All of this has been said about *ātmā* by those who know the *śāstra*. This being so, knowing the *ātmā* as it has been revealed so far, corrects our thinking. I thought I was the *kārya-karaṇa-saṅghāta*, body-mind-sense complex and, therefore, a mortal, a doer, an enjoyer, a *sukhī*, a *duḥkhī*, one moment happy and the next unhappy. Knowing the *ātmā* as it is, as *sat-cit-ānanda*, all the previous notions about *ātmā* are given up.

Thus, Kṛṣṇa told Arjuna, '*Śocituṁ na arhasi*, you have no reason for grief.' The literal meaning of '*na arhasi*' is 'you do not qualify.' We do not qualify to be sad because we know that *ātmā* is not subject to death and that there is only one *ātmā*, not many.

Arjuna had told Kṛṣṇa that he was grieving because Bhīṣma and Droṇa would die. To this, Kṛṣṇa responded by saying that Arjuna did not qualify to have any grief because no one really dies. If no one really dies, what is the use of grieving? People keep going. Even though they all disappear, they come back in different forms. Given this explanation, Arjuna could well have come back with, 'I am not really worried about the *ātmā*. It may be eternal, but I cannot shake hands with *ātmā*. Nor can I enjoy a talk with *sat-cit-ānanda-ātmā*, whereas I can with Bhīṣma. I am going to miss *sat-cit-ānanda* in the form of Bhīṣma. I am not grieving for the sake of *ātmā*.'

Thus, if Arjuna's grief was not for *ātmā*, it was for *anātmā*. Even then, Kṛṣṇa said, grief is useless. *Anātmā* has to be either *nitya* or *anitya*. Obviously, it cannot be *nitya*. As *anitya*, *anātmā* is constantly born and is always dying. To be born means it has to give up the previous form and giving up the previous form is what we call death. Therefore, birth itself implies death and every death implies birth. Kṛṣṇa then presented this argument

Verses 26&27

The insignificance of a lifetime

अथ चैनं नित्यजातं नित्यं वा मन्यसे मृतम् ।
तथापि त्वं महाबाहो नैवं शोचितुमर्हसि ॥ २६ ॥

atha cainaṁ nityajātaṁ nityaṁ vā manyase mṛtam
tathāpi tvaṁ mahābāho naivaṁ śocitum arhasi (26)

mahābāho – O mighty armed (Arjuna)!; *atha ca* – and if; *enam* – this; *nitya-jātam* – constantly born; *vā* – or; *nityam* – constantly; *mṛtam* – dead; *manyase* – you think; *tathā api* – even then; *tvam* – you; *evam* – thus; *śocitum* – to grieve; *na arhasi* – ought not

And if you take this (*ātmā*) to have constant birth and death, even then, Arjuna, the mighty armed! you ought not to grieve (for the *ātmā*) in this manner.

Whether you look upon this *ātmā*, in keeping with the body, as always born, continously born, birth after birth, or as dying all the time, death after death, you do not qualify to have any grief. The point Kṛṣṇa was making here is that if *ātmā* is being born all the time, why be afraid of death? Bhīṣma and everyone else will be born again in some other form. And if *ātmā* is always dying, which death are you crying for? There is no new death for which you qualify to be sad. What is dying keeps dying. You only see a fact.

Thus, there is no question of sorrow with reference to birth or death. The *asat* cannot be stopped by you. How are you going to stop that which is bound by time, *anitya*? No one is going to stop it. In fact, as Kṛṣṇa tells him later, the people Arjuna was grieving for were already as good as dead! Therefore, he was not going to destroy anyone nor could he hope to keep alive the people for whom he was grieving.

However, if Arjuna could take them all as *ātmā*, there would be no death for himself or anyone else. Moreover, if he continued to take *ātmā* to be *anātmā*, the body, *deha*, he could not do anything about its going. He would have to say that people were either always born or always going. To think that they were always born would not cause him any sorrow and if they were always going, there is no new going because what is going is always going! Since there is no new going, what is there for Arjuna to cry about?

For the one who is born, there is death and for the one who is dead, there is birth. Even in this sense, Kṛṣṇa said there is no room for sorrow:

जातस्य हि ध्रुवो मृत्युर्ध्रुवं जन्म मृतस्य च ।
तस्मादपरिहार्येऽर्थे न त्वं शोचितुमर्हसि ॥ २७ ॥

jātasya hi dhruvo mṛtyurdhruvaṁ janma mṛtasya ca
tasmādaparihārye'rthe na tvaṁ śocitum arhasi (27)

jātasya – of that which is born; *mṛtyuḥ* – death; *dhruvaḥ hi* – is certain indeed; *mṛtasya ca* – and of that which is dead; *janma*- birth; *dhruvam* – is certain; *tasmāt* – therefore; *aparihārye arthe* – with reference to an unalterable situation; *tvam* – you; *śocitum* – to grieve; *na arhasi* – ought not

For that which is born, death is certain and for that which is dead, birth is certain. Therefore, you ought not to grieve over that which cannot be altered.

There being no possible alternative, one who is born, will be gone. Kṛṣṇa, Rāma, and other *avatāra*s and prophets are all gone simply because they were born. This statement would only have made Arjuna sadder because everyone he was concerned about had been born and, therefore, would die. It was not that he wanted them to be eternal. He just wanted them to live a few more years. 'Why do you want them to live a few more years?' Kṛṣṇa may have asked, 'Is there any guarantee that, even if they live a little longer, you are also going to survive? This is your problem, Arjuna.'

There is an interesting story in the tradition about King Parīkṣit that bears this out. A curse was placed on him that he would die in a week. He went to Vyāsa's son, Śuka, who was a *jñānī*, and told him that he had only one week to live. In response, Śuka just laughed. 'Why are you laughing?' the king asked, 'I am going to die in a week!' Śuka then explained why he was laughing. 'You are lucky,' he said, 'You say you are going to die in a week. It means that you know you are going to be alive for seven days, whereas I have no such guarantee. '

Arjuna could have died before any of the people for whom he was grieving. Before he sent out his first shot, he could have had a heart attack and died. Anyone may die at any time. When death will come is anyone's guess; no one is going to live for very long, especially when compared to the age of a rock, for example, which has been around for millions of years. If the rock had a tongue and a memory, it could tell many stories. It could deride human life and call us pygmies, recalling the days of dinosaurs and other huge mammals. 'These days,' the rock would say, 'everything is so miniature in comparison, people and elephants alike!'

Fifty, sixty, or eighty-five years of life is nothing. By the time we are eighty-five most of our cells are already gone and the rest are old and worn out. They are unable to register anything new and even what had registered previously does not come out. Regardless of what recall button is pushed, nothing comes up. The floppy disk is worn out. It was too flimsy to last very long anyway. What are a few more years? It is better to live only a few years with a floppy disk that works well, so that when you press the button, something happens. Even a vague answer that comes quickly is better than no answer at all. One thing is certain, a little earlier or later means nothing in the eternal flow of time. A hundred years in this eternal flow is nothing! In spite of this, however, the human being still claims to have a biography!

If we compare our lifespan to that of a rock, we will always have freshness about ourselves. The calcium and other minerals in our bones definitely have a better story to tell! They at least have a story to tell. What story do we have? The body, therefore, is nothing but a few things brought together, which necessarily falls apart in a relatively short span of time.

Another way of looking at the meaning of one's lifespan is with reference to a star. The star that we see tonight may be two hundred light-years away. The light we see left the star two hundred years ago. During the time that it took the light to reach our eyes, the star may have died. It means that the star we see today may already be dead. Nothing travels as fast as light, as far as we know. In fact, all our concepts of time are related to the speed of light. It seems to be the constant with which we measure motion and everything else. This is the nature of the world and one hundred years is nothing but a flicker in the eternal flow of time. We come like a flicker and go like a whimper!

Life is a flicker

Life is like the flicker of a firefly, flicker… gone… flicker… gone… flicker… gone. Each birth and death represents one flicker.

This flicker is our biography! We then divide it into childhood, teenage, adulthood, problems, and so on. One flicker is all we have and, within this, there are so many things we have to do. We have to celebrate, cry, marry, divorce, and retire also, all within this flicker, this beep! The one positive note here is that there is always another beep available even for the dead who, as we have seen, are born again and again. Maybe we will beep in heaven also. There, we may beep slowly for some time until that too is over and the next beep occurs. Therefore, this life is but a flicker, a glow, and then it is gone.

Kṛṣṇa was saying here that life follows a rule, that is, if the born dies, the dead will certainly be born. Conversely, if the dead are born, the born will certainly die. These are two different points of view, with the constant being the certainty. Therefore, what is there to cry about? With reference to a matter that cannot be altered, you do not qualify to be sad because you cannot bring about any change. If you could change this fact, it would be different, but you cannot.

Whereas, *ātmā* is always there and does not elicit any sorrow from you. For *ātmā*'s sake, you need not be sad. Nor do you need to be sad for *anātmā*'s sake, either.

This line in the *Gītā* is, therefore, a very important one in that, it says, 'Let me accept what I cannot change.' The only alternative available is not to accept and to grieve. The point that Kṛṣṇa is making here is that something that cannot be changed does not deserve any sorrow on your part. He emphasises his point still further in the next verse.

Verse 28

There is nothing to grieve about life travelling between birth and death

अव्यक्तादीनि भूतानि व्यक्तमध्यानि भारत ।
अव्यक्तनिधनान्येव तत्र का परिदेवना ॥ २८ ॥

avyaktādīni bhūtāni vyaktamadhyāni bhārata
avyaktanidhanānyeva tatra kā paridevanā (28)

bhārata – O Bhārata (Arjuna)!; *bhūtāni-* – beings; *avyaktādīni* – being not manifest in the beginning; *vyakta-madhyāni* – manifest in the middle; *avyakta-nidhanāni* – not manifest in the end; *eva* – indeed; *tatra* – there; *kā* – what; *paridevanā* – grief

> Bhārata (Arjuna)! All beings are unmanifest in the beginning, manifest in the middle, and (again) unmanifest in the end. What indeed is there to grieve about?

The beginnings of all living beings, including the elements themselves, are all unknown. They are not available for perception. We do not know what they were before or what happens to them after death. We do not see the soul leaving the body, despite claims to the contrary. In fact, after death we do not know what happens; we do not see souls travelling. If we did, we would probably coax them back, promising to treat them better, and so on, even when they do not want to return. If we had our way, we would quite likely push these souls back into their bodies and then, afterwards, quarrel with them as before!

Perhaps it is to avoid such problems that we do not know what happens after death. We only know what is between birth and death. Even that is something like a travelling arrow. It emerges from darkness, *avyakta*, passes through a lighted area *vyakta*, and disappears into the darkness again, *avyakta*. It is not known before and it is not known later. In between, it dazzles in light. This is what we call life and it is all life is about – a beep, glow or flicker. Before the glow or flicker, we do not see the glow-worm or the firefly. In fact, we never see it; we only see the light. And, after the light has gone, again we see nothing.

Life is like a moving arrow, travelling between birth and death; so what is there to talk about? It is not even something that is staggered; it is just passing, always moving. Why the lamentation for this moving arrow? You cannot stop it anyway. In this glow, what is there to retain? That which is always eternal is always there and, in between, there is some kind of life, *mithyā*.

So what is there to lament about? If there is something that is always there and that thing has a problem, then it can be lamented about. However, what 'is' is not subject to lamentation. It is reality, the truth, *satya*, and it is limitless *ānanda*. Therefore, it is not subject to lamentation at all. Whatever else may be there is also not worth lamenting about.

People lament because of self-ignorance

People do lament. Even though life is just a beep in the eternal flow of time, they do have problems. They are concerned about their childhood, their marriage, old age, retirement, and what will happen to them after retirement. Within this one beep, all these divisions are made.

People continue to lament only because of self-ignorance. And this ignorance remains because there is no means of knowledge for knowing the self. The orientation of the individual is, 'I am small; I am a nobody.' Even those who claim to know, those who call themselves saviours and who say that you must be saved, confirm that *ātmā* is small, subject to sin, and so on. The world also confirms these notions by its very dimensions and its overwhelming strength. Because you have a particular dimension and limited powers, you find that you are helpless against bugs and certain other forces that are so overwhelmingly strong. You find that you have to conform to these forces. Against them, you always feel that you are a nobody. Thus, everything confirms your notion that, 'I am small,' and this conclusion about the 'I' is the problem.

Introducing the next verse, Śaṅkara agreed with Kṛṣṇa that *ātmā* is not easily understood. Arjuna is not the only one who laments. He is not the only person subject to sorrow. Sorrow is universal.

The significance of Śaṅkara's commentary

Because we will be drawing on Śaṅkara's commentary throughout our study of the *Gītā*, a brief explanation on the place that this commentary holds in the teaching tradition is in order here. The word '*bhāṣya*' refers to a commentary of an original work. The *Gītā* is an original work and, therefore, Śaṅkara's commentary of it is a *bhāṣya*. For a work to be original in our context, it must have the status of a scripture, *śruti*, meaning the *Upaniṣads*.

If the *Gītā* did not have the status of *śruti*, any commentary of it would be called only a *vyākhyāna*. But Śaṅkara's commentary is not a *vyākhyāna*. It is a *bhāṣya* because the *Gītā* has the status of the original work. Any commentary on the *Upaniṣads*, of course, is a *bhāṣya* because the *Upaniṣads* are *śruti*, providing what has been written is something more than the simple meaning of the verses. A commentary becomes a *bhāṣya* when it gives the meaning and also defends the meaning that is given.

A person who has written a *bhāṣya* is called *bhāṣya-kāra*. *Ṭīkā-kāra* refers to a person who has written *ṭīkā*, explanatory notes, for a *bhāṣya*. These notes serve to introduce the topic by explaining the sentences of the *bhāṣya* or a particular word in a sentence. A *ṭīkā* is not an independent work because it follows the *bhāṣya*, line by line, sentence by sentence.

There is also another type of work called *vārtika*, which is an independent exposition in verse form on the *bhāṣya* itself, not on the original. A *vārtika* is not a *ṭīkā* because it either goes beyond the *bhāṣya* or it is a further explanation of the *bhāṣya*. The person who writes a *vārtika* is called *vārtika-kāra*.

There is a *sampradāya*, tradition, in which certain people are recognised according to these categories. In Vedanta, by *vārtika-kāra*, for instance, we mean Sureśvara, the oldest of *bhāṣya-kāra*'s four disciples. Again, when we say *bhāṣya-kāra*, we mean Śaṅkara. Patañjali is known as *Mahābhāṣya-kāra*, the *Mahābhāṣya* being the commentary on the *sūtras* of Pāṇini on grammar, *vyākaraṇa-sūtras*.

Ṭīkā-kāra generally refers, in this tradition, to Ānandagiri, who wrote a *ṭīkā* for all of Śaṅkara's commentaries. There are many *ṭīkā-kāra*s. Anyone who comments upon the *bhāṣya*, sentence after sentence, as a traditional teacher does, becomes a *ṭīkā-kāra*. Knowing, then, that the words *bhāṣya-kāra* and *bhāṣya* refer to Śaṅkara and Śaṅkara's commentaries, respectively, we can proceed.

Verse 29

Ātmā is a wonder all the way

आश्चर्यवत्पश्यति कश्चिदेनमाश्चर्यवद्वदति तथैव चान्यः ।
आश्चर्यवच्चैनमन्यः शृणोति श्रुत्वाप्येनं वेद न चैव कश्चित् ॥२९॥

āścaryavat paśyati kaścidenam
āścaryavadvadati tathaiva cānyaḥ
āścaryavaccainam anyaḥ śṛṇoti
śrutvāpyenaṁ veda na caiva kaścit (29)

kaścit – some one; *enam* – this self; *āścaryavat* – as a wonder; *paśyati* – looks upon; *tathā* – similarly; *eva* – indeed; *ca* – and; *anyaḥ* – another; *āścaryavat* – as a wonder; *vadati* – speaks; *anyaḥ ca* – and another; *enam* – this; *āścaryavat* – as a wonder; *śṛṇoti* – hears; *kaścit* – someone; *ca* – and; *śrutvā api* – even after hearing; *enam* – this; *na veda* – does not understand; *eva* – at all

> One looks upon the self as a wonder. Similarly, another speaks of it as a wonder and another hears it as a wonder. Still another, even after hearing about this (self), does not understand it at all.

Śaṅkara begins his *bhāṣya* on this verse by saying that *ātmā* under discussion, *prakṛta-ātmā*, is not easy to understand, *durvijñeya*. *Prakṛta* is a technical term, meaning the topic under discussion, which is *ātmā* here. Although one has to recognise *ātmā* as Brahman, it is not easy and, therefore, not everyone comprehends it. The cause for this *bhrānti*, confusion, between *ātmā* and *anātmā* being *sādhāraṇa*, universal, everyone is to be sympathised with. No one is an exception. Arjuna was not the only one lamenting his lot. Knowing this makes us feel that we are in good company.

Modern group therapy does the same thing. You may start off thinking that you are the only one with a particular problem. But when you participate in group therapy, you discover that everyone is undergoing the same experience. Then you realise you are not alone; there are many people who have the same problem for which there is a cause. In the beginning, then, there is validation, which is a good thing.

Here too, Arjuna was given a boost. It was as though Kṛṣṇa was saying, 'You are not the only one lamenting, Arjuna. Everyone has the same problem because ignorance is common to all. It is not the personal problem of any one person.' Ignorance of *ātmā* is common to all and remains so because *ātmā* is not easily understood. This verse explains why *ātmā* is so difficult to understand.

Ātmā is always a wonder, *āścaryavat*. When I understand *ātmā*, it is a wonder and when I do not understand, it is a wonder to me how anyone can understand it. This wonder takes several forms. *Ātmā* is something never seen before, *adṛṣṭa-pūrva*, something that appears all of a sudden to one who has been taught by a *guru*, something that is striking. The student understands and looks at *ātmā* as a wonder, *āścaryavat paśyati*. Why? Because one now looks at oneself as a wonder.

When I suddenly discover that I am the whole and everything is centred on me, everything is me, it is definitely a wonder. First, this reality of myself seems to be an impossibility. Then it becomes a vague possibility, and finally it is real, true.

Anything that is experienced by me is myself. I am all the sounds; I am all the forms and colours; I am all the smells and sources of smell; and I am all the tastes and sources of tastes. Not only am I the food, I am also the one who eats the food. Otherwise, I would be eaten up. I am even the one who made the Vedas. I am not merely a reader of the Vedas; I am its author. I am the one to be understood by means of the Vedas. I am the one who is Lord Brahmā, the creator of the entire cosmos.

Previously, we thought that we were under the rule of the ruler whose law is the rule of *dharma*. For every *kalpa*, eon, there is said to be one such ruler. Thus, we are presently under *Vaivasvata-manu*'s law. This Manu is the son of Lord Sūrya. We have been under the ambit of this law, but now, having understood *ātmā*, we say, 'I am Manu, *ahaṁ manuḥ*,' Anyone, who was there in the past, was me and, in the future, anyone who is going to be there is me. Anything that is here now is also me. This is entirely a wonder because, previously, I could never have believed that I was everything, the truth of the whole creation. The opposite definitely seemed to be the case.

This *darśana*, vision, of *ātmā*, the knowledge of *ātmā*, is a wonder *āścarya*. And when we listen, *śravaṇa*, to the explanation of this *ātmā*, it is another wonder. To hear that I am the truth of everything, *satya*, the source of all happiness, anyone's happiness, *paraṁ-brahma*, is a wonder. Every creature in the world picks up small flakes of happiness, *ānanda*, all of which are from the original mountain or ocean of *ānanda*, which is me. Thus, when the teacher talks about *ātmā*, he or she describes it as a wonder, *āścaryavat anyaḥ enaṁ vadati*.

Ātmā is a wonder all the way! It is *sat-cit-ānanda* and, at the same time, it has created this entire world without undergoing any change. Talking about *ātmā* is itself a wonder because we are talking about something that is not available for words. That it is infinite and appears as though finite, without undergoing any change, without assuming any particular *nāma-rūpa*, is a wonder. All the *nāma-rūpa*s are Brahman alone and that Brahman is me, the *ātmā*. That the teacher can talk like this and get away with it is definitely yet another wonder! And, after listening to the teacher, the students also talk among themselves about what a wondrous thing the *ātmā* is. Everything about *ātmā*, therefore, is a wonder.

Lastly, it is a wonder that it cannot be understood even after having heard about it, *śrutvā api enaṁ veda na ca eva kaścit*.

Just as a very subtle joke is not understood, people do not understand *ātmā* at all. It has to be explained to them. Brahman appearing as a *jīva*, the bondage for the *jīva*, and the freedom from the bondage, *mokṣa* are all nothing but a big joke, the greatest joke ever, in fact. Therefore, life itself is a joke, as can be seen by analysing any one thing.

Life is like a very subtle joke

If you analyse a thought, there is no thought at all. Where does any given thought begin and where does consciousness end? Whatever you confront in the world is nothing but your thought. That there is a world for you is because you have a thought. When you ask, how far is any given thought true, where does the consciousness end, where does the thought begin, you will find that there is only consciousness. There is no thought. There is no beginning of the thought, there is no form of the thought. All that is there is consciousness.

This is both the beauty and the joke of *ātmā*. The whole thing is a continuous joke. There is, as though, an original joke, and then, afterwards, a variety of secondary jokes, one after the other. Marriage is a joke and children are secondary jokes. Childbirth itself is a joke and so are the birth pangs. Thus, there is one continuous joke within which there are lamentations.

If the original joke is not understood, you will not understand other jokes. The original joke should be understood as a joke; then all other jokes become jokes quite naturally. The last joke, perhaps, is that there will always be someone who, after listening to Vedanta will say, 'Please tell me what the teaching is!' It is like the man who listened to a musician sing *bhūpalī*, the name of a particular melody, *rāga*, in Hindustani music for an hour. He was nodding his head as though he understood the music very well. At the end of the rendering, however, the man said to the musician, 'Panditji, please sing *bhūpalī* next!'

Similarly, there is always someone in the audience who, at the end of a Vedanta talk, will say, 'I did not understand anything. I saw nothing in it at all.' If someone else expressed his or her appreciation of what was said, the first person may accuse that person of having been swept away, of not having retained his or her independent thinking, of having lost himself or herself in a sea of meaningless words. Faced with such criticism, the person who understood may begin to doubt whether there had ever been a time when he or she had thought independently!

That some people can listen to the teaching about *ātmā* and not understand is another wonder. Because it is a wonder, it is not easy to understand. Only a few people can understand such wonders. Even a simple joke is not understood by everybody, much less the *ātmā* joke! Because it is too big a joke, no one can say it is easy to understand. Therefore, it is no wonder that, having listened to talks about *ātmā*, some people do not understand. Or, that people do not understand can also be taken as a wonder, since what is to be understood is themselves.

All that is being talked about is oneself, a self-evident fact. We experience this *ātmā* all the time. Only because of *ātmā* do we experience the world. Everything in the world is unlike *ātmā*. This *ātmā*, as *ānanda*, is very evident in moments of joy when we discover ourselves to be full, *pūrṇa*. Yet, even when it is pointed out that we are that whole, we do not understand, which is another wonder, *śrutvā api enaṁ veda na ca eva kaścit*.

The difficulty in understanding

Why is it that people cannot understand? It is not calculus or something that requires an intellectual preparation and acumen. All that is required here is to see what is being said. Yet, some do not see it. This is because seeing oneself is not like seeing an object. It is not knowledge of an object, like a pot, which depends upon another object, clay, only one of which you may understand. To see yourself is knowledge of you as something that is not subject to negation; it is knowledge of the whole. *Ātmā* is therefore to be understood as the whole, that which is free from all attributes, which is yourself. All attributes are incidental.

What is to be known here is very clear and, in itself, does not require any intellectual discipline, unlike calculus. Even a wise person, in order to learn calculus, has to start from one plus one equals two, and it will take the person ages to understand calculus. *Ātmā* on the other hand, is very simple. All that is required are your experiences in life.

That you have been constantly seeking is a fact. That there is no answer to this seeking is another fact. You have tried various pursuits and none of them has yielded what you wanted.

This is also a fact. In between, you had some moments of joy, which is another fact. These two latter facts are the ones that you have to analyse in order to understand yourself, the *ātmā*. Because you have assimilated certain experiences, you cannot say that you have no raw material to analyse. The three states of experience, waking, dream, and deep sleep, themselves provide you with enough data. That one state cancels another state is enough data. Therefore, it is not that you lack materials or data. All you require is someone to lift your vision, for which a *pramāṇa*, means of knowledge, *ācārya*, a teacher, and *upadeśa*, vision, are there. Now, you should be able to see the fact; then understanding should take place.

To see an object is no problem. Your eyes are there, the object is there, and you see it. Similarly, if the teaching is available and *ātmā* is available, then knowledge should take place. There should be no hindrance to your gaining the knowledge. Yet, seeing may not take place and this not seeing is described in this verse as a wonder. Kṛṣṇa pointed out here that seeing is a wonder and not seeing is a greater wonder. That a person can come out of the whole teaching untouched, unscathed, as it were, is definitelya wonder.

The one who knows ātmā is a wonder

You can also take the verse differently, using the word *āścaryavat* to mean that the person who knows *ātmā* is like a wonder. The affix '*vat*' means 'like.' And, therefore, *āścaryavat* means 'like a wonder.' Among millions of people, only one person may be a seeker and, even among the seekers, only one person may see the truth of what is said. Understanding *ātmā* is not easy. Therefore, one who knows *ātmā* without any doubt whatsoever, who sees it directly, *yaḥ ātmānaṁ paśyati*, is a wonder because he or she has had to reverse an entire process.

Our natural trait is to follow the beaten track, in our ways of thinking, in our pursuits, and so on. We constantly strive to make something of ourselves because, initially, we condemn ourselves as useless. We try to set the *ātmā* up nicely by the pursuit of a *saṁsārī*. First, we think of the *ātmā* as a *saṁsārī*. Then we look for some means of support so that the *saṁsārī* can be better, so that he or she can develop some spine, some character, and so on. We think of *ātmā* as so drooped that it requires some kind of a support system in order to be acceptable. This is the nature of people. They are like flowing water that finds its own level. In this way, people tend to follow the beaten track.

Some may follow it better than others. If one person makes money in a particular pursuit, another may try to make the same money in another pursuit. But this is all really one beaten track with only minor variations. Nevertheless, such people are called creative, whereas the really creative person is one who questions the very seeker. He asks himself, 'Am I a *saṁsārī*?' If one assumes that one is a *saṁsārī*, any pursuit is a beaten track. The one who questions whether he or she is a *saṁsārī* reverses the whole process. It is something like water climbing up the mountain. Water flowing down is nothing; it is natural. However, water that begins to flow upwards is truly a wonder, an *āścarya* to behold. All of humanity would gather to see water climbing up a mountain.

Even to start the process of self-enquiry is a big thing; certain grace is definitely required, otherwise starting is not possible. Just as it requires a lot of horsepower to send water up a hill, so too, for a person who has been following the beaten track to question whether he or she is a *saṁsārī* requires a lot of horsepower, God power or grace. And if the person discovers the truth, he or she is definitely a wonder.

The one who talks about ātmā is also a wonder

The one who knows, then, is an *āścarya* and the one who talks about it is another *āścarya* because there is nothing really to talk about. When someone comes and says, 'I am overcome by sorrow,' the person who knows the truth cannot really talk about it because he or she does not see any sorrow or problem at all. It is also a wonder that someone who knows there is no problem takes the person who has sorrow seriously enough to talk to him or her about it. Starting out as Kṛṣṇa did, saying that there is no reason for sorrow, *aśocyān anvaśocaḥ tvam*, creates some elbow room in which to talk. Otherwise, the one who knows cannot talk at all.

If Kṛṣṇa had simply said, 'I am *ānanda;* you are *ānanda;* we are all *ānanda,*' there would be nothing to talk about. To tell a person who says he or she is sad, 'No, you are *ānanda*' leaves no room to talk, although the statement is true. To say that sorrow has no basis requires proof and Kṛṣṇa had seventeen chapters in which to prove that what he said was a fact. He knew that to start by saying, 'You are *ānanda,*' would give him no room to talk. Instead, Kṛṣṇa talked as though there was a problem and he 'as though' solved it also.

Thus, the talking itself is an *āścarya* because what cannot be talked about is talked about. What cannot be verbally mentioned is mentioned. What cannot be captured by words is presented by words. This is indeed a wonder. The one who teaches is also a wonder and the one who listens is another wonder. Can you tell an ordinary, practical person who asks you what you are studying that you are learning self-knowledge? No. If you did, your sanity would undoubtedly be questioned.

The self is something that is impossible to talk about and the one who comes to listen, the one in many millions, is a wonder. Such a person thinks that knowledge of the self is very important, whereas everyone else thinks of it as nonsense. They think those who take three years to study self-knowledge are wasting their time. They will say that you are frittering away the prime of your life, that you could have had two children in the same amount of time!

There are so many aspects to this wonder, the wonder with a capital 'W.' Any way you look at it, it is a wonder. The one who is able to see *ātmā* is a wonder. Or, we can say that the one among many who sees the *ātmā* does so with wonder. Also, there is no wonder that even after listening to the teaching, there are those who do not understand. This second intrepretation is offered by Śaṅkara in his commentary on this verse.

Verse 30

Kṛṣṇa sums up his original statement

देही नित्यमवध्योऽयं देहे सर्वस्य भारत ।
तस्मात्सर्वाणि भूतानि न त्वं शोचितुमर्हसि ॥ ३० ॥

dehī nityam avadhyo'yaṁ dehe sarvasya bhārata
tasmāt sarvāṇi bhūtāni na tvaṁ śocitum arhasi (30)

bhārata – O descendant of Bharata (Arjuna)!; *sarvasya dehe* – in the body of all; *ayam* – this; *dehī* – indweller of the body; *nityam* – for ever; *avadhyaḥ* – indestructible; *tasmāt* – therefore; *tvam* – you; *sarvāṇi* – all; *bhūtāni* – beings; *śocitum* – to grieve; *na arhasi* – ought not

> Bhārata (Arjuna)! This *ātmā*, the indweller of the bodies of all beings, is ever indestructible. Therefore, you ought not to grieve for all these people.

Here, Kṛṣṇa sums up his original statement that he made in verse 11, that there is no cause for grief. *Ātmā* is *sat* and therefore *nitya*, meaning that it is not subject to birth, death, change, and so on. In the live physical body of any being, there is a *dehī*, an indweller of the body, *deha*, and this *dehī*, called the *jīva-ātmā*, is not subject to destruction; it is *avadhya*.

Vadhya means that which is subject to destruction, that which can be destroyed. *Avadhya* means that which is not subject to destruction. The *dehī* is not subject to destruction at all; it is *nityam avadhyaḥ*. It is always indestructible, meaning that even when the body is destroyed, *ātmā* is not destroyed. This is the point that Kṛṣṇa wanted to establish. The *dehī*, the indweller of the body is not destroyed even when the body is destroyed. This being so, Kṛṣṇa told Arjuna that, with reference to all living beings, *sarvāṇi bhūtāni*, 'You do not qualify to be sad, *tvaṁ śocituṁ na arhasi*.'

Kṛṣṇa backed his statement with all possible arguments. For the body, *deha*, which is *anitya*, there is no way that it will not be destroyed and for the *nitya-ātmā* there is no way of destroying it. Either way, therefore, there is no room for grief based on death. Nor is there any room for grief on the basis of any other situation, as has already been pointed out, because any situation that causes you sorrow is not a permanent situation. Therefore, *duḥkha* also comes and goes, as does *sukha*. Because there is no content to *duḥkha* we cannot even say that a particular object or situation causes it. It is one's thinking with reference to a particular object or situation that actually causes *duḥkha*. There can be physically painful or uncomfortable situations, but these are different from sadness. Here, we are dealing with sadness, not mere physical pain.

Sadness does not depend on what you have or do not have. It is a particular way of thinking. Sorrow is something centred on oneself and this topic is the subject matter of the *Gītā*. Thus, there is this refrain, 'You should not grieve, *na tvaṁ śocituṁ arhasi*.'

Having stated that there is no reason for sorrow, Kṛṣṇa then takes up the same topic from other standpoints. In fact, he exhausted every possible standpoint. Introducing the next verse, Śaṅkara says that from the standpoint of ultimate reality, *paramārtha-tattva-apekṣāyām*, sorrow or delusion is not possible, *śokaḥ mohaḥ vā na sambhavati*. And it is also not possible from the standpoint of relative reality.

Arjuna may well have said to Kṛṣṇa, 'I am worried about Bhīṣma and the others and you are telling me that *ātmā* does not die. Bhīṣma is my grandfather, a man whom I respect. Therefore, I cannot kill him. Just to think of it causes me sorrow and all you say is that he is *ātmā*, he is eternal, etc. What are you doing to me? When I am sorrowful because someone is dead, you cannot come and tell me that no germ can kill the *ātmā* when, in fact, the germs killed the person. It just does not work. Here, too, what you are saying is too much for me.'

Arjuna would not really have argued in this way because he himself had asked for self-knowledge. Until he asked Kṛṣṇa to teach him, Kṛṣṇa did not teach; he only encouraged him to fight. Only when Arjuna asked, did Kṛṣṇa begin to teach him. Because Arjuna wanted *śreyas*, he told Kṛṣṇa that he was his *śiṣya* and, therefore, Kṛṣṇa taught. Even though this was not Arjuna's thinking here, Kṛṣṇa nevertheless exhausted the topic. He did not allow any standpoint, even relative standpoints, to go unattended. In this way, from both the absolute and the relative standpoints we can understand Kṛṣṇa's statement that there is no reason for sorrow. Kṛṣṇa then continued.

Verse 31

Arjuna's duty

स्वधर्ममपि चावेक्ष्य न विकम्पितुमर्हसि ।
धर्म्याद्धि युद्धाच्छ्रेयोऽन्यत् क्षत्रियस्य न विद्यते ॥ ३१ ॥

svadharmam api cāvekṣya na vikampitum arhasi
dharmyāddhi yuddhācchreyo'nyat kṣatriyasya na vidyate (31)

sva-dharmam – one's own duty; *api ca* – and also; *avekṣya* – looking at; *vikampitum* – to waver; *na arhasi* – you cannot; *hi* – for; *dharmyāt yuddhāt* – than a righteous war; *kṣatriyasya* – for a *kṣatriya*; *anyat* – any other; *śreyaḥ* – good; *na vidyate* – does not exist

And also, from the standpoint of your own duty, you cannot waver. For, there is nothing greater to a *kṣatriya* than a battle for the cause of *dharma.*

Shifting from the absolute standpoint, Kṛṣṇa then takes up the relative standpoint of *dharma,* what is right, what is to be done. This was a natural outcome of Arjuna's earlier and numerous comments on *dharma.* He had said that societal confusion would be the result of this war and he would be the cause for the confusion. He had said, 'We have heard, O Kṛṣṇa! that those men who have destroyed the family duty live in hell.'[10] Thus, Kṛṣṇa looked at it from the standpoint of *dharma* as well as from other standpoints, including worldly gain, as we shall see.

Avekṣya means 'seeing'– seeing from the standpoint of *sva dharma,* seeing what is to be done by oneself. Again, Arjuna was being told here that he was not eligible to develop this

---

[10] *Gītā* 1.44

trembling hesitation, *na vikampitum arhasi,* looking at the situation from the standpoint of his *sva-dharma,* his duty.

First of all, Arjuna was a *kṣatriya,* soldier. Secondly, he was a crown prince, which meant that, along with his brothers, he was supposed to protect *dharma.* He was not just a recruited soldier with only certain prescribed duties to do. He was a royal person, belonging to the royal family, and also one of the crown princes. Arjuna's duty was to uphold law and order. He had to administer and protect the kingdom. That was his job, his *dharma.*

When the Pāṇḍavas came back to claim their country after their thirteen years of exile, Duryodhana refused to give their kingdom back. All their efforts at a compromise failed. He refused to give them even a needle point of land let alone their country. Therefore Duryodhana was the usurper. Every day that Duryodhana occupied the throne, he did so illegally and this was a*dharma.* Kṛṣṇa told Arjuna that being a *kṣatriya,* he could not just sit and allow *adharma* to continue. Therefore, from the standpoint of his own *dharma,* Arjuna ought not to waver or hesitate about what he had to do, *svadharmam api ca avekṣya na vikampitum arhasi.*

A soldier is especially trained in warfare and must practice continually during peacetime to 'keep the powder dry' and to keep his wits sharp. If he has to retire before a war actually occurs, his skills go unused, although it was his and others' good fortune that there was no war. Not to fight is also proper if there is no cause to fight. But as Kṛṣṇa said, if that same soldier gets a chance to use his training legitimately, there is no greater opportunity than that to show his skills.

Generally, when such chances come, there is always some legitimacy about them. To shoot someone merely because he or she spoke out of turn is definitely illegitimate. But here, for Arjuna, there was a legitimate chance, *dharmāt anapetaṁ dharmyam*, that which was not against *dharma*. The battle, *yuddha*, was based purely on *dharma* and the one who brought Arjuna to it deserved to be punished. This, then, was a *dharmya-yuddha*, an expression that is often misused.

Here, the *dharmya-yuddha* was, first of all, to establish *dharma*. Also, the person who had flagrantly violated *dharma* by usurping the kingdom deserved to be punished. Thus, Kṛṣṇa as much as said to Arjuna, 'The battle is right in front of you, Arjuna. You now have a chance to demonstrate your weapons and skill, and it is your duty to do so.'

Arjuna's weapons had gone unused for a long time. They had been stockpiled and maintained so that they would not become rusty. Most of his missiles were in the form of *mantra*s and Arjuna had to repeat these *mantra*s daily because they were the power behind his weapons. This was how the weapons were kept alive and was how Arjuna 'kept the powder dry.'

Arjuna had done what was required and now a time had come when all of his acquired skill was to be used for the purpose for which it was learned and stockpiled. He did not learn all this to destroy people or to demonstrate his prowess, but to protect *dharma*. And now was his chance to do so.

So, from the standpoint of his own *dharma*, as to what had to be done, there was no room whatsoever for lamentation or hesitancy. This was one argument that Kṛṣṇa put to him.

Another argument Kṛṣṇa put forward was that for a *kṣatriya* especially one of Arjuna's stature, there was nothing more appropriate for him to do. 'What is to be done by you, Arjuna, is to be done by you and this *yuddha* is something that is to be done by you,' said Kṛṣṇa.

Verses 32-34

Arjuna's chance to protect dharma

यदृच्छया चोपपन्नं स्वर्गद्वारमपावृतम् ।
सुखिनः क्षत्रियाः पार्थ लभन्ते युद्धमीदृशम् ॥ ३२ ॥

yadṛcchayā copapannaṁ svargadvāram apāvṛtam
sukhinaḥ kṣatriyāḥ pārtha labhante yuddham īdṛśam (32)

ca – and; *pārtha* – O son of Pṛthā (Arjuna)!; *yadṛcchayā* – by chance; *upapannam* – has come; *apāvṛtam* – opened; *svarga-dvāram* – the gates of heaven; *īdṛśam* – of this kind; *yuddham* – battle; *sukhinaḥ* – lucky; *kṣatriyāḥ* – *kṣatriya*s; *labhante* – get

> Pārtha (Arjuna)! Only lucky *kṣatriya*s get this kind of battle, which has come by chance and which is an open gate to heaven.

Yadṛcchā means 'chance,' something that happens without your willing or wanting it. Here, Kṛṣṇa told Arjuna that the gates of heaven were open to him. This was something that had come to Arjuna without his desiring it. It is said that a person who dies performing his or her duty goes to heaven. It is a *karma-phala* promised by the scripture. Therefore, Kṛṣṇa said, 'When you perform your duty properly, *svarga*, heaven, will be the result. The gates of heaven have opened for you without any prayer on your part.' Kṛṣṇa also told Arjuna in this verse that this kind of battle, *yuddham-īdṛśam*, is not gained by ordinary people, but only by the very lucky ones, *sukhinaḥ kṣatriyāḥ labhante*.

A question may arise here, does this mean that the *kṣatriya*s in Duryodhana's army were unlucky? No doubt, they were also going to fight, but they had conflicts because they were supporting a usurper. Unlike Arjuna, they were not able to fight with a clean heart. Of course, they were soldiers and they had their own reasons for fighting. They may even have said it was their duty and perhaps it was true. Yet, for them the inner conflict was unavoidable. As soldiers, they could only do what they were commanded to do. Therefore, they too were doing their *sva-dharma*, but at the same time it was not totally *dharmya* because their leader was a usurper.

The entire army of Duryodhana, including Bhīṣma and Droṇa, were not totally convinced that what they were about to do was according to their *dharma*. They were there primarily because they were obliged to Duryodhana. The war was foisted upon them and was not, therefore, totally in keeping with *dharma*, whereas for Arjuna it was.

While no one enjoys a war, a *kṣatriya* who has to protect *dharma* could never have a better chance to prove himself as a *kṣatriya* Arjuna was a warrior. Therefore, Kṛṣṇa may have said, 'Only lucky *kṣatriya*s get a clean *yuddha* to fight. It is no longer a question of your ambition for a kingdom because you were already willing to accept a house with five rooms. You have explored every possible way to avoid this war, but in spite of all your efforts, war has been declared and it is definitely a *dharmya-yuddha*. Even from the standpoint of *dharma*, Arjuna, you have no cause to grieve.'

When Kṛṣṇa began to teach Arjuna, his original statement was, *aśocyān anvaśocaḥ tvaṁ*.[11] Having established it as a fact, Kṛṣṇa then told Arjuna that he is aggrieved for no reason, that grief has no real basis. This was Kṛṣṇa's argument. First he dealt with it absolutely and then from simple, relative standpoints, based purely on one's own duty, *sva-dharma*.

If we look at Arjuna's conflict from the standpoint of the *dharma-śāstra* we find that performing one's duty produces certain *karma-phala*. The *dharma-śāstra* deals with what is to be done and what is not to be done, what is right and what is wrong. It talks about the immediate result, *dṛṣṭa-phala* of right action in the sense that the action produces no conflict. Avoidance of conflict is the immediate result. The *dharma-śāstra* also talks about *adṛṣṭa-phala*, an invisible result credited to one's account and enjoyed by the person later.

The war, *yuddha*, for Arjuna was in keeping with his duty. Therefore, the war itself was like the gates of heaven opening for him. Any *dharma* can only produce so much; going to heaven, of course, is a relative result. And, as though, by accident, without any prayer on his part, this result was assured to Arjuna. All he needed to do was to walk into the war and do what was to be done. Only the lucky ones get such an opportunity, not everyone.

---

[11] *Gītā* 2.11

Kṛṣṇa then continued with the same argument:

अथ चेत्त्वमिमं धर्म्यं सङ्ग्रामं न करिष्यसि ।
ततः स्वधर्मं कीर्तिं च हित्वा पापमवाप्स्यसि ॥ ३३ ॥

atha cettvam imaṁ dharmyaṁ saṅgrāmaṁ na kariṣyasi
tataḥ svadharmaṁ kīrtiṁ ca hitvā pāpam avāpsyasi (33)

atha – but; *cet* – if; *tvam* – you; *imam* – this; *dharmyam* – in keeping with *dharma*; *saṅgrāmam* – war; *na kariṣyasi* – will not do; *tataḥ* – then; *sva-dharmam* – your own duty; *ca* – and; *kīrtim* – honour; *hitvā* – forfeiting; *pāpam* – sin; *avāpsyasi* – you will incur

But, if you refuse to engage in this war that is in keeping with *dharma*, then, forfeiting your own duty and honour, you will gain only sin.

Here, Kṛṣṇa told Arjuna that if he did not undertake this battle, which was in keeping with *dharma*, he would be destroying his own *dharma*, his duty. Destroying what is to be done by you simply means that you do not do it.

Also, the name and fame, *kīrti*, that Arjuna had thus far gained would be destroyed. He would incur sin alone. Arjuna had said earlier that he would incur sin by fighting this battle, but Kṛṣṇa was now telling him that by not fighting he would incur sin in the sense that he would be guilty of a dereliction of duty. Not fighting itself would not incur sin, but running away from his duty was an action, a *karma*, that would incur sin. Therefore Kṛṣṇa said, '*pāpam avāpsyasi*, you will incur sin, Arjuna. And you will lose your name also.'

Arjuna had gained fame previously because of his earlier contact with Lord Mahādeva, Lord Śiva, who appeared in the form of a hunter. Arjuna had hit a boar and was going to take it away when Lord Śiva appeared there and claimed that it was his. He incited Arjuna to fight with him. Although Arjuna realised that he was up against someone more than an ordinary hunter, still he was equal to Lord Śiva in the fight. Pleased with Arjuna, Lord Śiva blessed him with a weapon. Because Arjuna had encountered Lord Śiva and engaged him in battle, Arjuna had gained a great name, all of which would be lost. Therefore Kṛṣṇa says, '*kīrtiṁ ca hitvā pāpam avāpsyasi*, you will lose your name as well as incur sin.'

Not performing an action is not a sin

Not performing an action that has to be done is considered sinful. However, it does not constitute sin. Not doing anything cannot attract a punitive response. How can it? Only action can produce a result; inaction cannot. Inaction can only maintain the absence of some result, absence in the sense that if you had done something, there would have been a result. If you do not do what is to be done, you do not directly produce any result, but there will be a result nevertheless.

For instance, if you do not bathe, shower, or launder your clothes, whether you see the result or not, others will see it. The result will be very clear. This is what is meant by *dṛṣṭa-phala*. If you do not tidy up your room, you will see the results in just two days. It will be a mess. It is the natural entropy that is a part of the creation. Not doing something, then, can attract *dṛṣṭa-phala*. *Adṛṣṭa-phala* accrues only when you do it, rightly or wrongly.

To say that if you do not perform an action, you incur sin is a very loose statement. The point is that when you do not do what is to be done, you will do something else instead and that action may attract *adṛṣṭa-phala*. Running away from the battlefield is an action. A retreating action, on Arjuna's part, giving up his duty and doing something that was not his duty, would definitely attract *adṛṣṭa-phala*. That Arjuna could not avoid this *pāpa*, then, was another argument based on *dharma* put forward by Kṛṣṇa.

At the same time, Kṛṣṇa said, Arjuna would also lose his name. Arjuna may have replied, 'How can I lose my name? People will praise me. They will say that Arjuna was so compassionate that he gave away the kingdom and walked into the forest. He could have had the kingdom easily because he had the weapons to destroy the arrows of Karṇa and Droṇa. Yet he gave away the kingdom. What a compassionate man Arjuna is!' But Kṛṣṇa said that it would not happen that way at all.

अकीर्तिं चापि भूतानि कथयिष्यन्ति तेऽव्ययाम् ।
सम्भावितस्य चाकीर्तिर्मरणादतिरिच्यते ॥ ३४ ॥

akīrtiṁ cāpi bhūtāni kathayiṣyanti te'vyayām
sambhāvitasya cākīrtirmaraṇād atiricyate (34)

api ca – and also; *bhūtāni* – beings; *te* – of you; *avyayām* – unending; *akīrtim* – infamy; *kathayiṣyanti* – will speak; *sambhāvitasya* – for the honoured; *akīrtiḥ* – dishonour; *ca* – surely; *maraṇāt atiricyate* – is worse than death

Also, people will speak of your unending infamy. For the honoured, dishonour is surely worse than death.

Bhūtāni refers to one's fellow beings. Not only great men were included here. They too would talk, of course, along with the recent recruits who had come to fight and who did not even know how to button their uniforms properly. They would tell all kinds of stories, *kathayiṣyanti*, about Arjuna, each creating his own version. Their imagination would run wild and rumours would quickly spread. They would use words that would bring Arjuna into disrepute, *akīrti*, and people would continue to talk about it for all times to come.

Even children of subsequent generations, listening to the *Mahābhārata* would giggle when the topic of Arjuna would come up because he was the one who ran away. They would ask, 'Which Pārtha are you talking about? The one who ran away from the battlefield?' Thus, Kṛṣṇa told Arjuna that not only those on the battlefield would talk ill of him, but all the ordinary people would do the same.

For someone who had no name or fame, there would be no problems. No one would care whether he ran away from the battlefield or not. People would only assume that such a person was one of those soldiers who ran away. But if Arjuna ran away, it would be front-page news because he was held in such high regard. *Akīrti*, ill fame is not the same as loss of fame; it is the opposite of fame, and is worse than death for the one who was held in high esteem by society.

The argument here, then, is that if Arjuna cared about *dharma*, he should not leave the battlefield and, if he did leave, he would incur *pāpa*. Even if he did not care about incurring *puṇya-pāpa* or about his own *dharma*, but cared only for his own name and fame, the ill-fame would be worse than death because no one can live with ill-fame which is not at all legitimate. To have earned ill-fame is one thing, but if it is unearned, undeserving, Kṛṣṇa said, it is worse than death.

Verses 35&36

How Arjuna's retreat would be perceived

Arjuna might as well have asked, 'How will I have ill fame just by going away?' To this, Kṛṣṇa said:

भयाद्रणादुपरतं मंस्यन्ते त्वां महारथाः ।
येषां च त्वं बहुमतो भूत्वा यास्यसि लाघवम् ॥ ३५ ॥

bhayādraṇāduparataṁ maṁsyante tvāṁ mahārathāḥ
yeṣāṁ ca tvaṁ bahumato bhūtvā yāsyasi lāghavam (35)

mahārathāḥ – the great warriors; *ca* – and; *tvām* – you; *bhayāt* – due to fear; *raṇāt* – from the battle; *uparatam* – one who has retreated; *maṁsyante* – will consider; *yeṣām* – of whom; *tvam* – you; *bahumataḥ* – highly esteemed; *bhūtvā* – having been; *lāghavam yāsyasi* – you will fall in (their) esteem

The great warriors will consider you as having retreated from the battle due to fear. And you, having been so highly esteemed by them, will fall in their esteem.

The word *mahārathas* refers to Karṇa, Duryodhana, and others. Karṇa was Arjuna's arch enemy and along with Duryodhana, was supported by others of great valour. In this verse, Kṛṣṇa told Arjuna that they would look upon him as one who had run away from the battlefield out of sheer fright at the sight of Karṇa and Duryodhana's army.

These were not ordinary men; they were people who counted in the society. To them, Arjuna had always been a great man. Even Duryodhana considered him to be the greatest, which is why they were afraid of him. But although they had always held Arjuna in such high esteem, *yeṣāṁ ca tvaṁ bahumataḥ*, they would now consider him a lightweight, *lāghava*. They would look upon him as a feather that is easily blown away. He would become an ordinary person to them.

Kṛṣṇa knew that Arjuna was a great man and that his problem was one of affection and sympathy. That is why he told Arjuna that they would look upon him as the one who ran away. Kṛṣṇa knew that Arjuna's desire to run was not due to fear and that, in fact, he was not running away. Rather, Arjuna was giving up the fight, according to his own arguments, out of sympathy. But Kṛṣṇa knew that no one would understand that. There was neither *dharma* involved, nor prudence. Kṛṣṇa, therefore, told Arjuna that running away would be neither a prudent nor an ethical action. He would lose all of the name and fame that he had earned thus far, which would prove to be worse than death.

People would make fun of Arjuna. If he went to Rishikesh and sat under a tree, the pilgrims would come to see Arjuna who had run away from the battlefield. And, having become a *sādhu* there would be no recourse for Arjuna. At least if he had remained as he was, people would be afraid of him. But no one is afraid of a *sādhu* because he has taken the oath of *ahiṁsā* and, therefore, cannot seek restitution. Kṛṣṇa said, "People will come and talk ill of you, Arjuna, and will say, 'What kind of a *sādhu* are you, Arjuna, to have gone against *dharma*?' You will have to live with their accusations and you are not going to enjoy that."

Further, Kṛṣṇa says:

अवाच्यवादांश्च बहून्वदिष्यन्ति तवाहिताः ।
निन्दन्तस्तव सामर्थ्यं ततो दुःखतरं नु किम् ॥ ३६ ॥

avācyavādāṁśca bahūn vadiṣyanti tavāhitāḥ
nindantastava sāmarthyaṁ tato duḥkhataraṁ nu kim (36)

ca – and; *tava* – your; *ahitāḥ* – enemies; *tava* – your; *sāmarthyam* – prowess; *nindantaḥ* – belittling; *bahūn* – many; *avācya-vādān* – unutterable things; *vadiṣyanti* – will say; *tataḥ* – than that; *duḥkhataram* – more painful; *nu kim* – is there anything

And belittling your prowess, your enemies will say many unutterable things about (you). Is there anything more painful than that?

Duryodhana and other enemies of Arjuna would not think that he went away out of compassion. Even if Duryodhana knew it to be so, he would definitely not say it. Simple psychology was involved here. Duryodhana was a ruler and, already, there was talk that Duryodhana was occupying the throne illegitimately. The subjects were not happy with Duryodhana on that score, even though he introduced a lot of welfare schemes to win them over. They knew in their hearts that Duryodhana was just trying to convince them that he was a good person, when in fact he was a usurper and was occupying the throne illegitimately. Everyone knew this.

Also, if Arjuna were to go away out of compassion, which would have been the case, Dharmaputra would definitely have followed him. Bhīma and the other Pāṇḍavas would have done the same. Therefore, Duryodhana would be victorious without a shot and would definitely not have allowed the news of Arjuna's real reasons to spread because he would not want the people to look upon Arjuna and the Pāṇḍavas as truly great. To allow this to happen would not have been good psychology on Duryodhana's part because he would have wanted to draw the attention of his subjects towards himself. As a ruler, he was the person to be looked up to, not anyone else. Duryodhana could not afford to have anyone else greater than himself be looked up to by the people. His government would fall and the subjects may have started a revolution in an attempt to oust him.

Duryodhana would see to it that he was projected and Arjuna demeaned. He would say that Arjuna ran away out of sheer fear. The esteem people had for Arjuna would go and they would think that, because he ran away from the battlefield, Arjuna deserved to live in the forest. No one would respect such a person because they knew *dharma* and Duryodhana would make sure that people would talk. Kṛṣṇa therefore told Arjuna, '*avācya-vādān-bahūn vadiṣyanti tava ahitāḥ*, your enemies will use words about your capacity and courage that are impossible for me to repeat.' '*Tataḥ duḥkhataraṁ nu kim*, what can be more painful than that?'

Even the simple soldiers, the fresh recruits would talk in the victory parties hosted by Duryodhana. One soldier would say Arjuna ran away as soon as he looked at him. Another would say Arjuna became frightened when he put his hand on his moustache. Another would say that all he had said to Arjuna was, 'Get out!' and he fled in fear. Such people would also no doubt talk about Kṛṣṇa in the same way. Having involved Kṛṣṇa in the battle, Arjuna was now thinking of running away! Everyone would say that Kṛṣṇa, as Arjuna's driver, ran away too. Thus, Kṛṣṇa may have said, 'On top of everything else, Arjuna, you have also brought me into this mess.'

Verses 37&38

Arjuna is told to get up and fight

हतो वा प्राप्स्यसि स्वर्गं जित्वा वा भोक्ष्यसे महीम्।
तस्मादुत्तिष्ठ कौन्तेय युद्धाय कृतनिश्चयः ॥ ३७ ॥

hato vā prāpsyasi svargaṁ jitvā vā bhokṣyase mahīm
tasmād uttiṣṭha kaunteya yuddhāya kṛtaniścayaḥ (37)

hataḥ vā – or if destroyed; *svargam* – heaven; *prāpsyasi* – you will gain; *jitvā vā* – or conquering; *mahīm* – the earth; *bhokṣyase* – will enjoy; *tasmāt* – therefore; *kaunteya* – O son of Kuntī!; *yuddhāya* – to fight; *kṛta-niścayaḥ*- having resolved; *uttiṣṭha* – get up

Destroyed, you will gain heaven; victorious, you will enjoy (this) world. Therefore, Kaunteya (Arjuna)! get up, having resolved to fight.

Here, Kṛṣṇa presented two possibilities to Arjuna. He said, 'Suppose, Arjuna, you are destroyed, *hata*, in the process by Karṇa's or someone else's arrow, then you will gain heaven, *prāpsyasi svargam*. That is the rule. The *dharma-śāstra* says so. Therefore, when you perform your *karma* and in the process you die, you are not the loser. You gain *svarga*. And after *svarga*, you gain better *janma* because you have done what is to be done. So there is no sin.'

Earlier, Arjuna had put forth an argument based on sin. He had said, 'I would create confusion in the society and therefore would commit sin.' Here, Kṛṣṇa was telling him that this was not true. *Pāpa* would not come to him. In fact, he would gain *svarga*. *Pāpa* takes one to *naraka*. But now because, Arjuna would have died while performing his duty, he would definitely go to *svarga*.

On the other hand, if Arjuna won the battle, having won, *jitvā*, he would enjoy the kingdom. Therefore Kṛṣṇa said, '*jitvā vā bhokṣyase mahīm*.' Either way, he was not the loser. In the battles that Arjuna fought, these were the only two possibilities, either death or victory. Those days, wars were fought to death. Because there was no retreating from battle, men were either victorious or they died in the process. That was the *dharma*.

Therefore, lovingly addressing Arjuna as Kaunteya, Kṛṣṇa said, '*tasmāt uttiṣṭha*, please get up!' He asked Arjuna to get up because Arjuna had been sitting in the chariot determined not to fight and Kṛṣṇa wanted him to stand up and fight. Telling him to get up was psychological as well as physical. He told

Arjuna to get up, not to run away, having made a favourable decision to fight, *yuddhāya kṛta-niścayaḥ*, to either defeat the enemy or die.

Once he was finished with this argument, Kṛṣṇa moved on to a more general standpoint. Arjuna's situation involved a fight. But, because the *Gītā* is a *śāstra*, his situation had to be converted into something that was common, universal.

Therefore, he said:

सुखदुःखे समे कृत्वा लाभालाभौ जयाजयौ ।
ततो युद्धाय युज्यस्व नैवं पापमवाप्स्यसि ॥ ३८ ॥

sukhaduḥkhe same kṛtvā lābhālābhau jayājayau
tato yuddhāya yujyasva naivaṁ pāpam avāpsyasi (38)

sukha-duḥkhe – pleasure and pain; *lābha-alābhau* – gain and loss; *jaya-ajayau* – victory and defeat; *same* – same; *kṛtvā* – having made; *tataḥ* – then; *yuddhāya* – for battle; *yujyasva* – prepare; *evam* – thus; *pāpam* – sin; *na avāpsyasi* – you will not incur

Taking pleasure and pain, gain and loss, victory and defeat to be the same, prepare for battle. Thus, you will gain no sin.

Taking pleasure and pain with equanimity, as though they are one and the same, is the seed for *karma-yoga*. The same applies to gain and loss, victory and defeat, success and failure. Kṛṣṇa sowed the seed here and discussed it later. The whole *Gītā* is based on the psychology of *rāga-dveṣa*s, likes and dislikes.

Rāga and *dveṣa* are the known causes for our sorrow. There may be hundred unknown causes, but they can be reduced to *rāga* and *dveṣa*. *Karma-yoga* was being propounded here by Kṛṣṇa who said, in so many words, 'Do not fight for the sake of *rāga* or *dveṣa*.'

We should not fight just because we do not like someone, nor should we fight just because we like to fight. *Rāga-dveṣa*s are not involved here, only *dharma* and *adharma*. Arjuna was not fighting out of spite, whereas Duryodhana was fighting because of both *rāga* and *dveṣa*. He had *rāga* for the kingdom and *dveṣa* for the Pāṇḍavas. He had always been jealous of them and could not stand to see them ruling. Thus, Kṛṣṇa acknowledged that Duryodhana was fighting out of *rāga-dveṣa*s, whereas Arjuna must fight against *rāga-dveṣa*s. Kṛṣṇa also told Arjuna that in fighting this war, in reality, he was not fighting against Duryodhana but was fighting against *rāga-dveṣa*s. Therefore, the battle was one of *dharma-adharma*.

'Do what is to be done,' Kṛṣṇa said. Here, because what was to be done, happened to be a fight, he said 'Fight!' Because Arjuna was doing his *sva-dharma*, Kṛṣṇa assured him that he would incur no sin, *na evaṁ pāpam avāpsyasi*. In fact, by performing this action, he would gain only *puṇya* and not *pāpa*. To fight this battle was to uphold *dharma* so that *rāga-dveṣa*s would not rule. This, then, is the entire psychology of the *Gītā*.

Let *rāga-dveṣa*s not be the deciding factor. Let the sense of right and wrong prevail in its place. Let the sense of what is to be done and not to be done be the deciding factor. Then you become a *yogī*, as we shall see later. Taking the opposites, pleasure and pain, gain and loss, victory and defeat, as the same, striving to do what is right and thereby incurring no sin, is *karma-yoga* in seed form, *bīja-rūpa*, planted here in this verse. Later in this chapter and elsewhere in the *Gītā*, Kṛṣṇa picks it up again.

Kṛṣṇa had talked to Arjuna mainly about *ātmā*, saying that *ātmā* is something whose very nature is existence, that it is not subject to death, and so on. In fact, he taught Arjuna the nature, *svarūpa*, of *ātmā*. This is called *sāṅkhya*[12] meaning both Brahman and the knowledge of Brahman. The *jñānī*s who have this knowledge of Brahman are also called *sāṅkhya*s.

In the next verse, Kṛṣṇa tells Arjuna that, thus far he had talked about *sāṅkhya*, the nature of *ātmā*. Now he would elaborate upon *karma-yoga* which had been said only in seed form, that is, briefly thus far. In this way, he introduced the two different topics of the *gītā-śāstra* namely *sāṅkhya-yoga* or *jñāna-yoga*, and *karma-yoga*. Because this is an important section of the *Gītā*, Śaṅkara comments upon it in some detail.

Verse 39

Kṛṣṇa elaborates upon karma-yoga

एषा तेऽभिहिता साङ्ख्ये बुद्धिर्योगे त्विमां शृणु ।
बुद्ध्या युक्तो यया पार्थ कर्मबन्धं प्रहास्यसि ॥ ३९ ॥

---

[12] सम्यक् ख्यायते सा वैदिकी सम्यग्बुद्धिः सङ्ख्या। तया प्रकाश्यत्वेन सम्बन्धि तत्त्वं साङ्ख्यम्। (आनन्द गिरि)

...तद्विषया बुद्धिः ... साङ्ख्य बुद्धिः,...सा साङ्ख्य बुद्धिः, येषां ज्ञानिनाम् उचिता भवति ते साङ्ख्याः। (शङ्कर भाष्यम् २.११ उपक्रम भाष्यम्)

eṣā te'bhihitā sāṅkhye buddhiryoge tvimāṁ śṛṇu
buddhyā yukto yayā pārtha karmabandhaṁ
prahāsyasi (39)

saṅkhye – with reference to self-knowledge; *eṣā* – this; *buddhiḥ* – wisdom; *te* – to you; *abhihitā* – has been told; *yoge tu* – but with reference to *yoga*; *imām* – this (wisdom); *śṛṇu* – please listen; *pārtha* – O son of Pṛthā!; *yayā* – with which; *buddhyā*- wisdom; *yuktaḥ* – endowed; *karma-bandham* – bondage of action; *prahāsyasi* – you will get rid of

This wisdom with reference to self–knowledge has so far been told to you. Now, Pārtha (Arjuna)! Listen also to the wisdom of *yoga*, endowed with which you will get rid of the bondage of action.

In verses 11 through 30 of this chapter, the knowledge taught by Kṛṣṇa to Arjuna is *sāṅkhya*, meaning Brahman, the nature of reality of *ātmā*, whereas verses 31 to 38 are purely contextual and have nothing to do with the nature of *ātmā*. These eight verses are, therefore, unconnected to the topic under discussion and are not referred to in the present verse as the knowledge given thus far. They can, however, be brought under *yoga* or *dharma*.

Although not *sāṅkhya-śāstra*, they are contextual in the flow, representing a particular argument from the standpoint of one's *dharma* alone, entailing simple worldly reasoning. The argument presented is not from the standpoint of *paramātmā*; it relates only to what is to be done at a given time.

In verse 11 through 16 of this chapter, Bhagavān Kṛṣṇa introduced the topic under discussion, that is, the nature of *ātmā* and then went on to explain it in depth. Because its subject matter is *sāṅkhya* the chapter is called *sāṅkhya-yoga*. *Sāṅkhya* alone is not discussed here; other topics are also mentioned. For instance, Kṛṣṇa talks about *karma-yoga*, as we are about to see. *Sāṅkhya* however, is definitely the predominant topic throughout the chapter.

It is unlikely that Vyāsa actually gave the *Gītā* chapters their titles. They were probably added by others to indicate the central topic of each chapter. In all the chapters, the topics indicated by their titles are discussed along with other topics. In fact, although the twelfth chapter is called *bhakti-yoga*, there is an even more extensive discussion on this topic, *bhakti*, in the eleventh chapter where Arjuna praised Lord Kṛṣṇa. Similarly, in the chapter entitled *dhyāna-yoga*, there are just a few verses about *dhyāna*, meditation.

Up to the point we have reached in this chapter, *sāṅkhya* has been taught and this particular verse is a provisional conclusion of the topic. For those who study *vedānta-śāstra* it is very important to know why Kṛṣṇa concluded the topic here as he did. The reason is that there are two *śāstra*s within the *gītā- śāstra*, namely the *karma-śāstra* and the *mokṣa-śāstra*. *Mokṣa-śāstra* is Vedanta and the *Gītā* can be considered a *mokṣa-śāstra*. *Karma-śāstra* is the *karma-kāṇda*, which discusses the various *karma*s, rituals, *sādhana*s, means, to gain *sādhya*s, various ends. *Karma-kāṇda* is also Veda but *karma* is its subject matter. The subject matter of *mokṣa-śāstra* is *jñāna*, knowledge.

The difference between karma-yoga and sāṅkhya-yoga

Mokṣa-śāstra can be viewed from two standpoints with reference to the two possible lifestyles, namely *karma-yoga* and *sāṅkhya* or *sannyāsa*. Both are meant for *mokṣa* alone. Because the difference between *karma* and *karma-yoga* must be clearly understood, Kṛṣṇa talked about it. Doing *karma* for the sake of self-purification is *karma-yoga*. It indicates that the person has *viveka*, discrimination, and knows that he or she wants *mokṣa* because, to gain *mokṣa*, one requires a certain mind. And to gain that mind one performs *karma*s, actions, with an attitude. That attitude converts it into *yoga*. Merely doing *karma* is not *yoga*.

For example, there is a set of prayers called *nitya-karma*s, that are to be done daily. One of these prayers is *sandhyā-vandana*. *Vandana* means salutation or prayer, and *sandhyā* refers to three times of day that the prayer is to be performed, in the morning as the sun rises, at noon, and in the evening as the sun sets. The literal meaning of *sandhyā* is 'a time when two periods of time join, meet.' For example, it indicates the time when the day has not yet begun because the sun has not risen, but the night has already rolled away. Similarly another *sandhyā* is when the sun has already set, but the night has not yet come. The third *sandhyā* is in the middle, exactly at noon, neither forenoon nor afternoon. These *nitya-karma*s can be done for the sake of some result later or for the sake of purifying the mind, *antaḥ-karaṇa-śuddhi*.

Why would anyone want *antaḥ-karaṇa-śuddhi*? Because *antaḥ-karaṇa* is necessary for gaining self-knowledge. Therefore, *karma* is performed as an indirect means for *mokṣa* to prepare the mind for gaining the knowledge. When the prayer is done for *antaḥ-karaṇa-śuddhi*, the person has no other result in mind. One only asks that the Lord be pleased with the *karma* and bless him or her with a purified mind. *Karma* may be performed out of joy or out of a concept of duty, as a prayer. When it is performed as a prayer, for the sake of *antaḥ-karaṇa-śuddhi* and *mokṣa*, it becomes *yoga*.

Number of topics come under *karma-yoga* including prayer, devotion, *samādhi*, and *aṣṭāṅga-yoga*, for the sake of *samādhi*, all of which are stated in Śaṅkara's *bhāṣya* to this verse. The verse itself reveals that there is a division or difference between the two subject matters, *sāṅkhya* and *karma-yoga*. If this division is not clear, the entire *Gītā* will appear to be full of contradictions and the listener will be confused. Whereas if the division is clear, understanding is possible. The listener will know what is meant when it is said that for *sannyāsī*s there is only *jñāna-yoga* and for those who are seekers, *karma-yoga* is the means for gaining *mokṣa*.

The subject matter of this knowledge is *sāṅkhya*, a discriminative presentation of what is real and what is not. Every step of the unfoldment is based on discrimination. For example, *deha*, the body, is subject to death, whereas the *dehī*, one who dwells in the body, is not, and so on. The discrimination is presented because people usually think that when *deha* is destroyed, *dehī* is also destroyed. When one is not mistaken for the other, there is discrimination and it is this knowledge that has been given with reference to the reality of *ātmā*. Thus Kṛṣṇa said, 'So far, whatever I have taught you is with reference to *sāṅkhya* – *sāṅkhye eṣā buddhiḥ mayā abhihitā tubhyam*.'

What does knowledge do? It removes ignorance; it is the cause for the removal of ignorance. It cannot do anything else. Ignorance itself is the problem, it being the cause for false pursuits and sorrow, *saṁsāra*. To think that heaven will be an answer to one's problem is *moha*, delusion. *Moha* is thinking that sorrow can be removed by reaching somewhere or gaining something or the other. Knowledge of the reality of *ātmā* removes this ignorance, and therefore, is the direct cause for *mokṣa*.

Karma-yoga is an indirect means for gaining knowledge

Is there also an indirect cause for *mokṣa*? The *bhāṣya* says that there is, and it will be taught. That there are two different topics is clear. Kṛṣṇa himself says, '*sāṅkhye buddhiḥ abhihitā; yoge tu imāṁ śṛṇu*, this wisdom with reference to self-knowledge has so far been told to you; now listen to the wisdom of *yoga*.' Śaṅkara deals with this point thoroughly because, even in his time there was a great deal of controversy about whether the *gītā-śāstra* talks about *karma*, *jñāna*, or a synthesis of the two. There were many such notions, in one form or other. Therefore, *bhāṣya-kāra* spends a considerable amount of time here pointing out the distinction and then saying, 'Now listen to what I am going to say about *karma-yoga*.'

Any discipline is useful because it helps one gain certain composure, mastery over the opposites, as we saw in the preceding verse. Therefore, all disciplines are called *yoga*.

This composure is necessary for the mind to be able to receive the knowledge. To gain the composure you require *karma-yoga. Karma-yoga*, therefore, becomes an indirect means, not a direct means, for gaining knowledge.

You cannot say, 'I will take *karma-yoga* and you take, *jñāna-yoga* and we will both reach the same end.' It is not like that. If *karma-yoga* is presented as a means for gaining knowledge that will destroy ignorance, you may ask why the study of *śāstra* alone cannot do that. The reason is that study of the *śāstra* is capable of delivering the goods only when the *antaḥ-karaṇa* is ready. Therefore, preparing the *antaḥ-karaṇa* is what is meant by *karma-yoga* and is what is going to be discussed here.

Kṛṣṇa praised *karma-yoga*, telling Arjuna that it was as important as *jñāna. Karma-yoga* is not something less than *jñāna* since, without it *jñāna* will not take place. To create a value for *karma-yoga* in Arjuna, Kṛṣṇa praised it in this way. Kṛṣṇa told Arjuna that the knowledge of *karma-yoga* would enable him to destroy the bondage of *karma* –'*karma-bandhaṁ prahāsyasi*.'

Karma here means *dharma-adharma, adharma*, which means *puṇya-pāpa*, the good and bad actions that alone bind the individual. Therefore, it is called *karma-bandha*, the bondage of *karma. Karma* itself is bondage which is destroyed by knowledge made possible by *karma-yoga*.

Now a question may arise here. That is, knowledge destroys only ignorance, *ajñāna;* how is the *karma* destroyed? It is because, with the destruction of ignorance, doership is destroyed, causing *karma*s to fall apart.

So, both *sannyāsa* and *karma-yoga* play a role in the destruction of *saṁsāra*. However, the difference between the two must be clearly understood. Otherwise, it will be said that there are various paths, like the four paths advanced by some, *jñāna-yoga, bhakti-yoga, karma-yoga*, and *haṭha-yoga*. It is also incorrect to say that there are as many paths as there are people.

Addressing this lack of clarity in understanding, Śaṅkara says that because of the grace of Īśvara, you find yourself with a purified mind, the teaching, and the teacher; because of all of this, you gain knowledge. He says, being endowed with this *karma-yoga*, '*īśvara-prasāda-nimitta-jñāna-prāpteḥ*, by gaining knowledge by the grace of the lord,' you will get out of the bondage of *karma*. A life of *karma-yoga* prepares the mind, and knowledge releases you from bondage. But to say here through *karma-yoga* you are released from bondage is to praise *karma-yoga*, which is an indirect means for *mokṣa*. Knowledge is to understand that 'I am Brahman.' There is no other way. The Lord's grace, *īśvara-prasāda*, is in the form of the *guru*, the *śāstra*, the teaching, the type of mind that is required, and conducive circumstances, as well.

It has been everyone's experience that there can be a number of obstacles in any undertaking. In fact, by the time people come to this teaching, they have met with many obstructions in life and have experienced a lot of pain. This is how they come to the teaching, and the obstructions continue. For this undertaking also, then, the grace of Īśvara is required. Thus, you need to be prayerful.

Karma-yoga makes everything possible so that you can gain knowledge which destroys the bondage of *karma*. How many *yoga*s are there for *mokṣa*, then? Only one; knowledge, *jñāna*. There are two lifestyles, *karma-yoga*, living the life of a *karma-yogī* and *sannyāsa*, living the life of a renunciate. This is the vision of the Veda, the only vision that can account for the entire *śāstra*. And Śaṅkara states it very clearly, presenting very well what the *śāstra* says.

Both lifestyles imply knowledge and that knowledge is *mokṣa*. There is no doubt whatsoever here. To gain that knowledge you require a properly prepared mind, for which you require Bhagavān's grace. Therefore, you invoke the Lord's grace so that you have everything ready for gaining the knowledge. This is the only way to remove *saṁsāra*, bondage.

Verse 40

Kṛṣṇa praises karma-yoga

नेहाभिक्रमनाशोऽस्ति प्रत्यवायो न विद्यते ।
स्वल्पमप्यस्य धर्मस्य त्रायते महतो भयात् ॥ ४० ॥

nehābhikramanāśo'sti pratyavāyo na vidyate
svalpam apyasya dharmasya trāyate mahato bhayāt (40)

iha – in this; *abhikrama-nāśaḥ* – waste of effort; *na asti* – is not; *pratyavāyaḥ* – production of opposite results; *na vidyate* – is not; *asya dharmasya* – of this *dharma* (*karma-yoga*); *svalpam api* – even very little; *mahataḥ bhayāt* – from great fear; *trāyate* – protects

In this, there is no waste of effort, nor are the opposite results produced. Even very little of this *karma-yoga* protects one from great fear.

Karma-yoga, not *karma* itself, is involved in the pursuit of *mokṣa*. A person does *karma-yoga*, not for *karma-phala*, but for *mokṣa*. Here, *abhikrama* indicates the beginning of an undertaking and *nāśa* means destruction. You can always begin cultivation, but you may not be able to reap the harvest. Water may not be available, there may be no rain, or the pests may come in large numbers. Anything can happen between these two events. There may even have been floods or too much rain at the wrong time. All of these can destroy whatever cultivation that has been undertaken. But, in this verse, Kṛṣṇa says that, there is no destruction for this undertaking, *abhikrama-nāśaḥ na asti*.

Any *karma* that you undertake has numerous obstacles, but *karma-yoga* has none. It is purely prayer. All the *karma*s that you do form a prayer, as it were. Prayer itself is the result because, to the extent that you are able to pray, your *antaḥ-karaṇa* is taken care of. You are praying for the sake of purifying your mind, *antaḥ-karaṇa-śuddhi*, and the prayer itself produces the result. The result is not later. That you are praying is itself the result of prayer.

Karma-yoga is an attitude

Karma-yoga is an attitude; it is not just action. If it were an undertaking, it would be a problem because it might not end properly. There could be obstructions in between, or something could happen to prevent you from achieving the desired end. For example, if you perform a *vaidika-karma*, scripturally enjoined *karma*, the undertaking can be destroyed altogether by not doing the ritual properly, that is, there will be *abhikrama-nāśa*. Certain omissions and commissions may be there. If something was done incorrectly or if you did not distribute the proper gifts, *dakṣiṇā*, that was required, there would be no result at all. Therefore, in *karma* there can be *nāśa*, destruction, meaning that the desired end cannot be fulfilled at all. This is not the case for *karma-yoga* because you are not interested in the result, *karma-phala*. You are interested only in *antaḥ-karaṇa-śuddhi*, so that you can gain *mokṣa*.

The word '*pratyavāya*' used here has two meanings. Any undertaking that you have not completed due to your own omission has a *pratyavāya-doṣa*, a defect. The desired result is not achieved because the action, a prescribed treatment, for example, is incomplete, inadequate. Suppose you start a treatment, do it for one or two days, and then discontinue it. It creates problems because the treatment must be applied for a prescribed period of time for it to work. Only after a certain point should it be discontinued. To do otherwise will cause *pratyavāya* because you will not get the desired result. Not carrying out the prescribed treatment is a *pratyavāya*, a defect, and not doing it at the right time is also a defect, the second meaning for *pratyavāya*. If treatment is not taken at the right time, your condition may become complicated, yielding results that you did not expect at all and that may be most undesirable. Similarly, when an important *karma*, ritual, is performed, there are a number of satellite rituals to be followed. If these are not followed, there is either no result or a wrong result.

In *karma-yoga*, however, such problems do not exist because we are not talking about *karma*. *Karma-yoga* is an attitude and, being an attitude, if it is with you, it is with you. To the extent that you have it, you have it, and with this attitude, you continue to do *karma*. Previously you did *karma* and now also you do *karma*. It is the change in attitude that brings about the result and makes it *yoga*.

The discipline called *karma-yoga*, this attitude, even in the smallest degree, *svalpam api*, protects you from great fear, the great fear of *saṁsāra – trāyate mahataḥ bhayāt*. Once you have started living a life of *karma-yoga*, you have started a different journey. Till then, you were going in one direction as the water flows, so to speak. Now, it is as though the water has reversed its flow and flows towards the mountain top, instead of away from it. Through *karma-yoga*, you have reversed the process. Once you have started the reverse process, there is nothing to stop you, no matter how many obstacles remain. If you do not complete the journey in this lifetime, then you simply continue it in the next, the *Gītā* assures you.

You might ask how having *karma-yoga* in the smallest degree can help remove the *saṁsāra-bhaya*. It is because that small measure, that shift in attitude, has already initiated the reverse process of the journey. Even if the person dies while pursuing *mokṣa-mārga*, according to Kṛṣṇa, it does not take much time at all to complete it, as we will see in detail in the sixth chapter. The very fact that you reversed the process shows that you are well on your way; that the journey is all but over.

By assuring us that, the reversal itself is a great blessing, the *Gītā* praises *karma-yoga*. In the next verse, Kṛṣṇa talks about one's understanding with reference to the clarity of the end in view.

Verse 41

The means and end are one

व्यवसायात्मिका बुद्धिरेकेह कुरुनन्दन ।
बहुशाखा ह्यनन्ताश्च बुद्धयोऽव्यवसायिनाम् ॥ ४१ ॥

vyavasāyātmikā buddhirekeha kurunandana
bahuśākhā hyanantāśca buddhayo'vyavasāyinām (41)

kurunandana – O descendant of Kurus!; *iha* – with reference to this (*mokṣa*); *vyavasāyātmikā* – well-ascertained; *buddhiḥ* – understanding; *ekā* – is one; *avyavasāyinām* – of the indiscriminate; *buddhayaḥ* – notions; *hi* – indeed; *bahu-śākhāḥ* – many branched; *ca* – and; *anantāḥ* – innumerable

> With reference to this (*mokṣa*), Arjuna, the descendant of Kurus! There is a single, well-ascertained understanding. The notions of those who lack discrimination are many branched and innumerable indeed.

The vision of the *Gītā* is that you are already free and you cannot be improved upon. Since you are already *paraṁ-brahma*, it is knowledge alone that liberates you. To gain it, you should find a teacher and ask for the knowledge. In spite of the availability of such teaching, however, there is no guarantee that you will gain the knowledge because the place where it must occur may not be ready. Knowledge has to take place in the mind. Physically, you may be a mature person, an adult, but it does not mean that the *antaḥ-karaṇa*, mind, is ready for the teaching. Certain *viveka*, maturity, is necessary.

The teaching may be given for the asking, but the mind must be ready for it. You must be desirous of the knowledge, not out of curiosity, but out of *viveka*, discrimination, on your part; only then can you ask for this knowledge and hope to receive it. The mind that is necessary in order to receive the knowledge is accomplished by *karma-yoga*.

You can choose a lifestyle of *karma-yoga*, performing *karma* with a prayerful attitude. Or you can choose a life of renunciation involving only *sāṅkhya*, knowledge. *Sāṅkhya* and *sannyāsa* go together, since *sannyāsa* is taken for the sake of pursuing knowledge to the exclusion of any other activity. By simply becoming a *sannyāsī*, you do not become enlightened. A *sannyāsī* also has to gain knowledge. Similarly, merely by *karma-yoga* you do not gain liberation. You need to gain knowledge. Knowledge, therefore, is common to both. Knowledge liberates, for which you require a mind that has been made ready by *yoga*. A *sannyāsī* may follow the *aṣṭāṅga-yoga* upto its final limb of *samādhi*. But it too comes under *karma-yoga* because it is an action to be done to purify the *antaḥ-karaṇa* for the sake of gaining knowledge. Any technique that helps to acquire steadiness of mind is useful and may be employed even by a *sannyāsī*.

In this verse, *vyavasāya* means *niścaya*, clarity, with reference to what you seek and how you are going to go about gaining it. The *buddhi*, mind, therefore, is said to be *ekā*, single-pointed. There is also only one goal, *mokṣa*, in the form of *jñāna*, knowledge. That the goal, the end, is clear, is itself a very big accomplishment. To see that *mokṣa* is the destiny of a human being, 'this is exactly what I am seeking, which is freedom, freedom from a sense of limitation, and that freedom must be centred on myself alone, that it cannot be outside of me,' means that the goal is clear. You need to see that you are already free and that if you were bound, you could never be free. If you are already free, you should know it to own it. This is the kind of knowledge you need to have first, 'that there is such a thing as freedom I am seeking and it is in the form of *jñāna*.'

If there are hundred seekers and all of them are very clear about what they want, all of them are committed to the pursuit of knowledge, then all these minds have only one goal. *Śraddhā* is common to all of them. Only in preparing the mind can there be differences. Once the mind is prepared, it does not meander. It is like a river with two banks; it has a direction. If the banks themselves are not defined, if they are all over, there will be islands everywhere, just like the river *Godāvarī* before it reaches the sea.

Similarly, like a meandering river, the *buddhi* will meander all over if you do not know where you want to go. Everything will seem to be all right. Or, everything will seem to be important, which means there will be confusion about priorities. If everything seems to be as attractive as everything else, then everything will have the uppermost place on the list of items to be fulfilled. Because they have no *vyavasāyātmikā buddhi*, people are confused about what is to be done first and what later.

However here, whether it is with reference to *karma-yoga* or *jñāna*, the focus is the same because it is knowledge, and knowledge cannot differ. Knowledge is centred on the object and is as true as the object. Therefore, knowledge cannot differ regardless of whether it is my knowledge or your knowledge. One plus one is two for both of us. Because it depends on a valid means of knowledge, knowledge of a given thing does not differ. So too, knowledge for one who takes to *karma-yoga* is the same knowledge as that pursued by a *sannyāsī*. A *karma-yogī* does not do *karma* for the sake of *karma* or *karma-phala*. No one is interested in performing an action for the sake of action. Inaction would be preferable. Action is performed because the person is interested in something. We need to be clear about what this is. A *karma-yogī* does not perform *karma* for *karma*'s sake, nor because it is going to produce a particular result in terms of security and pleasure, and thereby make one a better person. Such a person no longer thinks that way, although one may have thought so originally. A *karma-yogī* like a *sannyāsī* is a *mumukṣu*, seeker, who has a desire for *mokṣa* only. One does not become a *karma-yogī* otherwise.

Without knowledge seeking is endless

Everyone does some kind of *karma* or the other. Who does not? Some are doing more while others are doing less, but everyone performs *karma* with certain ends in view. These ends are numerous, *bahuśākhāḥ*; there are many branches in the sense that each one goes his or her own way. The ways are not just one or two; they are *ananta*, endless, countless. If you go after money, there is no end to the search. If you want power, it too is endless. Pleasures are the same. Whatever you seek, you find the pursuit is endless.

Those who do not have *niścaya*, who are not clear with reference to what they want, have meandering minds, *bahuśākhāḥ buddhayaḥ*. There are too many branches, pursuits, too many channels, and too many expressions. They are indeed countless. Both the means and the ends are countless in number because the same ends can be achieved by different means. For instance, if you take money, or power, there are many gates including 'Watergate,' through which you can gain power and lose it also. A gate can take you in and it can push you out too. Inlets can become outlets. Thus, there are many ways to accomplish the same end because whenever an end is away from you, you can accomplish that end in different ways.

When the mind is not clear, priorities are always a problem. Everything seems to be equally important, whereas for the person who has clarity about what is to be known, there is *ekā buddhi*. With reference to *yoga* too it is *ekā buddhi* because *karma-yoga* is born of *nitya-anitya-vastu-viveka*, discriminating knowledge between what is eternal and non-eternal. All you have to do is to take care of your *rāga-dveṣa*s, likes and dislikes. These have to be neutralised and, to do this, you require *karma-yoga*. If you do not have *karma-yoga* and become a *sannyāsī* or simply pursue knowledge on your own, then too your *rāga-dveṣa*s still have to be taken care of. It does not mean that you should not pursue knowledge. The pursuit of knowledge itself may help you take care of *rāga-dveṣa*s. In fact, no one takes care of every *rāga-dveṣa* and then pursues knowledge. You pursue knowledge and take care of *rāga-dveṣa*s. This was what Arjuna did.

Karma-yoga is something more than an ethical life

Arjuna had been living a life of *dharma*, but it was not totally *karma-yoga*. He had great ambitions. Only in the battlefield did he become a *mumukṣu*. He had fought with Lord Śiva only for the sake of a weapon. He worshipped Lord Śiva because he wanted a blessing in the form of a missile, all for the sake of personal glories. Living a life of *dharma*, an ethical life, Arjuna legitimately sought these personal glories.

Karma-yoga is not merely living an ethical life because you can legitimately aspire for money, power, heaven, and so on. Legitimately, you perform various *karma*s and earn your living ethically. Following sound work ethics and personal ethics means that your life is proper. But such a person is not necessarily a *mumukṣu*, the one who has already discriminated between the real and the unreal, who has *nitya-anitya-vastu-viveka*. *Nitya* means that which is eternal, which is always there, and *anitya* is ephemeral, non-eternal. That 'I am seeking eternally' is knowledge, which you gain in time after you have gone through enough rounds of experience to enlighten yourself. You see that experiences come and go and all that happens is that you become a permanent seeker, an experience hunter. Either you grow out of one experience and want a new experience or you want to repeat the experience. Either way, the experience is *anitya*. The result of any *karma* is always *anitya*.

A person who has thus discovered a dispassion towards the experiences of life is a *mumukṣu*, who can take to a life of *sannyāsa* or *karma-yoga*. Those who take to either lifestyle are *mumukṣus* who have minds that are *ekā*, because of *niścaya- svabhāva*. There is a determination; there is clarity. *Niścaya* does not mean determination in the sense of resolve; it means that there is no doubt. There is clarity with reference to what you want to know.

If you want to know whether a pumpkin is made out of plastic or is real, you ascertain the difference and have *niścayātmikā buddhi* with reference to that object. There is clarity. However, a doubt is created when someone says that what you thought was real is made out of plastic. You can believe that it is real, but the mind is not *niścayātmikā*. You have to ascertain whether it is real with your own *pramāṇa*, with your own hands and nose. You touch it and smell it. Nowadays, a pumpkin can be made to smell and feel like a real pumpkin, so you may also have to scratch it. Once you know it is real pumpkin, then you have *niścayātmikā buddhi*.

From the above example, you can understand that *niścaya* is clarity, not determination. What determination or resolve is there in knowing a pumpkin? Determination is something entirely different. You determine or resolve to achieve something. Here, very well-ascertained knowledge is what is meant by *niścayātmikā buddhi*, clarity with reference to the *lakṣya*, what is to be accomplished in life.

Any target is called a *lakṣya*. Any implied meaning is also *lakṣya* as we have seen before. What is aimed at here is *lakṣya* and the *lakṣya* is very clear. The means also are very clear. You do not choose *karma-yoga* thinking that it will deliver the goods. You choose it knowing well it is *jñāna* that delivers the goods. A *karma-yogī* pursues knowledge while, at the same time, living a life of *karma-yoga*. In this, the *karma-yogī* has *niścaya*, clarity, about the goal. The person has no delusions whatsoever. He or she may practice *āsanas*, *prāṇāyāmā*, and various other disciplines. A number of rituals may also be performed. However, whatever is done is meant for only one purpose.

This integration is clear to the *karma-yogī* because he or she knows that *karmas* by themselves will not produce knowledge. The purpose of the various disciplines is clear. This is what clarity is about. No *karma* is discounted or dismissed; nor is it mistaken for a means to an end that it cannot produce. Therefore, a *karma-yogī* will not complain later that he or she tried everything, none of which helped at all.

People actually say, 'I tried all this and it did not work. It is all a trip.' They do not know what they tried it all for. Whatever one tries can help in some way or other if it is done properly. It is also true that something that helps one person may not help another. For instance, two people may have the same disease with the same symptoms, but only one will be helped by a particular treatment while the other may actually be harmed by it. There are hundreds of disciplines and cures for varieties of diseases, but they do not help everyone because each has its own limitation. No one really knows what a particular medicine will do. Researchers may have watched its effect on rats, but how it will act on a human being, in a male body as opposed to a female body, an Indian stomach as opposed to a Western stomach, they do not know. What happens when you eat meat instead of brown rice is not really known either. It is all guess work and prayer. Because everything has its own limitations, there is no last word.

As long as you understand that you do something for a certain purpose and do not have any delusion about it, everything is fine. You do not become a faddist. Nor do you think that this or that will deliver what it cannot. Only *jñāna* will deliver. And for the sake of *jñāna*, you have to do what is to be done, which requires, *vicāra*, enquiry. It is the thing that produces the knowledge that will deliver. If, for the sake of knowledge, you think you need to do something to be able to know, then do it.

Śaṅkara says here that *viveka* being there, the mind is single-pointed, *ekā buddhiḥ bhavati*. Suppose, the *lakṣya*, the human end, is not very clear, what kind of *buddhi* will there be? It will be a *buddhi* that is dissipated in many pursuits without any definite direction. Those who have no *vyavasāyā* are those with no *viveka-buddhi*, discrimination. They definitely do not have the knowledge born of *pramāṇa* through the study of the *śāstra*. They have no such clarity and, for them, there are many branches, *bahu-śākhā*s, countless means and countless ends, all of which are in the *buddhi*, so that the person wants to do many things, at the same time finally not doing even one of them properly. Time management, therefore, becomes an enormous problem.

To say, 'This job I will do now and the other I will do later,' means you have only one *buddhi*, to say nothing of having only one body! Suppose you want to do all of them and are not very clear about which one you want to do first, what happens is that you cannot even start! Similarly, when it is very clear to you that this knowledge, freedom, is what you want in life, then everything becomes *karma-yoga* for you, even marriage. In fact, marriage is *yoga*. Here both the partners together live a life of *karma-yoga*, preparing themselves for this knowledge.

Having pointed out the difference in understanding, Kṛṣṇa talks about those who are not clear about the end to be accomplished in life.

Verses 42&43

Without clarity priorities are a problem

यामिमां पुष्पितां वाचं प्रवदन्त्यविपश्चितः ।
वेदवादरताः पार्थ नान्यदस्तीति वादिनः ॥ ४२ ॥

कामात्मानः स्वर्गपरा जन्मकर्मफलप्रदाम् ।
क्रियाविशेषबहुलां भोगैश्वर्यगतिं प्रति ॥ ४३ ॥

yāmimāṁ puṣpitāṁ vācaṁ pravadantyavipaścitaḥ
vedavādaratāḥ pārtha nānyad astīti vādinaḥ (42)

kāmātmānaḥ svargaparā janmakarmaphalapradām
kriyāviśeṣabahulāṁ bhogaiśvaryagatiṁ prati (43)

pārtha – O son of Pṛthā!; *avipaścitaḥ* – the non-discriminating people; *veda-vāda-ratāḥ* – those who remain engrossed in the *karma-kāṇḍa* portion of the Veda; *anyat* – anything else; *na asti* – is not; *iti* – thus; *vādinaḥ* – those who argue; *kāmātmānaḥ* – those who are full of desires; *svargaparāḥ* – those with heaven as their highest goal; *bhoga-aiśvarya-gatim prati* – for the attainment of pleasure and power; *janma-karma-phala-pradām* – leading to a better birth as a result of their actions; *kriyā-viśeṣa-bahulām* – many special rituals; *yām imām* – these; *puṣpitām* – flowery; *vācam* – words; *pravadanti* – utter

> Pārtha (Arjuna)! The non-discriminating people, who remain engrossed in *karma* enjoined by the Veda (and its results), who argue that there is nothing other than this, who are full of desires with heaven as their highest goal, utter these flowery words that talk of many special rituals meant for the attainment of pleasures and power and of results in the form of (better) births.

Those who see clearly are *vipaścits*. *Avipaścits* are the opposite, those who do not see clearly. They have no *vyavasāyātmikā buddhi*. There are people who may see, but not clearly, and there are those who do not see at all. Kṛṣṇa is talking here about people who see, but not very clearly, who study and believe in the veracity of the Vedas, but miss the most important teaching of the Vedas namely *ātma-jñāna*. They believe in the existence of the soul after death because it is stated so in the Vedas. They believe in the efficacy of various rituals mentioned in the Vedas for accomplishing various ends and also they believe in the ends like heaven and a better birth. They believe in the capacity of a given ritual to produce a particular desirable result.

Therefore, these are not ordinary people. They are people who have studied the *śāstra* and who believe in its validity. This is why Kṛṣṇa used the word '*avipaścit*' meaning that these people see and yet do not see. They are not to be dismissed because they have studied the scriptures. Śaṅkara criticises them here because they have the words and some arguments which they back up by quoting selected verses. They talk, argue, and try to convince others also, *yām imāṁ puṣpitāṁ vācaṁ pravadanti*. They use well known words, *prasiddhā vāk,* that are very flowery. There are some trees, like magnolia trees, in which, when they flower, nothing but the flowers can be seen. Although the leaves and branches are there, they are hidden by the flowers. These people are like those trees for they speak words which are as attractive as a flowery, blossoming tree, *puṣpitāṁ vācaṁ pravadanti*.

Śaṅkara also uses another expression, *śrūyamāṇa-ramaṇīya,* meaning 'very nice to hear.' As you hear the words, they are very pleasing and wonderful to the ear, but in fact, they are all just so much hype! Such words are used because people who do not have *ekā buddhi,* who have not ascertained what they have to accomplish in life, do not see things very clearly. Those, who do not have this *viveka,* revel in parts of the Veda that talk of means and ends and exclude the Vedanta portion. They are the *veda-vāda-ratā*s.

They may even study Vedanta but only use it for the sake of rituals. Such people revel in many of the *veda-vākya*s because they state clearly the results accrued and the *sādhana,* means, employed for gaining it. There are rituals for having children, restoring health, removing obstacles, and so on. How these elaborate rituals are to be done is also stated. In other words, there is an answer for everything in the *karma-kāṇḍa* of the Veda.

Believing in all these sentences and performing the *karma*s because you want to accomplish various ends is fine. But, the *veda-vāda-ratā*s argue that there is nothing other than *karma*. They say that you must do *karma* and you must accomplish all the various ends. They say that you should not fritter away this life and, of course, we say the same thing! You are given this life and you do not know about the next one. There may be a next life or there may not be. Even if a next life does exist, you may be born a frog and end up on a lab table for experimental purposes. The legs go to someone else's plate and the body goes to the anatomy department of some medical college! Therefore, this life is the only one you can count on.

The *veda-vāda-ratā*s say that *karma* alone is to be done. For them, the greatest gain, *mokṣa*, is *svarga*, heaven. They also talk about this life, saying that the greatest gain is wealth. In other words, the goal is one hundred percent success here and in the hereafter also! This is how they talk. Why do they talk this way?

The people being described here are those who are nothing but desires, *kāmātmānaḥ*. It is not that they have desires. They are made up of desires alone. There is a difference. Going to heaven is the highest end for them; they are *svargapara*s. There are desires and desires for them to fulfil here on earth and for the hereafter; heaven is the ultimate goal!

The result of *karma* is always another *janma*, birth, in one form or other. The *karma-phala*s that you have gathered, ends up in this way. Therefore, the flowery words, *puṣpitā vāk*, of those who talk about a better birth later, being the result of *karma* gathered. They talk words that are *janma-karma-phala-pradā*. These words are in the form of statements such as 'Next time you will be born a prince. You will be born with a golden spoon in your mouth,' and so on. *Kriyā-viśeṣa-bahulā* is yet another adjective used by Kṛṣṇa to describe the words spoken by such people, words that reveal the many and varied *karma*s for attaining pleasure and power, *bhoga-aiśvarya-gatiṁ prati*. *Bhoga* is pleasure and *aiśvarya* is power, overlordship. You want power and overlordship because you cannot accept the helplessness that you feel. So the words, 'Next time you will become a king,' or 'in your next birth, you will be Indra, the ruler of heaven,' are very pleasant to hear. People's minds seem to be carried away by them.

Thus, Kṛṣṇa lamented their plight here. Not only are they themselves carried away by these words, their conviction in their belief is such that they become missionaries and make sure they convince few other people too. The real reason for their missionary zeal is that they are not that sure. Their belief is only a belief, after all. Believers become missionaries because belief means there is a doubt and doubt means you require some strength. If you can manage to convince one person, then you feel secure. There is mutual strength and you help one another. Groups are created in this way so that each member will have the support of other members.

The minds of those who are carried away by these enticing flowery words do not stay with the pursuit of Vedanta. With reference to what you must gain, there is no real clarity because clarity cannot take place in the minds carried away by such words.

The idea here is that if you do not allow yourself to be carried away by words, if you look into them, you will find that they fall apart. And, if the words are not looked into, you will find that they are very pleasing and attractive. Therefore, people who have no discrimination are easily carried off by them.

Verse 44

Without viveka confusion is endless

भोगैश्वर्यप्रसक्तानां तयापहृतचेतसाम् ।
व्यवसायात्मिका बुद्धिः समाधौ न विधीयते ॥ ४४ ॥

bhogaiśvaryaprasaktānāṁ tayāpahṛtacetasām
vyavasāyātmikā buddhiḥ samādhau na vidhīyate (44)

bhoga-aiśvarya-prasaktānām – for those who pursue pleasure and power exclusively; *tayā* – by those words; *apahṛta-cetasām* – whose minds are robbed away; *vyavasāyātmikā* – well-ascertained; *buddhiḥ* – understanding; *samādhau* – in the mind; *na vidhīyate* – does not take place

> For those who pursue pleasure and power exclusively, whose minds are robbed away by these (flowery words), well-ascertained understanding does not take place in their mind.

Kṛṣṇa had already unfolded the knowledge of *sāṅkhya* and then he asked Arjuna to listen to the knowledge unfolded about *karma-yoga*. Thus, when Kṛṣṇa praised *yoga* in terms of *karma-yoga*, as he did here, *sāṅkhya* was not being discussed at all.

Often something is praised by comparing it to something else. In Kṛṣṇa's praise of *karma-yoga,* there was a comparison to pure *karma, karma* done with a particular result in mind, *karma* that is done thinking, 'I perform this *karma* for this given result alone.' The result of pure *karma* is always limited. It is not *karma* done for the sake of *antaḥ-karaṇa-śuddhi,* purifying the mind, so that *mokṣa* will be gained. When *karma* is done for *antaḥ-karaṇa-śuddhi,* then the commitment is to *mokṣa* alone and you become a *mumukṣu.* This is what we call *yoga.*

Karma is generally done for the sake of limited result, whether the *karma* is *laukika-karma,* worldly, or *vaidika-karma* scripturally based. *Karma*s that are done for gaining limited results are *kāmya-karma*s. The *śāstra* includes heaven also as a result of *kāmya-karma.*

The people under discussion, in this verse, know the Veda and quote it, but only for the purpose of establishing the glories of *karma* and their results. *Puṣpitāṁ vācaṁ pravadanti,* words that are very flowery and pleasing to the ear are used in this way by these people, and they talk about the various *karma*s that can be done for gaining *bhoga,* enjoyments, and *aiśvarya,* overlordship, meaning the wielding of power. Enjoyment and power are the only two purposes for which such people dedicate their entire lives. Committed as they are to their own desires, they also talk a great deal about it.

Aiśvarya means overlordship, implying different degrees of power. For instance, a policeman controls people's driving habits. It is one kind of *aiśvarya.* Then there is a police inspector who controls the policemen in his station, and a commissioner who controls the inspectors. There is also someone else above the commissioner. The power wielded by these people is in different degrees and represents different degrees of *aiśvarya.*

Those who are totally committed to *bhoga* and *aiśvarya,* who are engaged in the pursuit of enjoyment and power alone, are influenced by the flowery words that reveal various types of *karma*s, the means for achieving different ends. These words are not only Vedic but also colloquial words drawn from the 'hype' available in the language at that time. Hearing these flowery, seductive words their minds are robbed away. They become *apahṛta-cetasaḥ.* In such people, the discriminative knowledge is totally covered that nothing is clear.

Naturally, such people do not see through these words. They do not see the limitations of the words because their *viveka,* discriminative capacity, is covered. For them, there is no *vyavasāyātmikā buddhi,* no clarity about what they want in life. That *ekā buddhi,* that is always the same, is not there for them. Therefore, there are hundreds of ends to be accomplished and a variety of means also, resulting in confusion. Where there is confusion, priorities are always a problem because you find that you cannot grab everything at the same time. In such circumstances, the mind can never be steady.

Here, in this verse, Kṛṣṇa says that people who are committed to *bhoga* and *aiśvarya,* whose minds are robbed away by enticing words praising the means and ends, do not have clear minds with reference to what is to be accomplished in life. Where such clarity does not take place? In the mind, *samādhau na vidhīyate.*

There is no other meaning for *samādhi* here because Kṛṣṇa was talking about *vyavasāyātmikā buddhi*, with reference to those who have no clarity, *niścaya*, about what they want, people whose minds meander. Therefore, this *vyavasāyātmikā buddhi*, which is *ekā buddhi*, does not take place in the minds of such people. Those who do have clarity have *ekā buddhi*, meaning that there is only one *lakṣya*, one goal, for them. *Mokṣa* is the only goal to be accomplished.

Śaṅkara explains the use of the word '*samādhi*' in his commentary on the verse when he says that everything in the world reaches your mind alone, *samādhīyate asmin*. In the mind alone, the sense objects, the experiences, the entire world that is in front of you, are experienced by you. The eyes may be open and seeing, but what they see has to reach the mind before any seeing actually takes place. Here, *samādhau* means 'in the mind' *antaḥ-karaṇe, buddhau*. And what is it that does not take place in the minds of such people? *Ekā buddhiḥ, vyavasāyātmikā buddhiḥ asmin samādhau na vidhīyate*. Instead, the *buddhi* is a meandering one wanting this and that, like the mind of an active, bright child who is taken to a toy shop and asked to choose only one toy! Total confusion is the result.

When a person who is already confused, studies the Veda, and finds that various actions will produce various results, his or her confusion becomes endless. It is like looking through a catalogue because one wants to buy some gifts. Before long, one finds that one needs something on every page! Not only does one find the whole world consists of so many alluring things, but one discovers through the *śāstra* that the unknown world contains many more equally enticing and attractive things. The mind is thereby robbed away for those who are committed to *bhoga* and *aiśvarya*, and their discriminative awareness is clouded. Therefore, Kṛṣṇa emphasised the importance of having *vyavasāyātmikā buddhi*.

Verse 45

Means and ends are not the only subject matter of the Veda

त्रैगुण्यविषया वेदा निस्त्रैगुण्यो भवार्जुन ।
निर्द्वन्द्वो नित्यसत्त्वस्थो निर्योगक्षेम आत्मवान् ॥ ४५ ॥

traiguṇyaviṣayā vedā nistraiguṇyo bhavārjuna
nirdvandvo nityasattvastho niryogakṣema ātmavān (45)

vedāḥ – the Vedas; *traiguṇyaviṣayāḥ* – have their subject matter related to the three qualities; *arjuna* – O Arjuna!; *nistraiguṇyaḥ* – one free from the hold of three-fold qualities; *nirdvandvaḥ* – one free from the (sorrow of) the pairs of opposites; *nitya-sattvasthaḥ* – one ever established in *sattva-guṇa*; *niryogakṣemaḥ* – one free from the anxieties of acquiring and protecting; *ātmavān* – one who is a master of oneself; *bhava* – be

> The subject matter of the Vedas is related to the three variable qualities. Arjuna! Be one who is free from the hold of these three-fold qualities, from (the sorrow of) the pairs of opposites; be one who is ever established in *sattva-guṇa*, who is free from the anxieties of acquiring and protecting, and who is a master of oneself.

Śaṅkara prefaces his commentary to this verse by saying that for the people who are committed to enjoyments and power, who do not have *viveka-buddhi*, the subject matter of the Vedas becomes *traiguṇya-viṣaya*. This is not a full definition of the Veda which contains much more, including Vedanta. What is meant here is that for those who are committed to *bhoga* and *aiśvarya*, the scriptures will be *traiguṇya-viṣaya* alone. Genreally, you look in the scriptures only for what you want to see. It is like going to a hardware store that has hundreds of things and you look only for what you want. Similarly, there are a number of topics in the scriptures and you look only for what you want.

The Veda provides you with legitimate means for achieving various ends. There are unknown means for known ends, known means for unknown ends, and unknown means for unknown ends. Heaven, for example, is an unknown end because it is not directly known to you. Another *janma*, a better birth, is also an unknown end that the *śāstra* says will be accomplished by a life of *dharma*. *Dharma* is a known means because what is right and wrong is not totally unknown to you. The Veda confirms what means are right and wrong to accomplish a desirable unknown end later, be it heaven or another *janma*.

Previously, you did not know that doing the right thing would get *puṇya*. And by doing the right thing, you not only get the result right here, *dṛṣṭa-phala*, but you also get *adṛṣṭa-phala*, a later result. In this way, the Veda talks about known means for gaining unknown ends. It also talks about unknown means for known ends, like having a child. The ritual that is provided has nothing to do with having a child and is only performed when other known avenues have been explored. If, after consulting doctors and following their advice, there is still no child, then there is definitely some *pratibandhaka*, obstacle. The only way remaining to remove the obstacle is through prayer. Therefore, the Veda gives a ritual, which is a prayer, not a broad-spectrum ritual, but a specific ritual meant solely for having a child.

So, the Veda reveals a variety of means and ends, known and unknown, but all of them are meant only for limited results. These are what people committed to *bhoga* and *aiśvarya* look for. For them, the Veda means only that part which relates to the three *guṇas*, *sattva*, *rajas*, and *tamas*, *traiguṇya-viṣaya*, meaning *saṁsāra*. *Sattva* will give you some happiness, *rajas* will give you agitation, and *tamas* will give you dullness and sorrow. Thus, these three qualities are what give you, *sukha* and *duḥkha*, joy and sorrow. *Saṁsāra* means, that which is within the fold of these three *guṇas*.

In this verse, Kṛṣṇa advised Arjuna straight away not to be one for whom *saṁsāra* is an end to be accomplished; he said, '*nistraiguṇyo bhava*.' In fact, *saṁsāra* cannot be an end to be accomplished; we already have it! We are already within the fold of the three *guṇas* and are seeking freedom from it.

A drowning man does not require more water. He is already drowning and will not want to get into the ocean. Similarly, we are already upto our necks in the ocean of *saṁsāra*. Thus, *saṁsāra* cannot be an end to be achieved at any time; it can only be a situation to get out of. Kṛṣṇa was as though telling Arjuna, 'Do not look into the Veda to find a better place in *saṁsāra*, be discriminative. You have come up to the Veda. Yet, you are trying to perpetuate your *saṁsāra*. It is meaningless. May you, therefore, become one for whom *saṁsāra* is not there, '*nistraiguṇyo bhava*.'

Śaṅkara gives the meaning in short, 'May you be free from desire, *niṣkāmaḥ bhava*.' That is, he says 'May you be free from the desire for pleasures and power.' Let these not be the end in view. Further, 'May you become free from the opposites, the causes of *sukha* and *duḥkha*, *nirdvandvaḥ bhava*.' Śaṅkara also explains *dvandva* and *nirdvandva*. The *hetus*, causes, for *sukha* and *duḥkha*, pleasure and pain, are referred to as opposites, meaning of the word '*dvandva*' here. The one who is free from the opposites is *nirdvandva*, free from the causes of *sukha-duḥkha*, etc. How can you be free from the causes of *sukha-duḥkha*? By not being dependent for your happiness on the presence or absence of anything. Cold and heat, for example, can make you unhappy. If they do, it means that you are dependent on their absence or presence for your happiness. It means that you are not *nirdvandva*.

Another set of opposites is *jaya* and *apajaya*, victory and defeat. They also become the *hetu*, the basis, for your *sukha-duḥkha*. In defeat, there is *duḥkha*, pain; in victory, there is *sukha*, elation. To this you may say, 'Granted I do not want pain, but why should I not be elated?' The reason is that if you are elated, you are definitely going to have pain also. Therefore, may you not let the opposites affect you, *nirdvandvaḥ bhava*. Since you cannot avoid them, may they not affect you. Although you cannot avoid winter and summer, you can allow them not to affect you by maintaining an attitude, a composure towards them. In this way, you need not be carried away by changing situations, which may not always be to your liking.

One whose mind, whose thinking, enjoys a predominance of the *sattvaguṇa* is *sattvastha*. When *sattva* is predominant, there is composure, discrimination, enquiry, and knowledge. *Rajoguṇa*, on the other hand, means agitation, ambition, and so on. Therefore, may your commitment always be to knowledge, *nityasattvasthaḥ bhava*, so that you can discover yourself to be *nistraiguṇya*.

Śaṅkara also explains what *niryoga-kṣema* means in his commentary to this verse. Gaining something that you do not have is *yoga*, something that is not with you, that you want to accomplish, which is desirable. *Kṣema* is protecting what you have already gained. Suppose, you do not have a job and you apply for one and go for an interview. This is done for the sake of getting a job and, therefore, you are doing *yoga*. Once you have the job, it becomes another job to retain it. The whole job of retaining a job is what is meant by *kṣema*. Similarly, earning money is *yoga* and hanging on to it, investing it, is *kṣema*. Having a child is *yoga;* bringing up and retaining the child, not losing it, is *kṣema*. Getting married is *yoga* and making it work is *kṣema*. Therefore, there is *yoga-kṣema* everywhere.

Your problems will always be related to either *yoga* or *kṣema*. Either you do not get what you want or you have lost what you had, or are losing what you have. From the hair on your head onwards, there are hundreds of things that you are losing which cause problems of anxiety, all of which are *yoga* and *kṣema*. Kṛṣṇa, therefore, said to Arjuna, 'May you be a person who has no concern or anxiety due to *yoga* or *kṣema*, *niryoga-kṣemaḥ bhava*.' The whole idea here is that for those who are only concerned with getting what they want and hanging on to it, engaging themselves in the pursuit of *mokṣa* will be very difficult. Kṛṣṇa did not say that you should not go for *yoga* and *kṣema*. Rather, he said, 'Let there be no concern born of *yoga* and *kṣema*.' In other words, 'May you be free.'

Further, Kṛṣṇa said, 'May you be one whose mind and senses are with you, may you be *ātmavān*, a master of yourself.' All of this is explained throughout the *Gītā*. Otherwise, Kṛṣṇa's words would have been merely advice and not teaching. This verse tells us what Kṛṣṇa was going to teach. Here, *ātmā* refers to the body, mind and senses and not to *sat-cit-ānanda-ātmā*, which is already you. Because you have a body, mind and senses, what is being said here is, 'May you have them; may they not have you! May you not be in the hands of your fancies. May your mind be with you. May you become free from indifference and mechanical thinking, *pramāda*. In other words, may you become alert; may you be together.'

Those who are committed to *bhoga* and *aiśvarya* see the Veda as having only the three qualities as its subject matter, *traiguṇya-viṣaya*, whereas it has much more to teach. For example, the contents of this verse are taught in the Veda. Vedanta is also a part of the Veda. Kṛṣṇa was saying that Arjuna had learned enough of the *traiguṇya-viṣaya* part of the Veda. Now it was time for him to study the other part, Vedanta.

Thus, he used the word, *nistraiguṇya*. He then went on to emphasise his point.

Verse 46

The end of seeking

यावानर्थ उदपाने सर्वतः सम्प्लुतोदके ।
तावान्सर्वेषु वेदेषु ब्राह्मणस्य विजानतः ॥ ४६ ॥

yāvānartha udapāne sarvataḥ samplutodake
tāvān sarveṣu vedeṣu brāhmaṇasya vijānataḥ (46)

sarvataḥ – everywhere; *sampluta-udake* – when there is flood; *udapāne* – in a pond or well (any small reservoir of water); *yāvān* – as much; *arthaḥ* – use; *tāvān* – that much; *vijānataḥ brāhmaṇasya* – for the *brāhmaṇa* who knows the self; *sarveṣu* – in all; *vedeṣu* – in Vedas

> For the *brāhmaṇa* who knows the self, all the Vedas are of only so much use as a small reservoir is when there is flood everywhere.

The reason Kṛṣṇa asked Arjuna to go beyond those parts of the Veda dealing only with *saṁsāra* is given in this excellent verse. The word '*brāhmaṇa*' means one in whom *sattva* is predominant. Therefore *brāhmaṇa* is a thinking person, a discriminating person. The word '*vijānataḥ*' qualifying *brāhmaṇa* refers to one who knows what it is all about. For an enlightened *brāhmaṇa*, *vijānataḥ brāhmaṇasya*, Kṛṣṇa says, the portion of the Veda relating only to *saṁsāra* is as useful as the water from a well when the entire countryside has been flooded, *sarvataḥ samplutodake*.

When the wells and ponds themselves are under water, you need not look to them for water!

The various means and ends talked about in the Veda are limited, and any result you derive from the *karma*s enjoined is also going to be limited. The wise person is one who knows he is limitless, *paraṁ-brahma*. When a person is limitless *ānanda*, where is the necessity of looking for *ānanda*? The very nature, *svarūpa*, of the person is *ānanda*. One who has this knowledge does not look for *ānanda*, just as a sugar crystal does not require any sugar to make itself sweeter. Nothing can become sweeter than sugar. Once something has crystallised into sugar, it cannot be sweetened any further. The very crystallisation indicates that the sweetness saturation has been reached. The American system of government may be better than the Russian system, but their sugars are both the same.

In the same way, you are *ānanda* by nature. When you are *ānanda*, you do not require any source of *ānanda*, much less any source of security. But this is exactly what you are seeking through all these means and ends. Therefore, the various means and ends mentioned in all four Vedas will only be of as much use, *tāvān sarveṣu vedeṣu*, as the small ponds and wells are when there is water, water, everywhere! When the ponds and wells are already flooded by water, where is the pond or the well, in fact!

All that Kṛṣṇa said in the previous verses was to create in Arjuna an interest in *karma-yoga*, which Kṛṣṇa has not yet talked about. He had only talked about *sāṅkhya*, knowledge. After asking Arjuna to listen to what he had to say about *karma-yoga*, he began praising it, saying that there was no possibility of losing anything or incurring any wrong result by its practice because *karma-yoga* is not mere *karma*. He then pointed out that people do *karma*s because they do not know what they really want. Since what they want is not very clear, they go after enjoyment and power. However, when what is wanted is very clear, the mind is settled. The storm is over and there is no more interest in experimentation. There is no more trying to see if this or that will do it. All experimentation stops because there is clarity with reference to what is wanted, which itself is a great blessing.

Then it becomes a question of whether you want to live a life of *sannyāsa* or *karma-yoga*, the only two lifestyles open to you. Between the two, you have a choice. In fact, there is very little choice because it depends upon where you are. *Sannyāsa* may not be advisable at all; therefore, *karma-yoga* is preferable. Both have a common goal; both are meant for *mokṣa* in the form of knowledge. A *sannyāsī* works for *mokṣa* and so does a *karma-yogī*.

Although Kṛṣṇa has talked so much about *karma-yoga*, he has not actually said what it is. In the next verse, he explains it.

Verse 47

Choice is only in action – never in the result thereof

कर्मण्येवाधिकारस्ते मा फलेषु कदाचन ।
मा कर्मफलहेतुर्भूर्मा ते सङ्गोऽस्त्वकर्मणि ॥ ४७ ॥

karmaṇyevādhikāraste mā phaleṣu kadācana
mā karmaphalaheturbhūrmā te saṅgo'stvakarmaṇi (47)

karmaṇi – in action; *eva* – only; *te* – your; *adhikāraḥ* – choice; *phaleṣu* – in the results; *mā kadācana* – never; *karma-phala-hetuḥ* – the author of the results; *mā bhūḥ* – do not be; *akarmaṇi* – in inaction; *te* – your; *saṅgaḥ* – attachment; *mā astu* – let it not be

> Your choice is in action only, never in the results thereof. Do not think you are the author of the results of action. Let your attachment not be to inaction.

Śaṅkara takes the *karma* mentioned in this verse as purely *vaidika-karma*, scripturally enjoined *karma*, because that was what was under discussion. We shall look at it as any *karma*, rather than strictly *vaidika-karma*, since *karma-yoga* allows for it and Śaṅkara has said nothing to rule out the propriety of this approach.

The word '*adhikāra*' here means choice, your right, something over which you have power. This choice is only with reference to *karma*, the actions you perform. However, *mā kadācit*, at no time, is there a choice with reference to the results of actions, *phaleṣu*. Thus with reference to all actions, you have a choice, but with reference to the results thereof you have no choice whatsoever. This is a very simple statement of fact. Even for *vaidika-karma* there is a choice; you can do it, you need not do it, and you can do it differently. This capacity to do, not to do, and to do it differently makes you a *karma-adhikārī*. An animal, on the other hand, is not a *karma-adhikārī* because it does not have a choice in its actions, but is motivated only by its instincts.

When Kṛṣṇa told Arjuna that he did not have any choice over the results of action, he was not giving him a piece of advice; it was a statement of fact. A statement of fact is not an advice; it is teaching. That water boils at 100° centigrade is a statement of fact. Here, also, with reference to actions and their results, the statement, '*karmaṇi eva adhikāraḥ te mā phaleṣu kadācana*, your choice is only in action, never in the results thereof,' is a statement of fact.

The definition of *karma-yoga* in the *Bhagavadgītā* is two-fold. One is, *samatvaṁ* (*Gītā* 2.48). The other is *karmasu kauśalam* (*Gītā* 2.50). The first one is obviously one's response to pleasant and unpleasant results of *karma*. Therefore it is one's attitude with reference to *karma-phala*. The second one is choice of means in keeping with *dharma*. Among many means of *karma* to accomplish desired ends one has to choose the means in keeping with *dharma*. Therefore, the choice or discretion is the meaning of *karmasu kauśalam*. Both definitions are necessary and need to be understood. Only then can *karma-yoga* be properly understood.

Samatva and *kauśala* are defining words for *karma-yoga*. *Samatva* is based on the sentence in the present verse, *karmaṇi eva adhikāraḥ te mā phaleṣu kadācana*. *Samatva* means sameness and sameness of mind is *karma-yoga*. *Karma* is also definitely involved in *karma-yoga*. Otherwise there would be no *karma-yoga*. There can be *karma* without *yoga* but without *karma*, there can be no *karma-yoga*. If *karma-yoga* implies *karma*, then there must be sameness, *samatva*, with reference to *karma*. Let us see where this sameness is possible.

Sameness is not possible in *karma* itself because you cannot do the same *karma* during the entire day, day after day, throughout your entire lifetime. Cooking is one *karma*, eating is another, and stirring the food in the pot is yet another. Removing the pot from fire is a different *karma* altogether. The *karma*s are therefore endless–sitting, standing, switching the tove on, switching it off, and so on. Obviously, *karma*s cannot be the same because they are different.

Perhaps we can say that the *karma-phalas*, results of *karma*s, are the same. Again, it is not possible. For instance, when you heat water there is a result, and when you switch off the stove, there is entirely a different result. The water that was hot slowly becomes cold as it loses its heat. Thus, different *karma*s are done for different results. The results vary. If you do not get a different result when you switch the stove on and off, you have a different kind of problem in that the stove is not functioning properly. Normally, the results will be different. So, neither *karma*s nor their results can be the same. In fact, different *karma*s are done for different results.

Every *karma* is desire-based; every action presupposes desire.

Desires are not the same, and you do different *karma*s because you want different results. Desires are meant for results alone and the results are different. Thus, *samatva* is not in the *karma*, or its result, or the desire upon which the *karma* is based.

In fact, *samatva* can only be with reference to your attitude concerning the results of action. While you have a choice over your action, you are helpless with reference to the result. You are not Īśvara; you are just an individual with limited knowledge and power, with any number of desires. You have countless likes and dislikes, *rāga-dveṣa*s to be fulfilled. Therefore, you undertake various activities.

Karma is totally desire-based

Whatever be the nature of the *karma*s you do, they are all meant for fulfilling your *rāga-dveṣa*s commonly called desires. *Rāga* is with reference to what you want to have, what you want to retain, and *dveṣa* is with reference to what you want to avoid, what you want to get rid of. That you want is *kāma*, desire. What you want is defined in terms of either *rāga* or *dveṣa*.

Everyone has likes and dislikes. They form the nature of an individual and are common to all. They may reveal how cultured, how sophisticated a person is, but the fact that everyone has likes and dislikes is common. There is no exception. Because of the presence of *rāga-dveṣa*s alone, there are various activities and all the *karma*s undertaken are meant to produce the desired results because both *rāga* and *dveṣa* are result oriented. You want to accomplish this, 'this' being the result. It is not that you want to accomplish *karma*; you want to accomplish the result and for its sake, you do *karma*.

Since you perform a particular *karma* to accomplish a specific end, it seems as though you have figured out which *karma* will produce which result. But then you find that what you had figured out is not that predictable. In fact, you find that you can get exactly the opposite of what you thought you would get! What you want is one thing, but what you do seems to be either inadequate or inappropriate as it produces the opposite result. If you analyse any result, you find that it always falls into one of the following categories–exactly what you want, more than what you want, less than what you want, or the opposite of what you want.

If you want to cross the road and you do so, finding yourself on the other side, you got what you wanted. The result was as you expected. If you wanted to cross the road to catch a bus and, while doing so, someone offered you a ride right to where you were going, you got more than you expected from crossing the road. Had you not crossed the road to get to the bus stop, you would not have met the person who offered a ride. Or, having wanted to cross the road, you may have found yourself in the hospital, having only reached the middle!

The result can be entirely different from what you wanted. You may have wanted a job but, instead, the person who interviewed you for the job you did not get, sold you what turned out to be a winning lottery ticket. You did not get the job you wanted, but you did get something entirely different and, in this case, the most desirable, million dollars!

These situations are possible because you are not omniscient. Also, there is helplessness involved. Therefore, keeping your fingers crossed may not be enough; you may be better off by crossing your toes also!

What is up the sleeve of the future is always a wonder because you simply do not know what is coming next. You do not even know what your next thought is going to be, even after having lived for forty or fifty years! Yet, you talk about the future! This, then, is the helplessness of the *jīva*.

The limitations of the jīva

Wherever the *jīva* is, power wielded by that *jīva* is limited. Even Indra's wings are clipped. He does not have total overlordship because there are other domains where he is not even given entry. He may say, 'I am Indra!' and still be told to leave. Some one might say, 'You might be Indra in your own *loka*, but here you do not even have the status of a mosquito. Please go!' Thus, you find that no one's wingspan enables him or her to go everywhere. Such freedom and limitlessness in terms of knowledge and power, is not there for anyone. Your knowledge and power are both limited. For want of knowledge, you cannot avoid what you want to avoid. Knowledge is not limitless. If it were, there would be no problem. Exactly what you want to happen would happen. You would know that this action would produce that result.

Limitless knowledge means limitless power too. If you have limitless power, you do not need to do anything other than think a thought. The thought you have will shape itself perfectly. God did not commit a mistake when he thought that an avocado would be the fruit that has a big pit; it was meant to be that way. It would not be an avocado if it did not have a big pit. An apple, on the other hand, should not have a big pit; only then is it an apple. This is how the creation is.

When there is omniscience, the thoughts are clean and complete. Nothing needs to be done. Thus, God did not need six days to create the world. It is not that on the first day God did this and on the second, third, fourth, fifth, and sixth days he did a few more things. Or that, having created everything else, he found there was no light and had to put a sun up there. How could he have done the other things with no light? How could there be a first day without a sun? A day is due to the sun alone. Nor is it that God was doing a job that required him to do certain things on the first day so that he could paint on the next. On the third day he did not look at what he had done before, and decide that it was unsatisfactory, and rearrange the whole thing. God is not an architect! If the Lord is omniscient and omnipotent, what is required is just a *saṅkalpa*, thought.

Even we, as mere mortals, do better in our dreams! We think of a world and it is there in front of us. If we think of a mountain, the mountain is up! If we think of a lion on the mountain, the lion is there! If we think of an African jungle, it is there! We need not do anything nor do we have to go anywhere. It is all there; we created it. And if we want everyone to come and see our creation, they come in droves, in every imaginable means of transport, because we have the capacity to create them all in an instant. A capacity similar to this in the Lord, of course, is what is meant by omnipotence. That is why he is called a *satya-saṅkalpa*, one whose *saṅkalpa*, thought, is *satya*, true. When the thought is there, the whole thing is there. This is omnipotence.

The results of karma can never be predicted

However, for you, power and knowledge being limited, certain situations cannot be avoided. For want of power, you cannot avoid illnesses or accidents, like falling from a tree. You know that you are falling and you may even know that you are accelerating downward at a speed of 32 feet per second per second. You know very well, but so what? Down you come! It matters not whether one is a great physicist or an ignoramus who has no understanding of gravitation at all. All that is known is that he or she is coming down! But, for want of power, neither of them can avoid falling.

Limitation with respect to power and knowledge, then, is the status of an individual. If this is so, Kṛṣṇa's statement that your choice is only over action, *karmaṇi eva adhikāraḥ te,* is very important. You may say that there is really no choice because so much is determined by your past, and so on, but it is an endless debate. The point is that you do have a choice. To understand that much is enough. You can perform a given action, you need not do it, or you can do it differently; this is a capacity you have. Therefore, you do have choice, which is why you do not do certain things and you can force yourself to do other things, even though you do not feel like doing them. Or you can do them differently.

So as a human being you have *adhikāra,* choice, but you have no choice whatsoever over the results of action. Once you perform *karma,* the result is taken care of. What choice do you have? If you had a choice over the result, you need not have done the *karma* at all. If you had any power over the result, you would always be successful. Because you are not omniscient, you do not know that a *karma* will produce a particular result. No one knows the ways of *karma*. To know how *karma* is going to produce its result and what result it is going to produce is very difficult to figure out. This is because, your own past *karmas* may be inhibiting the results of the present *karma*. Thus, all we know is good and bad luck.

Sometimes you find yourself in the right place at the right time and, at other times, you are in the right place but not at the right time. In order to get the desired result, you have to be at the right place at the right time, but you do not always know which is the right time and place. You can only keep trying. It means that there seems to be an element called luck involved here. But, you do not call it luck; instead, you refer to it as previous *karma*. If the cause-effect relationship is understood, there is no question of luck. It is simply replaced by past *karma*. Being at the right place at the right time is *karma* and being at the wrong place is also *karma*. Therefore, you really do not know; you can only go by your choice, your free will.

The use of free will

You have a free will, just as there is a free wheel in a car. You can only go by that. Whether the brakes will work is anyone's guess. You can check them, but at any time, they can give way. That is why they have special ramps every few miles on the highways for runaway trucks whose brakes have failed. It is not that every truck driver takes to the road without first having checked the brakes, but that anything can go wrong at any time. It is because when things are put together, their tendency is to fall apart. Whether it is a human system or any other system, the tendency is always the same. This tendency to fall apart applies to relationships and houses too. In fact, you often spend more time maintaining your house than living in it!

Therefore, here, you can only go by your free will. There is nothing else you can do. What the result will be depends on so many unknown factors that it is always a question mark. Whether what you want from a particular *karma* will happen as you expected is anyone's guess. Since you do not have a complete choice over the results of action, you had better recognise this limitation. Limitation here is not helplessness. Helplessness is felt only when you do not accept the limitation and, therefore, it has a negative connotation, whereas acknowledging limitation is being objective. Therefore, dismissing the concept of helplessness from our minds, we recognise our limitations as individuals.

Because there is a limitation in knowledge and power, you cannot figure out exactly what you want. Nor do you know exactly what any given action will produce. When you understand this limitation, you can respond to the results of action in terms of *samatva*, sameness of mind. Any result can be responded to in either of two ways, dispassionately with *samatva* or like a yo-yo, elated because you got what you wanted or suicidal because you did not. And, if someone saves you from suicide, you will respond again like a yo-yo, feeling that you could not even commit suicide successfully, thereby developing yet another complex! This yo-yo response is because you think that you are the author of every result of action when, in fact, you are only the author of action.

Depression is created by some onerous responsibility you have assumed, one that is absolutely illegitimate. You take what does not belong to you and then smart under it because you cannot always produce what you want. This is a fact.

Then why do you not just accept the fact? All that is required is to accept it objectively, to accept that this is how the creation is. This is what you are made up of and no one else, even a Swami, is made any differently. All human beings have the same types of limitations. According to the *śāstra*, even the *deva*s have the same limitations, albeit with some small differences between them just as there are between human beings. Similarly, while the President of the United States definitely has more power than other people, yet he cannot appoint anyone he chooses as a judge. Once he realises that he does not have a majority, he begins to withdraw quietly, proving that even presidential power is limited. Everyone's thumb has its size! Even if it swells, it can only become so big.

You are only a karma-hetu

Similarly, everyone has power only to a limited extent. You can improve your power, but only to a limited degree. Knowledge also is limited and can be improved upon only in a limited way. Anything else, such as your skills, health, longevity, your environment, are limited and can be improved upon. But the improvement is always limited. Thus, there can only be an improved limitation. If this fact is understood clearly, then you do not take up the responsibility of authoring the results of action, as you like. If you think you are the author of the results of action, you cannot but have a sense of failure. Is it not true?

What is being discussed here is *yoga;* it is not *jñāna*. It is simply an empirical, pragmatic attitude and has nothing to do with *ātmā* and *anātmā*, the reality, Brahman, and so on. It is simply looking at yourself as you are in the world, seeing how the world is and your own position in the scheme of things. To convey this attitude to Arjuna, Kṛṣṇa said, '*mā karmaphalahetuḥ bhūḥ*, do not be the cause of the result of action, because you are not.'

Then what are you? You are merely the *karma-hetu*, cause of action, not *karma-phala-hetu*, the cause of the result of action. You are the author of *karma*, but not of the result thereof. Given this fact, the most appropriate thing to do is to take whatever result comes with an even attitude, *samatva*. By not getting what you want, you become wiser. Not getting what you want does not mean you have become a failure. It means only that your limited knowledge has improved somewhat. You have become wiser. Or, if the result is more than you expected, you are also wise. In addition, if you try again, thinking you will again get more, and the result is not as you expected, you say, 'What luck!' Still, you have become wiser. Whether you gain or do not gain, there is always wisdom to gain. There is definitely something to learn. To know that you are the author of the action, but not of the result thereof, produces *samatva*.

In this context, *samatva* is nothing more than a pragmatic attitude. To make it *karma-yoga*, we have to go one step further because *karma-yoga* implies the acceptance of Īśvara. Unless you accept Īśvara, there is no *karma-yoga*. There are people who are pragmatic and who take whatever happens in their stride and then proceed because they know it is all in the game of living and doing. They are more or less pragmatic, more or less objective, because, of course, they have their bad days. This is simple *samatva*.

Karma-yoga requires the recognition of Īśvara

Samatva as *yoga*, on the other hand, requires one more aspect, recognition of Īśvara. Once you say the result of your action is not within your control, and that it is taken care of, the next question is, what is it that takes care of it? The results are taken care of by laws, the body of which we call either the law of *dharma* or the law of *karma*. In fact, it is law of *karma*. Other than the physical laws that you know and do not know, there does seem to be another order of law. You always find orders within orders. For example, when you lift your hand, physical laws are naturally at work, but there are also many other laws involved. Lifting the hand involves will. You have a thought and up it goes! There is nothing physical about this aspect of lifting your hand. You need not push any button.

Although you find that this physical body, anatomical structure, is standing on this earth according to physical law, it is born into this world by biological as well as physical laws. There are also physiological and psychological laws. You find, then, that there are laws within laws so that when you perform a simple *karma*, even your past *karma*s may infringe upon the result that you want from this particular action. You really do not know if this happens or not. Whether you find yourself lucky or unlucky, you appreciate that there is some law at work. Whatever is the law that governs the *karma* and its result is the law of *karma* and that law of *karma* includes various other laws too.

No law is created by you. You are not the author of any law. If you were, you would not be helpless. You would always be able to accomplish whatever you wanted. There would be no problem. You could even reorganise the law to suit you. You would not even need to cover the distance to reach a place; the place would come to you. Or, you could think about being in a place and you would be there immediately. However, it is not the case. Therefore, we try to go by the laws and, at the same time, we do not know very much about them.

As one who knows very little, you can only go by the known laws and know that the laws are not authored by you. Then the question may arise as to who authored them? Certainly not your grandfather. He and his father and grandfathers before him were themselves born of these laws. They existed because of the laws and they left the planet because of the same laws. The laws that bring people into being also take care of them and, then, take care of them for good! You find these laws always operating and no given person can be considered to be the author of them. To recognise the author, then, is to take one more step.

You must first recognise that the author of the laws produces the results of action and that the laws themselves do not. When you go one step further and recognise the author as Īśvara, the Lord, you have the beginnings of *karma-yoga*. There are still more steps to go, but this, at least, is the beginning, 'the creation is not created by me.' Therefore, whoever did create it is Īśvara and this same Īśvara is the giver of the results of action.

When you receive money from someone, month after month, the postman is the one who actually gives you the money.

However, it does not mean that the postman is a benevolent person who goes about distributing money to everyone like Santa Claus. There is someone other than the postman who is to be thanked. Similarly, *karma-phala,* the result, is produced by the law and the law itself is produced by another intelligent being. That all-intelligent being, Brahman, is Īśvara, the Lord, with reference to the creation. He is the Overlord, in fact, the top man, and the boss, not limited by time, space, or anything.

The Veda comes in here to address the question of the author and his creation. From that Brahman alone, the five elements are born; therefore, with reference to the creation, Brahman is considered to be Parameśvara. Not only is he Parameśvara, the author, the maker of the creation, *nimitta-kāraṇa,* he is also the material. This is another important point. Because *jagat,* the world, is *mithyā* having no independent existence apart from Brahman, it requires only a *mithyā* cause, called *māyā*. *Māyā* also being *mithyā*, has no independent existence apart from *satya,* Brahman, whereas *satya* does not depend upon anything for its existence. In *māyā* there is *satya.* Being *mithyā* the *jagat* is also *satya* and so are we. It is not that originally there was Brahman and now we have to cross over everything to reach that Brahman. Everything is Brahman. Wherever there is *mithyā* there is *satya* and that *satya* is the *adhiṣṭhāna,* basis, for everything.

Therefore, that Parameśvara, who is *paraṁ-brahma,* who is the *nimitta-kāraṇa,* cause of the creation, who is *sarvajña,* omniscient, and *sarvaśaktimān,* omnipotent, is also the *upādāna-kāraṇa,* material cause of the creation. Thus, he is not only the maker of the results of action, but also the very law, the very result of action, in fact. Because our topic is *karma-yoga*, we will not go beyond this point here since, to do so, becomes *jñāna*. We say, then, that Īśvara is the maker of the laws and that the laws are not separate from him. The result of action–coming as they do from the laws that are not separate from Īśvara, the Lord – come from Īśvara. It is this recognition of Īśvara that converts the simple *samatva* to *karma-yoga*.

Without Īśvara, what we have been discussing is nothing more than a pragmatic approach to life. But here, we are dealing with a purely religious approach, which is entirely different because it recognises Īśvara, the Lord, as the *karma-phala-dātā*, giver of the results of action, and oneself as only the doer of action, *karma-kartā*. Therefore, to be a *karma-yogī*, one has to accept Īśvara.

Īśvara now has one more definition, one who has all-knowledge, *sarvajña*. And when we say *sarvaśaktimān*, we mean that he is all-powerful and has all skills, being the creator of everything. Another defining word we have seen is *karma-phala-dātā*, the giver of the fruits of action. These definitions eliminate the problems that arise when it is said that God created all beings. I may naturally ask why God created a person blind and another lame. If I am told that, being God, he is justified to do whatever he likes and that I should not question him, I will definitely ask why God's creation is even talked about since it is obviously nothing to boast about, especially when I am also told that he is all-compassion! I am asked to worship and love him, but when I look at this creation with so much human suffering, God's compassion falls apart for me. Then I am told that he is justified in whatever he does and I am supposed to love him. How can I?

The explanation for human suffering

The answer to all of this is that not only is he the creator, he is also the creation. The *jīva*, the individual, is non-separate from and, therefore, not different from Parameśvara. The individual self, *ātmā*, is Brahman and, therefore, all that is there is *ātmā* that is Brahman. *Ātmā*, the *jīva*, is not created. When you say a person is created, it is only with reference to a given physical body at a given time. The *jīva* is due to ignorance alone and, ignorance being beginningless, the *jīva* is *anādi*, beginningless. The *sūkṣma* and *sthūla śarīra*s, subtle and gross bodies are born in the sense that the subtle body always adapts itself to the gross body. You also find that the *sūkṣma-śarīra* is always in keeping with the *sthūla-śarīra* it adapts itself to. Thus, only a cat's *sūkṣma- śarīra* is present in a cat's body, and not a human *sūkṣma-śarīra*. Otherwise, the cat will not mew at you; it will talk to you, saying 'Come on, it's morning. Get up!'

You find that in this world of living beings, in each unit of creation, there is a *sthūla-śarīra*, which is in keeping with one's *karma-phala*. Īśvara as the *karma-phala-dātā* is not to blame. Nor do you need to justify Īśvara's action either. To do so would only be justifying your own! You did it; you got it. You asked for it; you had it, and you have it also. You will continue to have it because you keep asking for it. Therefore, no one else is responsible for what comes to you. Every *jīva* is responsible for what that person is. This is the kind of responsibility that is assumed by the *jīva* here. You have a capacity, a free will, to perform action. You can do whatever you want to do, but the result is always something that is taken care of by the law that is Īśvara.

Why at all is this understanding necessary? To answer this question, you have to go a little more into the human psyche, defined here in the *Gītā* as a psyche that operates on the basis of its own *rāga*s and *dveṣa*s, likes and dislikes. The entire *Gītā* psychology is dealt with in terms of *rāga* and *dveṣa* alone. No other norms are used. *Rāga* and *dveṣa* can be in a spelt-out form or in an unspelt form. You may not know that you have a liking for something until you happen to see it closely. Otherwise, how is it that even though you meet so many people every day, one day you suddenly meet someone you like a lot. Of all the people you have met and known, why this particular one? In fact, it is a wonder to your family and friends that you chose this person as a life-partner when someone else, whom they thought more suitable, was already after you!

There are lot of likes and dislikes embedded in you that are not shaped properly. You may call them unconscious, subconscious, or whatever, but still, they are unshaped likes and dislikes, meaning that they are not very clear to you. But they are evoked when situations appear before you. All these are included in the term *rāga-dveṣa*s. *Rāga* is that which is pleasing or desirable to you and *dveṣa* is that which is undesirable in your view. Both *rāga* and *dveṣa* are purely according to you alone, they are totally limited to the individual. Wherever psychology is involved, you must always know that it is according to you alone. When you say this person did something wrong to you, it is only according to you. In fact, if you ask the person he or she will say you got what you deserved. Thus, it is always a matter of perception, yours and the other person's.

Avoidance of the undesirable is also a fulfilment

What should you do when your whole life is dedicated to the altar of *rāga-dveṣa*s? To fulfil *dveṣa*, you must stall what you do not want to happen, and when you succeed, you are very happy that you avoided it. Some people have become great devotees simply by avoiding what could have been a very serious accident. They say that God saved them. When you avoid something unpleasant, it is a great relief. People talk as though it is a great accomplishment when, really, you did not accomplish anything. The incident that could have created a problem for you simply did not happen. Yet you are so relieved that you become a devotee! Why? Because something was avoided. Thus, avoidance is a fulfilment, too.

So you see that what you do not want and you have, you have to get rid of. What you want to have, you should have; and what you already have that is desirable to you has got to be retained. This is *rāga-dveṣa*. Therefore, your activities are nothing but *rāga-dveṣa*s. Your psychological problems are also nothing but *rāga-dveṣa*s; what else are they? If you had no *rāga-dveṣa*s, you would have no problems, just like in deep sleep. Until you sleep, you may have *rāga-dveṣa*s – the pillow may not be comfortable, the room may be chilly or you may have hundred other complaints. But, once you have gone to sleep there are no likes and dislikes.

This *rāga-dveṣa* argument is simple and complete. Some things should be kept simple because more you complicate them, more the problems are there. This applies especially to psychological problems which are based on your anxiety to fulfil likes and dislikes and, also, on the judgements you make with reference to their non-fulfilment.

The necessity for *karma-yoga* is because people are in the hands of *rāga-dveṣa*s. Their behaviour, activities, responses and prejudices, cultural, racial, and otherwise, are controlled by their likes and dislikes. Prejudices and preferences come under *rāga-dveṣa*s, whether they are binding or non-binding. It is said that even gods have preferences. When we worship Lord Gaṇeśa, for example, we offer him a sweet *modaka* that we say he likes. It is based, of course, on our own like. Thus, we impute our own *rāga-dveṣa* to Bhagavān too. We say Gaṇeśa likes this, Śiva likes that, and so on, so that we can deal with the deity as a person. We cannot deal with someone without preferences, but the idea is that our preferences should be non-binding.

Preferences should be non-binding

In everyone's life there are preferences that are non-binding in nature and those that are binding. Preferences that are binding in nature are the ones we have to deal with. About those that are non-binding, we need not do anything. In fact, the *gītā-śāstra* does not deal with them at all because they are not a problem. Whenever the *Gītā* talks about *rāga-dveṣa*s, it does so in terms of one's binding likes and dislikes only. Even Kṛṣṇa, the Lord, who taught the *Gītā*, had preferences. For instance, he always chose the flute; he did not come with a guitar or a *vīṇā*. We know that he knew what he was talking about, as evidenced by his life. Whether we take him as a wise man or as Īśvara, the Lord, we cannot say that he had *rāga-dveṣa*s, even though he had his preferences.

This is to point out that there are non-binding and binding *rāga-dveṣa*s and we must deal with the binding ones. The binding *rāga-dveṣa*s are those whose fulfilment is a must for you and in whose non-fulfilment you feel you are a loser, struggler, a seeker, all-empty inside. You are a seeker because you have hope; you want to fulfil your likes and dislikes. These *rāga-dveṣa*s are binding in nature and they make you act. Action does not take place without reason. When you undertake a course of action, there is definitely a like or dislike involved. *Rāga-dveṣa* is commonly called want or desire, *kāma*. These likes or dislikes are behind every kind of action.

We are talking here about the person who has just entered into a life of *yoga*, for which the cause is *karma*. Therefore, *yoga* should definitely include your likes and dislikes. When you say, 'I am a *karma-yogī*,' you have to accept that you havelikes and dislikes to fulfil. To do this, you have to undertake activities which produce results and these results are not always what you want because you have control only over your actions, but not over the results. The results come from Īśvara. First you accept Īśvara and then you accept Īśvara as the *karma-phala-dātā*, the giver of the fruits of action. When you do this, you have a purely religious attitude, the attitude of a *bhakta*, devotee.

The recognition of Īśvara as the *karma-phala-dātā* is what makes you appreciate Īśvara in your daily life. Even when you fall down and incur an injury, Īśvara's grace is at work. That you fell down and hurt yourself does not mean that his grace is absent. Under the law of *karma*, you escaped greater injury; you did not break altogether. You can fall down and receive a small injury, not be injured at all, or end up in the hospital, never to return! All these are possibilities. Therefore, as a devotee, we see Īśvara working constantly.

The attitude of a bhakta

No matter what the *karma-phala* is, you confront Īśvara. When you open your mouth to talk, when your tongue is able to produce the words that tumble out one after the other, it is because Īśvara is at work. *Karma* you can do, but *karma-phala* is something that takes place because of the laws that are the Lord. Therefore, every action producing a result, even a small action like opening and closing the eyelids, is the work of the Lord. In every action, there is an intended result that sometimes happens and sometimes does not. It is according to the laws. Therefore, as a *bhakta*, a devotee, you continuously confront Īśvara as you receive your *karma-phala*.

Since every result comes from Īśvara, you take it as *prasāda*, a Sanskrit word that does not have an exact English equivalent. The word 'grace' has a somewhat intangible connotation, whereas *prasāda* covers both the tangible results and the intangible, the grace. When you offer a fruit to the Lord, it comes back to you, given to you from the altar. The fruit that comes back is called *prasāda*. For an English word for *prasāda*, to exist, the concept must be there; and it is not there. A dieting person may refuse a laddu, but not when he or she comes to know that it is from Tirupati Venkateśvara. What converted the laddu into *prasāda*? The tangible laddu becomes *prasāda* because the person now knows that it comes from the Lord.

Therefore, what converts a *karma-phala* into a *prasāda* is purely your recognition that it comes from the Lord. It is not just a statement; it is seeing, understanding. This is where the word 'experience' can be used, if at all. It is a way of looking at the whole thing. Recognition that Īśvara is the *karma-phala-dātā* converts every *karma-phala* into *prasāda*. Therefore, *prasāda* is not an object; it is a way of looking at an object.

Prasāda is purely symbolic. If a person with diabetes eats laddus, his blood sugar levels will definitely rise, not because he is eating *prasāda* but because he is eating laddus. *Prasāda* is an attitude, a way of looking at an object, which itself is born of understanding that it comes from the Lord. Therefore, *prasāda* can be anything, a fruit, leaf, sugar crystal, laddu, or even a child. Because, in India, a child is looked upon as *prasāda*, there are many people who are named as Prasad. Anything that comes to you as *karma-phala*, as a gift from the altar of Īśvara is *prasāda*, which includes the attitude with which you receive it. *Prasāda* is not received and then cast away disrespectfully; it is received in a certain manner. It is this *prasāda*, then, that brings about *samatva*, sameness of mind.

Once everything is *prasāda*, you have nothing really to complain about. You have only something to learn. Therefore, when the *karma-phala* comes, you take it as *prasāda*. If it is more than what you wanted, you take it as *prasāda*. If it is less than what you wanted, it is still *prasāda*. And if it is exactly what you wanted, opposite to what you wanted, or different from what you wanted, it is still *prasāda*. As every *karma-phala* comes, there is sameness in your reception of it. This is what Kṛṣṇa is saying here when he tells Arjuna not to be the cause of *karma-phala*. The *karma-phala-hetu* is Īśvara, not Arjuna. Arjuna is the cause of action, but not the cause of its results.

Further, Kṛṣṇa said, '*akarmaṇi saṅgaḥ mā astu*, let there be no attachment to inaction.' Action itself is not the problem. It is your response to the result of action that is the problem. Thus, inaction here means fear of action, not of action as such, but fear that the results you want will not come. Even before you begin doing an action, you expect to fail. Therefore, Kṛṣṇa told Arjuna that *karma* itself is not binding. Nor does *karma-phala* bind. It is the response to the *karma-phala* that makes *karma* seem like a bondage. Thus, let there be love for action, but let the results be received by you as *prasāda*.

Verse 48

Definition of karma-yoga

योगस्थः कुरु कर्माणि सङ्गं त्यक्त्वा धनञ्जय ।
सिद्ध्यसिद्ध्योः समो भूत्वा समत्वं योग उच्यते ॥ ४८ ॥

yogasthaḥ kuru karmāṇi saṅgaṁ tyaktvā dhanañjaya
siddhyasiddhyoḥ samo bhūtvā samatvaṁ yoga ucyate (48)

dhanañjaya – O Dhanañjaya (Arjuna)!; *yogasthaḥ* – being steadfast in *yoga*; *saṅgam* – attachment; *tyaktvā* – abandoning; *siddhyasiddhyoḥ* – with reference to success and failure; *samaḥ* –

the same; *bhūtvā* – being; *karmāṇi* – actions; *kuru* – do; *samatvam* – evenness of mind; *yogaḥ ucyate* – is called *yoga*

> Remaining steadfast in *yoga*, Dhanañjaya[13] (Arjuna)! perform actions abandoning attachment and remaining the same to success and failure. This evenness of mind is called *yoga*.

The recognition in your life that Īśvara is the *karma-phala-dātā* brings about an attitude, called *samatva*. *Rāga* and *dveṣa* are the cause for attachment, *saṅga*, which prompts you to say, 'This should or should not happen to me.' The *rāga-dveṣa*s become a *saṅga* with reference to any *karma-phala* that is going to affect you. Then only is it *rāga-dveṣa*. But if you have the attitude of *samatva*, *rāga-dveṣa*s are neutralised. They are rendered incapable of creating any kind of reaction in you. The *rāga-dveṣa*s manifest themselves through various *karma*s and in time by your attitude of *samatva*, they become neutralised. This is what is meant by *karma-yoga*.

Staying or abiding in *yoga*, being *yogastha*, means enjoying this attitude of *samatva*. The evenness of mind with reference to both *siddhi*, success, and *asiddhi*, failure, is called *yoga*. It is what makes you a *yogī*. *Samatvam yogaḥ ucyate* is a separate sentence in this verse that defines *yoga*.

As stated earlier, there are two definitions for *karma-yoga* in this chapter. The first one is this one, *samatva*, whereas the other one is, *yogaḥ karmasu kauśalam*.

---

[13] *Digvijaye prabhūtaṁ dhanam ajayad iti dhanañjayaḥ* – one who acquired large wealth during his conquest tour is Dhanañjaya.

Scripturally enjoined karma and the four āśramas

*Vaidika-karma*s, scripturally enjoined actions, are made up of many rituals. These rituals can be divided into four categories – *kāmya-karma*s, meant for producing given results desired by a given person; *nitya-karma*, daily rituals; *naimittika-karma*, occasional rituals; and *prāyaścitta-karma*, rituals to right any wrongs done.

There is a ritual called *putrakāmeṣṭi* for those who want children. Daśaratha, Rāma's father, had no children. Being a king, he had to have children so that there would be someone to rule the kingdom after his death. Naturally, he wanted children. Therefore, he performed the ritual, *putrakāmeṣṭi* and had four children. *Putrakāmeṣṭi* is still done and known to work, even in fairly recent times. Perhaps, any ritual in any religion will work if the person performing it has *śraddhā*, faith, in it. *Putrakāmeṣṭi* is a very expensive ritual, so that only a rich man can do it. We see here how the Veda can be very tricky. This kind of *karma* or ritual is an example of *kāmya-karma*, a ritual performed purely for a given desired result.

Even though *kāmya-karma* was designed and unfolded by the Veda, which tells you that a given *karma* will produce a particular result, it does not mean that *kāmya-karma* is for *antaḥ-karaṇa-śuddhi*. Particular rituals are mentioned for particular results and are purely for desired objects, *kāmya*, such as the desire for a child. Similarly, there are many rituals mentioned in the Veda whose result is said to be heaven and they too are *kāmya-karma*s.

Then there are *nitya-karma*s and *naimittika-karma*s, which can be considered together. *Nitya-karma* means a ritual or prayer that is to be done every day. Which rituals or prayers are to be done, depends on a person's status. An unmarried person, *brahmacārī*, has two fold *karma* to perform. The first is a prayer, *sandhyā-vandana*, enjoined by the Veda to be done three times a day, at sunrise, at noon, and at sunset. The second is a fire ritual, *samidhādāna*, performed once in the morning and evening, wherein the prayer is, 'May I become brilliant. May I learn. May I be a person who has total control over myself.'

For a married person, a house-holder, *gṛhastha*, the *nitya-karma*s differ. *Sandhyā-vandana* continues, whereas *samidhādāna* is replaced by *agni-hotra*, another fire ritual, which is also a *nitya-karma*. This *karma* has to be performed twice a day, morning and evening. On the day of marriage, the fire is lit and it is not allowed to die until the person takes *sannyāsa* or dies. If the married person dies before *sannyāsa*, this same fire is used for the cremation of the body. Thus, the life of a house-holder is a dedicated, religious life. The person can do anything inbetween, but these *nitya-karma*s have to be performed every day without fail.

When a married person withdraws from the duties of a house-holder and enters the next stage of life called *vānaprastha-āśrama*, a few more *karma*s are added. These are of the nature of meditation. In this third stage of life, *sandhyā-vandana* and *agni-hotra* rituals must still be performed. There is no way of escaping these *karma*s, except by *sannyāsa* or death. In *sannyāsa* the vow or commitment, *dīkṣā*, taken earlier to perform these rituals is given up and the person is no longer bound to do these *karma*s. One's hair and the various accoutrements of the earlier initiation are also given up, including the *gāyatrī-mantra*.

Only the '*om-kāra*' remains and a few essentials. By saying that he is no longer interested in gaining heaven, having children, and so on, and by saying that no one should be afraid of him thereafter, a man becomes a *sannyāsī*. It is a very serious commitment! But until *sannyāsa*, he must definitely perform the various rituals enjoined by the Veda.

Performing these *nitya-karma*s, you do gain results in the form of *puṇya* or *antaḥ-karaṇa-śuddhi*. But the main point here is that they are to be done daily and generally they are done. *Naimittika-karma*s, on the other hand, are those rituals to be done on particular occasions, at a particular time, on a particular day, like on the anniversary of the death of one's mother or father. Such a ritual called *śrāddha*, which must be performed monthly on the new moon day and a more elaborate ritual is done on the anniversary date itself. This, too, is done until *sannyāsa*. *Śrāddha* is not done daily and is only done if one's father or mother has passed away. Because these *karma*s are done on a particular occasion, *nimitta*, they are called *naimittika-karma*s.

*Naimittika-karma*s are generally performed by house-holders, although the *śrāddha-karma*, mentioned above, is done by everyone except *sannyāsī*s. Other *naimittika-karma*s performed by house-holders include the rituals done, on the day when the northern and southern Solstices begin. Eclipses of the sun and moon are also recognised in this way, based on ancient methods of calculation. It has been said that if you think the *śāstra* is false, wait for an eclipse!

Finally, *karma*s that are done to right a wrong, called *prāyaścitta-karma*s, are performed when what is not to be done was done or there was some omission during the performance of any ritual. Thus, a particular *karma* can neutralise the results of wrong action, be it an omission or a commission. An example of *prāyaścitta-karma*s is *cāndrāyaṇa* wherein you regulate the amount of food you eat for one month. Beginning on the full moon day, you take the amount of food that you would ordinarily eat. The next day, you cut it down by one-fifteenth and the second day, by another fifteenth, continuing in this way until the new moon day, during which you eat nothing at all. Then you begin again on the first day after the new moon, on the *prathamā*, by taking one-fifteenth, then two-fifteenths on the second day, adding increments of one fifteenth portion each day until the full moon day, when again you eat as before. During this entire period, certain rituals are performed. *Prāyaścitta-karma* then is the fourth type of *karma*, a *karma* of atonement.

The purpose of karma-yoga

In *karma-yoga*, you give up *kāmya-karma* and perform *nitya-naimittika-karma*s as an offering to the Lord, as well as for purifying the mind. According to the definition of *kāmya-karma* stated above, *kāma* is always involved. This *kāma* is given up in *karma-yoga*. Śaṅkara says here that by performing these various *vaidika* rituals for the sake of *antaḥ-karaṇa-śuddhi*, you become a *karma-yogī*. Otherwise, you are only a *karmī*. When you perform *karma* for a particular end alone, you will gain only that end. You will not gain the mind necessary for gaining knowledge that is *mokṣa*, because you have no *vyavasāyātmikā buddhi*.

If, however, you have *vyavasāyātmikā buddhi*, all your *karma*s are directed towards one goal, *mokṣa*. And for *mokṣa*, you require an *antaḥ-karaṇa* that is prepared. *Mokṣa* is not gained through *karma*; *karma* is only for preparing the *antaḥ-karaṇa*. Thus, preparing the *antaḥ-karaṇa* through *karma* becomes *yoga* for you.

In the *Gītā*, the word '*karma*' is usually used with reference to *vaidika-karma*. However, when Arjuna was asked to do *karma*, it was not a ritual to be performed. He was to fight; it was his duty. Śaṅkara also confirms this. Fighting is 'to be done,' obligatory *karma* of a *kṣatriya*. Thus, *karma-yoga* covers all activities. And if *karma* is taken to mean any action performed, which is the actual meaning of the word, then you have to look at *karma* from the standpoint of your entire life. The actions then referred to will be those activities that you perform in the attempt to fulfil all your *rāga-dveṣa*s.

Since you do have *rāga-dveṣa*s, and they need to be neutralised, what will you do? You cannot just command yourself to give up your *rāga-dveṣa*s as you would do with a hat. *Rāga-dveṣa*s are there; they are not just given up. They constitute the person. However, when you perform actions with a sameness of attitude, *samatva*, towards the results of your actions, your *rāga-dveṣa*s are neutralised. This attitude is *karma-yoga*.

The attitude of *samatva* mentioned in this verse is not with reference to the action itself; it is with reference to the *phala*, result, of any action. This attitude is present in the Vedic culture and is called *prasāda-buddhi*. We have seen that even children are named Prasad because they are thought of as *prasāda*.

If your son is *prasāda*, then you are also *prasāda* to your parents. Your physical body is not only *prasāda* to others, but also to you. A house is *prasāda*, the food cooked, offered to the Lord, and then eaten is also *prasāda*. This *prasāda-buddhi*, attitude is an important aspect of *karma-yoga*.

It is important to note here that any translation that says you should perform action without expecting a result has no basis in the Veda. Such an interpretation serves only to create additional complexes. Try as you might, you find that you cannot do *karma* without expecting some result. The truth of the matter is that no one can perform action without expecting a result. Even a dull-witted person cannot engage in an activity without expecting a result. Therefore, this meaning of *karma-yoga* must be abandoned.

Another definition of karma-yoga

Although this verse presents a particular line of argument, the fact is that this is not the only way of looking at it. Let us, therefore, look at the other definition of *yoga*, *yogaḥ karmasu kauśalam*. *Karmasu* means 'with reference to actions.' Thus, with reference to actions, *yoga* is *kauśala*, meaning the state of mind or the disposition of a *kuśala*, who is an expert.

Different meanings are given to this word, *kauśala*. It is the abstract noun of *kuśala*, expert, the qualities that make an expert. Thus, it has been said that *kauśala* is expertise or skill. From this meaning, a modern translation for this second definition of *yoga* has come about. People say, 'Skill in action is *yoga*,' which seems to convey that it is efficiency of some kind. Although efficiency is always desirable, it is not what *karma-yoga* is about. The inappropriateness of this translation will become clear as we proceed.

Here, the 'skill-in-action' interpretation, meaning that if you are very skilful in action you are a *karma-yogī*, must also be abandoned. This is a secular translation designed to bypass Īśvara. There are people who read the *Gītā* without recognising Īśvara at all. Those who want *karma-yoga* without recognising Īśvara as the *karma-phala-dātā* simply cannot have it. There is *karma-yoga* only when Īśvara is recognised. *Karma-yoga* is a religious attitude, a devotee's attitude. There is no way of escaping this. There is no such thing as secular *karma-yoga*.

They say that when there is skill in action, when there is efficiency, the person is a *karma-yogī*. A *yogī* may be efficient in whatever he does, but how can he be efficient if he is given a new job or is just beginning to learn driving, for example? He has not yet acquired the necessary skill and, therefore, he will be inefficient in this respect. Thus, a *karma-yogī* can definitely be inefficient in a given area. Conversely, merely because a person is efficient in a given area does not mean that he is a *yogī*. A pickpocket, for example, is very efficient in picking pockets, whereas if you try to do it, you will get caught. Even before you pick, you will be picked up! Picking pockets is not easy. Not only do you have to be skilful in getting an object out of someone's pocket, you also need to be a master of deception in order not to be accused. Such a person may be skilful in action, but this is definitely not *karma-yoga*. A *yogī* in action may be skilful, but this does not mean that skill in action is *yoga*.

The meaning of kauśala

What does *kauśala* mean in this definition? To understand this, let us go back to the first definition, *samatvaṁ yogaḥ ucyate*, where *yoga* is defined as sameness. Suppose a man says to the Swami, 'I have my *rāga*s and *dveṣa*s. For instance, I like my neighbour's money. He has plenty of it and has converted it into gold, which he keeps in his safe. I definitely have a *rāga* for his money and I also have a *dveṣa* for this man. I dislike him because he is so blatant about his riches. He thinks he is such a big shot that he is always showing off. Therefore, I detest him but I love his money! I want to fulfil my *rāga-dveṣa*. Also, I happened to listen to your talk yesterday. Until then, I had never heard of *karma-yoga*.'

'Now I want to ask you, will I continue to be a *karma-yogī* if I carry on with my plan? I have been working on a tunnel between my house and the room in which my neighbour's safe is located. I know how to open the safe. I know how the whole thing has to be done. I have only one hour's work left and then I will be there in the room. I was going to do it last night but, having listened to your talk, what I was doing started to bother me. I want to be a *karma-yogī*. It looks to me as though I can continue with my plan and still be a *karma-yogī* because you say I have a right, a choice, over my action. I have already sent my wife and children away and I will not give you their address. I am telling you only this much, hoping that you will not tell anyone. I intend to join them tomorrow. Tonight I am off. My house is already empty and, since I have been renting it, I have nothing more to claim from it. Therefore, everything is set and I am going to work'

'Of course I am taking a risk. You say that Īśvara is the *karma-phala-dātā*, giver of the fruits of action. So I am going to work one more hour tonight so that I can clear out the safe. Of course, I do not know what is going to happen. There may be nothing in it at all. My neighbour may have already cleared it out and put the gold elsewhere. Or, the gold may be there but I may get caught. I may be shot or beaten up. I may be handed over to the police and have to be in jail for a number of years. Anything is possible. Or, I may get away with it also. My hope, of course, is that I will get away with it. Therefore, whatever comes, I am going to take it as *prasāda*. If I get all the gold, fine, it is *prasāda*. And if I am beaten up, I will take every stroke as *prasāda*. Will that be okay? Do you think I am a *karma-yogī*? Do you think that when the Lord says in the *Gītā* that a *karma-yogī* is very beloved to him, is he referring to me? That is what I want to be. I want to be beloved to the Lord. If I take everything as *prasāda*, will I be beloved?'

It is for this person's sake that we have the definition, *yogaḥ karmasu kauśalam*. *Kauśala* is discretion in your *karma*, in your choice. It is not an untethered choice without norms. It is choice with discretion, meaning that your choice should be in keeping with certain norms. This is another important aspect of *karma-yoga*. The first definition is with reference to the results of action, *karmaphale samaḥ bhūtvā*, which defines *karma-yoga* as an attitude of *samatva*. Whereas, this definition is with reference to the action itself, *yogaḥ karmasu kauśalam*.

Kauśala is your capacity to interpret correctly. This capacity to interpret with reference to norms for human interaction is the discretion, the expertise. The norm for human interaction is *dharma* and the opposite is *adharma*. *Dharma* and *adharma* form the standard norms. They are not absolutes in that they have to be interpreted according to the given situation. The person who can interpret them properly is *kuśala*. *Dharma* and *adharma* are not to be interpreted according to convenience, but must be in line with what is proper. Proper interpretation of *dharma* is what is meant by *kauśala*. *Kauśala* is *yoga* because, again, you are not in the hands of your *rāga-dveṣa*s when you exercise discretion in your choice of action.

Dharma and adharma are universal

The man in the story has *rāga-dveṣa*s. His *rāga* is for the money and the *dveṣa* is for his neighbour to whom the money belongs. He wants to go by his *rāga-dveṣa*s. And they are totally against *dharma* and *adharma*. What should not be done, he is doing. Therefore, he is going against *dharma*, which means he is doing *adharma*. But could it not be said that this is all a man-made order? No.

Suppose, in a particular country there is no law against stealing. Does it mean that if someone takes away what belongs to another, would it still be called as not stealing? No, it would still be called stealing. This is not the same, as the man-made convention that traffic shall proceed on the right. We proceed on the right because to do otherwise is a definite risk to life and limb, and it is also illegal. Even if you say you are ready to take the risk, the police will not let you because you are not the only one involved. Other people will be in danger. We can then describe convention as man-made.

But is the law against stealing man-made? No, the law that stealing is not right is not man-made and therefore it is universal. If no one had anything that was his or her own, there would be no stealing. Even though there would be people, there would be nothing to steal and therefore no one can steal from the other. However, everyone has something of his or her own and, therefore, there is going to be stealing. Even a Swami has a begging bowl and a *mālā*. These are two important *liṅga*s, symbols, of a *sādhu* and he is supposed to carry them. There are thieves for this too, especially now that they have become rare and therefore costly. Thus, even *sādhu*s can lose few of their possessions because, as long as anyone has something that is his or her own, there is such a thing called stealing. This is universal.

Like *adharma*, *dharma* also is universal, and is not man-made. *Dharma* is something that is commonly sensed by a human being and is meant for human interaction. I live and let live. I want to be left alone in the sense, I do not want the few possessions I have to be stolen. And, at the same time, I let others live in the same way.

There is a particular order that is sensed commonly and this order, called *dharma*, is the very basis upon which you are supposed to interact with your fellow beings. The scriptures confirm this and also say that if you go against the order, your action produces *pāpa* for you. The scriptures do not tell you what is right and wrong, *dharma* and *adharma*, 'Thou shalt do this; thou shalt not do that,' and so on. They merely confirm what you already know. You do not need anyone to tell you this. Indeed, your knowledge is such that you tell everyone else!

Scriptures the world over merely confirm the existence of a common sense *dharma*. It is not that they came into the world at a particular period of time and, finding there was no *dharma*, established one. People knew what was right and wrong before the scriptures came along.

Choice in action implies norms

Common sense *dharma* is there for a human being because he or she has a choice in action. This choice implies a set of norms, which must be known. If these norms, the *dharma*, were not there, the creation would be defective. You could not have been given a choice without being given the norms that go with the choice. It would be something like giving a Ferrari without brakes to someone who is drunk and who also does not know how to drive!

Having been given a choice, the norms should be common to all without any education being necessary. This is an important aspect of *dharma*. To be given a choice, but no knowledge of the norms, would also be a defect in the creation. If you did have to be educated about these norms, then no one would have the same opportunity to receive this education. If so, then some people would be stealing or getting hurt because they never knew they should not steal or get hurt. They were never taught. Therefore, without any education, you know that you should not steal or get hurt. I also know that others do not want to be stolen from or be hurt. This, then, is the common norm.

What is equally common to you and me is the norm on the basis of which we can choose our actions. What you do not want from others, you find others also do not want from you. Therefore, there is a common norm, *dharma,* and the person who is able to interpret his or her to-be-done actions in terms of *dharma* has *kauśala.*

Let us now complete the story of the man who wants to continue his plans to steal his neighbour's money and take the result as *prasāda.* He will only be fulfilling one part of the *karma-yoga* definition. The other part will remain unfulfilled because there is no *kauśala.* He is not even interpreting; he is going against the very *dharma.* If someone wanted to rob him, how would he take it? He would not allow it, which means that he should not rob anyone else because it is a wrong action. If everyone were simply to say, 'so what?' to all the norms, what we would have is only confusion. Even today, the society is not that confused, that we are prevented from conducting our lives. People more or less do follow some norms. If everyone were to do exactly what they wanted, they would be hitting others, robbing them, and so on, all of which would be going against *dharma.* There would be no order, only confusion, and no one could live his or her life.

There is order in the world, even today, which is why we are able to live peacefully. Some of us do not even have gates or fences because there is *dharma.* Since there are boundaries that people seem to follow, we cannot say there is no *dharma.* Of course, there is *adharma* too, and because choice is there people are sometimes going to abuse their power of choice.

The man who wants to rob his neighbour has to be told, along with Arjuna, that he must conform to *dharma,* even though his likes and dislikes prompt him to do otherwise. What happens to likes and dislikes then? They are curtailed at the level of action. They must be aligned with *dharma* and *adharma*. If there are lingering likes and dislikes, which are not in conformity with *dharma* and *adharma*, there is no one in your heart to claim them. You do not follow them; you do not join them. They rise and they die a natural death. There is no one to claim them because you have no connection with them. They simply rise as fancies and die as fancies. You go only by what is right and wrong.

Summary of the definition of karma-yoga

To summarise, we have a two-part definition for *karma-yoga, samatvaṁ yogaḥ ucyate* and *yogaḥ karmasu kauśalam*. With reference to the results of your actions, there is *samatva*, sameness, in your response. Gaining this attitude of *samatva* depends upon the recognition of Īśvara as the *karma-phala-dātā*, the giver of the fruits of actions. Whatever result you gain, the laws do not cheat you in any way. Therefore, as a *karma-yogī* you have the same attitude, towards both desirable and undesirable results of your actions, *karma-phale samatva-buddhiḥ*. Then, with reference to action itself, because there is choice involved, as a *karma-yogī*, you exercise your choice based on norms. These norms are indicated by the rules of *dharma* and *adharma*. They are universal, common to all, *sāmānya-dharma*.

Even universal laws require interpretation

Although common to all, *sāmānya-dharma* must be interpreted to accommodate given situations so that it is appropriate to the situation. This interpreted *dharma* is referred to as *viśeṣa-dharma*.

Ordinary laws also have similar provisions. That you should keep to the right in traffic is a law that is universal in the United States. Suppose a huge truck is coming towards me in the same lane. By keeping to the left the truck driver is doing the wrong thing and I am doing the right thing. But, I am driving a very small, lightweight car. By keeping to the right, I am right, but if I refuse to interpret the law and do not budge an inch because I am right and he is wrong, I will certainly suffer the consequences.

Suppose, however, I swerve to the left, making sure that I am not going to hit anyone in the process, and then return again to the right when I have avoided the truck, then I have saved the situation. If a police officer sees me going to the left, he or she will not give me a citation, but will go after the truck driver instead. I interpreted the law rightly and the officer will probably congratulate me for escaping serious injury or death.

Every law has an exception. No one has ever made a law, including Bhagavān, without there being an exception. For example, Newton's law of gravitation applies only in some areas. If you are in a spaceship, peanuts cannot be eaten in the same way as they are eaten here. Instead of going into your mouth when you toss them up, they will go to the right or to the left. Even though Newton's law is really Bhagavān's law, still it does not operate in the same way in all places at all times. Thus, there are no absolute laws.

That there are no absolute laws, however, does not mean that there is no universality. *Dharma* is universal because you feel the same way as others feel. However, even what is universal has to be interpreted according to the situation. Although you expect people to speak the truth to you and people expect the same from you, sometimes you may have to tell a lie in order to save someone's life. This is *viśeṣa-dharma* or interpreted *dharma. Viśeṣa-dharma* is when someone other than yourself is the beneficiary of the lie. Thus, the differences between *dharma* and *adharma* with reference to speaking truth depends on whether you are the beneficiary of the lie.

Other examples of *viśeṣa-dharma* are those *dharma*s imposed by the scriptures, which are only valid insofar as a given place, time, or culture is concerned. For instance, a *brāhmaṇa, kṣatriya* and a *śūdra* have respective duties to perform within the framework of the Vedic culture only. Therefore, these duties are *viśeṣa-dharma.*

Sāmānya-dharma and *viśeṣa-dharma* should always be the governing factors when exercising your choice with reference to a given action. You cannot go by your *rāga-dveṣa*s alone. When you do go by *dharma* and not by your *rāga-dveṣa*s, you are living an ethical life. Such a life, however, may not be *yoga. Yoga* comes into the picture only when Īśvara is taken into account.

The role of Īśvara in karma-yoga

The *Gītā* does not discuss Īśvara immediately. It only does so in the third chapter. Another verse, in the eighteenth chapter, explains the role of Īśvara in *karma-yoga.*

यतः प्रवृत्तिर्भूतानां येन सर्वमिदं ततम्।
स्वकर्मणा तमभ्यर्च्य सिद्धिं विन्दति मानवः ॥ १८.४६ ॥

yataḥ pravṛttirbhūtānāṁ yena sarvamidaṁ tatam
svakarmaṇā tamabhyarcya siddhiṁ vindati mānavaḥ
(Gītā 18.46)

Through one's duty, worshipping him from whom is the creation of the beings, by whom all this is pervaded, a human being gains success.

The Lord is not only the creator but also the creation. Therefore, the creation is non-separate from Īśvara who is both the efficient and the material cause of the creation. No *kārya*, product, is separate from the material of which it is made. The status of being both efficient and material cause is, therefore, what is meant by Īśvara, which is why the creation is non-separate from the creator.

The creator, on the other hand, is independent of the creation in the sense that even without the creation, the creator remains. At the time of dissolution, for example, the entire creation goes back to Īśvara who alone remains. The creation is like the dream world you create, without which you remain as you are. While the dream world is not independent of you, you can be without it, as you are in deep sleep. Similarly, the creation is not separate from the creator, the Lord.

Anything in the world that is naturally created can be looked at as *īśvara-sṛṣṭi*, just as anything you make may be said to be *jīva-sṛṣṭi*, because your free will is involved. There is, however, only some truth in you being the creator of anything.

When you say that the house you built is your own creation, you find, upon analysis, that the statement is not totally true. Because your will and effort are involved, there is some truth to it. But, the earth that the house is standing on is not created by you. Nor are the laws, which allow the house to stand. The materials that are necessary to build and maintain the house are also not created by you. In this way, you come to see that your 'creation' depends on many aspects, which are not created by you. Therefore, nothing is really created by you although, for the time being, you can assume that there is such a thing as *jīva-sṛṣṭi*.

The laws of creation are not separate from the creator

Your physical body is not created by you. The powers that are necessary to create are not created by you. These are *īśvara-sṛṣṭi*, alone. *Īśvara-sṛṣṭi* includes law of *dharma* too. These laws are not created by you; they are only sensed by you. Gravitation is sensed by people and by monkeys as well. Birds also seem to sense it. They know that when they want to fly, they must flap their wings in order to take off into the air. Every creature seems to know at least some of these laws because they do what they have to do.

The laws that are instinctively known by animals are known to us by common sense. The law of *dharma* is also known to you in the same way. Without any education whatsoever, without being taught, you know what is right and wrong. Although this knowledge is generally called 'conscience' it is actually your simple common sense knowledge of *dharma* and *adharma*, what is right and wrong. It is basic knowledge that everyone has, about a fact that is already there in the creation. Just as other laws exist as part of the creation, the law of *dharma* also exists as part of the creation.

If the Lord is the creator, and the creation is non-separate from the creator, then the law of *dharma*, being a part of the creation, is also non-separate from Īśvara. Therefore, *dharma* becomes Īśvara. The law of *karma* also becomes Īśvara in the same way, which is why we worship the Lord as *dharma* and have even given him two hands and two legs, in the form of Rāma.

When we say Rāma was an *avatāra*, we do not need any history. Whether Rāma existed or not is irrelevant because he is looked upon only as the Lord. He is *dharma* personified. History is necessary only for those who have problems with reference to what is historical. Their concept of the Lord being what it is, such people require history, but we do not require it.

Name and form are given only for the sake of worship and meditation, and that is how Rāma, Kṛṣṇa, and others are presented. In fact, Lord Kṛṣṇa is nothing but joy personified with two hands, two legs, a head, with a flute in hand and a peacock feather on his head. Therefore, whether Kṛṣṇa existed or not does not mean anything. Kṛṣṇa is a particular name and form given to Parameśvara whose nature is joy, *ānanda-svarūpa*. Similarly, Rāma portrays the Lord as *dharma*. Thus, we look at the Lord from various aspects in the creation and represent these aspects with many different gods called *devatā*s.

What happens when you look upon *dharma* as Īśvara? If you merely conform to *dharma*, you are an ethical person. But if you look upon *dharma* as the Lord, you worship that Lord by doing what is to be done at a given time and place. *Dharma* is something already established and you come to sense it. Therefore, what is to be done by you, you do. Kṛṣṇa says that by doing *karma* that is to be done by us, we are worshipping him. How can it be? This is also something we need to know.

Everything in the creation has its own dharma

With reference to this cycle of creation, the Lord is the creator. The world is born of him and sustained by him. It is not that he created the world and then went to sleep. The creation is ON! Every moment new cells are born, new things are born. You yourself are born and new children are born. A continual process of *sṛṣṭi*, creation, *sthiti*, existence or sustenance, and *saṁhāra*, dissolution, is going on.

This second, a recognised unit of time, is born. And as it is born, it is, and it is also gone. This, 'born-is-gone' is a continuous process. The various living beings on this planet, trees, insects, animals, and human beings, do exactly what is expected of them. In this way, everything goes well. A tree that has to change its colours before winter comes, does so and it keeps doing so, because it is a sugar maple tree and that is what a sugar maple tree has to do. Being programmed, the tree does exactly what it has to do. If it has to make chlorophyll, it makes chlorophyll. If it has to take in carbon dioxide and give out oxygen, it does exactly what it has to do, which is why a sugar cane continues to be sweet and a lime continues to be sour. All vegetation grows upon the same earth and may even belong to the same species. Yet, one may be sour and the other sweet, if, for example, a particular orange happens to be a 'lemon!'

An orange is an orange and a lemon is a lemon. If one orange turns out to be a lemon, there is a reason for it; it is because some programming is there. It is not that an orange tree decided to have some fun, wanting to see the face of the person who bites into an orange and discovers it to be a lemon. The tree does not make any such decision to produce a sour orange. Being programmed as it is, it behaves and contributes to the creation exactly as it must because the creation is ON!

Īśvara himself is in the form of the very world, the very creation. Therefore, every blade of grass is what it is, and it is Īśvara. Everything in the vegetable kingdom is Īśvara's creation and, having a particular form, does exactly what is expected of it because members of the botanical world do not have free wills.

The world of animals is the same. A snail is always a snail, an oyster is an oyster, a jackal is a jackal, a lion is a lion, a cow is a cow, and a turkey is a turkey. All of them are exactly the same. They do not call themselves snails, lions, and turkeys. A cock will fight like a cock which is why it is a cock. Similarly, monkeys behave like monkeys, exactly as they should, programmed as they are. They all seem to be fine and are intelligent enough. Even turkeys know how to survive when left to their own devices. The fact that they cannot survive the month of November is only due to the way people choose to celebrate 'thanksgiving'!

Human beings are not programmed

It is only when you come to human beings, including a small child, that you find a difference. When you call a puppy, it wags its tail and comes every time because it connects your calling it by name with a cookie or some other treat in your hand. But, if you call your young child by the same name, whether you hold out a cookie or not, the child may or may not come. Why? Because the child is much more than a pup. He or she is a complete person with a will of his or her own, asserted from childhood onwards. This is always a problem for parents, especially when they want the child to perform for guests, for instance. If the child is at all concerned about what others will think, there is no way he or she will perform.

Even as an adult, most of your worries are based on what others will think, a problem not shared with other living beings. When a cow wants to make a noise, it does so without bothering about what anyone will think. If a dog wants to bark, a donkey wants to bray, or a lion wants to roar, they too do not concern themselves with what others will think. Wherever there is water, all the frogs in the vicinity will gather every evening and put on a 'concert.' The racket they create is so dreadful that you cannot sleep. But, the frogs are not at all concerned with what you or anyone else thinks of their music. Only human beings have this problem because they have free will and a self-image, half of which depends on what others think. Therefore, they are entirely different and are not going to do exactly what is to be done unless they decide to do so.

In the process of growth, a person picks up hundreds of *rāga-dveṣa*s. Such fancies are always there and we find that convenience is usually the order that we follow. This is why we often do not bother about, 'No Trespassing' signs, and cut across a rectangle diagonally, thereby creating a path, even though it is someone's private property. Once there is a path, a right to it also seems to be established! This is what is meant by the term, 'grandfather rights.' We also see evidence that convenience is our nature wherever there is a sign saying, 'Post No Bills.' There will even be a bill stuck right on top of the very sign, perhaps so that the problem will disappear!

Convenience is often the governing factor. We want what is convenient, what is pleasant. Easy gratification is exactly what human beings go for. If some work, pain, or effort is involved, we want to avoid it. The human disposition is like that, going after easy, quick gratification, wanting only what pays off immediately. This is our nature. We have therefore created in ourselves a number of *rāga-dveṣa*s, which prompt us to perform various actions that are not often in keeping with *dharma* and *adharma*. To go against *dharma*, the Lord, is to go against the order that is the Lord, and this is *adharma*.

Doing one's own duties is worship

Since creation operates according to this same order, there is definitely a reason that you were born. Your parents may not have wanted you, but somehow you were born. Even if you feel unwanted, still you are here because, without you, this world is definitely incomplete, which is why you are here. It is as simple as that.

If you see a purpose in everything in the world, why should you take your presence in this big politic of humanity as anything other than important? Even in your own body politic, everything has a role to play. Just as a tree is there, you are also there. You are important. You have roles to play and things to do. Īśvara's job is going on and you are a cog in his wheel. This being the case, naturally you have to do your job. You have to know that at this time and place, this is the job that you have to do. This is called *sva-karma*. Just as every animal and every tree contributes to this great creation, you too make your contribution. Whatever be your *sva-karma* that very *karma* becomes an offering to Īśvara.

Offerings to the Lord need not always be in the form of flowers. Bhagavān says that by doing what is to be done by you at a given time, you are worshipping him. Because of your recognition of Īśvara, whatever action you perform is your *arcana*, offering, contribution to the Lord. You offer your actions unto the Lord, who is in the form of the creation and who continues to do the job of creation. You are one of his limbs. You perform your role, which is an important one. Otherwise, you would not be here. It is something like a symphony orchestra where, even though it looks as though some of the musicians could be removed, each person has a significant role to play according to the composer. One person may only play one note every fifteen minutes, but that is his or her role to play in the overall scheme of the symphony. Similarly, each of you has your own job to do and when you do it, you are in harmony with Īśvara, the Lord. This is why, whenever you do exactly what you have to do, you find satisfaction. Even if it is something you do not want to do, once you do it, you feel great about it. Why? Because you are in harmony with Īśvara. Recognising this, you become a *yogī*.

This recognition is not ordinary; it is a vision. To be in harmony with the world, with what is to be done, with the law of *dharma* that govern *karma*, is *karma-yoga* – *yogaḥ karmasu kauśalam*. Therefore, you choose your *karma*s recognising Īśvara as *dharma*. Then your actions become a form of *arcana* to Īśvara. This attitude results in *antaḥ-karaṇa-śuddhi*, purification of the mind. Once this happens, it takes no time for self-knowledge to take place. Since *antaḥ-karaṇa-śuddhi* is what is required, the necessary steps have been completed, *karma-yoga*, *antaḥ-karaṇa-śuddhi* and *jñāna*. These steps are mentioned throughout the *Gītā*, and Śaṅkara also mentions them repeatedly in his *bhāṣya*. Through *karma-yoga*, the mind is purified, and when the mind is pure, knowledge takes place and *mokṣa* is gained. *Karma-yoga*, therefore, is for *mokṣa* alone.

Verse 49

Those who perform action only for results are misers

दूरेण ह्यवरं कर्म बुद्धियोगाद्धनञ्जय ।
बुद्धौ शरणमन्विच्छ कृपणाः फलहेतवः ॥ ४९ ॥

dūreṇa hyavaraṁ karma buddhiyogāddhanañjaya
buddhau śaraṇam anviccha kṛpaṇāḥ phalahetavaḥ (49)

dhanañjaya – O Dhanañjaya (Arjuna)!; *hi* – therefore; *buddhi-yogāt* – as compared to *buddhi-yoga* (the *yoga* of proper attitude); *karma* – action; *dūreṇa avaram* – is far inferior; *buddhau* – in the *buddhi-yoga* (of proper attitude); *śaraṇam* – refuge; *anviccha* – seek; *phala-hetavaḥ* – those who perform action only for results; *kṛpaṇāḥ* – misers

> Action (based on desire) is, therefore, far inferior to that performed with the proper attitude of *karma-yoga*. Seek refuge in this *buddhi-yoga* (of proper attitude), Dhanañjaya (Arjuna)! Those who perform action only for the results are misers.

Buddhi-yoga means *karma-yoga*, the attitude of sameness towards all results, *samatva*. *Karma* done under the spell of *rāga-dveṣa*s is far different from *karma-yoga*, which involves proper attitude and commitment. The result of such *karma* is received in keeping with one's *rāga-dveṣa*s and not with *samatva-buddhi*. This kind of *karma* is thus far inferior, *avaram*, to *buddhi-yoga*, *karma-yoga*.

Therefore, Kṛṣṇa told Arjuna to take refuge in *karma-yoga-buddhi* – *buddhau śaraṇam anviccha*, go for it, pray for it. Why? Because people who perform *karma* for the sake of the results alone, not for *antaḥ-karaṇa-śuddhi* and *mokṣa*, are *kṛpaṇāḥ*, misers. They want only *bhoga*, enjoyments, and *aiśvarya*, power. For them, there is no *karma-yoga*, which makes them misers because they do not make use of their *buddhi*.

In his commentary on this verse, Śaṅkara defines misers, referring to them as *dīnāḥ*, helpless weaklings. Misers are those who have money but do not have the heart to spend it, either on themselves or on others. Those who have no money are not misers because they have no money to spend. Those who do have money and spend when there are occasions to spend are also not misers. A man who has money and spends more than what he has, who does not spend judiciously, is a spendthrift and is just as much a problem as the one who has money and does not spend it at all. A miser cannot spend because he is so afraid that his money is going, going, going. Therefore, he always keeps saving, saving for the winter of his life, retirement. Sometimes, such a person dies before retirement and his brother-in-law gets everything! Misers have no heart to spend because their priorities are not clear. They are not clear about what money is for.

The meaning of the word miser, *kṛpaṇa* is extended here to the disuse of one's *buddhi*. Śaṅkara quoting the *Bṛhadāraṇyaka-Upaniṣad* discusses the meaning of the word *kṛpaṇa*.[14]

Why is such a person a miser? Because he or she was given an intellect, *buddhi*, and does not use it. The *buddhi* is the discriminative power one is endowed with as a human being and is the greatest wealth, the greatest treasure, that one can have. Therefore, its primary use should be for gaining self-knowledge. Even though everyone has a good chance to use the *buddhi*, a miser hoards it or fritters it away and dies not having made proper use of the greatest wealth that he or she was endowed with. And although the money misers leave can be enjoyed by others, no one can enjoy their *buddhi*s after they are gone.

---

[14] Refer to page 25

Misers are people whose aims are only small results, not *mokṣa*. Therefore, for them there is no *karma-yoga* or *sannyāsa*. There is only miserliness. We have seen that, according to the vision of the Veda, there are only two possibilities, to be a *karma-yogī* or to be a *sannyāsī*. There is no accommodation for a third kind of person. Those who are neither *karma-yogī*s nor *sannyāsī*s have to become *karma-yogī*s; otherwise, they are misers. Therefore, Bhagavān said, 'Take to *karma-yoga*.'

Verses 50&51

Karma-yoga is discretion in action

बुद्धियुक्तो जहातीह उभे सुकृतदुष्कृते ।
तस्माद्योगाय युज्यस्व योगः कर्मसु कौशलम् ॥ ५० ॥

buddhiyukto jahātīha ubhe sukṛtaduṣkṛte
tasmād yogāya yujyasva yogaḥ karmasu kauśalam (50)

buddhi-yuktaḥ – the one who is endowed with the *samatva-buddhi* (sameness of mind); *iha* – here, in this world; *ubhe* – both; *sukṛta-duṣkṛte* – *puṇya* and *pāpa*; *jahāti* – gives up; *tasmāt* – therefore; *yogāya* – to *karma-yoga*; *yujyasva* – commit yourself; *yogaḥ* – *karma-yoga* (is); *karmasu* – in action; *kauśalam* – discretion

> One who is endowed with the sameness of mind, gives up both *puṇya* and *pāpa* here, in this world. Therefore, commit yourself to *karma-yoga*. *Karma-yoga* is discretion in action.

The idea already expressed is that you should not be attached to inaction but rooted in the sameness of mind that is *yoga*; you should perform action. In his commentary on this verse, Śaṅkara explains that *samatva-buddhi* that is talked about is with reference to *karma-phala*, the fruits of action. What is gained by following *dharma*, right and wrong, and not mere *rāga-dveṣa*s, is also stated here. Here, in this world, while alive, the person gains *yoga-buddhi* which means *samatva-buddhi.*

Two *buddhi*s have been talked about, *sāṅkhya-buddhi* and *yoga-buddhi. Sāṅkhya*, Knowledge, was already discussed and now *yoga* is under discussion. *Buddhi-yukta* means *yoga-buddhi-yukta*, who is a *karma-yogī*, committed to a life of *karma* with the *buddhi* of *yoga*. What does this person do? Here, *iha*, in this world, while alive, one gives up both *puṇya* and *pāpa*, *sukṛta-duṣkṛte. Sukṛta* means that which is well-done, a *karma* that is proper, and *duṣkṛta* means the opposite.

Both proper and improper actions produce results and the results are also called *sukṛta* and *duṣkṛta*. Therefore *sukṛta-duṣkṛte* means *puṇya* and *pāpa*. The verse says that the *karma-yogī* gives up both *puṇya* and *pāpa* here, in this life. But can the results of action be given up even by a *karma-yogī*? No. Because he has *kartṛtva*, doership, the *karma-yogī* cannot give up the results. He can only become a master of his likes and dislikes so that he has freedom from them. In this way, he can be in harmony with Īśvara and, having a mastery over himself, he can enjoy composure, but nothing more because he is a *karma-yogī.*

A *karma-yogī* has *kartṛtva*, whereas a *sannyāsī*[15] does not. When you look upon yourself as a doer, you have doership

---

[15] Here by the word *sannyāsī*, we refer to a *jñānī*. Śaṅkara often uses the word *sannyāsī* in this sense.

and when you have doership, you cannot escape from the results of action, which always accrue to the doer. Because a *karma-yogī* has *kartṛtva* he is not a *jñānī*. If he has *kartṛtva*, he definitely has *puṇya-pāpa*. Whether he likes it, *puṇya-pāpa* will be there for him. Both the current *puṇya-pāpa* and the old are standing in his account. Thus, the question of how one gives up *puṇya-pāpa* would naturally arise here. This has to be properly understood.

When *karma-yoga* is there for a person, knowledge is not far away. As long as *karma-yoga* is there, there will be *antaḥ-karaṇa-śuddhi*, which will soon be followed by knowledge. Śaṅkara points out this order again here and says, *sattva-śuddhi-jñāna-dvāreṇa*. The *karma-yogī* gives up *puṇya* and *pāpa* here in this world, while he is alive, by means of *sattva-śuddhi*. The word '*sattva*, has two meanings. It is one of the three qualities, *sattva, rajas, tamas*. And it also means *antaḥ-karaṇa*, the mind. Here it is used in the sense of *antaḥ-karaṇa*. Therefore *sattva-śuddhi* here means purification of the mind.

First, *karma-yoga* takes care of *antaḥ-karaṇa-śuddhi*. Then knowledge is gained, there is *jñāna-prāpti*. This order is one of the important points in the *śāstra* that we have to know clearly. Otherwise, what is being said will be confusing. Because people are confused, they think that *karma-yoga* is just another means through which *puṇya-pāpa* is destroyed. And they say the same thing about *jñāna*. This 'different means' approach is how people get lost and become confused.

By performing *karma* with the proper attitude, you prepare yourself to be totally freed by knowledge. And that knowledge is gained only when the *antaḥ-karaṇa* is *śuddha*, pure. *Karma-yoga* takes care of it because *karma-yoga* purifies the mind. So, whenever you come across expressions in Śaṅkara's *bhāṣya*, like *sattva-śuddhi-jñāna-dvāreṇa ubhe sukṛta-duṣkṛte iha jahāti*, you must understand the order. Once the *antaḥ-karaṇa-śuddhi* is taken care of, that is, the *aśuddhis*, impurities, of the mind are taken care of, you are no longer under the enthralment of your likes and dislikes. Because you enjoy a composure, *ātma-jñāna* self-knowledge, is not far away.

Concerning this point, Śaṅkara says that a *karma-yogī* is a *karma-yogī* only for the sake of *mokṣa*. A person is only a *karma-yogī* for *ātma-jñāna*. Therefore, you continue to listen to the teaching and reflect upon it so that it will become a reality.

What, then, should Arjuna or anyone else do first? To ask whether you should become a *karma-yogī* or a *sannyāsī* is like asking if you should join a university or get a Ph.D. *Karma-yoga* is a step for gaining knowledge. There is no choice here. Therefore, Kṛṣṇa says, 'Commit yourself to *yoga* – *yogāya yujyasva*.' This is the same as saying, 'You have just started this enquiry, Arjuna. Therefore, prepare yourself by engaging in *karma-yoga*, which means doing what you have to do with the attitude of a *karma-yogī*.' Kṛṣṇa also made it clear that *yoga* in no way implies avoidance of action.

Exercising discretion in one's choices

In this verse, we are told that with reference to our actions, we must use our discretion, *kauśala*. What is not to be done is avoided and what is to be done is done properly.

And any action we do is done with the attitude that it is our offering to the Lord, *īśvara-arpaṇa-buddhyā*. This is *yoga*. Discretion, then, is with reference to the choices involved in action and involves our appreciation of Īśvara as well.

Inaction is not going to solve the problem, even though we will see later that *sannyāsa* is referred to as *sarva-karma-sannyāsa,* giving up of all actions, something that is not physically possible. Even a great *jñānī* performs actions. Then there are Swamis – the sitting ones, the standing-on-one-leg ones, and many others, all of which imply actions. Therefore, no one can avoid action totally. Renunciation of all *karma*s is strictly in terms of knowledge. By knowing that he or she is not the performer of any action, a *jñānī* is said to have given up actions. A person who has this knowledge of *ātmā* is a *sarva-karma-sannyāsī*.

Kṛṣṇa was telling Arjuna here that *sarva-karma-sannyāsa* has nothing to do with inaction; it has concerns only with knowledge. This knowledge can only take place in a person whose mind is clear, *śuddha*. Such a person is either a *karma-yogī* or a *sannyāsī*, who has taken to the life of renunciation. Knowledge is possible for both *sannyāsī*s and *karma-yogī*s.

Kṛṣṇa told Arjuna that while a choice between *yoga* and *sannyāsa* is possible, he did not think Arjuna was ready for *sannyāsa*. That meant, according to Kṛṣṇa, that Arjuna was ready only for *karma-yoga*. Therefore, as we saw in verse 48, Kṛṣṇa told Arjuna, '*yogasthaḥ kuru karmāṇi saṅgaṁ tyaktvā dhanañjaya*, Arjuna, remaining steadfast in *yoga* and abandoning attachment, perform actions.'

How could Arjuna live a life of a *sannyāsī*, a life of contemplation, when he was emotionally involved with his own people? Like others who have too many irons in the fire, Arjuna had too many arrows in his quiver. Therefore, it would be better if he exhausted them all and then see what was to be done.

Further, Kṛṣṇa said:

कर्मजं बुद्धियुक्ता हि फलं त्यक्त्वा मनीषिणः ।
जन्मबन्धविनिर्मुक्ताः पदं गच्छन्त्यनामयम् ॥ ५१ ॥

karmajaṁ buddhiyuktā hi phalaṁ tyaktvā manīṣiṇaḥ
janmabandhavinirmuktāḥ padaṁ gacchantyanāmayam (51)

buddhi-yuktāḥ – those who are endowed with the proper attitude of *karma-yoga; manīṣiṇaḥ* – the wise; *karmajam* – that which is born of *karma*; *phalam* – result; *tyaktvā* – giving up; *janma-bandha-vinirmuktāḥ* – free from the bondage of birth; *anāmayam* – free from all afflictions; *padam* – the end that is accomplished by knowledge, *mokṣa*; *hi* – indeed; *gacchanti* – go to

> The wise, endowed with the attitude of *karma-yoga*, having given up the results of action, free from the bondage of birth, indeed accomplish the end that is free from all afflictions.

Suppose a *karma-yogī* gains knowledge and thereby gives up all *karma-phalas*, that is, all the *puṇya-pāpas*, does that not mean that the person is empty, possessing nothing? Will he or she then be a nobody? At least if such a person had gathered lot of *puṇya*, he or she would have been an entity to be reckoned with.

But now, it seems that the person will be empty. This assumption is refuted in the present verse.

People who are endowed with *karma-yoga-buddhi* first gain *antaḥ-karaṇa-śuddhi*. Then knowledge takes place, which results in the giving up of *puṇya* and *pāpa*. Giving up the *puṇya* and *pāpa*, and as mentioned in the previous verse, *karma-phalaṁ-tyaktvā*, he gains *mokṣa* through knowledge. The first line, here, is a restatement of the previous verse and connects it with the previous verse and tells that the *karma-yogī* also gains *mokṣa* eventually.

Birth is bondage

How do *karma-yogī*s give up the results of action? A *karma-yogī*, having sameness of mind towards the desirable and undesirable results of actions, is said to give up the results and, in time, becomes wise. Such a person gains self-knowledge and is a *manīṣī* or a *jñānī*. Having become a *manīṣī*, the person becomes free from the bondage of birth, and becomes *janma-bandha-vinirmukta*.

When the doership is not there, the result of action will also not be there. The result of *puṇya-pāpa* is *janma*, birth, which itself is bondage. You cannot say that you are only bound after birth. You are bound inside the womb. No matter how much you twist and turn, you have to wait nine months before you can come out. Thus bound, you are born. Once you are born, you are also bound in that you have to wait at least another eighteen years to have a life of your own. After that, of course, you are bound to a hundred different things. Therefore, birth is bondage all the way!

From this bondage of birth, the wise are liberated. Śaṅkara makes it quite clear here that liberation does not happen after death, but while you are living. He says, *jīvantaḥ eva vinirmuktāḥ*, while living they are liberated. Unless you are liberated now, while you are alive, you are not going to be liberated later when you are dead. All that you can be is a ghost! If you are liberated here, there will be no problem, to yourself or to others. But if you are not liberated, and you become a ghost, you will be just another entity knocking around for people to channel through! Here in the world, you confused people by giving wrong advice and so on, and then later, as a spirit, you come through the channels, continuing to give out wrong information!

So, it was said that while you are alive, you are completely freed from the bondage of birth and death, commonly referred to as the cycle of *saṁsāra*. You may say that you do not care whether you are born again. If it happens, fine, and if it does not happen, that too is fine. You are only interested in 'right now.' You are not interested in any investment for later since no one knows what later really is. After death, all you see are the ashes, nothing more. And if the body is not cremated, it is buried deep enough that there is no chance of your coming out, even if, life is still there! Grass will be planted on top so that there will be no chance of oxygen reaching you! This you know very well.

Whatever happens after death is a matter of belief alone. Some logic may be there, but still, it is only a belief. You are only interested in what happens here. You do not care if your *karma-phalas* go or not. How do you know if *puṇya-pāpa* is really there for you? Therefore, you do not care about all this. But, you do care about your harmony with the world and you can understand the value of sameness of mind towards the results of action and discretion with reference to the choices involved in your actions. These things are all very clear to you. But please do not tell me that you will be freed from birth and death. You do not care about all that; You are only interested in what you can get now. This could be an argument. This is being answered now.

Liberation is not after death

This verse tells us what we can accomplish here, while we are alive, not in the form of sense gratification, but in terms of a pursuit that is meaningful in this life itself. Here *pada* means that which is to be accomplished. It also means 'a word' that by which something is known. Mere sound is not *pada*. From the word, a given object must be understood. What I say, you must be able to understand. Only then is there a language. The word has a meaning and that meaning is understood by everyone. Any word in any language is a *pada*. It is not used in this sense here in this verse. Here it means that which is accomplished by knowledge.

Pada in this sense is famous in Sanskrit literature. For example, there is a mention, *viṣṇoḥ paramaṁ padam*, meaning the greatest abode of the Lord Viṣṇu, who is all-pervasive. That all-pervasive *viṣṇoḥ padam* is *mokṣa*, liberation or freedom and that freedom is gained now, while living.

In the verse under study, *pada* is qualified by another word, *anāmaya*. Any problem is called *āmaya*. *Anāmaya* is defined by

Śaṅkara as *sarva-upadrava-rahita,* that which is free of all problems. It includes the problems starting from nagging onwards. Any kind of affliction is *upadrava.* Thus, *anāmaya* means that you are free from all afflictions. 'I am afflicted' is a notion that everyone has. You are a product of your own past; and, therefore, you are afflicted. Everyone has this notion about himself or herself and, from this notion, the person becomes free.

Knowing that you are limitless Brahman, you are not afflicted by anything because there is nothing other than Brahman. There is nothing else to afflict you. Therefore, you are free of all afflictions. When? While living here in the world. This knowledge, then, is really something! It is more than just something; it is the thing! And whatever you do is only for the purpose of gaining this self-knowledge.

In the next verse, Kṛṣṇa told Arjuna that he would attain this when his mind was no longer deluded.

Verses 52&53

A dispassionate minds gains self-knowledge

यदा ते मोहकलिलं बुद्धिर्व्यतितरिष्यति ।
तदा गन्तासि निर्वेदं श्रोतव्यस्य श्रुतस्य च ॥ ५२ ॥

yadā te mohakalilaṁ buddhirvyatitariṣyati
tadā gantāsi nirvedaṁ śrotavyasya śrutasya ca (52)

yadā – when; *te* – your; *buddhiḥ* – intellect; *mohakalilam* – impurity of delusion; *vyatitariṣyati* – crosses over; *tadā* – then;

śrotavyasya – for what is yet to be heard; *śrutasya* – for what has been heard; *ca* – and; *nirvedam* – dispassion; *gantāsi* – you shall gain

> When your intellect crosses over the impurity of delusion, then you shall gain a dispassion towards what has been heard and what is yet to be heard.

Delusion is in the form of absence of *viveka*, discrimination. The *aviveka*, lack of discrimination, makes you go towards objects and not towards the *ātmā*. Your mind goes towards objects as though they are going to take you to *ātmā*. Even though the solution to your problem is you, you always think of it as being elsewhere, outside of you.

There is no greater delusion in this world than wanting a solution to a problem that is centred on the 'I' and expecting the solution to be outside of the 'I.' This *mahā-moha*, great delusion is due to a lack of understanding of what I am about, what the world can give, what my problem is, what I really want, and so on. The *kalila*, impurity, of this delusion is what is given up by *ātma-anātma-viveka*, discriminating between *ātmā* and *anātmā*.

The verse goes on to say that when your mind is no longer under the spell of *moha*, you gain *vairāgya*, dispassion, with reference to what you have heard and what you have yet to hear. You have heard about many means and ends. These are *śruta*. They are on your list of things to do later. Then there are a few more means and ends that you have not yet heard about. They are to be heard later, *śrotavya*. They come under the heading of *śrotavya* when you think, 'I think I should read this and find out...' Dispassion towards what you have heard and will hear extends also to everything that is known to you; such dispassion is really very beautiful.

Suppose you decide to gain self-knowledge, *mokṣa*. You have developed a great value for this knowledge and have completely dismissed everything that you have so far come to know as desirable ends. Because they do not solve your problem you no longer have a value for them and have dismissed them. The only thing you want now is *mokṣa*. Suppose, someone comes and tells you that there is something more interesting than *mokṣa*, what will you do?

One's dispassion can be shaky

If we are practical people, we may have to give up self-knowledge. It means that our *viveka* is incomplete and our *vairāgya* is shaky. Everyone has *vairāgya* until something more interesting comes along. Similarly, our plans for gaining self-knowledge vanish along with our dispassion, when we are confronted with something we think of as rosier and more promising than *mokṣa*. We give up *mokṣa* and go after whatever it is. This is a clear indication that discrimination is lacking. It is not that dispassion is lacking. Our discrimination is lacking and therefore our dispassion is shaky!

I was once asked what I would do if, having devoted my life to Śaṅkara, a new philosopher came along and dismissed what Śaṅkara had said. I replied that Śaṅkara was a teacher and I am not a Sankarite. I am a *sādhu*, a *sannyāsī* in this tradition of teaching, *sampradāya*. For us, Śaṅkara is only a link. He never said that he was starting a new philosophy. He was just a teacher, a link in the chain. This is reflected in the verse that all students of Vedanta chant daily.[16] It says, 'I salute the lineage of teachers, that begins with Sadāśiva, which has Śaṅkara in the middle, and that has my teacher at its end.'

There is no Śaṅkara-ism here. There is only teaching and a *pramāṇa*, means of knowledge, in the form of words called the *Upaniṣad*s, also known as Vedanta.

Suppose someone tries to say something that is better than what Śaṅkara said or something that proves what Śaṅkara said was wrong. For a person with discrimination, there will be no context for such statements because Śaṅkara says exactly what is said in the *Upaniṣad*s. They tell you that you are Brahman, that you are the whole. Who is going to improve on this? Who is going to dismiss it? No one can dismiss it and no one can improve it. Try dismissing that you are the whole. The teacher is very clear about it and the *śāstra* is very clear about it. That you are the whole is not subject to your dismissal because you already know that only through the *śāstra* can you appreciate that you are the whole. How then, are you going to dismiss it? It is not available for any other *pramāṇa*. That you are the whole is already established by the *śāstra*, and that it cannot be dismissed is very clear.

---

[16] Refer to Volume 1 - page 49

If the statement, 'I am the whole,' cannot be dismissed or improved upon, I cannot be enticed by a new philosophy which gives me a supposedly better idea about me. Already the *Upaniṣad* has given me the last word. It says I am limitless, I am infinite, I am Brahman, I am the whole, I am all that is here. Who is going to improve on this? No one can improve *sat-cit-ānanda*. Nor can anyone dismiss it because it is me. There is nothing better possible. Anything that I am going to come to know later will not disturb my dispassion either. I will have the same dispassion towards what I come to know in the future as I have towards what I know now. Whatever comes will be from the world, which has no independent existence apart from Brahman. Nothing can come from outside the world and nothing more can come from Brahman because it is *eka* one. Knowing this is what is meant by *viveka*, discrimination.

Once you do not have *moha* in you, when your values are very clear, when you understand the delusion of human pursuits, then you will discover in yourself a dispassion, *nirveda*, towards what is to be heard, *śrotavya*, and what has been heard, *śruta*, whether it is from the Veda or from any other source. This was the point Kṛṣṇa wished to make very clear to Arjuna in this verse.

श्रुतिविप्रतिपन्ना ते यदा स्थास्यति निश्चला ।
समाधावचला बुद्धिस्तदा योगमवाप्स्यसि ॥ ५३ ॥

śrutivipratipannā te yadā sthāsyati niścalā
samādhāvacalā buddhistadā yogam avāpsyasi (53)

yadā – when; *te* – your; *śrutivipratipannā buddhiḥ* – mind distracted by the Vedas (which present various means and ends to be gained); *acalā* – firmly established; *samādhau* – in the *ātmā* (oneself); *niścalā* – steady; *sthāsyati* – will remain; *tadā* – then; *yogam* – self–knowledge; *avāpsyasi* – you will gain

> When your mind is no longer distracted by the Vedas (which present various means and ends to be gained) it will remain steady, firmly established in the self. Then you will gain self-knowledge.

This verse points out a further gain brought about by dispassion and also sums up the whole teaching. The Veda, *śruti,* talks about various means for achieving various ends. These means and ends are described vividly and so elaborately that your mind becomes confused, *vipratipannā*. There seem to be so many means and ends for you to accomplish and they keep on increasing. Thus, the list of things to be done also keeps on increasing and you become confused by the *śruti.*

When, however, your mind becomes one, meaning when you have determined what is to be gained, you are not easily shaken by the various means and ends enjoined by the *śruti.* Just as any hype about a particular brand of shampoo has no effect on a bald-headed person, you will not at all be shaken by anything because you have already set your heart on an end that includes all means and ends.

We have seen that all means and ends are limited and what we are really seeking is freedom from any limitation whatsoever. When we know this, everything becomes very simple. The mind being definite about what it wants, it stays without being shaken, without being assailed, swayed, or swept away by anything, no matter how seemingly attractive it may be, *sthāsyati niścalā*.

Not only is such a mind unable to be swayed, it is single-pointed, *ekā*, with reference to the goal. This attitude of the mind is *karma-yoga*. When your goal is very clear to you, the hold that your *rāga-dveṣa*s previously had on you is released and your *buddhi*, mind, is steady.

Śaṅkara defines *samādhi* in his commentary on this verse as, '*samyag ādhīyate cittam asmin iti samādhiḥ*, that into which everything resolves, *ātmā*. He thus makes it very clear that the word *samādhi* means *ātmā* in this context. When your mind is no longer distracted by the various ends and means prompted by your *rāga-dveṣa*s because the goal is very clear to you, it will remain steady, firmly established in *ātmā*. Then you will gain self-knowledge.

The first line of the verse itself indicates that the person is a *mumukṣu*, who seeks *mokṣa*, liberation. A *mumukṣu* may continue to be in the field of activity as a *karma-yogī*, or he or she may take to a life of renunciation as a *sannyāsī*. These are the only choices a *mumukṣu* has. When the mind is no longer swept away or confused by the *śruti*, which talks about various means and ends, it becomes steady and definite about what is to be accomplished, *mokṣa* through knowledge of the self. This steadiness is *karma-yoga* and the *karma-yogī* is a *mumukṣu*.

The possibility of doubt

There can be some doubts here. Is *ātmā* always free or is it always bound? Is *ātmā* limited or free from limitations?

Is *ātmā* mortal or is it free from time? Is *ātmā* the truth of everything or is it one of the many things in the world? Is *ātmā* the very cause of everything that is created here or is it a product of creation? Is *ātmā* identical with Īśvara or separate from Īśvara? Is *ātmā* separate from every other *ātmā* or is there only one *ātmā*? Is *ātmā* separate from the world or is it non-separate? Does *ātmā* undergo a change to become the world or does it always remain the same, even though it is the cause of the world? These are examples of possible doubts, the list being in no way complete.

None of these doubts is there for a *mumukṣu*. When your *buddhi* remains without any *vikalpa*, doubt, there is *jñāna*, knowledge, which is real *yoga*. *Jñāna* can be called *yoga*, a means of knowledge can be called *yoga* and a state of mind can also be called *yoga*. Here, the context does not permit us to take the word *yoga* as simple *karma-yoga*. It can only be *jñāna*, the real *yoga*, which Bhagavān defined later as 'dissociation from association with pain, *duḥkha*.' It means that there is nothing you have to do except be yourself.

You have been associating with *duḥkha* all along because of *aviveka*, lack of discrimination that causes you to take on limitations of things that are different from you. Then you say, 'I am limited.' This indeed is *duḥkha* and is *duḥkha-saṁyoga*. Due to *aviveka*, lack of discriminative knowledge, there is *duḥkha* for you. Dissociation from association with *duḥkha* is brought about by removing the *aviveka*, by *viveka* between *ātmā* and *anātmā*. When the *viveka* is very clear, meaning you know very clearly that everything is you and that you are free from everything, then there is real *yoga, paramārtha-yoga*. This *yoga*, called *jñāna*, is what Arjuna would gain. Thus Kṛṣṇa said, *yogam avāpsyasi*.

Śaṅkara gives the meaning of *yoga* as *viveka-prajñā*, thus making it clear that the word *yoga* in this verse is nothing but discriminative knowledge of *ātmā* and *anātmā*. When true discrimination is lacking, sorrow is the result.

Having talked mainly so far about *karma-yoga* and *sāṅkhya*, in this verse, Bhagavān summed up everything he had said so far. The first line, '*śrutivipratipannā te yadā sthāsyati niścalā*,' refers to *karma-yoga*. The second line, '*samādhau acalā buddhiḥ tadā yogam avāpsyasi*,' refers to *sāṅkhya-yoga*. Having thus summed up and perhaps thinking he had done a good job, Lord Kṛṣṇa might have paused for Arjuna to respond.

Arjuna did not say, as he would in the eighteenth chapter, that his delusions were gone, that he knew what was to be done and was going to do it. He did not say this until the end of the *Gītā*. If he had said it here in the second chapter, the *Gītā* would, of course, be over! Kṛṣṇa would have said, '*Oṁ tat sat!*' and completed the *Gītā*. However, since the *Gītā* was a *saṁvāda*, dialogue, Kṛṣṇa talked to Arjuna and Arjuna asked questions because this particular subject matter has to be understood, not just blindly believed. There is no use in Arjuna walking away thinking, 'Kṛṣṇa told me that I am eternal. Therefore, I must be eternal.'

A belief requires no explanation at all; you just believe. The only requirement is that the belief be stated. Why people write about belief is beyond our comprehension. The belief need only be stated honestly. Stating a belief is exactly what a belief is. If there is something to support the belief, it can also be stated. However, when something is to be understood, it will either remain not understood or it will be understood, regardless of the number of books written on the subject. In other words, it can be understood by reading only one book and, in spite of reading every book on the subject, it can remain not understood.

Here, the subject matter is to be understood. In fact, Kṛṣṇa himself will say later on in his dialogue with Arjuna, 'May you gain this knowledge by asking proper questions.' If you ask the right question you get the right answer. Even if you ask the wrong question, as Arjuna did in the next verse, you may get the right answer!

Verse 54

Arjuna's first question

अर्जुन उवाच ।
स्थितप्रज्ञस्य का भाषा समाधिस्थस्य केशव ।
स्थितधीः किं प्रभाषेत किमासीत व्रजेत किम् ॥ ५४ ॥

arjuna uvāca
sthitaprajñasya kā bhāṣā samādhisthasya keśava
sthitadhīḥ kiṁ prabhāṣeta kimāsīta vrajeta kim (54)

arjunaḥ – Arjuna; *uvāca* – said;

keśava – O Keśava!; *sthitaprajñasya* – of one in whom the knowledge is firm; *samādhisthasya* – of one whose mind abides in the self; *bhāṣā* – description; *kā* – what; *sthitadhīḥ* – one whose mind is not shaken by anything; *kim* – how; *prabhāṣeta* – would speak; *kim* – how; *āsīta* – would sit; *kim* – how; *vrajeta* – would walk

Arjuna said:

Keśava (Kṛṣṇa)! What is the description of a person of firm wisdom, one whose mind abides in the self?

How does such a person, whose mind is not shaken by anything, speak, sit, and walk?

Śaṅkara introduces this verse by saying that Arjuna, desiring to know the characteristics of a person who knows *ātmā*, asked a question, 'How does such a person speak, sit, and walk?'

The word '*sthitaprajña*' refers to a person who has no doubts, vagueness or error with reference to the knowledge of *ātmā*. Thus, the knowledge stays, becomes *sthita*. A person's knowledge can also be so erroneous that there seems to be no doubt or vagueness, but the error will show in time. Here, the knowledge stays without error. The word *sthitaprajña* being in the masculine gender, means the person for whom the knowledge stays and not the knowledge itself. The word for knowledge is *prajñā*, which is in feminine gender.

Prajñā can mean knowledge of anything, such as archery, for example. Śaṅkara therefore clarifies the knowledge being spoken of as, well-established, well-rooted knowledge that I am the whole, *paraṁ-brahma aham asmi*. The topic here is *paramātmā*, not archery, and the person for whom the knowledge of *ātmā* being *paraṁ-brahma* is steady, is called *sthitaprajña*.

This person is also described as one who is in *samādhi*, *samādhistha*, one whose mind is abiding in *ātmā*, is awake to *ātmā*. Arjuna wanted to know how Kṛṣṇa would describe such a person. He asked, *sthitaprajñasya kā bhāṣā*? Śaṅkara puts this question in another way, '*katham asau paraiḥ bhāṣyate*, how is this person described by others?'

Bhagavān used the word *samādhi* in the previous verse, not *sthitaprajña*. It was Arjuna who coined this latter word and his question reveals that he seemed to know what it was all about, at least in the first line! He asked for a description of a wise person, a *sthitaprajña*, which was an excellent question. He also used the word *sthitadhī*, meaning a person whose *buddhi* remains firm. But then he asked, '*kiṁ prabhāṣeta*, does this person talk? *Kim āsīta*, does he or she sit? *Kiṁ vrajeta*, does he or she walk?' Śaṅkara did not think that these questions as worded were Arjuna's real questions.

To ask, 'Does a wise person talk?' would have been meaningless because Kṛṣṇa had been talking all along. It would also have meant that Arjuna had a doubt whether Kṛṣṇa knew what he was talking about and, therefore, whether he was a *sthitaprajña*. Because *kim* can mean 'what' or 'how.' Śaṅkara took Arjuna's questions to mean the latter. How does a wise person talk, sit, and walk?

When someone asks you a question, you either answer the question or you answer the person. When you answer the person, you still answer the question, but it is the spirit of the question that you address. When you answer the person, you consider what the person had in mind while asking the question. Before talking, a person has a sense to convey, which is why one talks. Therefore, the listener tries to understand the intention or the sense of what the speaker is attempting to convey. This is listening and is very important, whether you are reading what someone has written or are listening to what someone is saying. A person may not always say what he or she really wants to say. A person's look may be enough for you to see his or her language. This sometimes happens without the eyes also, like when you hear two or three words and understand the whole sentence. It depends on your capacity to see what the speaker wants to say.

The spirit of Arjuna's question

When Lord Kṛṣṇa answered Arjuna, he did not answer his question. Instead, he answered the person, as we will see. If Kṛṣṇa had answered the question, what could he have said? Would he have described *sthitaprajña* as one who walks very slowly or quickly because the person is a *sthitaprajña*? Suppose the *sthitaprajña* does not have any legs? Or, would Kṛṣṇa have said that a *sthitaprajña* talks very slowly because he or she is very alert? Or, that being very alert, *sthitaprajña*'s words are carefully measured and come only in half-minute intervals, the person being so rooted in the self!

What does all this mean? How does it make any difference? Some people think that if you talk very slowly, you are wonderful. They think that the words of a wise person who talks slowly come from infinity and, therefore, they take time! They come from such depths, it seems! People can be very easily fooled by those who pose as wise by saying very little and speaking very leisurely.

There is yet another popular description of a wise person, 'Words just tumble out. The physical organ is incapable of keeping track of the pace of the quicksilver mind of the wise. It is so mercurial. No God has made an organ of speech that can keep pace with it. The person has such enormous energy!' Then there is another type of wise person, it seems, who, having reached *ātmā*, does not talk at all. He or she is always in *samādhi*. People come and the person just looks at them without even blinking! Why? Because he or she is a *sthitaprajñā*, of steady wisdom!

We see that if Arjuna's question had been taken literally, no answer would have been possible unless Kṛṣṇa himself believed in such definitions of a wise person. Therefore, the second line of Arjuna's question did not mean anything to Kṛṣṇa, but there was a spirit to it; that is, how does a wise person interact with the world? How does he or she talk and go about in the world? Is there any indication that this person has wisdom? Is there anything that betrays or reveals the wisdom he or she has? Will there be any difference in how this person interacts with the world and how an ordinary person interacts? There should be some difference. Therefore, what is it that characterises the person's wisdom? This was the spirit of Arjuna's question and it was this question that was answered in the verses to come.

Verse 55

Kṛṣṇa's reply

श्रीभगवानुवाच ।
प्रजहाति यदा कामान्सर्वान्पार्थ मनोगतान् ।
आत्मन्येवात्मना तुष्टः स्थितप्रज्ञस्तदोच्यते ॥ ५५ ॥

śrībhagavān uvāca
prajahāti yadā kāmān sarvān pārtha manogatān
ātmanyevātmanā tuṣṭaḥ sthitaprajñastadocyate (55)

śrībhagavān – the Lord; *uvāca* – said;
pārtha – O Pārtha!; *yadā* – when; *sarvān* – all; *manogatān* – as they appear in the mind; *kāmān* – desires; *prajahāti* – gives up; *ātmani* – in oneself; *eva* – alone; *ātmanā* – with oneself; *tuṣṭaḥ* – one who is happy; *tadā* – then; *sthitaprajñaḥ* – a person of ascertained knowledge; *ucyate* – is said to be

Śrī Bhagavān said:

When a person gives up all the desires as they appear in the mind, happy in oneself with oneself alone, Pārtha (Arjuna)! that person is said to be one of ascertained knowledge.

The characteristics stated here and in the subsequent verses of the chapter are with reference to a person who has already attained this knowledge. Both the definitions, *lakṣaṇa* of a *sthitaprajña* wise person, and the *sādhana*, means for becoming wise, are discussed.

Although Arjuna only wanted to know who is a *sthitaprajña*, the *sādhana* is also taught because, throughout the *śāstra*, the characteristics of a wise person are also said to be the means for preparing one's mind for the knowledge of *ātmā*. In his commentary, Śaṅkara referred to a *sthitaprajña* as one who is accomplished, one who has made it, a *kṛtārtha*. The characteristics of one who has made it by gaining this knowledge become the *sādhana*, the means, for gaining the knowledge. Thus, the wise person's spontaneous expressions in life, the attitude and disposition with which he or she interacts with others, are the characteristics that establish the norms to be followed by the seekers of this wisdom.

These characteristics are to be cultivated because they are the means by which the seeker becomes a wise person. Without these *sādhanas*, a person does not become wise. Thus, in the beginning, there is *sādhana* and later, the *sādhana* becomes an expression. Sympathy, love, freedom, giving, and so on are *sādhanas* in the beginning. They are means for self-purification and maturity, eventually becoming the natural expressions of the same person. It is not that the person tries to be sympathetic, loving, and giving; one is naturally sympathetic, loving, and giving. However, for the person who has not yet made it, makes an effort to give. This is necessary because, along with the giving thought, there is also the opposite thought in the form of a reluctance to give. In the mind of the person, the question, 'Why should I give?' still arises. If the ego is there telling you not to give, then you are not a giving person. Thus, giving, love, sympathy, consideration, and so on, are the spontaneous expressions of a wise person, which become the*sādhanas* for the person who wants to be wise, the *mumukṣu*.

The *sādhana* itself is to be accomplished by *yatna,* effort. If you succeed in acquiring these characteristics, then you become firmly established in knowledge. You gain *jñāna-niṣṭhā*. What was accomplished with effort becomes the natural expression of a wise person. That is the rule. Therefore, all universal values, being natural to the *sthitaprajña* are *sādhana*s for a *mumukṣu*. They became natural to the *sthitaprajña* because they are one's natural expressions. But, in the beginning, the person deliberately cultivated them. To become wise, you have to follow them; only then can you gain *jñāna-niṣṭhā*. Thus, these values are both the qualifications and the qualities you need for knowledge to take place and, in time, they become very natural to you.

The qualities represented by universal values are not like a boat that you use to cross the river and then leave behind once you have reached the other side. Even though these qualities are the means for preparing your *antaḥ-karaṇa* for knowledge, they become natural expressions because you continue to be a person with such a mind. You interact with the world as before, but now you interact spontaneously because these qualities have become natural to you. Thus, in the beginning, they are in the form of *sādhana*s, the means for accomplishing self-knowledge whereas, later, they are like ornaments, very natural, spontaneous expressions of the person.

Bhagavān Kṛṣṇa included both the definition of a wise person and the means for becoming wise in his response to Arjuna's request for a description of a *sthitaprajña* because they are one and the same. Śaṅkara makes the same point in his commentary introducing this verse. Kṛṣṇa also indicated that giving up all desires, *sarvān kāmān*, does not mean that the *sthitaprajña* has no desires, but that as they arise in his mind, *manogatān*, he gives them up, *prajahāti*. It means the desires are not pursued. In this way, the wise person gives up all desires.

Now the question may arise, if a man gives up his desires, does it not mean that he will have no happiness, *ānanda*? We know that a man is happy only when he fulfils a desire. But, here, he gives up desires as they arise in his mind and at the same time continues to live. If his desires disappear and he disappears with them, there is no problem. But if he gives up desires and continues to exist in this world, it seems that he has no way of being happy. What recourse does he have, except to become high on drugs or a mad man who is always laughing at nothing!

In order to answer this question, we have to take two things into consideration. First, people are not happy and, secondly, people are always busy fulfilling their desires in order to be happy. They are always hopeful that happiness will come because they do become happy occasionally. 'Tomorrow will be better,' they say. 'Everything will be wonderful when this is over.' It seems therefore, that people who pursue their desires are always working for happiness, whereas those who have given up desires have no way of being happy. And no one can remain for a long period without being happy.

Bhagavān corrected this train of thinking by saying that such a person is happy with oneself, *ātmani eva ātmanā tuṣṭaḥ*, in himself or herself, the wise person is happy. Everyone is happy in oneself anyway, but always because of something else. Here, without any external props or circumstances, without expecting or depending upon any condition whatsoever, the person is happy.

The analogy of a sugar crystal is useful here. Simply by being a sugar crystal, a sugar crystal is sweet. It does not require a sweetening agent to be sweet because it is already saturated with sweetness, which is why it is sugar crystal. Therefore, it cannot be sweetened further. Similarly, one who is happy, *tuṣṭa*, does not depend on any other object or situation to be happy. By one's own awakening to oneself alone one is happy. Such a person is called *sthitaprajña*.

Śaṅkara explains here that *sthita* means well established and *prajñā* is that knowledge which is born of *viveka*, the discriminative enquiry into and analysis of *ātmā* and *anātmā*. Therefore, the one for whom this knowledge is well- established is called a *sthitaprajña* or a *vidvān*, a wise person.

Arjuna wanted to know what a *sthitaprajña* was and this was Kṛṣṇa's definition. It is an excellent and complete definition. A *sthitaprajña*, Kṛṣṇa said, is one who, being awake to the fact of *ātmā*, being happy for no other reason, gives up desires that arise in one's mind.

The difference between binding and non-binding desires

Kāmas, desires, are divided into two types, *rāgas* and *dveṣas*. *Rāga-dveṣas* being nothing but desire, the common word for both of them is *kāma*, 'I want' is *kāma*. 'I want such-and-such' can be either something you want to acquire or protect or something that you want to avoid or get rid of. Either way it is *kāma*, 'I want.' This want can be in the form of *rāga* or *dveṣa*, depending on whether you want to acquire something or get rid of something.

*Rāga-dveṣa*s are also of two types, binding and non-binding. Whenever the *śāstra* talks about *kāma* in the form of *rāga* or *dveṣa*, it is referring only to those that are binding. When you give up *kāma*s as they arise in the mind, you do so for a reason. Otherwise, giving them up is not possible. That a man who gives up desires in his mind and who is happy in himself, is called a wise man, *sthitaprajña*, seems to mean that the first condition is a necessity for the second condition. Thus, in order to be happy with yourself, you have to give up desires. How is that possible? Unless you are happy with yourself, how can you give up desires?

If, in order to give up desires, you have to be happy with yourself, and in order to be happy with yourself you have to give up desires, you are in an unenviable position. It is something like a mentally unbalanced man who is advised that unless he marries, he will not be cured. In other words, the diagnosis and the treatment are one. Because no father will give his daughter in marriage to a mad man, he will not be able to marry and unless he marries, he cannot be mentally well. We seem to have the same situation here. But do we? According to some modern translations, it may look that way, but not according to Śaṅkara.

Non-binding desires are not the problem

First, Śaṅkara created a problem by saying that a person who gives up his desires is like a mad man. Otherwise, how can he be happy? Then, he said, a man who is happy in himself, by his own awakening to himself, does not need any desire to be fulfilled in order to be happy. What desires are being referred to here? Only those desires whose fulfilment is meant to make the person happy and not those that are non-binding in nature.

Non-binding desires may include a desire to do, to write, to teach, to give, to just simply stay put, and so on. Only binding desires are being considered here, not non-binding desires. If a wise person gives up desires, where does that leave Śaṅkara, who wrote the commentary on giving up desires? Was he a wise man? Was Kṛṣṇa, who taught Arjuna, a wise man? Was Vyāsa, who wrote the *Mahābhārata* in which the *Gītā* appears, a wise man?

If only those who have given up desires are wise, none of these men can be considered to have been wise. Kṛṣṇa seemed to have a desire to teach. In fact, Kṛṣṇa but pounced on Arjuna! He did not even mind that he was in the midst of a battlefield. Kṛṣṇa's knowledge seems to have been bottled up inside him and it came pouring out for Arjuna's asking in one long, continuous flow! Aside from his desire to teach, Kṛṣṇa seemed to have some other desires, too. For example, when he was asked to drive Arjuna's chariot, he agreed.

Had Kṛṣṇa given up every desire that arose in his mind, he could not have driven the chariot. But he did drive it.

He also took up the flute and played songs. If this desire had been given up, all the *gopīs* would be still, waiting to hear his music and he would be still sitting with his flute poised. He would not have even had the desire to remove his hands from the flute!

Since Kṛṣṇa presented himself as one who performed various actions and since doing presupposes desire, he could not have been a *sthitaprajña* by his own definition. Vyāsa also must have had a lot of desires to have written this great magnum opus, huge work, *Mahābhārata*. To have kept on writing as he did, Vyāsa must have had a very special mind indeed, and many desires as well. People often have the desire to accomplish some enormous project or the other, but then after a while they give it up. They begin but do not complete it. Not Vyāsa. He began and finished every chapter. Thus, according to the definition, he could not have been a *jñānī*. In fact, no teacher can be a *jñānī*. So, they must all be *ajñānīs*. If the desire is not there, a wise person cannot teach. Which means that only the 'otherwise' can teach, but they have nothing to teach! Unfortunately, the explanations put forward in some modern commentaries of the *Gītā*, based on incorrect translations, have created a lot of problems in understanding what is meant by giving up desires. If this were not the case, there would be no misunderstanding because what was said originally by Kṛṣṇa is very clear.

As Kṛṣṇa told Arjuna in the third chapter, a wise person is not bound by his or her desires and is not subject to any kind of mandate. Desires are only binding if you take yourself to be a *kartā*, a doer. Only then do you have things to do, and only then can there be dereliction of duty. If, on the other hand, you do not look upon yourself as a *kartā* and are awake to the knowledge of yourself, there is no question of the self being a doer. Therefore, there is no doership and nothing to be done. Lord Kṛṣṇa told Arjuna that because he had no desires, he had nothing to do. Because Kṛṣṇa is everything and everything is him, what is there to be accomplished? Nevertheless, he was always active, meaning that all the activities he performed were non-binding.

If activities are non-binding, the prompting factor of activity, *kāma* must also be non-binding. Here, in the *Gītā*, non-binding *kāma* is not the topic; only binding *kāma* is discussed.

The placement of the words '*yadā*, when, and *tadā*, then' in this verse is also significant. The word 'then' comes much later and until it comes, the force of the word 'when' continues. When a man gives up desires as they arise and being happy with himself in himself, only then can he be called a *sthitaprajña*. The force of 'when' is the same for both conditions 'when he gives up desires' and 'when he is happy' with himself, in himself, depending on nothing for his happiness.

Therefore, one gives up desires arising in one's mind that are binding in nature, the desire to be secure, to be happy, to be somebody, and so on. A person who is secure with himself or herself gives up such desires naturally. *Tuṣṭa* in the verse does not merely mean happiness; it implies security too. he insecure cannot be *tuṣṭa*, happy. Therefore, one who is secure is also happy. Giving up all desires is possible only when one is happy with oneself. Thus, the definition of *sthitaprajña* is complete.

What else can be said? One who is happy with oneself is a wise person who can totally accept the self because the self is acceptable. The self is perfect; it is not imperfect. Perfection means that there is no sense of imperfection whatsoever. The self is free from any sense of imperfection and the whole creation, the universe, is non-separate from the self. Because the self is complete, *pūrṇa,* it cannot be improved upon. Just as the sweetness of sugar cannot be improved upon, so too, the fullness of *ātmā* cannot be improved upon. Being awake to that fact, the person is happy.

Wisdom alone makes one wise

This, then, is the *lakṣaṇa,* the definition, of a wise person. To be wise requires wisdom, nothing else! How a wise person walks, talks, and sits means nothing. Anyone can learn to walk in a way. And if the definition of a wise person is that he or she talks slowly, then everyone who talks slowly would be a *jñānī*! The speed at which one talks or how one walks means nothing. Wisdom alone makes one wise, just as being friendly is the only way to make friends. There is no other way.

Similarly, some people ask how they can develop love. All that is to be done is to love. What else can you do? You cannot discover love outside of love. If you want to discover more love, be loving. Create conditions that will help you discover love, conditions that are not inimical to the discovery of love. People often create conditions in themselves, knowingly or unknowingly, that are inimical to the discovery of love. If you avoid doing this, you will find that you are loving.

Love is nothing but the expressed form of fullness, *ānanda*. Just as wheat flour takes on names such as bread, rolls, and muffins, so too love is subject to various forms. The different names given to wheat represent modifications of the wheat. Similarly, love is a simple emotion, which is a modification or manifestation of *ānanda*. If you analyse love, you will find nothing but *ānanda*. The manifest form of *ānanda* is love and love itself turns into such natural qualities as sympathy, compassion, and giving, depending upon the situation. And when that same love is distorted in any way, it becomes *kāma* leading to negative emotions such as greed, anger, depression and so on. These, are nothing but one expression of *ānanda*, love, which is why we say love is Bhagavān, meaning that the expressed form of *ānanda* is Bhagavān.

What is Bhagavān? The essential form of Bhagavān is *sat-cit- ānanda*. And the expressed form of *ānanda*, Īśvara, the Lord, is love. The modifications of this love can be either positive or negative. Sympathy and compassion are examples of positive modifications of love, whereas negative modifications are anger, greed, jealousy and so on. What is there is one *ānanda*, expressed or unexpressed. Unexpressed it is the *svarūpa*, the very nature of fullness, which is the definition of *ānanda*; expressed, it becomes love, *prema*. We shall see more of this definition later.

Here, the *sthitaprajña* is one who discovers the *ānanda* in him or her. The person knows that there is nothing other than oneself. When one says, 'I am the whole,' it means that the person is himself or herself the fulfillment of all desires.

We shall see, as we proceed how the discovery of oneself and the fulfillment of desires are not separate, but identical.

Verse 56

What we need to follow in order to be wise

दुःखेष्वनुद्विग्नमनाः सुखेषु विगतस्पृहः ।
वीतरागभयक्रोधः स्थितधीर्मुनिरुच्यते ॥ ५६ ॥

duḥkheṣvanudvignamanāḥ sukheṣu vigataspṛhaḥ
vītarāgabhayakrodhaḥ sthitadhīrmunirucyate (56)

duḥkheṣu – in adversities; *anudvignamanāḥ* – not affected; *sukheṣu* – for pleasures; *vigataspṛhaḥ* – one who is without yearning; *vīta-rāga-bhaya-krodhaḥ* – one who is free from longing, fear, and anger; *muniḥ* – the wise person; *sthitadhīḥ* – one whose knowledge stays; *ucyate* – is said

> The one who is not affected by adversities, who is without yearning for pleasures, and is free from longing, fear and anger, is said to be a wise person whose knowledge stays (unshaken).

Arjuna's question, as we have seen, was answered completely in the previous verse. Being awake to yourself and in yourself alone, you discover your joy, your fulfillment. You discover it by yourself, meaning through knowledge. Without self-knowledge, you cannot discover happiness in yourself. How can you discover happiness in yourself by yourself when the self is unhappy? Generally, you are happy if your desire is fulfilled, but here you are happy with yourself without fulfilling any desire.

The nature of *ātmā* is free from any sense of limitation and the person who is awake to this particular fact, the *sthitaprajña* is free from unhappiness. As desires arise in your mind, you are not affected by them because of being happy with yourself. This, then, was how Kṛṣṇa described the characteristics of a person of wisdom when Arjuna wanted to know how a wise person responds to the world.

Even though our response to the world does not necessarily reveal how much wisdom we have, still Arjuna thought that the spontaneous expressions of a wise person interacting in the world would reflect those values to be cultivated assiduously by a seeker and would, therefore, serve as a handy reference. Knowing how a wise person expresses himself or herself in the world is not for judging whether a person is wise or otherwise. It is not that we have a matrix of norms indicating the exact behaviour of a wise person, against which everyone is measured. It is only to know what we need follow in order to be wise.

What was it that the wise person followed before becoming wise that made him or her wise and that continues as the spontaneous expression of the person? This is what Arjuna really wanted to know, because the characteristics of a *sthitaprajña* become the very means, the *sādhana*, to be followed by a *mumukṣu*. Kṛṣṇa understood this to be the spirit of Arjuna's question and answered it accordingly.

The three-fold source of sorrow

Duḥkha, sorrow or pain, has three sources, *ādhyātmīka*, *ādhibhautika* and *ādhidaivika*. *Ādhyātmīka* is pain for which the source is your own body, mind, and senses, from stomachache onwards. The second source of sorrow, *ādhibhautika,* is situation around you, including the people and bugs that irritate you. Finally, *ādhidaivika* is the pain or sorrow caused by disasters such as as earthquakes, lightning and so on. This kind of pain is not created by any human being, but is from a source that is absolutely divine, natural phenomena over which you have no control whatsoever. You may try to control mosquitoes with sprays that will destroy them, but there is nothing you can do to prevent an earthquake.

So, while the source of sorrow is three-fold, there are not different types of sorrow. Sorrow may express itself in hundred different ways – weeping, howling, kicking, moaning, and so on. But the sorrow itself is one and the same. The word '*duḥkheṣu*' in the verse is in the plural because the source of sorrow is three-fold, as explained by Śaṅkara in his commentary on this verse. And those whose minds are not affected or shaken by sorrow arising from these three sources of pain are said to be wise.

Because the sources of pain are always active, pain is possible for a wise person, but he or she is not affected by it. What, then, is the response of a wise man when his head aches? 'Will his head ache?' is the first question. Or, let us start from the very beginning, 'Does he even have a head?' Yes, and because the wise man continues to have a head, it may ache. Now, when his head aches, does he know it or not? After all, he is *sat-cit- ānanda*. Being *sat-cit-ānanda*, what happens when there is headache? Does he recognise it? The verse indicates that he does by saying, when such pain occurs, the wise man is not affected.

When you recognise *duḥkha*, there is *duḥkha* for you. But what happens afterwards? You are shaken by pain or sorrow and then you become disturbed, *udvigna-manāḥ*. Any disturbance from the three sources described above can make it a reality. The headache is there, you recognise it and then you worry about it until your whole head and everything else aches! You may even become a pain to everyone around you! You were the only one with a neck pain, but you talk so much about it and make such a fuss that your pain also becomes everyone else's pain in the neck.

A wise person's response to sukha

What about pleasure, *sukha*, then? There are people who can remain quiet when *duḥkha* comes, but jump around like a football when something pleasant happens. The word '*sukheṣu*' here refers to any happy, pleasant situation, regardless of its source, which can also be described in the same three-fold manner. *Sukha* can come from your own sensory pleasure, from some external event, or yearning for such pleasures, *sukheṣu spṛhā*. But does a wise person not laugh when something funny is happening? Yes, but there is no 'Encore! Once more!' from the person, no longing. Recognising both pain and pleasure, the wise person is not carried away by either of them, *sukheṣu-vigata-spṛhaḥ duḥkheṣu anudvigna-manāḥ*. This characteristic, then, becomes a *sādhana* for a *mumukṣu*.

Śaṅkara in his commentary to this verse gives the example of fire. If you feed the fire with more wood, it will grow even more, *anuvivardhate*. In keeping with the fuel that has been offered, it grows to a big conflagration. When you first light a fire, it always starts as a flame, but set one match to a tank of gasoline and you have an instant conflagration. Thus, more the fuel, more the fire! Unlike the fire, Śaṅkara said, the wise person's *sukha* resolves in his or her fullness. The idea here is, since there is no yearning for *sukha*, the person's desires do not get out of hand.

Kṛṣṇa also said in this verse that one who is not swept away by either *sukha* or *duḥkha* is free from likes, fear, and anger; he is *vīta-rāga-bhaya-krodhaḥ*. Freedom from *rāga* implies freedom from *dveṣa* also. They are a pair. When one is mentioned, the other one is automatically understood to be included; in other words, they go together.

The happiness of those who are not in the hands of *rāga-dveṣa*s is not determined by their *rāga-dveṣa*s. Their *rāga-dveṣa*s do not affect their being happy with themselves; the *rāga-dveṣa*s no longer have any teeth! They may be baby *rāga-dveṣa*s or old *rāga-dveṣa*s, but either way, they do not bite because they cannot bite. They can only be enjoyed, which is why the *rāga-dveṣa*s of the wise are referred to as non-binding. They are toothless.

Absence of fear

Once *rāga* is gone, fear also goes. Fear exists only when desire is there and desire is there only when *rāga-dveṣa* is there. *Kāma* indicates duality. It is due to the notion, 'I am this much alone. Everything else is other than me and I have to get it.' Thus there is duality, meaning that there is a difference between *jīva*, the individual, and Īśvara, the Lord, *jīveśvara-bheda*. Naturally, then, there will be fear because difference between individual and the Lord implies duality between individual and the world. And duality between individual and the world means duality between individual and individual. Once you accept a duality between individual and Īśvara, you will find difference, *bheda*, everywhere.

If you think that you are different from Īśvara, you will think that you are different from the world and from everyone else in the world. And in this world of duality, you are an insecure person; therefore, the fear of danger from another source will always be there because the 'other' will always be there. Fear comes from duality only. Any fear means that duality is there because you recognise the source of fear as something other than yourself.

You can even be afraid of yourself if you have created a split in yourself. There is an 'ideal I' and an 'actual I' and the 'actual I' is always frightening to the 'ideal I.' This is also the reason why you are afraid of an insane person, provided you are sane, of course! Similarly, you may find that you are afraid of a person who is sad.

There can be no fear if there is only one *vastu*. A second thing is necessary for fear to occur. Therefore, the one who has no duality is not only free from *rāga-dveṣa*, but is also free from fear.

Anger also goes

A wise person is free from anger. Anger is nothing but another form of *rāga*. The desire itself is transformed into anger.

First, the desire is in a benign form and then it gets transformed into another form, an ugly form, anger. We will be seeing this later in the chapter, *kāmāt krodhaḥ abhijāyate*. When what you want is not accomplished due to some obstruction, that very *kāma* turns into anger whose target is the obstruction. Whatever is obstructing your desire becomes the object of your anger.

Many murders take place because the object of a person's love becomes the object of his or her anger. A man does not kill the loving woman; he kills only the obstinate, unwilling woman. And then he will cry for the loving one! Thus, when a person becomes an obstruction to your desire, that same person becomes the object of your anger. Anger is a mutilated, transformed, deflected form of *kāma*. Therefore, if you are free of *kāma*, desire, you will be free of *krodha*, anger.

Duality and fear

The word '*bhaya*,' fear, was put between the words *rāga* and *krodha* because of its special significance, which is dealt with very well in the *śāstra*. The only way to be free of fear is by swallowing duality. And you cannot swallow duality unless there is no duality. Because there is no duality, it can be swallowed, but only through knowledge. It is the only way to get rid of fear. Wherever there is duality, there is fear–fear of mortality, fear of being put down, fear of being small, fear of not making it, and so on. Fear can exist only as long as there is a seeker-sought relationship, the very relationship implying duality between the seeker and the sought and, in the final analysis, duality between oneself and the Lord.

Any small division whatsoever is enough to cause fear. Even to say, 'Īśvara is everything and I am a part of him' is enough! In fact, upon analysis, you will find that this concept is the very point from which everything becomes different. This difference is born of *avicāra*, a lack of enquiry or non-thinking. And if, after enquiry, duality is still there, it is a tragedy. Because the *Upaniṣad*s expect this kind of thinking or non-thinking, they address the topic thoroughly, pointing out that as long as there is any division whatsoever, fear cannot be avoided.

A *muni* is a thinking person, a person of enquiry, and the knowledge, *dhī*, of the *muni* stays, *sthita;* that is, it does not swing and sway. The *muni* does not think *dvaita*, duality, one day and *advaita*, non-duality, the next, just because someone has put forth a cogent argument. In fact, *dvaita* is not knowledge; it is a belief. Regardless of the number of objections raised, *advaita* is something you know. You may not be able to communicate it to someone else, but you know because it is you. It is not something you have to believe. It is a freedom from notions; *advaita* is all that is there.

We have seen that the person whose knowledge stays is a *sthitaprajña*, a wise person. *Sannyāsī* is also a word to point out *jñāna-niṣṭhā*, whose knowledge is firm and abiding. This word was brought in by Śaṅkara here because he did not think that one could be a *jñānī* without being a *sannyāsī*. As we proceed, we shall see that Śaṅkara's *sannyāsa* is always *jñāna*, nothing less.

Verse 57

A jñānī is unattached to anything

Further, Kṛṣṇa said:

यः सर्वत्रानभिस्नेहस्तत्तत्प्राप्य शुभाशुभम् ।
नाभिनन्दति न द्वेष्टि तस्य प्रज्ञा प्रतिष्ठिता ॥ ५७ ॥

yaḥ sarvatrānabhisnehastattat prāpya śubhāśubham
nābhinandati na dveṣṭi tasya prajñā pratiṣṭhitā (57)

yaḥ – the one who; *sarvatra* – in all situations; *anabhisnehaḥ* – without attachment; *tat tat* – whatever; *śubhāśubham* – the pleasant and unpleasant; *prāpya* – gaining; *na abhinandati* – does not rejoice; *na dveṣṭi* – does not hate; *tasya* – his; *prajñā* – knowledge; *pratiṣṭhitā* – is well established

The one who is unattached in all situations, who neither rejoices on gaining the pleasant nor hates the unpleasant, his knowledge is well established.

The *muni* discussed in the last verse is the person referred to here. A *muni* is a *jñānī*, who has the capacity for *vicāra* and, therefore, knowledge. Such a person is said to be unattached to anything, *sarvatra anabhisneha*. *Sneha* means affection or love. The literal meaning of this word in Sanskrit is anything viscous, like oil or glue. If you touch it, it sticks to you. Thus, anything sticky is called *sneha*.

Affection is considered to be *sneha* because the person for whom you have affection sticks to you. Even if the person is away from you, he or she is always with you in your thoughts. Because there is sharing involved, the other person's joys and sorrows become your joys and sorrows. You are deeply affected by the person and, therefore, there is *sneha*, affection, between the two of you.

Affection need not be a problem. However, attachment, *abhisneha*, is definitely a nuisance. When a mother has affection for her child, there is no problem because the child needs the affection in order to grow well. To be fondled, talked to, listened to, and cared for, all of which is *sneha*, is very important for the child's growth. But what usually happens is that affection becomes attachment and attachment means there is a strangulation of some kind. Instead of being an object of your affection, the person becomes an object to be possessed and controlled.

The need to control is a common problem everywhere. It is also a very old problem, which is why Kṛṣṇa addressed it in this verse. Attachment is not there for a wise person. His or her heart is never caught anywhere. It is always free and in its own place. In fact, most of us have empty hearts because that which is our heart has been distributed in little bits to various places – a little bit in the furniture, another bit in the carpet, and still other bits in your bank balance and a variety of other things. What that is left is a ticking heart! Everything else has been liberally distributed around and about. In this way, we lose our hearts in quite a few places, and even say so, 'I lost my heart.'

Where will your mind be? Where the heart is, because that is where you are. Wherever the emotional attachment is, the mind will run right to it. Thus, the heart being in a hundred different places, the mind, attempting to keep pace with it, necessarily goes to the same hundred places and, in fact, finds it quite difficult to cope with all the travel!

A person who has a wound involving pain and a little swelling will look at the wound every few minutes and stroke it ever so gently. Because there is pain and a lot of healing activity going on, the wound receives all of the person's love and attention. The mind goes there because the heart is there. The whole system naturally wants to fight it out and will certainly not allow the mind to dwell upon the meaning of *sat-cit-ānanda* at this time! Thus, our attachment is towards many things and many places, including heaven, none of which attracts the wise.

Any description of heaven that you can think of, no matter how seemingly perfect, will not interest a wise person. He or she is not caught up anywhere, whose heart is with him or her and never gets lost. Such a person may have love, friendship, affection and care, but nothing more. This is why the prefix '*abhi*' is added to the word *sneha*. That the wise person may have affection, but no attachment, is evidenced throughout the *Upaniṣad*s and the *Gītā*.

Kṛṣṇa definitely had affection for Arjuna when he said, 'O, my friend! I am teaching you because you are my devotee and I am your friend.' He talked to him very fondly. We find many expressions in the *Upaniṣad*s like, '*somya*, O Pleasing one!' etc., referring affectionately to a student. The point is that, while there is affection, there is no attachment. Attachment helps no one, definitely not the *mumukṣu*.

The verse also tells us that the wise person does not dance for joy over desirable situations or detest undesirable situations, *śubhāśubham tat tat prāpya na abhinandati na dveṣṭi*. *Śubha* means that which is good, auspicious, pleasant, and desirable. *Aśubha* means that which is unpleasant like death, disease, and so on. To detest an undesirable situation is nothing but refusal to accept a fact. A wise person does not react to a given situation, meaning that he or she accepts it as it is, and therefore does not subject himself or herself to sorrow.

In the face of both pleasant and unpleasant, the auspicious and inauspicious, the wise person is the same, *samaḥ*. For a *yogī*, it is a matter of attitude, born of an understanding, whereas for a *jñānī*, it is a natural, spontaneous expression. This is the only difference.

In his commentary on this verse, *Śaṅkara* confirms that the one who remains the same in the face of both pleasant and unpleasant situations is well-established in knowledge. This is because the person is free from the swings of joy and sorrow, elation and depression. There are no stock-market highs and lows because the person's knowledge is born of *ātma-anātma-viveka*, discrimination between the real and the unreal. Kṛṣṇa describes the same person further in the next verse.

Verse 58

A wise person is able to withdraw the sense organs at will

यदा संहरते चायं कूर्मोऽङ्गानीव सर्वशः ।
इन्द्रियाणीन्द्रियार्थेभ्यस्तस्य प्रज्ञा प्रतिष्ठिता ॥ ५८ ॥

yadā saṁharate cāyaṁ kūrmo'ṅgānīva sarvaśaḥ
indriyāṇīndriyārthebhyastasya prajñā pratiṣṭhitā (58)

yadā – when; *ca* – and; *ayam* – this person; *kūrmaḥ* – turtle; *aṅgāni* – limbs; *iva* – like; *indriyārthebhyaḥ* – from sense objects; *indriyāṇi* – sense organs; *sarvaśaḥ* – completely; *saṁharate* – is able to withdraw; *tasya* – his; *prajñā* – knowledge; *pratiṣṭhitā* – is steady

> When, like the turtle that withdraws its limbs, this person is able to completely withdraw the sense organs from their objects, his knowledge is steady.

This verse was also in response to Arjuna's question about how a *sthitaprajña* interacts with the world, the word '*ca*' connecting it to the previous verse. The wise person's capacity to manage his or her mind and senses is what is now being discussed.

A person may have *jñāna*, but for that knowledge to be steady, one must be able to withdraw the sense organs from the sense pursuits at will. Although the senses themselves are not harmful, they are referred to as the villains by the *śāstra* and by ourselves. For example, we make such statements as, 'I am okay, but my sense organs take me for a ride. My eyes alone take me to New York's 42nd Street. My ears also take me places. My sense organs are turbulent. They are the ones doing all the mischief. I am in their hands, the victim of my sense organs.'

The sense organs are not to blame

In fact, the sense organs are not to blame at all. They are purely reporters. They do not ask you to do anything. Otherwise, you could not go into a shopping mall and come out without everything sticking to you. The senses themselves are not turbulent; they only report and they keep reporting because it is their nature to report. Reporting is their job. The eyes tell you what is there. If it is a sentence, they help you read it. If it is a colour, they help you see it.

It is not the sense of smell that tells you that this is sweet and so on. It only reports the smell. You are the one who decides whether it is sweet or not. Otherwise, who would like blue cheese? If the senses had sweetness, they would never develop a liking for a strong smelling cheese called blue cheese. You develop a liking for it, not the senses. They only report the smell. And when they report the smell of blue cheese to some people, those people run! The senses are not responsible for your going for the blue cheese. Your mind is the cause. Thus, the senses themselves are not to blame.

Please remove the blame from the senses. They are given to you simply for reporting; they do no harm. The reason they are presented as villains is because they report there are problems. If they did not report, there would be no desire, no pursuit, and therefore no problem. But, because they report, there are fancies and you go along with the fancies. These fancies are many and the reports of the senses are constant. They keep coming all the time, reports of new objects, changing objects, new scenes and changing scenes.

Because the senses are a means of knowledge, a *pramāṇa*, it is their job to report what is happening. For example, if there is a sound, your sense of hearing immediately tells you that it is a sound. Because of the various sense data, you get yourself started and, before long, find yourself caught up in fancies. Because the reports of the senses lead to fancies, the senses seem to be a problem, but they are not. Even the fancies that happen in your mind are not in themselves a problem. But, because you go along with the fancies, the senses are considered to be turbulent and are thought of as villains.

The senses are not villains. If they report something and there is a fancy for it, you go along with the fancy until you find that you have no time for anything else. And because there are so many fancies, you are totally lost. The verse under discussion here refers to the person who is able to withdraw the senses at his or her will in order to gain steadiness in the knowledge of the self. When a person is able to gain or command the capacity to dismiss fancies at will, then his or her knowledge is steady because there is nothing for the person to regret. A *sthitaprajña* goes only by what he or she wants, meaning what is considered to be right, and is not dictated by fancies.

To go by what you want means that you decide. The decision itself may be right or wrong, but you go by it and not by your fancies. The one who does not go by fancies, who is able to withdraw one's sense organs at will, is not in the hands of the senses. Sense pursuits do not happen for such a person without his or her signature and sanction. This person then gains *jñāna-niṣṭhā*, steadiness in the knowledge of the self.

Anyone can withdraw the senses

We must remember, here, that the person under discussion is a *sthitaprajña*, whose knowledge is firm and remains.

Otherwise, anyone who is together could be taken as *jñānī*, which is not true. The person we are discussing is either a *sthitaprajña* or one who is committed to *sthitaprajñatva*, one who wants to be a *sthitaprajña.* For both, the capacity to withdraw one's senses from anything, at will, is important. This capacity has already been accomplished by a *sthitaprajña*, whereas for the one who wants to be a *sthitaprajña*, it is yet to be gained.

Kṛṣṇa used the example of a *kūrma*, turtle, with reference to withdrawing the sense organs. A turtle is able to withdraw its limbs at will and then send them out again. Because the turtle cannot move quickly, it is given a protection. It has the extraordinary capacity to withdraw its neck, legs, and tail in under its thick shell whenever it apprehends danger. The thickness of the shell prevents the detection of any scent of a living being underneath. This is Bhagavān's gift to the turtle and is also an indication of Bhagavān's sense of humour and justice. If he had given every living being four good legs, it would have meant that he had run out of imagination. Instead, Bhagavān is showing you that there is yet another way – without big legs or fast movements the turtle too can survive by withdrawing its limbs into itself, into its shell.

Similar to the turtle, a human being is not helpless in the hands of the senses because the person also has a thick shell into which he or she can withdraw. In fact, for some people their shell is so thick that nothing enters! If the mind is taken away by fancies, what can the senses do? But you can see hundred different things without wanting any of them. You simply see them in the same way as you see nature's autumn colours. What do you want out of them? Nothing. You just enjoy them from a distance, appreciating them as they are. In the same way, the senses need not create a problem. If there is fancy, it comes as a fancy and goes as a fancy. It is only when you want something that problems arise. By means of the turtle example, Kṛṣṇa is describing the capacity to withdraw the senses at will, from their objects and into oneself. And for the one who has knowledge, this capacity will enable that knowledge to become steady, to gain *niṣṭhā*.

For the one who has prepared oneself for knowledge by developing the capacity to make the mind and senses behave in this way, the knowledge is not going to be far away. And if the person is not so prepared, let him or her try to make the mind and senses behave by the practice of withdrawing them from the sense objects. It is as simple as that.

The information in this verse is not provided in order to judge anyone, but so that you may understand how the mind and senses are meant to function.

Verse 59

Knowledge alone removes the longing

विषया विनिवर्तन्ते निराहारस्य देहिनः ।
रसवर्जं रसोऽप्यस्य परं दृष्ट्वा निवर्तते ॥ ५९ ॥

viṣayā vinivartante nirāhārasya dehinaḥ
rasavarjaṁ raso'pyasya paraṁ dṛṣṭvā nivartate (59)

nirāhārasya – for the one who does not feed the sense organs; *dehinaḥ* – for the one who indwells this body; *viṣayāḥ* – senses; *vinivartante* – come back to oneself; *rasa-varjam* – leaving the longing behind; *param* – Brahman; *dṛṣṭvā* – having seen; *asya* – of this person; *rasaḥ* – the longing; *api* – even; *nivartate* – goes away

> For the one who does not feed the senses, the senses come back to oneself, with the longing remaining behind. Having seen Brahman (when the self is known) even the longing goes away.

There is the possibility of a doubt here. Does this capacity to withdraw one's senses from the sense objects at will give the person *jñāna-niṣṭhā*? No. Even a complete fool can practice this technique. A *yogī* also actively engages in this discipline of withdrawing the senses. The sense organs can be withdrawn as a turtle withdraws its limbs. Therefore, you cannot say a person is a *jñāna-niṣṭhā* merely because he or she can withdraw the senses and sit with himself or herself. Śaṅkara presents this doubt here in order to deal with it.

One can withdraw the senses, but the rasa lingers on

Even though you may not go along with your fancies, the taste for them will still be there. Therefore, is this not the practice of suppression, rather than a withdrawal? We have seen how people blow up. The senses definitely get them sooner or later, if not today, then tomorrow. Why, because everything is suppressed inside. When the value for something is inside you, you will definitely deliver yourself into the hands of your senses eventually. Because you are not their master, the senses will get you. If you think you have enslaved them, you need only wait for situations to present themselves. You will find yourself enslaved by your senses in no time. They will take you for a ride. In the wink of an eye, you will be gone totally.

So, even an ordinary person can withdraw the senses, but the taste, *rasa*, and value for the fancies will still be there. Such a person feels that sense enjoyments are important and without them, one cannot be happy. Because this person is told that sense enjoyments are all very painful, he or she decides not to go after them. Then the person might begin practising withdrawal of the senses, but finds that the *rasa* does not go away. Even those who already have a value for meditation and learn to withdraw the senses in order to discover *ānanda* in themselves, or gain inner contentment, may continue to have a value for the enjoyments of the senses.

The question is, when would the taste, the subjective value, for sense enjoyments go? The subjective value is an emotional value. Suppose a person is not a fool and has *viveka*. He is intellectually convinced that sense enjoyments are of no use, because they do not provide any real security or lasting pleasure. Even if this person has no intellectual value for sense enjoyments, he or she may still have an emotional value. Therefore, when and how will this emotional value go?

The emotional value is very important and must be recognised as such. Emotion is a part of your life, part of your expression. Therefore, you cannot dismiss it, nor is it necessary to do so. And emotion does need to be respected because it has a power that can be overpowering. You can be completely overwhelmed by emotion and, therefore, you need to know how to tackle it.

An emotional value, which is a subjective value, is different from an intellectual value, which is objective. Intellectually, your analysis can be clean, 'These are sense objects. They do not contain any joy or security. I am insecure and remain so, whether I have sense objects, whether I have money. Therefore, I need to discover security within myself.' This you may know. Though you know that money does not make you secure, you still have an emotional value for it. And even if you do not have an emotional value for money, an intellectual value will definitely be there because you do need to buy a few things. Therefore, to say that money has no value is not correct.

That money does not give you security is a fact, but money does give you a house, health, haircuts, and a variety of other necessities and comforts. Money is not something that has no value whatsoever. Because it has an objective value, it cannot be dismissed totally.

With reference to its emotional value, money is used to measure success. If someone comes to see you in a new car and your car is battered, you find yourself wanting to have a new car. When money is used to measure your success, there is always a feeling that you have not made it. 'I did not do this and I did not do that' is one of many inner tapes indicative of a subjective, emotional value that cannot be dismissed.

How can you withdraw from that *rasa*, that taste, that is always there? To suppress the value is not the answer because suppression is nothing but a volcano that blows its top one day. Whenever there is suppression, this problem arises. Here, Kṛṣṇa told Arjuna how the subjective value is dealt with.

The word '*viṣayas*' usually means sense objects, but in the present context it stands for the senses, the topic discussed in the previous and following verses. Based on similar expressions found in the *śāstra*, Śaṅkara, in his commentary on this verse, converts sense objects into sense organs. Here, the sense organs belong to a person who does not take to any sense object, who denies himself or herself sense objects, who does not have any sense pursuits, *nirāhāra*. *Āhāra* means 'sense objects' and refers to that which is taken by you. Food is *āhāra*[17] because it is eaten, taken, by you. The one who does not feed the sense organs is therefore called *nirāhāra*. Kṛṣṇa also referred to this person as a *dehī* meaning one who is alive in a physical body.

Śaṅkara makes the point here that the person who engages in a rigorous discipline of sense withdrawal can either be a *vivekī* or an *avivekī*. He or she can even be deluded, a fool, *mūrkhaḥ api*. In all cases, the sense organs that are withdrawn from the sense objects come back to oneself, *viṣayāḥ vinivartante*. But even though the sense organs come back and sense objects are no longer with the person, the taste for the sense objects remains, *rasa-varjaṁ vinivartante*. In other words, the subjective

---

[17] *āhriyate iti āhāraḥ*. *Āhāra* is that which is taken in. Therefore, it can mean food or any sense object in general.

emotional value for them is still there. If the person is deluded, an intellectual value will also be there, impelling the person to perform rigorous disciplines, *tapas*, merely because someone said that they should be done.

The difference between a *vivekī* and an *avivekī*, then is, the *vivekī* will only have subjective value, not intellectual value, whereas the *avivekī* will have both subjective value and intellectual value.

In general terms, *rasa* is a sense and is commonly used to mean *rāga*, liking. Śaṅkara describes it in the same way. Anything that is pleasing to you may be referred to as *rāga* or *rasa*. This is the value that remains inside a person's heart and mind, even after having withdrawn the sense organs from it. This *rasa* too goes away, Kṛṣṇa said, when the self is known, *raso'pi paraṁ dṛṣṭvā nivartate*. This means that when a *vivekī*, who pursues self-knowledge and is judicious about his or her present pursuits, withdraws the senses, there is no suppression. The *vivekī* is only living a life of meaningful discipline. Whereas, for a person who practices sense withdrawal without pursuing this knowledge, the withdrawal does amount to suppression.

The literal meaning of the word *dṛṣṭvā* is, 'having seen,' but here it is used purely in the sense of knowing. What is to be known is 'I am that, *tat paraṁ-brahma aham eva*.' It is not any other *jñāna*. Brahman is myself; there is no difference between the two. Knowing that 'I am Brahman does not imply a knower-known difference. And in the wake of this knowledge, the *rasa* goes away, *nivartate*, meaning that it does not take the person for a ride. How the emotional value for sense objects can capture one's mind is explained by Kṛṣṇa in the next verse.

Once you can no longer be taken for a ride by the *rasa*, the knowledge of sense objects does not create any kind of craving or longing in you. It is *nirbīja*, seedless, and therefore does not sprout, meaning that it does not set you up so that you are carried away by your fancies. However, when the clarity of vision is not there, when knowledge is not there, elimination of *rasa* is not possible. Therefore, *samyag-darśana*, knowledge in the form of clear vision, has to be well established, steady and firm. 'May you work on gaining this vision, again and again' is what is meant here because, if you give up working for this vision, the erroneous vision you have will not go away.

People generally plan to work for clear vision only after they have fixed up everything in their lives, but it does not work that way. There is no 'fixing up of everything' without the vision. So, the pursuit is two-fold, *yoga*, self-mastery, and *jñāna*, self-knowledge.

Removing the sense objects also does not work

Taking the word '*viṣaya*' to mean sense organs, as we have just done, is the simple way of looking at this verse. Now, we will look at it by taking *viṣaya* to mean sense objects. Suppose the sense objects have gone away because you withdraw yourself from the sense world. Previously, you lived in Manhattan and now you are living in the mountains a day and a half away from anyone. You are completely alone. No objects will come to you, no newspapers, radio, or people. You have not even allowed yourself a television set. Having denied yourself these sense pursuits, you are a *nirāhāra*.

However, although the sense objects have gone away, the taste for them will still be there. You will find yourself wondering about what everyone else is doing. Then you will begin to think that you should go back to the city for some time. After all, you will say, even Freud does not condone suppression. And then there are those who will send you letters now and then, pointing out that what you are doing is wrong. This is the prime of your life. Everyone is making money in the stock-market and you are losing opportunities to do the same, something you will certainly come to regret for the rest of your life, all of which will remind you that you are a nobody. Their comments will begin to make a lot of sense to you because you have *rasa* inside. A value for money is there, in fact, the only reason you are able to stay where you are is because you have money.

Alcohol is another example of something for which the *rasa* remains. You may have given it up, even the bottles may have walked away, but the *rasa* will still be there. It will only go when you have something more intoxicating, with more of a kick in it, something more profound, beautiful, and useful. In other words, more powerful, which is why alcoholics require prayer. Without prayer, they cannot easily get rid of the problem. An alcoholic who turns into a sober person can be a saint because he or she has mastered prayer and knows what it is all about. When an alcoholic finds something more powerful than alcohol, the *rasa* for alcohol within the person goes away.

The need to acknowledge emotional values is seen in the alcoholic who thinks that he or she can stop drinking at any time. The alcoholic may even advance the advantages of alcohol in terms of one's health. Of course, when you begin to take alcohol, you are still the master. You can take it or you need not take it. Sometimes you take it and other times you dismiss it. No problem. But alcohol is not an ordinary substance. It is something that takes charge of you in time, so that eventually you have no power over it. It is more powerful than a *rākṣasa*, a demon. From here on, although you may argue that you can stop at any time, in fact, you cannot! You are no longer talking; the alcohol is talking.

First, the person takes the bottle and then, after some time, the bottle calls the person. If it is six o'clock, the time set aside for 'Happy Hour,' and the person is elsewhere, the bottle calls, 'Where are you?' He replies, 'I am here in the office working.' Then the bottle says, 'This is not the time tobe in the office. Come here!' Faithfully, the person goes. 'Come and sit down,' the bottle says, and the person sits down. 'Pick me up!' it says. Once the bottle is in his or her hand, it says, 'Come on, tilt!' Then the person tilts, everyday! There was a time when the person took the bottle; now the bottle takes the person. All decisions about where to go and what to do are made by the bottle, and not by the person.

Where, then, is the question of 'not taking alcohol' being your decision? This is no longer the case. You lost this freedom a long time ago. The only way to stop drinking is to accept that you have no power over alcohol. You have to know it. The acknowledgement alone is the beginning. There is no other way. Once you acknowledge that alcohol has a power over you, there is a chance of you regaining this freedom, provided, of course, that you really decide to stop drinking. You need to acknowledge that you are not going to drink any more. And once you stop taking alcohol, the bottles you have in your cupboard will go away. You will not want to keep them. But the smell of alcohol, the craving for it, will still be there in your head, which is where support groups come in. Otherwise, you may start drinking again and lose yourself totally, after which there is no chance.

Only when people find themselves secure, when they know that they are everything, do the *rasa*s lose their hold. Then, the world can no longer take such people for a ride.

To understand what Kṛṣṇa was saying here, we need not alter the meaning of the word *viṣaya* to mean sense organs. It can be looked at from the perspective of sense objects also.

Verse 60

One needs commitment and constant effort to gain firmness

यततो ह्यपि कौन्तेय पुरुषस्य विपश्चितः ।
इन्द्रियाणि प्रमाथीनि हरन्ति प्रसभं मनः ॥ ६० ॥

yatato hyapi kaunteya puruṣasya vipaścitaḥ
indriyāṇi pramāthīni haranti prasabhaṁ manaḥ (60)

kaunteya – O son of Kuntī!; *hi* – because; *yatataḥ* – of the one who makes effort; *api* – even; *vipaścitaḥ* – of the one who sees clearly; (*api* – even); *puruṣasya* – of the person; *indriyāṇi* – sense organs; *pramāthīni* – powerful; *haranti* – take away; *prasabham* – forcefully; *manaḥ* – the mind

> Indeed, the powerful senses forcefully take the mind away, Kaunteya (Arjuna)! of even the person who makes effort, who sees clearly.

A person who has given up sense pursuits does not feed the sense organs. By using the will, one simply does not pursue sense objects. Only when the senses are with the person, meaning under his or her control, can steadiness in self-knowledge be accomplished. Thus, in the beginning, the will is used to keep the senses in one's own hands.

Anything that is within your control or power is called *sva-vaśa* or *ātma-vaśa*, the word *vaśa* meaning 'within one's hands.' The money in your own pocket that you can spend as you wish is *sva-vaśa*. If however, your money is in the hands of someone else, it is *para-vaśa*. Naturally, you do not have the freedom to spend it as you would like. The other person must give it to you first. Thus, anything in the hands of another is called *para-vaśa* and the one who delivers oneself into the hands of someone else or something is called *para-vaśa*. For example, a person who is totally overpowered by emotion or who is completely controlled by another person is *para-vaśa*. He or she has no freedom.

Still discussing how one becomes a *sthitaprajña*, who is steadfast in the knowledge, Kṛṣṇa said that, first, one's mind and senses have to be with oneself alone. Even though a person is a *vivekī* and has certain knowledge, there is still something to be taken care of because the *rasa* for sense objects is still there. If these are not taken care of, the person will deliver oneself into the hands of *rāga-dveṣa*s.

The word '*yatataḥ*' in this verse means, 'of the person, *puruṣa*, who is making effort.' One may make effort and be a fool, *mūrkha*, but this is not the person being discussed here. The person who makes effort is one who has *viveka*, who sees things clearly, *vipaścit*. Even this person's mind is not steady; it is the mind that is in the hands of the senses and fancies. But he or she is not an armchair *vivekī*. This person has a commitment and makes efforts in order to gain firmness, *niṣṭhā*, in knowledge. This, then, is the kind of mind that is being discussed here.

The sense organs can be turbulent, vicious, and very powerful. They can really shake you up. In this verse, Kṛṣṇa told Arjuna that the sense organs can even take the mind of a *vivekī* away, meaning that they can take charge of his or her mind. Why? Because *rasa*, the taste for sense objects is still there inside the person. As long as *rasa* is there, the sense organs will continue to take charge of the person's mind. As we saw earlier, the sense organs imply the various fancies that one has because he or she still has a value for sense objects. Thus, when we say that the sense organs take the mind away, we mean that the *rasa*s rob the person of his or her *viveka*. By the time the person realises what has happened, the sense organs, meaning the *rasa*s, have already taken the person for a ride!

The use of the word '*hi*' in the verse indicates that all of this is very well-known. The appetites that are there do not ask for any sanction; they forcefully, *prasabham*, take care of you! Therefore, what should you do? The only answer for these *rasa*s is to gain steadiness, *sthairya*, in this knowledge. In the next verse, Kṛṣṇa told Arjuna that this is done by contemplating upon what is.

Verse 61

The necessity for contemplation

तानि सर्वाणि संयम्य युक्त आसीत मत्परः ।
वशे हि यस्येन्द्रियाणि तस्य प्रज्ञा प्रतिष्ठिता ॥ ६१ ॥

tāni sarvāṇi saṁyamya yukta āsīta matparaḥ
vaśe hi yasyendriyāṇi tasya prajñā pratiṣṭhitā (61)

yuktaḥ – the one who is endowed with discrimination; *tāni* – them; *sarvāṇi* – all; *saṁyamya* – keeping in one's hands; *matparaḥ* – in contemplation of me; *āsīta* – may the person sit; *yasya* – whose; *vaśe* – under control; *indriyāṇi* – sense organs; *hi* – indeed; *tasya* – his; *prajñā* – knowledge; *pratiṣṭhitā* – well-established

> May one who is endowed with discrimination, keeping all the sense organs in one's hands, sit in contemplation of me. For the one who has all the sense organs under control, the knowledge is well -established.

The advice given by Kṛṣṇa in this verse is, *tāni sarvāṇi saṁyamya yukta āsīta matparaḥ*. In the compound '*matparaḥ,*' *mat* refers to Īśvara, meaning, in me, Īśvara, and the word *para* means to be committed to. *Āsīta* means, 'may he sit.' Kṛṣṇa says, 'Withdrawing the senses, *tāni sarvāṇi saṁyamya*, may he sit committed to me, Īśvara.'

The person is advised to contemplate upon the one who is *ātmā*, the self, of everything, the *satya*, truth, of everything, who is limitless, who is the inner self of all beings, not just one's own body-mind-senses, but the being of all beings, the existence in all forms of existence. This is the ultimate end to be accomplished and is the Lord, the cause for everything, the truth of everything, which is oneself alone.

Therefore, let the one whose ultimate end, the innermost self, *pratyagātmā* which is the self of all, sit in contemplation, having withdrawn the senses to oneself. Such a person must be a *vivekī*. He or she must already be endowed with the ability to discriminate between the real and the unreal. Some knowledge must be there. Otherwise, sitting in contemplation will not work. If a person sits without *viveka*, what will he or she do? What will the advice, 'Contemplate on Me,' mean to such a person? His or her understanding of this advice will definitely be different because the person does not know what it is all about.

Only when a person has enough enquiry, *śravaṇa*, and understanding, is one endowed with the capacity to discriminate. Only then will the person know what is to be contemplated upon. The question, 'Why should I contemplate?' comes from *rasa*. The vision is stifled; it is knowledge with lot of obstructions, *sapratibandha-jñāna*. The knowledge we are talking about here is that of a *sthitaprajña*, one who is well-established in knowledge. The knowledge is possible only when *rasa* goes and *rasa* goes only by constant contemplation. It takes its own time. Thus, may the person sit in contemplation.

There are different forms of contemplation wherein the same *pratyagātmā*, inner self, is seen from different angles, *pūrṇa-ātmā*, limitless self; *asaṅga-ātmā*, detached self; *sākṣi-ātmā*, self as witness; *akartṛ-ātmā*, action-free self; *abhoktṛ-ātmā*, self that is free from the sense of being an enjoyer; and *ānanda-ātmā*, self that is ever-full, is to be recognised in these different ways. By contemplating upon *ātmā* in this manner, the *rasa*s go. How can they remain? If you know, 'I am all this, *aham idaṁ sarvam*,' the *rasa* cannot be there. Thus, *rasa* goes away in time and knowledge becomes well established and clear, *tasya prajñā pratiṣṭhitā*.

Śaṅkara introduces the next two verses by saying that Kṛṣṇa points out exactly how a person gets into trouble when he or she is completely taken over by the senses, meaning the *rasa*s. This analysis applies to everyone, *vivekī*s and *avivekī*s alike. There is a common psychology here, the psychology of desire–how desire originates, how its pursuit begins, how it destroys your objectivity, and so on – all of which is set out in the two important verses that follow.

Verses 62&63

Attachment destroys one's objectivity

ध्यायतो विषयान्पुंसः सङ्गस्तेषूपजायते ।
सङ्गात्सञ्जायते कामः कामात्क्रोधोऽभिजायते ॥ ६२ ॥

क्रोधाद्भवति सम्मोहः सम्मोहात्स्मृतिविभ्रमः ।
स्मृतिभ्रंशाद् बुद्धिनाशो बुद्धिनाशात्प्रणश्यति ॥ ६३ ॥

dhyāyato viṣayān puṁsaḥ saṅgasteṣūpajāyate
saṅgāt sañjāyate kāmaḥ kāmāt krodho'bhijāyate (62)

krodhād bhavati sammohaḥ sammohāt smṛtivibhramaḥ
smṛtibhraṁśād buddhināśo buddhināśāt praṇaśyati (63)

viṣayān – objects; *dhyāyataḥ* – for the one who dwells upon; *puṁsaḥ* – for the person; *saṅgaḥ* – attachment; *teṣu* – with reference to them; *upajāyate* – is born; *saṅgāt* – from attachment; *sañjāyate* – is born; *kāmaḥ* – desire; *kāmāt* – from desire; *krodhaḥ* – anger; *abhijāyate* – is born; *krodhāt* – from anger; *bhavati* – comes; *sammohaḥ* – delusion; *sammohāt* – from delusion; *smṛti-vibhramaḥ* – loss of memory; *smṛti-bhraṁśāt* – from loss of memory; *buddhi-nāśaḥ* – ruin of the mind; *buddhi-nāśāt* – from the ruin of the mind; *praṇaśyati* – one is destroyed

> In the person who dwells upon objects, an attachment is born with reference to them. From attachment is born desire and from desire, anger is born.

From anger comes delusion and from delusion comes the loss of memory. Because of the loss of memory, the mind becomes incapacitated and when the mind is incapacitated, the person is destroyed.

Every desired object has its own peculiarities, its enticing qualities and desirable attributes. The object is not desired for itself. It is desired because it is seen as desirable. The person being discussed in these two verses meditates on the peculiarities and desirability of various objects, instead of meditating on *pratyagātmā*, the inner self.

One who dwells on a particular object and its merits develops certain longing, love or affection for the object. The word 'object' here refers to anything that you think of and, therefore, includes people as well. First, you come into contact with an object or a person and then, when the encounter is over, it is over, unless, of course, the object or person keeps coming back into your head. There is no reason, as to why certain objects come back into your head. They just do; and when they do, you dwell upon them.

An object that comes back into your head and goes away again is not a problem. Any experience leaves some memory, *smṛti*, and, because of the impact of the experience, the whole scene may be played back in your mind. This, in itself, is not the problem. What happens, however, is that you begin to like the object and begin to dwell upon its desirability. Even at this stage, there is no real problem.

Dwelling upon the object is what is meant by meditation here, meditation meaning constantly thinking about something. It may be something about a person that you keep dwelling upon such as the person's dress, jewellery, voice, speech, mannerisms, decorum, thinking, hair, nose, eyes, or height, all of which represent the countless varieties of objects upon which you can meditate. Meditation is the flow of thoughts about an object and anything connected to it, *sajātīya-vṛtti-pravāha*.

Kṛṣṇa was not talking about the person who meditates on *sat-cit-ānanda-ātmā*, even though the person he was discussing may be smiling while meditating. The smile is only because of the memory of some compliment or other. It is a smile of elation and this elation is what is meant by attachment, *saṅga*. There is certain love, affection that has developed for another person or an object, a sense of being pleased with the object. Otherwise, there would be no attachment. Once a smile comes at the thought of the object, it means that attachment has already been established.

You cannot discover affection for anything without first dwelling upon it. A person may develop affection for a cat merely by continuing to think about it and caring for it. An attachment can also develop so that without the cat, you find that life is empty. If life is full only when it is full of cats and dogs, definitely you will find life full of cats and dogs!

This kind of attachment can occur towards any object, a carpet, furniture, house, anything! Is it any wonder, then, that there is affection and then attachment towards a person who talks back nicely in a sweet voice that utters pleasing words? If affection for and attachment to a mewing cat can be developed, of course a talking, smiling, thinking person is capable of evoking an even better response.

Affection itself is no problem. The problem is this, whatever you like you almost want to possess. This is why Kṛṣṇa said that desire is born from attachment, that attachment is the cause of desire. And because there are different types of objects, there are different types of desires – the desire to possess, the desire to own, the desire to experience.

To create a desire, all that is required is a casual glance at a Caribbean cruise brochure that came in the mail. In fact, the whole idea of direct mail is to create a desire in you. You may call it junk mail, but for those who send it, it is not junk. They know that someone will be attracted to the idea conveyed by the brochure and, to ensure that you do not forget, they also send you follow up literature. When the second brochure arrives, the pleasant memory that had been stored, based on the first brochure comes to mind and affection for the subject matter develops. From this affection alone comes the desire to go on a Caribbean cruise. In this way, the desire to experience, to own, to possess is created.

Not every desire can be fulfilled

Varieties of desires are born, depending on the objects for which you have affection and attachment. Desire is not a problem, but once a well-shaped desire has been formed, it is no longer in the fancy state, and you have to deal with it. You have to fulfil it and this causes you to take action. If you can fulfil the desire, there is no problem. More often than not, however, the desire is not fulfilled. This is where the problem arises.

Not every desire can be fulfilled; it is not that easy. There are many obstacles that prevent the fulfillment of some desires. The problem comes when the desires are not fulfilled, and you become angry. The desire itself turns into anger, *krodha*. Thus, desire is the cause for anger or, in the words of Kṛṣṇa, anger is born of desire.

If there is no expectation with reference to a desire, there will be no anger if the desire is not fulfilled. Suppose you want someone to do something for you and the person does not do it. If you knew that he or she might not do it, then there is no anger. But if you expected the person to do it, you will definitely be angry when it is not done. Even if the anger is not expressed, anger born is born.

The intensity with which you desire something is what determines the magnitude of your anger, and not the object itself. If your desire is such that it does not matter to you whether it is fulfilled, then anger will not be there. Even if it is, it will amount to very little. Whereas, if the intensity of the desire is great, the anger that comes from the desire not being fulfilled is not going to be easily managed either by you or by the person who happens to be between you and what you want. If the other person is an obstruction to what you want, then, your desire will turn into anger towards that person. If you expect the person to behave in a manner and he or she does not do so, then the person will definitely be the target of your anger. And if that person's behaviour is not according to your expectations because of another person, then your anger gets directed towards the other person. Sometimes, your anger against the second may be more than towards the first.

The nature of anger

Anger is always towards the obstruction to the fulfillment of your desire. If between you and the object that you desire there is an obstruction, that obstruction is the target of your anger.

The desire itself is deflected against this obstruction and this deflected ray of desire is what is called anger. This anger is like the vinegar that may result when you try to make wine. Both wine and vinegar have as their essence the grapes alone. But the wine turns into vinegar. How? It too has its own story.

The point here is not to avoid anger by avoiding desire. Rather, you have to remove the sting from your desire, for which a proper attitude is very important. That everything should happen as you want it to is not a realistic expectation. Such an expectation is due to *rāga-dveṣa*s alone, which have to be neutralised if you would like to be free of anger.

Nor is it a matter of controlling anger. What does controlling anger really mean? Anger is inside and you are simmering, simmering, simmering, until suddenly one day, it erupts like a volcano! Once anger is there, what happens is only too well-known. *Aviveka*, lack of discrimination, will definitely be there. In anger, you are not going to take time to consider whether an action is proper or improper. You are not going to spend time considering, 'Should I kick him or should I punch him?' Whatever comes first is what happens. Once anger is there, things just take place. What you do or say takes place of its own accord and depends entirely upon the past, your upbringing, and so on.

There is no question of control here. The very meaning of anger is that *viveka* with reference to what should and should not to be done, is lacking. From anger comes delusion, *sammoha*. What is being pointed out in these two verses is the process that takes place when you dwell on an object. There is no time involved here; dwelling on an object implies affection, desire, anger, delusion, and more.

Because of the delusion born of anger, *smṛti-vibhrama,* loss of memory, takes place. Here, *smṛti,* memory, refers to whatever you may have learned by studying the *śāstra,* from your teachers, elders, and life's experiences, whatever you have assimilated about right and wrong, what made you angry in the past, what happened, and so on. None of these you remember because delusion has come, and, along with it *aviveka.* Thus, there is a loss of memory with reference to the wisdom you had gathered from your past education and experiences.

Once the wisdom of your past experiences, *smṛti,* is not available, the mind is incapacitated. There is *buddhi-nāśa.* Your *buddhi* now, is incapable of analysing whether something is to be done or not to be done because whatever wisdom you had gathered is not available to you. Delusion is like an inner torpor, a blackout that makes you forget the wisdom you had. Therefore, your *buddhi,* intellect, is unable to do what it is supposed to do. It is incapable of giving orders to go ahead or stop in accordance with what is right and wrong. This is what the *buddhi* is supposed to do, but it is not available to do it.

In the absence of wisdom, impulse takes over

The *buddhi* is only available when wisdom is available. In the absence of wisdom, it behaves as though it is programmed;

impulse takes over. In other words, the *buddhi* is destroyed, *praṇaśyati*. The person is no more a human being and can be likened to an animal because he or she gives himself or herself over to impulses. The impulses take over and determine exactly what the person is going to do. It may be biting, kicking, screaming, hitting someone, or even committing suicide. When a person is controlled by impulse, anything can happen and whatever happens, just happens.

Until anger comes, the person can be careful, but once anger is there, all caution is gone. The verbs used in these two verses are very revealing in this regard. From attachment, desire 'is born' and from desire, anger 'is born.' At this point, however, the verb changes from 'is born' to 'takes place.' From anger, delusion 'takes place' and from delusion, the incapacity of the mind 'takes place.' This shows how the person has no more any control over the situation. Once anger is born, delusion, loss of wisdom, and the destruction of the person just take place. Control is possible only before anger; afterwards, what happens is history.

Given that meditating on desirable objects creates problems for you, the message of the *Gītā* is clear, instead of meditating upon objects, meditate upon the self. Instead of meditating upon your own problems and inhibitions, meditate upon the *pratyagātmā*, the inner self, because, if you do not, you will naturally meditate upon the objects, which is the cause of all of your problems.

Verse 64

A karma-yogī is a mumukṣu

रागद्वेषवियुक्तैस्तु विषयानिन्द्रियैश्चरन् ।
आत्मवश्यैर्विधेयात्मा प्रसादमधिगच्छति ॥ ६४ ॥

rāgadveṣaviyuktaistu viṣayān indriyaiścaran
ātmavaśyairvidheyātmā prasādam adhigacchati (64)

tu – whereas; *rāga-dveṣa-viyuktaiḥ* – free from likes and dislikes; *ātmavaśyaiḥ* – with those that are under his or her control; *indriyaiḥ* – with the sense organs; *viśayān caran* – moving in the world of objects; *vidheyātmā* - one whose mind is controlled; *prasādam* – tranquility; *adhigacchati* – attains

> Whereas, one whose mind is controlled, moving in the world of objects with the sense organs that are under his or her control, free from likes and dislikes, attains tranquility.

We have seen that even a *vivekī* cannot but dwell upon objects of *rāga-dveṣa*s, likes and dislikes, if he or she still has *rasa*, a value, for these objects. And this dwelling upon is also called meditation. One dwells upon objects of *dveṣa* in order to avoid them, for which one has to scheme and plan, whereas objects of *rāga* are dwelt upon in order to gain them.

Dwelling upon the desirability of objects is, indeed, the basis for all problems that come later. It is the cause for the affection and love that develops for the object. Once affection is there, it will naturally turn into a desire. If the desire is fulfilled, there is no problem, but if it is not fulfilled, the whole psychology of how one loses oneself comes into play, as Kṛṣṇa pointed out in the previous two verses. The present verse reveals how the problem created by unfulfilled desires becomes neutralised and, once again, points out the starting point for *mokṣa*, liberation.

The natural pursuit of a person's sense organs is in keeping with his or her *rāga*s and *dveṣa*s. Suppose the person is a seeker, a *mumukṣu*, meaning that he or she wants *mokṣa* for which self-knowledge is required, then all his or her pursuits cannot be dictated by his or her *rāga-dveṣa*s. The word '*mumukṣu*' is especially pertinent here in that it means one who is desirous of liberation, *moktum icchuḥ, mumukṣuḥ*. We have seen that *mokṣa* is one of the four pursuits open to a human being. But for a *mumukṣu*, *mokṣa* alone is important. He or she has already sought after and experienced pursuits of *artha*, security, and *kāma*, pleasure, or has learned about them by observing the pursuits of others. From all these, the person has developed *viveka*, discrimination, and because of this *viveka* alone, has become a *mumukṣu*.

Thus, the one who has *viveka* is a *mumukṣu*, whereas a person who is merely curious is not. The person who wants to be free must necessarily have lot of *viveka* for this particular desire. At the same time, he or she does have some *rāga-dveṣa*s. *Rāga-dveṣa*s do not just go away because the person has *viveka*. What does a *mumukṣu* do then?

This was exactly Arjuna's situation. During the war that eventually ensued, his son died and Arjuna took a vow that, before sunset, he would avenge his son's death by killing the person who was responsible. We see, then, that Arjuna had lot of grief. It was because *rāga-dveṣa*s do not go away overnight. Even though, in the eighteenth chapter of the *Gītā*, which preceded the above episode, Arjuna had said, 'No more delusion for me. I know exactly what it is all about.' He still had ambitions and therefore attachments. He had definitely been living a life of *dharma*, but *rāga-dveṣa*s were still in his heart. This is why one has to live a life of *karma-yoga* for a length of time.

The sense organs of a *mumukṣu* are freed from *rāga-dveṣa*s, meaning that they are not backed by, *rāga-dveṣa*s. It is because the *mumukṣu* has been living a life of *karma-yoga*. Such a person does not run away from the world. Where would he or she go? The *mumukṣu* goes about in the world, experiencing the sense objects. The word '*caran*' here generally means 'reaching' or 'going' in the sense of movement, but it can also have the sense of knowledge. In fact, any verbal root that has a sense of reaching or going has also the sense of knowing or experiencing. For example, the expression 'reaching Brahman' means understanding or knowing Brahman; there is no 'going' or 'moving' in the sense of reaching somewhere.

So too, in this verse, *caran* does not mean that the person is moving around in the physical sense. The word means 'experiencing' and takes the sense organs into account, the experience of seeing, hearing, touching, smelling, and tasting. The senses are open and the world of sense objects is there. The verse also describes the sense organs as being in the person's hands and not in the hands of *rāga-dveṣas*, *ātmavaśyaiḥ rāga-dveṣa-viyuktaiḥ indriyaiḥ viṣayān caran*. It means that one's pursuits are not dictated by *rāga* and *dveṣa*, but by *dharma* and *adharma*, what is proper and improper. The person decides what he or she wants and is not goaded by his or her likes and dislikes. In other words *rāga-dveṣa*s do not decide.

When your *rāga-dveṣa*s do not come between yourself and the sense pursuits, the determining factor for the sense pursuits is purely *dharma* and *adharma*. You then become one whose mind moves only according to your will. In other words, you are a person who is 'together.' Such a person is a *karma-yogī*, living a life of *karma-yoga* for the sole purpose of neutralising his or her *rāga-dveṣa*s.

Every *karma-yogī* is a *mumukṣu*. *Karma-yoga* is there only because the person has *mumukṣā*, desire for liberation. Because *karma-yoga* is meant for *mokṣa*, the *karma-yogī* pursues knowledge while engaged in freeing him or her from the hold of *rāga-dveṣa*. The latter pursuit makes the person *karma-yogī* and marks the difference between a *karma-yogī* and a *sannyāsī*. Whether the person is a *sannyāsī* or a *karma-yogī*, he or she is one who has the senses and mind together. Such a person gains satisfaction or tranquillity, *prasāda*.

We have already seen that *prasāda* is anything that comes from the Lord. But *prasāda* has another meaning too, namely, cheerfulness, satisfaction, tranquillity, which is what happens in the mind of one whose sense organs are in one's own hands and when one is free from the hold of *rāga-dveṣa*s. The satisfaction, the contentment, is with oneself. The mind is steady and there is an almost total absence of agitation and self-dissatisfaction. The person's knowledge is *sthira*, steady, and it stays. That *rāga-dveṣa*s are to be tackled is the whole psychology of the *Gītā*.

Verse 65

For a person of tranquil mind knowledge is well-established

प्रसादे सर्वदुःखानां हानिरस्योपजायते ।
प्रसन्नचेतसो ह्याशु बुद्धिः पर्यवतिष्ठते ॥ ६५ ॥

prasāde sarvaduḥkhānāṁ hānirasyopajāyate
prasannacetaso hyāśu buddhiḥ paryavatiṣṭhate (65)

prasāde – when the mind is tranquil; *asya* – his; *sarva-duḥkhānām* – of all the pain and sorrow; *hāniḥ* – destruction; *upajāyate* – is born; *hi* – because; *prasanna–cetasaḥ* – of the tranquil minded; *āśu* – soon; *buddhiḥ* – knowledge; *paryavatiṣṭhate* – is well-established

> For the person whose mind is tranquil, destruction of all pain and sorrow happens. The knowledge of one whose mind is tranquil soon becomes well-established.

One whose mind is under control directs the mind according to his or her will. Such a person experiences the world through sense organs that are not backed by likes and dislikes. In this way, the *rāga-dveṣa*s are neutralised and the person gains a mind which is cheerful, composed and tranquil.

For the person whose mind is tranquil, *duḥkha*s, pain and sorrow, are destroyed. Although the plural form of *duḥkha*s is used here, sorrows are the same. One person is crying because he lost the kingdom and someone else is crying because he lost his car. What is the difference between their two sorrows? Both of them are crying. Does *duḥkha* subject itself to division? No, sorrow is the same whatever the reason. Whether you lose your kingdom or your hair, sadness is the same. What Kṛṣṇa meant here is that any sorrow, whatever be its source, is destroyed for the person whose mind is tranquil.

In an earlier discussion, we saw the three sources of sorrow, *ādhibhautika-duḥkha*, sorrow caused by people and situations in the external world; *ādhidaivika-duḥkha*, sorrow caused by calamities over which you have no control; and finally, *ādhyātmika-duḥkha*, sorrow caused by your own body, mind and senses. Your own past memories or the condition of your physical body create *ādhyātmika-duḥkha*, whereas the *duḥkha* caused by your brother-in-law is an example of *ādhibhautika-duḥkha* Any natural calamity is *ādhidaivika-duḥkha*. Kṛṣṇa said, that these three-fold *duḥkha*s are destroyed, *sarva-duḥkhānāṁ hāniḥ upajāyate*. Although *duḥkha*s are destroyed when the mind is tranquil, the causes for *duḥkha*s themselves do not go away. They are merely incapable of causing *duḥkha*. The body may experience physical pain, but there will be no *duḥkha* because the mind is tranquil, *prasanna*. A tranquil mind means the *rāga*s and *dveṣa*s have been neutralised. Desirable and undesirable situations do not cause reactions.

*Duḥkha*s are said to be destroyed because the real nature of the self is tranquillity, and that tranquillity is manifest in the mind. The mind is stifled only because of *rāga-dveṣa*. The fullness of the self, which is its nature, *ānanda-svarūpa*, is inhibited from manifesting in the mind because of *rāga-dveṣa*s alone. When the *rāga-dveṣa*s are neutralised, *ānanda* is uninhibited and the mind is tranquil. Destruction of *duḥkha* is said to be born, *upajāyate*, here in the sense that it happens, it takes place.

Does mere tranquillity destroy all forms of *duḥkha*? No, destruction of *duḥkhas* can only happen when there is self-knowledge. *Duḥkha*s go away for the person who has a tranquil mind because knowledge for such a person is not far away. We are talking about a *sthitaprajña* here. This knowledge, the subject matter of which is *ātmā*, self-knowledge, is steady and, like space, it just stays; it does not move. The earth, air, and everything else moves, whereas space is always steady.

Similarly, the mind of a person with self-knowledge stays. And because the knowledge stays, the mind no longer causes any problem. The knowledge stays because there is nothing to oppose or inhibit it. It means that the very person stays in the form of knowledge. The mind of such a person becomes a useful instrument. Because the mind is tranquil, it no longer causes trouble.

To gain tranquillity, you have to take care of your *rāga-dveṣa*s. Whatever is required is what you have to follow, whether it is *karma-yoga* or something else. Only when tranquillity is there does knowledge stay. It means that the knowledge becomes clear, having been freed from all vagueness and doubts. Otherwise, you will always doubt your own knowledge. You will say things like, 'With this kind of mind, how can I say that I know?' The mind itself creates all kinds of doubts, which is the problem.

The mind has to gain the tranquillity that is the basis for self-knowledge and to do this, it has to free itself from the *rāga-dveṣa*s. Then the *duḥkha*s go away because the knowledge stays. Tranquillity is the condition that frees one's knowledge from all obstructions and because of that knowledge, sorrows are gone and the person is said to have gained *mokṣa*.

Verses 66&67

For the one who has no peace, there is no happiness

नास्ति बुद्धिरयुक्तस्य न चायुक्तस्य भावना ।
न चाभावयतः शान्तिरशान्तस्य कुतः सुखम् ॥ ६६ ॥

nāsti buddhirayuktasya na cāyuktasya bhāvanā
na cābhāvayataḥ śāntiraśāntasya kutaḥ sukham (66)

ayuktasya – for the one who is not tranquil; *buddhiḥ* – knowledge; *na asti* – is not there; *ayuktasya* – for the one who is not tranquil; *bhāvanā ca* – contemplation also; *na* – is not; *abhāvayataḥ* – for the one who is not contemplative; *śāntiḥ* – peace; *na* – is not; *ca* – and; *aśāntasya* – for the one who has no peace; *kutaḥ* – how; *sukham* – happiness

> For the one who is not tranquil, there is no knowledge. For the one who is not tranquil, there is no contemplation also. For the one who is not contemplative, there is no peace. For the one who has no peace, how can there be happiness?

This verse is Kṛṣṇa's way of praising a tranquil mind, that is, *prasannatā*. The word '*ayukta*,' here, means a person who does not have the cheerful, tranquil mind that was discussed in the previous verse. *Ayukta* is one who has not taken care of his or her *rāga-dveṣa*s sufficiently. It must be clearly understood that what is being said here is in no way meant as a judgement. If this is not understood correctly, a problem of self-judgement can arise as you listen to the *Gītā* and the *vedānta-śāstra*. 'I am useless!' you may say. Because there is already a tape inside, the self-criticism begins immediately. All that the Swami has to do is utter one negative statement and this inner tape switches on automatically, 'Because I am an *ayukta*, I will never get this knowledge.'

Since the tendency is to judge yourself, you must know that what is being said in the *Gītā* is not meant as criticism; its sole purpose is self-understanding. If, having heard what the *Gītā* says, there is something to be done, it is to be done. There is nothing more to it than that. If *rāga-dveṣa*s are there, they are to be taken care of, that is all.

The word '*buddhi*,' here means knowledge of the self, that by which you understand *ātmā*, the self. Adequate knowledge does not take place for one whose mind is in the hands of *rāga-dveṣa*s. For a *yukta*, the *rāga-dveṣa*s are neutralised and there is no problem, whereas for an *ayukta*, *rāga-dveṣa*s are there, causing his or her knowledge to be inadequate. In addition to the knowledge being inadequate, the pressure of *rāga-dveṣa*s, more often than not, will drive the person towards the desirable objects to be gained and retained and those that are to be avoided and eliminated.

There is nothing right or wrong about *rāga-dveṣa* pursuits. This is just to explain how the pressures of *rāga-dveṣa* work.

Because of the natural tendency of the mind towards objects of *rāga-dveṣa*s, there is no yearning for or commitment to self-knowledge. There is time only to nurse your *rāga-dveṣa*s. Even if you try to read the *Gītā*, your *rāga* will keep clamouring at you, 'What are you doing? What kind of book are you reading? It is not going to fulfil any of your *rāga-dveṣa*s. I have so many things to interest you.' In this way, the *rāga-dveṣa*s seated inside you, demand your attention so much so, that if you begin reading the *Gītā*, you will either fall asleep or feel like doing something else!

*Rāga-dveṣa*s being there, one's interest in the pursuit of self-knowledge will necessarily be stifled and one's commitment inhibited. Even if you want to contemplate upon the self in order to get rid of some of your problems, the pressure of *rāga-dveṣa*s makes contemplation very difficult. You find that you are unable to sit with yourself even for a short period of time.

For the person who cannot sit with oneself, who cannot contemplate, who cannot pursue self-knowledge quietly, there is no composure, no tranquillity. Whereas, for the one who can contemplate upon oneself, who can stay with oneself, there is tranquillity and love of oneself. Thus, the more one can be with oneself, the more tranquil one will be.

We are not talking about the commonly known self here. We are talking about the real self, the self that is beautiful. The more you begin to understand, the more you begin to love the self. The self, *ātmā*, is not other than you; therefore, self-love comes. And because the self is absolute, the love for it is absolute.

A lot is talked about the necessity of developing self-love. But how can you develop love for this limited self that you have with its crippling *rāga-dveṣa*s? Without feeling love for yourself, you cannot sit with yourself and, when you cannot sit with yourself, there is no tranquillity, all of which implies *aśānti*, absence of peace and contentment.

Only a tranquil mind can discover happiness

You may say that you do not want *śānti*, peace and contentment, but want only *sukha*, happiness. You may say, 'Some people may want *śānti* but I am an enterprising person. I want pleasure, joy, and happiness. For me *śānti* is useless!' But, *sukha*, happiness, is possible only in a tranquil mind. When you cannot sit with yourself, naturally you are agitated. When you are agitated, where is the possibility of *sukha* for you? When you are agitated, there is no *sukha*. A person who is *aśānta*, who does not have *śānti* cannot pick up any *sukha*. There is no way! *Sukha* is only with yourself. Therefore, the more you can stay with yourself, more tranquil you are, and more tranquil you are, the happier you are.

Happiness, then, is another word for tranquillity. Only the tranquil person can discover happiness. In fact, you discover happiness even in small things. You do not require a talk show to be happy. Everything in the world becomes amusing to the person who is tranquil. If you have tranquillity, the whole world is a continuous joke. You require nothing; it is all there, free of charge. Just open your eyes and you see the joke!

When inner tranquillity is there, you require nothing to be happy, whereas if it is not there, happiness cannot even be bought.

'Happy hour' does not buy you happiness; it only robs you of your money. It may be a happy hour for the owner of the bar, but not for anyone else. For both, you and your family, it is definitely an unhappy hour. When you cannot stay with yourself, where is the possibility of *sukha* for you?

You need to take care of your *rāga-dveṣa*s; otherwise they are a nuisance. Therefore, whatever is to be done to take care of them must be done. It may imply *karma-yoga, śravaṇa*, listening to the teaching, or *manana*, further analysis. How the knowledge takes place, what is required for it to be *sthira*, steady and why it can be *asthira*, unsteady, is what is being discussed in these verses.

इन्द्रियाणां हि चरतां यन्मनोऽनुविधीयते ।
तदस्य हरति प्रज्ञां वायुर्नावमिवाम्भसि ॥ ६७ ॥

indriyāṇāṁ hi caratāṁ yanmano'nuvidhīyate
tadasya harati prajñāṁ vāyurnāvam ivāmbhasi (67)

hi – indeed; *caratām* – of the wandering; *indriyāṇām* – of the senses; *yat manaḥ* – that mind which; *anuvidhīyate* – follows; *tat* – that; *asya* – his; *prajñām* – knowledge; *harati* – robs away; *vāyuḥ* – the wind; *nāvam* – a small boat; *iva* – just as; *ambhasi* – on the waters

> The mind that follows the wandering senses indeed robs the person of his knowledge, just as the wind carries away a small boat on the waters.

For the one whose mind is not resolved, and is therefore in the hands of *rāga-dveṣa*s, there is no knowledge. Even if knowledge is there, it is not adequate, as it has already been pointed out. This is because the mind follows, goes behind, the moving senses, which are engaged in their own spheres of activity. For example, the eyes have their sphere of seeing in forms and colours and the ears have their sphere in sounds. Thus, one finds that each sense organ has its own sphere of activity. As the sense organs experience the objects according to their own spheres, the mind naturally has some fancies that one goes after as they arise. In other words, one goes along with the sense cravings.

The person being discussed in this verse is one whose mind joins with the sense perceptions, with reference to which there are some inner cravings or fancies. A mind that joins the senses robs away your knowledge, the knowledge born of the discriminative enquiry of yourself. It means that whatever self-knowledge you may have had is as good as gone! Your mind, meaning the will, is one that says 'yes' to everything that is not to be done and 'no' to whatever has to be done. To illustrate this point, Kṛṣṇa used the example of the wind with its capacity to take a small boat away from its destination.

Robbed of self-knowledge, the mind is busy with objects alone. It has no time for self-knowledge. In fact, there is no time for anything because there are so many *rāga-dveṣa*s. Because situations do not happen as you want, there is nothing but concerns, one after the other. First, the pressure of *rāga-dveṣa* is in the form of undifferentiated concern and then the concern is in the form of desire, regret, disappointment, sorrow, despair, anxiety, and a constant sense of loss.

When the mind is occupied with objects, there is concern, whereas when it is occupied with the self, the *ātmā*, there is no concern, only tranquillity. The self will not run away. It stays put. Even if you come back after twenty years, *ātmā* will still be *sat-cit-ānanda*. Regardless of which book you read, *ātmā* will not grow into *asat-cit-ānanda*. *Ātmā* is always fullness, limitlessness, *ānanda*. If the object of your knowledge is *ātmā*, then there is *ānanda* for you.

Verse 68

Knowledge and mastery of the mind go hand-in-hand

Kṛṣṇa sums up what he had said with reference to one's knowledge becoming steady in the following verse.

तस्माद्यस्य महाबाहो निगृहीतानि सर्वशः ।
इन्द्रियाणीन्द्रियार्थेभ्यस्तस्य प्रज्ञा प्रतिष्ठिता ॥ ६८ ॥

tasmād yasya mahābāho nigṛhītāni sarvaśaḥ
indriyāṇīndriyārthebhyastasya prajñā pratiṣṭhitā (68)

tasmāt – therefore; *mahābāho* – O mighty armed (Arjuna)!; *yasya* – whose; *indriyāṇi* – senses; *indriya-arthebhyaḥ* – from sense objects; *sarvaśaḥ* – completely; *nigṛhītāni* – are withdrawn, mastered; *tasya* – his; *prajñā* – knowledge; *pratiṣṭhitā* – is steady

Therefore, Arjuna, the mighty armed! the knowledge of one whose senses are completely withdrawn (mastered) from their respective objects is steady.

The word '*tasmāt*' indicates that Kṛṣṇa was summing up this section that described the mind of a person who has some vision, and who is making an effort to make his or her knowledge steady. He explained that because the senses are turbulent, they could rob away the mind of such a person. How they do this was also discussed.

Kṛṣṇa addressed Arjuna here as '*mahābāho*, O, Mighty armed Arjuna!' One may be mighty armed with reference to one's prowess and skill, but what is needed for self-knowledge is to be mighty armed, that is, strong in the mind, which is more difficult. The prowess and skills that Arjuna had gathered to earn him the name 'Mighty-armed' were great in their own sphere in that he was able to control all external enemies, but his ability to control the inner one was the issue here.

To control the senses, to withdraw them from their respective objects, means to be able to withdraw them at will, just as the turtle withdraws its head and limbs into its shell whenever it senses any danger. If you want to release the senses, release them, if you want to withdraw them, withdraw them. It means that the senses are under your control. Only when you have the capacity to withdraw your senses at will, can your knowledge be steady. The idea here is that knowledge becomes steady only when the mind is freed from the pressure of your *rāga-dveṣa*.

To the extent you master your *rāga-dveṣa*s, to that extent your knowledge stays. Because your *rāga-dveṣa*s are neutralised, you can enjoy the benefits of your knowledge. The pressure of *rāga-dveṣa*s being less, the benefits of the knowledge are more. The knowledge is complete when *rāga-dveṣa*s have no say in your life, when they are neutralised, when it makes no difference to you whether a desire is fulfilled or not. Only then is there no hindrance to self-knowledge.

There is a trick to all this in that, as your knowledge grows in clarity, mastery of the mind over *rāga-dveṣa*s also takes place. With *karma-yoga* attitude, *rāga-dveṣa*s are mastered to an extent and the knowledge becomes clearer. Thus, there is a mutual kinship between the two.

The entire presentation of *yoga* in the *Gītā* is with reference to *rāga-dveṣa*s. The psychology of *Gītā* is *rāga-dveṣa* psychology and, as a psychology, the *Gītā* itself is adequate and complete. When we are dealing with normal people, *rāga-dveṣa* psychology is enough. It implies an order, *dharma-adharma*, which is looked upon as Īśvara, the Lord, the giver of the fruits of action, which bring about a neutralisation of your *rāga-dveṣa*s.

Taking care of *rāga-dveṣa*s itself brings about tranquillity, cheerfulness to the mind. As the cheerfulness increases, your knowledge becomes clearer. Conversely, as knowledge becomes clearer, your cheerfulness increases. In other words, the pressure caused by *rāga-dveṣa*s is less. Just as a bird requires both wings to take off, so too, we require both wings, enquiry and a proper attitude, to glide into this knowledge. One wing is as important as the other.

Verse 69

Ignorance and knowledge are like night and day

या निशा सर्वभूतानां तस्यां जागर्ति संयमी ।
यस्यां जाग्रति भूतानि सा निशा पश्यतो मुनेः ॥ ६९ ॥

yā niśā sarvabhūtānāṁ tasyāṁ jāgarti saṁyamī
yasyāṁ jāgrati bhūtāni sā niśā paśyato muneḥ (69)

sarvabhūtānām – for all beings; *yā* – that which; *niśā* – night; *tasyām* – in that; *saṁyamī* – one who has mastery over oneself (who is wise); *jāgarti* – is awake; *yasyām* – that in which; *bhūtāni* – beings; *jāgrati* – are awake; *sā* – that; *paśyataḥ muneḥ* – for the wise person who sees; *niśā* – night

> In that which is night for all beings, the one who is wise, who has mastery over oneself, is awake. That in which beings are awake, is night for the wise person who sees.

Kṛṣṇa had been answering Arjuna's question about how a *sthitaprajña*, person of wisdom, is defined and how such a person interacts with the world. Upon analysis, we find Kṛṣṇa's answer a very interesting one. First, he defined a *sthitaprajña* as one who is happy with himself by himself and thereby one who is free from the hold of desires.

One who is able to give up binding desires as they arise in one's mind, being happy with oneself, in oneself, is awake to the nature of oneself and is, therefore, wise. The wisdom of such a person is steady.

Although Arjuna expressed the second part of his question with the words, 'How does a wise person talk, sit, and walk?' the spirit of his question was, 'How does such a person interact with the world?' Taking the spirit of Arjuna's question into account, Kṛṣṇa replied that one's wisdom is steady only when one's mind is no longer a problem.

Kṛṣṇa said that *rāga-dveṣa*s are the cause for one's knowledge being stifled or inhibited. For the person whose sense organs are freed from *rāga-dveṣa*, and whose pursuits are not backed by *rāga-dveṣa*s, the knowledge remains because he or she has a cheerful mind, a mind that is not in the hands of *rāga-dveṣa*s. Kṛṣṇa then summed up by saying that for the one who has withdrawn the sense organs from the sense objects, who has the sense organs with oneself, if indeed this person has self-knowledge, that knowledge will be steady.

Having said all this Kṛṣṇa was not very happy with his reply to Arjuna's question because he knew that to know whether a person is wise, you yourself must be wise. How else are you going to know otherwise? Only a person who is wise knows what it takes to be wise. Arjuna thought that the characteristics of a wise person could be a kind of *sādhana*, a means for becoming wise. But how could he understand these characteristics if he himself was not wise? This is what Kṛṣṇa still had to convey to Arjuna.

Kṛṣṇa had talked about the person who is happy with oneself and, since a mad man can also be happy with himself, he also pointed out that a *sthitaprajña* must have knowledge. Recognising that his description of a wise person was not complete, Kṛṣṇa adds this very interesting verse. In essence, what he says is that a wise person is like a wise person and the 'other-wise' cannot really understand such a person without becoming wise. He illustrated his point by saying that what is night for all people is day for a wise person who has the mind and senses with him or her. Such a person is a *saṁyamī* here. The word '*yama*' means mastery or control over the mind and senses, and *saṁyamī*, one who has that mastery along with knowledge.

Further, Kṛṣṇa said, that which is day for everyone else is night for the wise person, called *muni* here. *Muni* means the one who sees things clearly, *mananaśīla*. For this person of clear vision, the state that everyone else thinks of as day is night. In other words, when all beings are awake, the *sthitaprajña* sleeps. And when they are asleep, the wise person is awake.

Does it mean that the wise person is some nocturnal being, like a bat, or a thief who prowls about at night? Not at all. Just as the darkness of night does not allow you to see objects as they are, night here represents darkness with reference to one's knowledge not being clear. The wise person is awake to what is night for all beings, the night of *avidyā*, ignorance.

What is not known to people is called the sleep of night, the sleep of darkness, or ignorance, *avidyā-nidrā*. In this sleep of ignorance, people are like somnambulists, sleepwalkers. This state is more than just sleep; such people are dreamers. They are sleeping, but awake, just like in dream. They are awake and perform different activities, yet they are asleep because they are not awake to realities.

If you are totally asleep or totally awake, you have no problem. The problem is when you are only half-awake, this being a state where mistakes are possible. In dream, a person is partly awake, meaning that there is some projection by the mind. The person is not identified with the body and the physical reality, but is identified with memories and thoughts, from which a dream world is set-up.

The reality of duality

In the dream world, everything is *dvaita*, dual, for the person. The knower is distinct from the known, the known is distinct from the knower, and the knowledge, of course is distinct from the knower, being something that the knower has and for which there is distinct object, that is, the known.

This division in dream is a reality for the dreamer. But, upon waking, all the three – the knower, known, and knowledge – become one and the same. The known objects in the dream are not separate from knowledge. The knowledge is not separate from the knower; and the knower is not separate from the waker. All the three that belong to the dream resolve into the waker, when the person who is dreaming wakes up. The waker was the knower, the known, and the knowledge in the dream. The knower is the waker, which is why one says, 'I dreamt.' The *ātmā*, the self of the knower that obtained in the dream, obtains also in the waking state, as evidenced by the expression of the experience as, 'I dreamt. I was the one who was dreaming.' In the dream, however, everything is a reality.

Even the Veda recognises *dvaita*, addressing you as a *kartā*, doer. Śaṅkara discusses this in his commentary to this verse. The Veda tells you to perform *karma*s and it also tells you what you will gain by doing them. There are very specific differences mentioned also. It says, 'This *karma* will produce this result if it is done in this manner by this person at this time.' Thus, rituals to be performed are set out in the Veda, all of which implies duality because it addresses a *kartā* who is different from the *karma* he does.

The Veda that says you are non-dual Brahman addresses you, in the earlier sections, as a person who wants certain results and who is going to get these results later. The connection between the person and the results is established by performing the prescribed rituals, the result of which is *puṇya*. This *puṇya* is what connects the person to the result. The people, rituals, and the results are different and therefore constitute duality.

Your perception also tells you that one object is different from another object. Perception gives rise to different types of knowledge and based on that knowledge you conclude that everything is different from you. The first part of the *śruti*, as we have seen, also confirms this difference by addressing you as a doer and not as *paraṁ-brahma*. If the Veda were to address you as *paraṁ-brahma*, it could not ask you to perform action. Thus, it can only address you as a doer.

The *śruti* deals with the person who is available right now. You are now a doer and that doer is addressed. Furthermore, the doer is told that he or she will be an enjoyer later if some *karma*s are performed. If they are not done, or not done properly, the person will have problems later. Even if a wrong action is done, the doer will still be an enjoyer, but the 'enjoyment' will not be very pleasant! In this way, the *śruti* keeps the person in view and talks about what is good and bad for the person, what should be done and what should be avoided.

Thus, it looks as though the *śruti* is for the doer alone and that duality is a reality. Naturally, then, the person looks upon himself or herself, in the waking state, as someone different from the world, just as in the dream. This is what is meant by the sleep of ignorance. Because of ignorance alone, the person is said to be sleeping. Sleeping here means that one is a dreamer. The person is not totally sleeping. He or she is awake doing various activities. There is even a valid *pramāṇa* available to the person, enabling him or her to know that some actions are right and others are wrong. As long as this sleep of ignorance continues, everything is valid for the person in the waking state, just as it is in dream. One doer is different from every other doer and one enjoyer is different from every other enjoyer.

The physical body is the place of enjoyment, the counter of experience from which you encounter the world; it is the point from which you operate. You are an enjoyer and a mosquito is also an enjoyer, you being the object of its enjoyment. Thus, you find there are many enjoyers and different kinds of enjoyments; there are different doers and different types of doing, which are valid. Therefore, pain and pleasure are valid. That 'I am a small person is valid, I am someone who is struggling to prove myself to be somebody is valid, and that the struggle never comes to an end is also valid.'

The vision of the wise and the other-wise

Everything seems to be valid to those who see themselves as distinct. But, amidst all this validity, one thing alone is not known, the *paramārtha-tattva*. *Tattva* means reality and *paramārtha-tattva* is the ultimate reality, the essential reality of everything. The differences that seem so real in dream and waking have no independent reality apart from this essential reality. What is essentially there, is only one thing and that is what I am, *tad aham asmi*. The knower is myself, the known is myself, the knowledge is myself, the doer is myself, the doing is myself, and the done is myself. The world is myself and the knower of the world is also myself. That the knower, known, and knowledge are myself is an entirely different vision altogether. In reality there is no difference whatsoever.

For a wise person, the *paramārtha-tattva* is one thing alone and it is oneself. This *paramārtha-tattva* is not recognised by those who are not wise. For them, everything is real. It means that there is more than one reality for such people, which is why the world is always too much for them. To think that everyone is different from you means that everyone is as real as you are. Words too will have their own realities so that everything is as real as everything else. Naturally, then, you find a world, which is dual. In other words, you experience *saṁsāra*.

While others are in this great sleep of ignorance, the wise person is awake to the *paramārtha-tattva*. He or she is awake to the reality of *ātmā*, the knowledge of which nullifies the division between the knower and the known since, in reality, there is no division. Therefore, '*aham idaṁ sarvam*, I am all this.' Previously, I was only one among the many. Now the vision is that, immanently, I am everything, and transcendentally, I am free from everything. To this fact, the wise person, the *saṁyamī* is awake.

Those who are not wise are awake only to divisions. These divisions are very real for such people, whereas for the wise person, the person of enquiry whose vision is very clear, any division is night. The *saṁsāra* that people complain about, he or she does not see at all. One person may say, 'I am sad,' but the wise person does not see any sadness. Others complain that the world is too much for them, but the wise person does not find it to be so. It is not that the world is too much. You are too much. You are everything.

Therefore, the vision of the wise person is, '*ahaṁ pūrṇaḥ*, I am limitless.' Whereas other people say, '*ahaṁ apūrṇaḥ*, I am limited.' This is their vision, which for the wise person is like night, because this is not their understanding at all. What is day to others is night for the wise and what is night for others is like day for the wise. So, the other-wise do not know the wise and the wise do not see like the other-wise because night and day do not meet. They cannot co-exist, one being the opposite of the other. When day breaks, night is gone. When night comes, day is gone. The day always ensures that night has gone before it comes. This is the role of dawn. Lord Sun tells the dawn, Aruṇa, messenger of the Sun, to go and make sure that the way is clear. Dawn then comes and clears the way. Thus, before the Sun comes, night has already gone. In this way, the Sun and the night do not meet.

Here is my[18] story about why the Sun rises every morning. Nārada, who is often found in mythological stories, was able to go to the gods without any passport or visa. Or, one could

[18] Swamiji

say that he had a cosmic passport, as it were, since he could go from one *loka*, world, to another. In this particular story, Nārada went from the earth to the Sun. The Sun asked Nārada what the people thought of him on earth.

Nārada responded, 'O Lord Sun! In India they do salutations to you early in morning. Do you not see that when you come up?'

The Sun replied, 'Nowadays very few do it, in the past, they did, but not now. But what is it that they say about me?'

Nārada told him, 'O Sun! You are always praised everywhere, except, of course, in the Sahara Desert and Saudi Arabia! When you come out, everyone is happy.'

The Sun then asked Nārada, 'What did you see that you liked on the earth?'

In response, Nārada told him that there was one person whom he thought the Sun should see someone that he had never seen before.

'Everyone praises you as omniscient, but I would have to say that you are not omniscient because there is someone I think you have never seen'

'What!' 'I am not omniscient! I am the Sun. I see everything. Who is it that you think I have not seen?'

'There is one lady called Miss Darkness,' Nārada told him.

'Where is this Miss Darkness?'

'You can see her on the earth,' Nārada replied.

'Where will I find her right now?'

'She is in India. If you go there, you will see her.'

Eager to see Miss Darkness, the Sun rose in the eastern sky. But Miss Darkness had gone to the west, to the Antipodes, the opposite side of the globe.

The Sun became angry. He really wanted to meet this woman and so set out after her again. But when he went to the Antipodes, Miss Darkness had already gone to the other side and when he went to that side, she was again on the opposite side. In this way, Sun continued to move around trying to find Miss Darkness and is still doing so, even today! When he comes to the east, Miss Darkness goes to the west. When he goes to the west, she comes to the east. They never meet each other, just as day and night never meet each other, because they are opposites. You cannot even compare the two; sun is like itself and so is darkness.

So too, a wise person is like a wise person, which means that no comparison is possible. Therefore, Arjuna did not become wiser by Kṛṣṇa's statement. For the wise person, what is reality is limitless; the self being everything is reality. The reality is that Īśvara is the self. For other people, Īśvara is located somewhere, in heaven perhaps, and is only a matter of belief. They think he sends people down and then meddles in their affairs. People have so many kinds of beliefs, because, for them, the statement, 'I am everything,' is not a reality. Therefore, there are different conjectures, speculations, faiths, and beliefs. We find that for the *ajñānīs*, the ignorant, everything is guesswork, whereas for the *jñānī*, the wise person, there is no problem. The *jñānī* sees no problem at all, whereas for the other person, everything is a problem.

For the wise person, everything is a glory. The physical body, the mind, and the world are *vibhūti*s, glories, *mama vibhūtayaḥ*, my glories. *Aham annam*, I am the food eaten, and again *aham annādaḥ*, I am also the eater of the food. I am the thinker and I am the object of thought. I am free from all these too. The ignorant are asleep to this vision of the reality and the wise are asleep to what the ignorant are awake to.

This is something like one person seeing a snake and another person seeing a rope in the same object. The person seeing the snake sweats and shivers in fear. Even the sound of the snake's rattle is heard by this person in spite of the fact that there is no snake. There is only a rope mistaken for a snake. Once a snake is seen, everything else comes along with it, the sound of the rattle, the sight of its head rising, and so on. For this person, the snake is a reality, whereas for the other person, all that is there is a piece of rope, and he or she does not see what the frightened person is fretting about. The one who sees the rope as rope will either treat the other person with compassion or simply walk away because he or she does not see a problem. Even if this person is told that there is a snake, he or she will only reply that there is no snake, there is only the rope.

This is strictly a matter of two different visions. How, then, is Arjuna going to understand a wise person? Kṛṣṇa was saying here that he could only do so by being wise. There is no other way. Being ignorant, you want to understand a wise person.

In fact, there is really no one called as 'wise person'. Wisdom is you. You are the wisdom. The wise person is one who knows himself or herself. If you know yourself you are a wise person. Until you know yourself, how are you going to understand a wise person? To be a wise person you have to be wise. There is no other way, then, of knowing the wise person.

In response to Arjuna's request for a description of a wise person, Lord Kṛṣṇa told him, the verse under study, that it takes wisdom alone to be a wise person. The wise person is awake to a reality to which everyone else is sleeping. This answer could only have created despair in Arjuna because he wanted to know the characteristics of a wise person so that, by emulating them, he himself would become wise.

The sleep of ignorance that prevents one from knowing a wise person was explained further by Śaṅkara in his commentary on this verse. For the wise person, there is no activity because he or she no longer takes the self to be a doer. This applies not only to the performance of Vedic rituals and prayers, *vaidika-vyavahāra*, but to worldly activities, *laukika-vyavahāra* as well, such as eating, cooking, dishwashing, bathing, laundering, vacuuming, conducting business and so on. The notions, 'I am doing this, I am the doer,' are no longer there.

When you look upon yourself as a doer, you perform rituals and if you do not perform them, you will do something else. And this something else may incur sin. With reference to the performance of rituals, then, the Veda only addresses the person who takes the self to be the doer.

A *brahmacārī*, a student, has to have the notion, 'I am a *brahmacārī*,' in order to perform the *karma* enjoined for *brahmacārī*s by the Veda. If a *brāhmaṇa* is enjoined to do certain *karma*, then the person doing it must look upon oneself as a *brāhmaṇa*. The same thing applies to other *varṇa*s and *āśrama*s. The Veda does not say that *sat-cit-ānanda* should perform *karma*. It says that a *brāhmaṇa*, a *brahmacārī*, or a *gṛhastha* should perform *karma*s.

Karma, then, is enjoined only for the one who looks upon oneself as, 'I am this, I am that,' and so on. It is not meant for the person who has *jñāna*, in whom self-knowledge has taken place. Once this knowledge has dawned, it stays. Self-knowledge is not a dawning knowledge; it is a fully blazing, mid-day sun. In the wake of this knowledge, worldly and scriptural *karma*s both go away because *vyavahāra*, activity, is born of the notion, 'I am the doer.'

Unless you consider yourself a doer, you cannot perform scriptural or worldly activities, activity itself being a product of self-ignorance. But for the one who has self-knowledge, this ignorance is not there and, thus, it is said that the *vyavahāra*, activity, goes away.

Does knowledge remove the product of ignorance or does it remove the ignorance itself? Śaṅkara deals with this question in his commentary on this verse. When knowledge takes place, the ignorance is removed. *Ātma-anātma-viveka-jñāna*, knowledge which is of the nature of discriminative understanding between the real and the unreal, is opposed to ignorance. Thus, when self-knowledge takes place, self-ignorance goes away. And when ignorance goes away, its broods, its products, also go away.

To take the classic example of seeing the rope as a snake, ignorance of the rope produces the snake. When the rope ignorance goes away, snake also goes away. We may ask, 'does the rope ignorance go?' It goes when the rope is seen, when it is known. Rope ignorance will go only in the wake of rope knowledge. Therefore, rope knowledge is the opposite of rope ignorance. When rope ignorance goes, anything that was there due to that ignorance will also go because when the cause of a problem is removed, the symptoms also disappear. Similarly, for the person who has knowledge, activities are gone. Such a person becomes *sarva-karma-sannyāsī*, who renounces all *karmas*.

The Veda sets out the *karmas* that have to be done and Śaṅkara clarifies as to who has to do them–the person who has notions such as, 'I am a *brahmacārī*, I am a *brāhmaṇa*, I am a married person, I am bound by time, spring, new moon day, full moon day, morning, evening.' The one who has these kinds of notions about oneself, who thinks that he or she is time-bound, place-bound, and group-bound, is the person whom the *śruti*, the Veda, addresses with reference to the performance of rituals.

If one knows, 'I am *sat-cit-ānanda*,' the *śruti* does not address such a person at all. In fact, it says that you are *sat-cit-ānanda*, but it reserves this particular statement for the last chapter, which is what we call Vedanta. Until then, the Veda talks exclusively about rituals and meditation, all of which are *dvaita*, dual. Only at the end of all this does it say, '*tat tvam asi*, you are that Brahman.'

The question may then be asked, 'Why did the *śruti* not say this in the beginning? If it had done so, I need not have done these *karma*s. I did the morning and evening prayers because the Veda said to do them, and I had faith in the Veda. Now I find that these *karma*s have become a colossal waste because, at the end of it all, the Veda tells me that I am Brahman and that *karma* is of no use. If *karma* will not give me *mokṣa*, why did it not say so in the beginning?'

The reason the Veda does not tell you right in the beginning that you are Brahman is because you have to be ready for this knowledge. By performing *karma* you are able to eventually get to the last chapter of the Veda and understand what it says. By not performing *karma* you will be neither a *jñānī* nor a devout person. You will only be driftwood with no moorings whatsoever. The rule is that those who are not ready for the knowledge should not be disturbed with it. We will see this later in the *Gītā*. Instead, people are encouraged to perform *karma* in order to prepare their minds for self-knowledge. They are told about *svarga*, heaven, in the beginning, so that they will perform the enjoined rituals for gaining *svarga*. In this way, they will definitely avoid *pāpa*, and *puṇya* will follow. The person who performs *karma* will have a value for *dharma-adharma*, right and wrong, and will come to believe that there is an *ātmā*, a self, other than the body. That much is enough in the beginning.

Once you respect *dharma-adharma*, the ability to discriminate between the real and the unreal will not be far behind. To respect *dharma-adharma* is not to be swayed by your *rāga-dveṣa*s. Therefore, the pressure of *rāga-dveṣa*s will be less. This is what is meant by *viveka*. *Viveka* begins as soon as you start to question what is what. First, there is an internal leisure and then *viveka* naturally comes. Once *viveka* is there, you will naturally turn to Vedanta. Only in this way can you proceed properly. Therefore, as long as self-ignorance is there, you should perform *karma*, whereas once there is self-knowledge, there is renunciation of *karma*, *sarva-karma-sannyāsa*.

Śaṅkara repeats this argument throughout his commentary on the *Gītā*. It is because there was a notion, prevalent in his day, that the Veda enjoins you to do *karma* and, at the same time, to gain the knowledge that 'I am Brahman'. This position maintains that both will give you *mokṣa*, and is refuted by Śaṅkara at every opportunity.

'Or, if either *karma* or *jñāna* is adequate for *mokṣa* why should anyone do the other? If *mokṣa* is something that I produce, why do I need *jñāna*? And, if *karma* is not going to produce *mokṣa*, there is no reason to do *karma*. If I am Brahman and I merely need to know it, which is Śaṅkara's contention, then *jñāna* is *mokṣa*, and I do not need to do anything.' Thus, the question, 'Why should I do *karma*?' The answer is that one performs *karma* for *citta-śuddhi*, to purify the mind. *Citta* means 'mind.' We have seen the word '*śuddhi*' with reference to *rāga-dveṣa*s.

Reality is already accomplished; it is not something to be created. Reality is. Whatever the reality, that is what is. It is to be recognised. Therefore even if you do millions of *karma*s, you do not create the reality that exists. Because of the prevalence in Śaṅkara's time of the synthesis argument of combining *karma* and *jñāna*, he goes all out to clarify the difference between *karma* and *jñāna*.

There are some topics that every teacher has to highlight, given the views of his or her time. In Śaṅkara's time, the *jñāna-karma-samuccaya-vāda*, the contention that *mokṣa* is not gained by knowledge alone, but by a combination of knowledge and action was widespread. Therefore, he found it necessary to refute it by continually pointing out the fallacies in it. This is the job of a teacher. Here, too, Śaṅkara points out that *karma* applied only until knowledge comes. For one who does not have knowledge, the *karma* enjoined by the Veda is a valid *pramāṇa*, whereas for the wise person, it is not. Once *jñāna* is there, the person is a simple *sannyāsī*, who is not a doer and therefore for whom no *karma* is enjoined by any *śāstra*.

A wise person cannot be emulated based on action

Since a wise person does not do *karma*, you cannot emulate him or her. You cannot say that because he or she does not do *karma*, you will also not do *karma*. The wise person does not perform *karma* because the need to do so is no longer there. Since you still need to perform *karma*, you cannot imitate a wise person in this respect.

Kṛṣṇa did not say that the wise person is one who does not do any *karma*. To say that this person has no duty whatsoever could be interpreted by a *mumukṣu* in such a way that he or she would not live a life of *karma-yoga* and, instead, would become nothing more than a lazy person. This is why Kṛṣṇa pointed out here that what is night for a wise person is day for everyone else, meaning that no *karma* is enjoined. What is *pramāṇa*, a means of knowledge, for you is not *pramāṇa* for the wise person. In fact, what Kṛṣṇa was saying here is that for the wise, there is no *pramāṇa* at all. Even the usefulness of the last *pramāṇa*, Vedanta, is over for them.

Vedanta says that you are Brahman. Until you know this, Vedanta is a *pramāṇa* and afterwards it, too, becomes *mithyā*. With knowledge, there is no means of knowledge, known, or knower, the differences between these three having been swallowed. The *pramāṇa*, the means of knowledge, is gone; it is Brahman, as are the *pramātā*, the knower, and *prameya*, the object to be known. The very knower is cancelled by the knowledge that says you are not a knower.

Resolution of knower-known-knowledge

Śaṅkara says that the final *pramāṇa*, the statement, '*tat tvam asi*,' itself goes away, having dismissed the *pramāṇa*. An example generally given to illustrate how knowledge works is the method of using a thorn to remove the thorn that is lodged in one's foot. Once the thorn is removed, we discard both the thorns. There is also a more interesting example used. When a body is cremated, a huge funeral pyre is made out of wood. If the person who died was rich, the pyre will be made of sandalwood, but this is the only difference.

When the pyre is ready, the body is placed on it, covered with husks and small pieces of wood, and then the fire is lit. Once the body has caught fire, the people who came for the ritual go away. But the ritual itself is still incomplete and continues the next day when the person performing the ritual comes to pick up the ashes and bones. This person is either the departed one's eldest son or a cousin, someone who is closely related. When this person comes to pick up the ashes, there should be no portion of the body left unburnt. It must be burnt thoroughly; there should be nothing remaining except the ashes and bones. Until this happens, the ritual is incomplete.

The person in charge of the cremation ground is the one who must ensure that the body is completely burnt. Because the body is not to be touched and, being in the fire, cannot be handled, a stick is used for this purpose. Once the person is sure that the body is completely burnt, he throws the stick into the funeral fire. Having done its job, the stick also gets burnt.

Similarly, the statement, '*tat tvam asi*, you are that,' is a *pramāṇa*. The *pramātā*, the knower, *jīva*, you, is told, 'You are Brahman.' If you are Brahman, there is no knower. After this knowledge takes place, the *pramātā* is just an 'as though' *pramātā*. There is no real *pramātā* any more. When the knower is told, 'You are not a knower, you are Brahman,' the knower is sublated. And when the knower is not there, where is the *pramāṇa*? It too goes. All three, the knower, known, and means of knowledge, are understood to be Brahman.

Duality goes in the wake of this knowledge, including the knower, the known, and the knowledge itself. The known, the *prameya*, is gone because there is nothing to know. Once knowledge takes place, all three, *pramātā*, *prameya*, and *pramāṇa*, become meaningless. Therefore, the knower-known-knowledge activities resolve in the wake of knowledge that I am Brahman.

This is what Kṛṣṇa meant when he said that what is day for everyone else is night for the wise person. Śaṅkara conveyed this alone in his commentary. All translations, therefore, should be read with this meaning in mind.

Emulate the values of a wise person

Any description of a person of steady wisdom, *sthitaprajña*, is useless, really speaking. You can only talk about the *prajñā*, wisdom, that makes a person wise. Unless you have this wisdom yourself, you cannot understand what a wise person is. Only a *mahātmā* knows a *mahātmā*. One who is not a *mahātmā* cannot appreciate one. Therefore, any description, other than an unfoldment of the wisdom that makes such a person wise, is really meaningless. Yet, Arjuna wanted a description. He also wanted to know how a wise person reacts to the world. In his response, Kṛṣṇa told Arjuna certain things, including the fact that one cannot emulate a wise person, except insofar as values are concerned.

The wise person may not perform Vedic rituals. For such a person, *karma*s are no longer necessary because the previous performance of the scriptural injunctions has found its fulfillment in wisdom. Whether the person has taken *sannyāsa* or not, he or she is a *sarva-karma-sannyāsī*. The doership is already negated in the person. There is no real doer. And when there is no real doer, there is no real *karma*. In this way, the wise person is not bound by duty of any kind.

To emulate a wise person, therefore, is dangerous. Kṛṣṇa mentioned the mind, values, control, and mastery of a wise person because these alone are to be emulated. In this way, Kṛṣṇa confirmed for Arjuna that the characteristics of a wise person, as demonstrated in his or her interactions in day-to-day life, can become the *sādhana*, the means, for a seeker.

Finally, Kṛṣṇa said that a wise person is as different from an *ajñānī* as day is from night, meaning that there is no way of unfolding what a wise person is. What is night for all the people is day for the wise and what is day for them is night to the wise. Arjuna was bound to be flabbergasted by this. He was definitely not going to be any wiser for having heard this particular verse. Therefore, out of sympathy and compassion, Kṛṣṇa followed his night-and-day example with another example, an illustration that Arjuna could hold on to, and one that would enable him to appreciate, in a way, what a wise person is.

Verses 70&71

The wise person

आपूर्यमाणमचलप्रतिष्ठं समुद्रमापः प्रविशन्ति यद्वत् ।
तद्वत्कामा यं प्रविशन्ति सर्वे स शान्तिमाप्नोति न कामकामी ॥ ७० ॥

āpūryamāṇam acalapratiṣṭhaṁ
samudram āpaḥ praviśanti yadvat
tadvatkāmā yaṁ praviśanti sarve
sa śāntim āpnoti na kāmakāmī (70)

āpūryamāṇam – brimful; *acalapratiṣṭham* – still; *samudram* – into the ocean; *āpaḥ* – waters; *yadvat* – just as; *praviśanti* – enter;

tadvat – so too; *sarve* – all; *kāmāḥ* – objects; *yam* – the one (the wise person) into whom; *praviṣanti* – enter; *saḥ* – he; *śāntim* – peace; *āpnoti* – gains; *kāmakāmī* – the desirer of objects; *na* – not

> Just as water flows into the ocean that is brimful and still, so too, the wise person into whom all objects enter gains peace, (remains unchanged) whereas, the desirer of objects does not gain peace.

There are two adjectives describing the ocean in this verse. The first one, '*āpūryamāṇam,*' refers to the ocean being totally filled with water. It requires no more water to be full because it is already filled to the brim. The second adjective, '*acalapratiṣṭham,*' describes the ocean as not moving from place to place in the same way that a river does, for example. Thus, the ocean is not only full but, being without motion, it is also well-grounded.

The verse also gives some more information about the ocean. While a pond depends upon a source of water for its existence, the ocean does not depend upon any other source of water for its fullness. It does not depend upon the rain for its oceanness, unlike the rain clouds that depend upon the evaporation of the ocean water for their cloudness. Nor does the ocean depend upon any entry of water. It does not become an ocean because river water enters into it. Thus, to be brimful, it depends on no other factor, no other source of water. The glory of the ocean, then, is within itself alone.

Water enters the ocean from all sides in the form of rain and rivers. But does the entry of these various forms of water bring about any change in the fullness of the ocean? If it does, then we can say that the ocean is not full, that it depends upon other sources for its oceanness. And if no change is brought about by the water entering into it, then the ocean is full by itself and the non-entry of water will make no difference in its fullness.

By itself, then, the ocean is full of water. Because it does not depend upon any source of water for its fullness, neither the non-entry nor the entry of water makes any difference to it. The ocean is not after the entry of water nor is it afraid of water entering into it. It has no fear of becoming flooded and thereby losing its name, ocean. Nor, in order to be ocean, does it covet water.

A pond, on the other hand, does depend upon rain or some other water to be a pond. If a pond is dependent upon a particular spring underneath it for instance, all that is required for it not to be a pond is for someone to put bore wells all around. The water table will go down, the spring will go dry, and there will be no water in the pond. A pond can also cease to be a pond if too much water enters into it. If its banks are broken, there will be water everywhere. No one will know where the pond is, unless they are wading in the water and suddenly step into it! Therefore, a pond will no longer be called a pond if there is too much water entering into it or if no water enters into it at all. Such changes are possible for a pond, whereas an ocean undergoes no change whatsoever, regardless of whether water enters or does not enter.

Just as the fullness of the ocean is not affected by the entry or non-entry of water, so too the wise person's peace of mind is not affected by objects that enter the mind. These objects enter into such a person just as water enters the ocean. But he or she is not affected by them because, like the ocean, the wise person is full, for no other reason than fullness being his or her own nature.

Everyone has this sense of fullness, if only for the time being, when something desirable happens. But, eventually, the person finds himself or herself not full. A wise person, on the other hand, does not depend on anything for his or her fullness because the self is already full, like the ocean. The self is *ānanda;* it has no limit. Thus, recognition of the self is the very reason for the person's being full. 'I am' is fullness. I am fullness. If I am fullness, then the meaning of the word 'I' is not found in a limited factor like the body, mind, or senses.

Therefore, the 'I' should be understood as it is, and it happens to be *ānanda*. The wise person is one who is happy without depending upon any object or situation. Like the ocean, the wise person is full by his or her own glory, by his or her own nature. The *ānanda*, fullness of a wise person, is not going to increase because of the entry of some desirable objects. And if such desirable objects do not enter, the wise person does not lose anything. In either case, no change is brought about in the person. He or she remains unchanged.

If desirable objects enter into the head of a person who is not full, they create havoc in the person because they have to be gained, experienced, or owned and there may be no way of doing so. Therefore, the person smarts, sweats, frets and fumes. When a person looks upon oneself as one who is lacking, desires only cause problems. And, if such a person is told to give up all desires, he or she cannot do it. Unless one is full, desires cannot be given up. They go away only when the person is full. Even if desires do enter the head of a wise person, they do not create any problems because whether the desires are fulfilled or not it is all the same to the person.

The word '*kāma*' in this verse is taken to mean objects, *kāmyate iti kāmaḥ*; they are desired and therefore called *kāma*s. If one does not know that one is *ānanda*, then one is elated when desirable objects enter and dejected when undesirable objects also enter. Whereas, for the wise person, there is no difference. He or she is *śānti* alone, meaning that there is no change in the person whatsoever. The emotional yo-yo is no longer there for him or her. There may be a ripple of laughter or even roaring laughter sometimes, just as the ocean seems to be very ecstatic at times and simply smiling at other times. There can be a smile, a laugh or tranquillity. For the ocean, the small waves are its smiles and the huge breakers are its roaring laughter. If it is not roaring with laughter or smiling, is the ocean gone? No, it is tranquil in its fullness. Therefore, it is the fullness that is laughing, the fullness already being there. It can be a laughing fullness, a smiling fullness, or a tranquil fullness.

The other person mentioned in this verse, the *kāmakāmī*, is one who has desires. This is not to say that one has a desire for desires. No one wants to have a desire for desires, but this person definitely has desires for desirable objects. Into this person's mind, also, sense objects enter; the world enters. When the desirable enters, there is elation and when the undesirable enters, there is depression. In this way, the emotions of the person go up and down like a yo-yo.

If a wise person can be likened to an ocean, the other-wise can certainly be likened to a miserable pond that we just saw in the example. When the rains come, there will be water. Provided there is not too much water or too little, the pond will remain. But if it is flooded or all its water dries up, the pond is gone. Similarly, for one who has binding desires, the entry and non-entry of desirable and undesirable objects bring about changes, which is not the case for the wise person. This verse, then, gave Arjuna some hope. The previous verse was a real description of a wise person in the sense that it takes wisdom to be wise and, therefore, one had better gain this wisdom. This was followed by the illustration in the present verse that likened the wise person to an ocean. Let all the desirable and undesirable objects enter, like so much water into the ocean! The wise person remains full while the *kāmakāmī* does not.

Kṛṣṇa was telling Arjuna here that the one who has binding desires will always have problems and by this illustration Arjuna would know what a wise man is like. Having said this, Kṛṣṇa then sums up the section on the *sthitaprajñā*, as well as the entire chapter, in the next two verses.

विहाय कामान्यः सर्वान्पुमांश्चरति निःस्पृहः ।
निर्ममो निरहङ्कारः स शान्तिमधिगच्छति ॥ ७१ ॥

vihāya kāmān yaḥ sarvān pumāṁścarati niḥspṛhaḥ
nirmamo nirahaṅkāraḥ sa śāntim adhigacchati (71)

yaḥ – the one who; *pumān* – person; *sarvān* – all; *kāmān* – binding desires; *vihāya* – having given up; *niḥspṛhaḥ* – devoid of longing; *nirmamaḥ* – without the sense of 'mine'; *nirahaṅkāraḥ* – without the sense of limited 'I'; *carati* – moves around; *saḥ* – he; *śāntim* – peace; *adhigacchati* – gains

> Having given up all binding desires, the person who moves around, devoid of longing, without the sense of limited 'I' and 'mine,' gains peace.

The wise person is one who has given up all binding desires and who moves freely in the world. Whether the person is a king like Janaka or a *sannyāsī* like Śaṅkara, there is no difference in the freedom of the person. The longing for this or that is gone because the person is happy with oneself. There is no more longing for situations in order to be secure and happy. Therefore, the sense of 'mine' is no longer there. Such a person does not have this kind of attachment to anyone or anything.

You hold on to people and objects and look upon them as 'mine.' It is like a child who says, 'Do not touch this. Do not take it away from me. This is my toy.' The only difference between the 'mine' you had as a child and the 'mine' you have as an adult is that the toys have been replaced with other, more sophisticated objects. In fact, you are nothing but bearded, grown-up child. The 'mine-ness' never goes; only objects are replaced. Thus, with reference to the few things and people, you say, 'This is mine.'

However, when you see that everything is yourself alone, everything changes. You are the father, the mother, and all the places. When everything is you, there is no 'mine.'

'Mine' means that 'yours,' 'his,' and 'hers' are also there. These are the reasons for all your problems. You become small in your own eyes. When 'I' and 'mine' are no longer there, you are wise because you know 'I am all of this'.

When you say, 'I am all of this' the sense of 'mine' is gone. The 'I' sense is also gone because when everything is me, there is no 'I.' People think this is vanity, but vanity only exists when you are small. When you say, 'I am everything,' there is no vanity. Vanity is only with reference to comparison and pride. When you take yourself to be 'this much,' there is quantifying in terms of your possessions, your capacity, your skills, and so on. Then there is *ahaṅkāra*, ego. But when the ego is enlightened and recognises, 'I am everything,' there is no *ahaṅkāra* at all! There is only reality, knowledge, Brahman.

Ahaṅkāra is nothing but a notion, the 'I' notion. When the reality is 'I am everything,' there is no ego. Ego is only when you compare yourself with another person, and say, 'He does not have as much as I have.' But there is no other person at all. All that is there is me. There is no ego, no doer; there is only *aham*, 'I.' That, 'I am a doer' is a notion, whereas 'I' is the self. Therefore, the person under discussion in this verse is one who has no 'I' or 'mine' sense because everything is oneself. If everything is oneself, where is the question of having a desire? Knowing this, then, the wise person has no binding desires.

How a wise person lives in the world

The use of the word, '*carati*,' here is very beautiful. The wise person does not run away from the world. Where would he or she go anyway? Having given up all binding desires, such a person continues to live in the world and may engage oneself in a variety of activities. But the activity itself means nothing. The person gains only *śānti*, meaning that he or she never changes. Other people move around because of the pressure of their desires, whereas the wise person is free from such binding, pressurising desires.

People who are impelled by desires will say, 'This has to be done; only then can I be happy!' The only difference between a wise person and these people is that the wise person is motivated but not driven by his or her desires. In spite of moving around and being active in the world, there is no appreciable inner change brought about in the person either by desire or by its outcome.

When the world enters into the *sthitaprajñā*, the person is *śānta*. And when he or she enters into the world, engaging in the activities of the world, then also there is nothing but *śānti*. This was said because of a doubt that can arise here. It is fine to say that the *sthitaprajñā* is full and when the world enters into such a person, it merely resolves into his or her fullness. He or she just sits in one place in this fullness and whatever world enters into the person, *śānti* alone prevails. What about the wise person who is active? Activity does not change the person's wisdom. There is no change because there is no doership or enjoyership, no 'I' notion, in the person. *Śānti* alone remains.

Let the person be engaged in the world or let the world enter into the person. Either way, it is the same. Whether one is enjoying or doing, there is *śānti*. When the world enters into the person or the person does something, one does not become an enjoyer or a doer. Enjoyership and doership are both negated in the wise person. Although there is a seeming enjoyership and doership, essentially, they are not there. This is what we call *bādhita*, meaning that, through knowledge, the reality of doership and enjoyership, centred on 'I' is sublated.

When Kṛṣṇa talked to Arjuna and when Śaṅkara wrote his commentaries, there was doership. But neither Kṛṣṇa nor Śaṅkara looked upon themselves as the doer. Doership, for the wise person, is just doing. The notion, 'I am the doer,' is not there. This means that the *sthitaprajñā* continues to be Brahman.

Verse 72

Kṛṣṇa concludes in praise of the brahma-niṣṭhā

एषा ब्राह्मी स्थितिः पार्थ नैनां प्राप्य विमुह्यति ।
स्थित्वास्यामन्तकालेऽपि ब्रह्मनिर्वाणमृच्छति ॥ ७२ ॥

eṣā brāhmī sthitiḥ pārtha naināṁ prāpya vimuhyati
sthitvāsyām antakāle'pi brahmanirvāṇam ṛcchati (72)

pārtha – O son of Pṛthā (Arjuna)!; *eṣā* – this; *brāhmī sthitiḥ* – the state of being in Brahman; *enām* – this; *prāpya* – having gained; *na vimuhyati* – is not deluded; *antakāle* – at the end of life; *api* – even; *asyām* – therein; *sthitvā* – remaining; *brahma-nirvāṇam* – liberation; *ṛcchati* – gains

> Pārtha (Arjuna)! This is (what is meant by) one's being in Brahman. Having gained this, one is not deluded. Remaining therein, even at the end of one's life, one gains liberation.

The *jñāna-niṣṭhā*, steady knowledge, that had been the topic of Kṛṣṇa's teaching from the beginning, is *brahma-niṣṭhā*, steadfastness in Brahman. In between, *karma-yoga* was pointed out and Arjuna's question concerning the definition of a *sthitaprajña* was answered, this same steady wisdom being again mentioned. *Jñāna-niṣṭhā* means steady knowledge and *brahma-niṣṭhā* is one whose knowledge is that *ātmā* is Brahman. This *brahma-niṣṭhā* is praised here in the last verse of the second chapter.

Sthiti refers to this *niṣṭhā*, steadfastness in the knowledge. Addressing Arjuna as Pārtha, the son of Pṛthā, Kṛṣṇa told Arjuna that being a *sthitaprajña* is the state, *sthiti*, of being in Brahman, born of the knowledge of Brahman. However, once we use the word 'state,' there is a problem because, being only a state, it will not always be the same. Previously, something was not and now this something is, in a particular state. Later, using the same logic, it will be lost when another state is gained, just as the previous state was lost when this state was gained.

When the waking state goes, dream comes. When the dream-state goes, sleep comes. When sleep also goes, waking comes. When this particular life is gone, another life comes. Because of centrifugal force, we find that certain things are in a particular state or position and when the force is gone, they are no more in the same position. Similarly, any state is subject to loss, subject to change. Otherwise, it would not be called a state.

It is important to note that we are not discussing *samādhi* here, which is a state. The question about what happens after one comes out of *samādhi* often arises. The final stage of *samādhi*, wherein there are no thought modifications whatsoever, the *nirvikalpa-samādhi* is a state and, therefore, will be lost.

Since Kṛṣṇa used the word '*sthiti*' here, one may question how long this state will last, if indeed it is ever gained. The word 'state' is used in this verse only for want of a better word and does not mean something that will be lost. This *niṣṭhā* is knowledge, knowledge of Brahman. It is not that *ātmā* goes into Brahman and sits there. All that is there is *ātmā*, the self, and the self happens to be Brahman. Therefore, it is something to be understood.

Knowledge of Brahman is not a state

There is no Brahman other than *ātmā*. *Ātmā* is Brahman. If *ātmā* is Brahman, it is a matter for understanding. It is not a state; it is knowledge, gaining which the person is no more deluded. Because knowledge is not a state, the wise person never dons the cloak of delusion again. Therefore, the old ignorance does not come back. Notions that were based on ignorance, such as 'I am a *jīva*, a mortal, a doer, an enjoyer,' also do not return.

You may fret about whether the false notions will come back again. You may think, 'Suppose the doer, the enjoyer, comes back. Again, I will have all the old problems. Then what will I do? I will have to find another *guru*. My present *guru* will send me away because, having taught me once, he will not want to teach me again. What will I do? Again, I will have to come back. I will have to assume another body and everything will start all over again!' There is no such problem because what we are discussing here is not a state; it is knowledge. Knowledge gained is gained for good. *Ātmā* is Brahman. When its *svarūpa*, its nature, is understood, there is no more *jīva*. The individual is gone. There are no more false notions about oneself and the old delusion does not return.

It is never too late to gain self-knowledge

Kṛṣṇa then said that, remaining in this knowledge of Brahman, the wise person gains *mokṣa* in this life itself; living, one is liberated. Also, there is one more piece of information given – liberation is possible even for a person who is in the last lap of his or her life. The person may be very old. The ears may no longer hear, the eyes may not see, the liver may not work, the heart may be palpitating, and the person may always be scratching his or her head in order to remember things, none of which matters at all.

Even if a person is old and is in the last days of his or her life, the person can know, helped by all life's experiences. The old problems are no longer there and everything has been tried anyway! It is only those who cannot even try any longer who tend to think of themselves as lonely. 'I cannot go out boating or fishing. I can no longer catch any salmon. They move too fast for me. Now it is deer season and all the deer escape from me. I cannot even drive a car and I am in an old age home. No one comes to see me except at Christmas time. My family asks me how I am and goes away again.' For such people, these are big problems, whereas if a person has some discrimination and has learned what life can teach, nothing is really a problem for him or her anymore.

Life is meant for all this. Children are born and call you 'Daddy' and then 'Grand-daddy.' When you are a Daddy, you are supposed to be a *vivekī*, one who can discriminate the real from the unreal. And when you are a Grand-daddy, you are supposed to be a grand *vivekī*! Naturally, then, such a person is ready. If all the people go away and you are left with yourself, it should not be a problem. By now, you should know that nothing is really with you, except some social security perhaps. There is no other security. Then, having some *viveka*, if you listen to the *śāstra* the knowledge will stick. Why? Because you are mature.

An old person has already gone through all the experiences that make one wiser. For such a person, one sentence, if presented properly, is enough. He or she should be mature by this time and, therefore, should have no emotional problems or *rāga-dveṣa*s. Such a mature person, even though close to death, can gain the knowledge.

Earlier in this chapter we saw the story about King Parīkṣit that bears this out. A curse was placed on him that he would die in a week. He went to Vyāsa's son, Śuka, who was a *jñānī*, and told him that he had only one week to live. In response, Śuka just laughed. 'Why are you laughing?' the king asked, 'I am going to die in a week!' Śuka then explained why he was laughing. 'You are lucky,' he said, 'you say you are going to die in a week. It means that you know you are going to be alive for seven days, whereas I myself have no such guarantee. Since you are sure you are going to live for seven days, it is definitely a matter for celebration. You are lucky. My God!

You can be Brahman by that time.' Seven days are more than enough time to change your whole perspective and, sure enough, in seven days this king became a *jñānī*. Thus, even if you are suffering from a terminal disease or are very old, it makes no difference. You can gain *mokṣa*, liberation.

Śaṅkara then completed the sentence. If a person about to die can gain *mokṣa*, anyone can. Even as a *brahmacārī*, before one enters the second stage of life that is marriage, a person who takes to this study can gain *mokṣa*. Then, for as long as one lives, the person lives in the knowledge of Brahman.

When the ears hear, the eyes see, the mind is thinking, and memory is a possibility, knowledge can definitely be gained. If a person whose memory is gone, whose eyes do not see, and whose ears do not hear can gain this knowledge, all the more possible is the knowledge for one whose body is healthy and whose mind is bright.

There being no doubt that knowledge is all that is to be gained for one to be liberated, the second chapter comes to an end.

ॐतत्सत् ।

इति श्रीमद्भगवद्गीतासूपनिषत्सु ब्रह्मविद्यायां योगशास्त्रे
श्रीकृष्णार्जुनसंवादे साङ्ख्य-योगो नाम द्वितीयोऽध्यायः ॥ २ ॥

oṁ tat sat.

iti śrīmadbhagavadgītāsūpaniṣatsu brahma-vidyāyāṁ yoga-śāstre śrīkṛṣṇārjunasaṁvāde sāṅkhya-yogo nāma dvitīyo'dhyāyaḥ (2)

Om, Brahman, is the only reality. Thus ends the second chapter called *sāṅkhya-yoga,* having the topic of knowledge, in the *Bhagavadgītā* which is in the form of a dialogue between Śrī Kṛṣṇa and Arjuna, which is the essence of the *Upaniṣads*, whose subject matter is both the knowledge of Brahman and *yoga*.

Alphabetical index of verses

Books by Swami Dayananda Saraswati

Public Talk Series :

1. Living Intelligently
2. Successful Living
3. Need for Cognitive Change
4. Discovering Love
5. The Value of Values
6. Vedic View and Way of Life

Upaniṣad Series :

7. Muṇḍakopaniṣad
8. Kenopaniṣad

Prakaraṇa Series :

9. Tattvabodhaḥ

Text Translation Series :

10. Śrīmad Bhagavad Gītā
    (Text with roman transliteration and English translation)
11. Śrī Rudram
    (Text in Sanskrit with transliteration, word-to-word and verse meaning along with an elaborate commentary in English)

Stotra Series :

12. Dīpārādhanā
13. Prayer Guide
    (With explanations of several Mantras, Stotras, Kirtans and Religious Festivals)

Moments with Oneself Series :

14. Freedom from Helplessness
15. Living versus Getting On
16. Insights
17. Action and Reaction
18. Fundamental Problem
19. Problem is You, Solution is You
20. Purpose of Prayer
21. Vedanta 24x7
22. Freedom
23. Crisis Management
24. Surrender and Freedom
25. The Need for Personal Reorganisation
26. Freedom in Relationship
27. Stress-free Living
28. Om Namo Bhagavate Vāsudevāya
29. Yoga of Objectivity

Bhagavad Gītā

30. Bhagavad Gītā Home Study Course (Hardbound - 9 Volumes)

Meditation Series :

31. Morning Meditation Prayers
32. What is Meditation?

Essays :

33. Do all Religions have the same goal?
34. Conversion is Violence
35. Gurupūrṇimā
36. Dānam
37. Japa
38. Can We?
39. Moments with Krishna
40. Teaching Tradition of Advaita Vedanta
41. Compositions of Swami Dayananda Saraswati

Exploring Vedanta Series : (*vākyavicāra*)

42. śraddhā bhakti dhyāna yogād avaihi ātmānaṁ ced vijānīyāt

Books translated in other languages and in English based on Swami Dayananda Saraswati's Original Exposition

Tamil

43. Veeduthorum Gitopadesam (9 Volumes)
    (Bhagavad Gītā Home Study Course)
44. Dānam

Kannada

45. Mane maneyalli Adhyayana (7 Volumes)
    (Bhagavad Gītā Home Study Course)
46. Vedanta Pravesike

Malayalam

47. Muṇḍakopaniṣad

Hindi

48. Ghar baithe Gītā Vivecan (Vol 1)
    (Bhagavad Gītā Home Study Course)
49. Antardṛṣṭi (Insights)
50. Vedanta 24X7
51. Kriya aur Pratikriya (Action and Reaction)

English

52. The Jungian Myth and Advaita Vedanta
53. The Vedantic Self and the Jungian Psyche
54. Salutations to Rudra
55. Without a Second

Biography

56. Swami Dayananda Saraswati
    Contributions & Writings
    (Smt. Sheela Balalji)

Distributed in India & worldwide by
MOTILAL BANARSIDASS - NEW DELHI
Tel : 011 - 2385 8335 / 2385 1985 / 2385 2747

Also available at :

ARSHA VIDYA RESEARCH
AND PUBLICATION TRUST
32 / 4 Sir Desika Road
Mylapore Chennai 600 004
Telefax : 044 - 2499 7131
Email : avrandpt@gmail.com
Website : www.avrpt.com

ARSHA VIDYA GURUKULAM
Anaikatti P.O.
Coimbatore 641 108
Ph : 0422 - 2657001
Fax : 0422 - 2657002
Email : office@arshavidya.in
Website : www.arshavidya.in

ARSHA VIDYA GURUKULAM
P.O.Box 1059. Pennsylvania
PA 18353, USA
Ph : 001-570-992-2339
Email : avp@epix.net
Website : www.arshavidya.org

SWAMI DAYANANDA ASHRAM
Purani Jhadi, P.B.No. 30
Rishikesh, Uttaranchal 249 201
Telefax : 0135 - 2430769
Email : ashrambookstore@yahoo.com
Website : www.dayananda.org

Other leading Book Stores:

Chennai:	**044**
Motilal Banarsidass	24982315
Giri Trading	2495 1966
Higginbothams	2851 3519
Pustak Bharati	2461 1345
Theosophical Publishing House	2446 6613 / 2491 1338
The Odessey	43910300
Bengaluru:	**080**
Gangarams	2558 1617 / 2558 1618
Sapna Book House	4011 4455 / 4045 5999
Strand Bookstall	2558 2222, 25580000
Vedanta Book House	2650 7590
Coimbatore:	**0422**
Guru Smruti	948677 3793
Giri Trading	2541523

PTO

Trivandrum:	**0471**
Prabhus Bookhouse	2478 397 / 2473 496
Kozhikode:	**0495**
Ganga Bookhouse	6521262
Mumbai:	**022**
Chetana Bookhouse	2285 1243 / 2285 3412
Strand Bookstall	2266 1994 / 2266 1719/ 2261 4613
Giri Trading	2414 3140

Made in the USA
Columbia, SC
27 May 2022

61006859R00257